Equity Investment Management

Equity Investment Management

How to Select Stocks and Markets

Stephen Lofthouse

JOHN WILEY & SONS

Chichester · New York · Brisbane · Toronto · Singapore

Published 1994 by John Wiley & Sons Ltd
              Baffins Lane, Chichester
              West Sussex PO19 1UD, England

              Telephone National Chichester (0243) 779777
              Telephone International (+44) 243 779777

Reprinted October 1994

Notice

Datastream is a registered trade name, trademark and service mark of
Datastream International Limited.

All data and graphs contained in this publication and which have been obtained
from the information system of Datastream International Limited ("Datastream") are
proprietary and confidential and may not be reproduced, republished, redistributed
or resold without the written permission of Datastream.

Data in Datastream's information system have been compiled by Datastream in
good faith from sources believed to be reliable, but no representation or warranty
express or implied is made as to the accuracy, completeness or correctness of the
data. Neither Datastream nor such other party who may be the owner of any
information contained in the data accepts any liability whatsoever for any direct,
indirect or consequential loss arising from any use of the data or its contents. All
data obtained from Datastream's system and contained in this publication are for
the assistance of users but are not to be relied upon as authoritative or taken in
substitution for the exercise of judgement or financial skills by users.

Library of Congress Cataloging-in-Publication Data

Lofthouse, Stephen.
      Equity investment management : how to select stocks and
   markets / Stephen Lofthouse
         p.   cm.
      Includes bibliographical references and index.
      ISBN 0-471-94169-7 (cased) — ISBN 0-471-94170-0 (paper)
      1. Portfolio management.   2. Investment analysis.   I. Title.
   HG4529.5.L63   1994
332.6—dc20   93–29957
                                                          CIP

British Library Cataloguing in Publication Data

A catalogue record for this book is available from the British Library

ISBN 0-471-94169-7 (cased)   ISBN 0-471-94170-0 (paper)

Typeset in 10/12 Times from author's disks by Text Processing Department,
John Wiley & Sons Ltd, Chichester
Printed and bound in Great Britain by
Biddles Ltd, Guildford and King's Lynn

Contents

Preface

This book is written for investment professionals and students taking professional examinations. It is equity-orientated and discusses how to:

- analyse stocks
- analyse markets
- construct a portfolio

Apart from the "How I Made My Second Billion" type of book, investment books fall mainly into two categories: (a) the academically rigorous and mathematically demanding textbook; and (b) the elementary textbook which explains the basics such as how to calculate a yield and the merits of buying gilts at the post-office. UK investment professionals tend to ignore the first type of book and have read the second. Yet most want to know more than the second type of book has to offer. This book attempts to satisfy that demand.

Key features include:

- complex theories are outlined in a simple and intuitive manner;
- statistical and mathematical notions are discussed in a way that will be accessible to readers with an arts background;
- the major UK and US empirical studies are discussed;
- practical implications of academic work are stressed;
- ample references are given to enable readers to pursue in greater depth the issues that especially interest them;
- stockbroking, consultant and trade sources, as well as academic, are drawn on.

Investment practitioners and students will benefit from reading this book:

- young fund managers and analysts will get a broad overview of the process of constructing a portfolio. My experience is that many young investment managers are familiar with the usual introductory investment and accounting material, know a great deal about individual companies and can even discuss the broad state of the economy and the prospects for the coming year, but nonetheless feel uneasy about investment strategy. How does one pick one share rather than another? There are many approaches, but is there evidence that supports these approaches? How does one decide whether the equity market as a whole is cheap or dear and how does one choose between different markets? How does one pull all this together? These topics are the subject of this book.

- experienced managers who do not have the time to read the academic or professional literature will be brought up-to-date on the latest empirical evidence.
- the book should help bridge the unhealthy divide in the investment profession between the quantitative specialist and the general manager or analyst. Many of the techniques quantitative practitioners use are discussed in this book, but in an informal and mainly non-quantitative manner.
- students will find a practical orientation to managing money rather than the typical textbook's orientation towards topics that can be treated in a rigorous manner, irrespective of practical relevance. It must be pointed out that the book does not aim to match an examination syllabus, but reflects the conjunction of my interests and topics about which something useful can be said.
- although written specifically for investment professionals and students, the book will be useful for private clients and trustees of investment funds who want to achieve a more informed dialogue with their investment manager.

A couple of features of the organization of the book are worth noting:

- There is a glossary of terms. This will be useful for readers with no statistics background, for readers who read chapters out of order, and for students who do not readily translate DJIA, for example, into Dow Jones Industrial Average.
- I have attempted to fully reference my sources but I have tried to minimize the disruptive effect of references. Accordingly, where it is obvious which work I am referring to, I have usually given just a page reference. I have included in the references at the end of the book a number of useful articles that I read while preparing this book but do not directly refer to. Anyone who wishes to read further on a topic should read works mentioned in the text and should also skim the references section to see if any related works are listed.

I am indebted to Jeremy Lang, Jane Raybould and Richard Bisson for comments on a draft of my manuscript, and Dugald Barr for comments on two chapters. None of these readers saw the final version and I am solely to blame for remaining errors. I am indebted to the British Library of Political and Economic Science and the Library of Congress for the use of their resources.

I am grateful to the authors and publishers who allowed me to reproduce copyright material. Chapters 31 and 32 are drawn by permission from an article I published in the *Professional Investor*. The copyright material on pages 30 (Table 8), 31 (Table 9), 49 (Tables 13 and 14), 102 (Table 25), 104 (Table 26), 116 (Table

28), 134 (Tables 31 and 32), 242 (Table 54) and 308 (Figure 42) is reprinted with the permission of *The Journal of Portfolio Management*, 488 Madison Avenue, New York, NY 10022. The copyright materials in Table 24, p. 98, and Figure 24, p. 184, are reprinted by permission of the American Association of Individual Investors, PO Box 11092, Chicago, Illinois 60611-9737. The copyright material on pages 21 (Figure 8), 29 (Table 7), 55 (Figure 12), 64 (Table 16), 65 (Table 17), 76 (Table 19), 83 (Table 21), 135 (Table 33), 191 (text quote), 193 (Table 46), 204 (Table 47), 205 (Table 48), 236 (Table 51), 237 (Table 53), 257 (Figure 35), 265 (Figure 36), 266 (Table 58), 314 (Table 64) and 315 (Table 65) is reproduced by permission of the *Financial Analysts Journal*. The copyright material on pages 92 (Table 23), 107 (text quote), 120 (Figure 21), 140 (text quotes) and 146 (Tables 38 and 39) is reproduced from the *Journal of Finance* by permission of Professor M. Keenan. Quotations on pages 156 and 158, from the *Review of Financial Studies*, are reproduced by permission of Oxford University Press, those on page 190, from *Continental Bank Journal of Applied Corporate Finance*, by permission of Stern Stewart Management Services, Inc., while those on pages 103, 155, 163 and 164 are reproduced by joint permission of the authors and Elsevier Science Publishers BV.

Stephen Lofthouse

PART ONE
Introduction and Basic
Financial Theory

In Chapter 1 we set out the four main tasks involved in managing an investment portfolio. The bulk of this book discusses these tasks in a practical manner. The remainder of Part 1, however, sets out some basic portfolio and capital market theory and background information. Portfolio theory deals the selection of optimal portfolios and capital market theory deals with equilibrium asset pricing models. Chapters 2 and 3 cover a large number of topics: risk and return, diversification, efficient frontiers, optimal portfolios, and the capital asset pricing asset model. The approach is informal and intuitive: the goal is to give the gist of some important ideas rather than provide a rigorous treatment. In Chapter 4 the efficient market theory is discussed and the implications it has for investors. Chapter 5 takes a broad look at the methods used by investment analysts and fund managers as they go about their tasks.

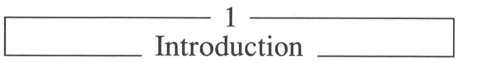

1
Introduction

The central task of investment management is to construct a portfolio. To do this, an institutional or private investor has to address four broad issues:

1. which asset classes to include in the portfolio;
2. what strategic weights to assign to those classes over the long term;
3. what short-term tactical weights to assign;
4. what selection strategies to use within each asset class.

This book discusses items 2 and 3, and 4 for equities.

The potential number of asset classes that could be included in a portfolio is large—cash, equities, bonds, property, gold, silver, art, etc. These asset categories can be further sub-divided. Equities can be split into: domestic and foreign; large and small stocks (including venture capital); actual stocks and derivatives (i.e., futures and options), and so on. Table 1 shows the asset allocation at a broad level of aggregation for large institutional funds in 1991 in the UK, US and Canada.

It is clear from Table 1 that equities and bonds dominate institutional portfolios. The UK is much more pro-equity than the other two countries: as well as having a large domestic equity weighting, 18.3% of UK funds are invested in overseas equities. Different countries adopt very different asset allocations.

Table 1 Asset Allocation of Large Funds: 1991

	UK Funds (%)	US Funds (%)	Canadian Funds (%)
Domestic Equities	54.7	42.2	24.9
Domestic Fixed Interest	9.1	35.2	46.3
Overseas Investments	21.2	4.5	8.7
Property	9.6	4.7	8.1
Cash and Other Short-dated			
Investments	4.9	6.4	10.6
Other	0.5	7.0	1.4

Source: Greenwich Associates (1991, p. 3). Greenwich Associates, Greenwich, CT 06830, USA. Reproduced by permission

The choice of possible asset classes to be included in a portfolio is not discussed in this book. Instead it is assumed that investors will be invested in the broad categories shown above. Property is omitted from the discussion because property investment is usually undertaken by specialist investment managers. Moreover most managers are not involved in asset allocation decisions that involve property versus other assets. Most private investors have sufficient exposure to property via their homes.

Having decided on the asset categories to be included in the portfolio, a decision must be made on the strategic asset weights. These weights can be viewed as those which would be applicable if the manager had no views about likely short-term market performance. They can also be viewed as the weights that the fund will actually have, on average, over a five-to-ten year period, assuming there is no reason to change them during that period. How these weights might be set is discussed in Chapter 22.

The strategic asset class weights should be set with a central value, and a range around that to set the bounds for short-term tactical deviations. Depending on the manager's view of short-term market prospects the manager will position the fund at the high or low end of the strategic ranges. Tactical asset allocation is discussed in Chapters 23, and 25–30. Table 2 shows a sample asset allocation guideline that an investment manager might work with. This guideline might be for the manager of a young pension fund that had no short-term liabilities and whose trustees were not risk-averse. It has been decided that the fund will invest only in the assets shown and that the appropriate strategic stance is to be entirely invested in equities with a 70/30 split between domestic and foreign equities. No weights have been set for individual foreign markets. The tactical range shows that if cash or fixed interest securities seem more attractive than equities on a short-term basis, up to 15% and 20% respectively can be invested in those assets. The current position shows how the fund is actually invested.

Table 2 Sample Asset Allocation Guidelines

Asset	Strategic Weight %	Tactical Range %	Current Position %	
Fixed Interest	0	0–20	0	
● UK: Conventional				
● UK: Index Linked				
● International				
UK Equities	70	50–80	75	
Overseas Equities	30	10–40	20	
● US				7
● Europe				5
● Japan				5
● Other				3
Cash	0	0–15	5	

The final issue in managing a portfolio is to select an investment style for constructing equity and fixed income portfolios. This book focuses on equity investment and share and sector selection techniques are discussed in Chapters 6 to 21. Fixed interest portfolios are not discussed. The share selection evidence is drawn from the UK and the US.

Tactical asset allocation for international markets is discussed in Chapter 29. Further discussion of international markets is contained in Chapters 31–33. Japan has the second largest equity market in the world and we discuss some of its unique features in Chapters 31 and 32. Chapter 33 looks at emerging markets.

Being a successful investor involves much more than knowing a few theories and pieces of empirical evidence. In the penultimate chapter of the book we look at some of the characteristics of investment winners and losers. The last chapter of the book considers passive investment management (trying to match the return from a benchmark), the alternative to the active investment management (trying to find mispriced securities and asset classes), discussed in the rest of the book.

The four broad tasks listed at the start of the chapter are probably listed in their order of importance in determining returns. However, we tackle them out of order and devote a disproportionate amount of space to share selection. This is done because most fund managers spend most of their time on share selection and, as we shall see, in practice share selection often affects returns as much as tactical asset allocation. Before share selection is examined, however, some background information and theory is presented in Chapters 2 to 5.

2
Portfolio Theory

Of all the possible portfolios, which offers the best combination of risk and return? That is the subject of this Chapter. The writer is aware that many people dislike diagrams and algebra. Chapters 2 and 3 have a lot of diagrams but the technical skills required are minimal, so please do not be scared off. All algebra is followed by the key ideas expressed in words. And if you get the gist of statistical notions, that is good enough to understand the text, you don't have to be able to use formulas.

THE SIMPLE ARITHMETIC OF RISK AND RETURN

We will introduce some notions of risk and return by looking at data most investors will be familiar with. In Figure 1 the annual returns, i.e., income plus capital gains or losses, from UK equities and gilts are shown. Figure 1 is quite informative: annual returns are variable, both equities and gilts have generated positive returns on average and equities have returned more than gilts. We would have more specific information if we calculated, from the data used to draw the chart, the average or mean return for both assets. The way most of us would do this is to add up all the returns for each asset and divide by the number of years. This is called the arithmetic mean and is 16.3% for equities and 6.4% for gilts for the period shown in Figure 1 (page 8)

There is another way of calculating an average and this is the geometric mean. This is often used in portfolio analysis. To see why, consider Table 3, which shows the changes in an index over a two year period.

Table 3   Hypothetical Returns

Year	Index	Annual Return
End–90	100	
End–91	200	+100%
End–92	100	−50%

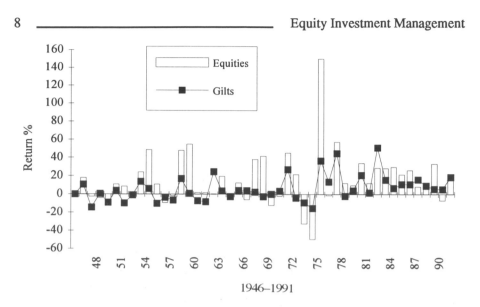

Figure 1 Annual Returns From UK Equities and Gilts: 1946–91. Source: Drawn from data in Barclays de Zoete Wedd (1992, p. 72) by permission

The arithmetic average annual return is (100%–50%)/2, i.e., 25%. This seems a little odd because the portfolio is worth exactly what it was two years ago. The geometric mean gives a more accurate description of this aspect of the data even if its definition is a little off-putting. The geometric mean is the nth root of the product of n observations. In plain language, the geometric mean is best thought of in investment terms as the rate of return that would make the initial investment, or index, equal to the ending investment or index value. For our example, the geometric mean is zero. If there is variability in a series, the geometric mean is always lower than the arithmetic mean. For Figure 1, the geometric mean is 13.1% for equities and 5.6% for gilts.

Which average is the correct one? The answer is that it depends on the topic of interest. If investors are interested in returns for *individual* years, the arithmetic mean is usually preferred. However if investors are interested in portfolio returns over an *entire period*, the geometric mean is usually preferred.

We now know the average returns—measured in two different ways—from UK gilts and equities. But what about the risks? It is usually assumed that risk is the uncertainty as to whether an asset will produce its expected return. If we look at Figure 1, we can see that while equities on average return more than gilts, returns are much more variable. There is a greater chance of an unpleasant surprise from equities than from gilts: they are riskier.

It is generally assumed that investors are risk-averse and that they will only accept risk for extra returns. Given the choice of a 10% return and a 20% return, both with the same odds of happening, they will go for the higher return. In general, investors will choose the highest return for a given risk. Offered a bet with a 50/50 chance of winning either £10 000 or losing £10 000, most investors would turn down the offer. The reason is that money, like most goods, has declining marginal utility. The benefit, or utility, you get from each addition of a good gets smaller and smaller. Say you have £50 000 in savings. If you take the bet you will end up with either £40 000 or £60 000. Diminishing marginal utility suggests that the pain from your savings falling to £40 000 would exceed the pleasure of them rising to £60 000. Diminishing marginal utility implies that most investors will be risk-averse. They will want the chance to win more than they might lose before taking a bet. Just how much more will vary from investor to investor, depending on how uncomfortable they are with the risk of losing money. In general, investors will bear risks, but only for extra returns.

If we examine several assets at the same time it is difficult to tell from a chart or list of figures which asset is the riskiest, or most variable. If we accept that the variability, or dispersion, of return is a measure of risk, then the solution is to calculate a statistic that quantifies the variability of the returns. The statistic usually calculated is either the standard deviation or the variance (the standard deviation is simply the square root of the variance so they both tell exactly the same story). To calculate the standard deviation for returns data, the deviation of each annual return from the arithmetic average is computed and then squared. The average of these squared values is obtained and the standard deviation is the square root of this average: the higher the number, the greater the variability. Calculating a standard deviation is easy: a computer spreadsheet will do the calculation for you if you can type "=STD" or some similar command. If you haven't used a personal computer, somebody in your office or college will be able to show you how easy it is. For gilts and equities, the standard deviations for the data shown in Figure 1 are 29.5% and 14.2%, respectively. Equities are much riskier than gilts. The most important thing to remember is that the larger the standard deviation, the greater the variability.

There is a second feature worth knowing about a standard deviation: it is an especially useful statistic if the distribution of the probability of an outcome has a normal distribution. A normal distribution is a bell-shaped curve, like that shown in Figure 2, in which the probability of an outcome is highest at the mean and tapers off sharply at high and low outcomes. With a normal distribution, two-thirds of the time an outcome will be within plus and minus one standard deviations of the mean, and 95% of the time an outcome will be within plus and minus two standard deviations. Financial data is not usually normally distributed, but it is often sufficiently close to a normal distribution that we can treat it as though it were. For the period 1945–91, the mean arithmetic return for gilts was 6.4% and the standard deviation was 14.2%. Thus, for gilts, the mean plus and minus one standard deviation was 20.6% and −7.8%. Broadly speaking, two-thirds of the time we would expect gilt returns to be within that range, and one-third of the time outside.

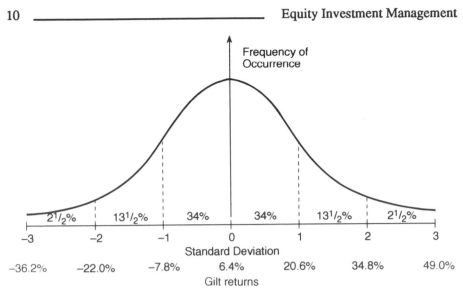

Figure 2   A Normal Distribution

EQUITIES: RISKY BUT REWARDING

In Table 4 a number of statistics that have been mentioned are brought together plus some new ones. This exhibit shows that UK equities have offered a higher return than gilts and have been substantially riskier (i.e., have larger standard deviations).

Table 4   Summary Statistics for the UK Market

Asset	Arithmetic Mean	Geometric Mean	Standard Deviation
		1946–91	
Equities	16.3	13.1	29.5
Gilts	6.4	5.6	14.2
Treasury bills	7.2	7.1	4.5
Inflation	6.6	6.5	5.3
		1919–91	
Equities	14.4	11.8	26.1
Gilts	6.3	5.6	13.0
Inflation	4.6	4.3	7.8

Source: Barclays de Zoete Wedd (1992, p. 3). Reproduced by permission

Equities have outpaced inflation and offered real (inflation-adjusted) returns, whereas gilts offered real returns for the entire period and negative returns after the Second World War. Notice that in this latter period Treasury bills offered higher returns than gilts and with lower risk (smaller standard deviation). Does this refute the view that higher risk is only borne for higher return? Probably not, for what happened after the Second World War was that bond holders suffered much higher inflation, and more variable inflation, than bonds were priced for. Treasury bills rates are refixed at short intervals and the purchasers were able to demand a return above the rate of inflation. Bond holders were locked in. Investors may desire a higher return as a reward for bearing extra risk but they will not necessarily achieve it. If they always got a higher return they would not be bearing risk. In academic jargon, the belief that investors require a reward for bearing risk is an *ex ante* (before the fact) theory rather than an *ex post* (after the fact) theory.

All around the world, equities are usually riskier than bonds, and have offered a higher return. For risk and return data for world markets, the reader should consult Ibbotson and Brinson (1993).

THE RISK REDUCTION EFFECTS OF DIVERSIFICATION

We have looked at risk and return for broad asset classes such as equities and gilts: these could be considered to be portfolios. The same approach to measuring returns and risks in terms of means and standard deviations can be applied to individual securities. However, the risk of a portfolio is not simply the weighted average risk of its components. The position is more complex, because forming a portfolio involves diversification, which usually leads to a reduction in risk.

To understand this, imagine two companies, one an accountancy partnership specialising in insolvency and the other an advertising agency. The insolvency partnership will do well in recessions and, let us assume, will do badly in good times. And vice versa for the advertising agency. Let us assume that good and bad times occur with equal frequency. If we assume some profit and loss figures, we might have the situation shown in Table 5.

Table 5 Profits and Losses for Two Companies

Economic Cycle	Advertising Agency	Insolvency Practice	Average
Growth	+100	−50	+25
Recession	−50	+100	+25

Although both companies deliver profits over an entire economic cycle, profits are very variable. Each company is risky. An investor owning either company would have variable profits, but if both companies were owned in equal amounts, profits would be stable. Diversification would eliminate risk because the returns from the two companies are negatively related. When one goes up, the other goes down. Diversification achieved by combining an advertising agency and a luxury car distributor would not work so well—both companies are likely to do well and badly at the same time.

Constructing a plausible example of perfect diversification is quite difficult—when the economy does badly, most companies and their stocks do badly. And vice versa when the economy does well. However, companies' profits do not move exactly in tandem, and selecting a basket of stocks at random will reduce risk.

In our simple two company example we chose companies whose returns were negatively correlated. When one did well, the other did badly. By holding both assets in a 50/50 ratio, the portfolio risk was totally eliminated. Because most assets move together to some extent, i.e., their returns are weakly positively correlated, diversification will only reduce risk and not eliminate it. Of course, if asset returns are perfectly positively correlated, diversification will not achieve risk reduction. In short, the risk of a portfolio is a function not only of the risk of each of the assets comprising the portfolio but also of the degree of correlation between the returns of the assets. With anything less than perfect correlation of returns, diversification will reduce risk. We can be a bit more specific. The expected return for a portfolio will be just the weighted average of the expected returns of the securities that are included. The portfolio risk or standard deviation is trickier. It will depend on all the securities' standard deviations and the proportion held in each security as well as their covariances, a statistical concept related to correlation. You will understand the main point if you think of correlation whenever covariance is mentioned.

THE EFFICIENT FRONTIER

Turning from the simple example of Table 5 to the real world we find that it is possible to construct innumerable portfolios. A portfolio could consist of a single share, or two shares, or 100 shares, or one share and one bond, and so on. Calculating the return and risk for each portfolio would be hard work. For a 1000 share universe, to calculate the risk and return for all possible portfolios would require 1000 expected returns, 1000 standard deviations and 499 500 covariances, a total of 501 500 estimates. (The formula is $(N^2+3N)/2$, where N is the number of securities.) This is not the sort of information the average analyst provides. Nonetheless, we shall assume all the calculations are made for all possible portfolios and we can plot the risk and return for each portfolio. Some of the portfolios are represented by the dots in Figure 3.

The dots (and all those that we omitted) represent the attainable set of portfolios. Consider portfolios A and B. Both have the same risk in terms of portfolio standard deviation. To read off the risk, just cast your eye down the dotted vertical line that passes through the two portfolios. Now look across to the left along the dotted horizontal lines to read off the returns. Portfolio A has a higher return than portfolio B and is said to dominate it. Portfolio A suffers the same risk but offers a

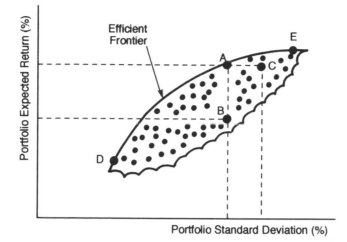

Figure 3   The Attainable Set and Efficient Frontier

better return. Compare now portfolios A and C. Both offer the same return but if we look down to the risk axis we see that C is much more risky. Portfolio A has the same return as C, but less risk. Portfolio A dominates C and all other portfolios with the same return. Portfolio A can be described as efficient: no other portfolio offers as much return as A with as little risk, or as little risk with as high a return. By a series of similar arguments we could establish all the efficient portfolios and thence the efficient frontier, which is shown as the curved line, EAD.

The efficient frontier traces out the portfolios that dominate other portfolios. Portfolios around A on Figure 3 will usually contain more assets than those around portfolios E and D. Which portfolio among the efficient frontier portfolios is optimal? The answer will vary with an investor's risk preference. Very risk averse or conservative investors will tend to choose portfolios near portfolio D, i.e., low risk and low return, while more aggressive investors will tend to choose portfolios near portfolio E, i.e., high risk and high return.

COMBINING RISKY AND RISK-FREE ASSETS

So far we have only considered risky assets. We shall now introduce an asset that has a known return for a given holding period, i.e., a fixed interest government security with a maturity equal to the investment holding period. This is usually assumed to be a Treasury bill. Such an asset will be risk-free—in the sense of having a certain return—and, because there will be no variability of return, it will have a standard deviation of zero. Whatever the return from a risky asset, the risk-free asset will offer an unchanged return, therefore it will have no correlation with the returns of risky assets. It can be shown that when a risky and a risk-free asset are combined, the expected return and standard deviation of the new portfolio will simply be the weighted average of each asset's return and standard deviation. For example, if a risk-free asset has an expected return of 5% and a zero standard deviation, and a risky asset has a return of 10% and a standard deviation of 10%, then the returns and standard deviations of various portfolio mixes of the assets will be as shown in Table 6. If the expected return and standard deviation data in Table 6 are plotted, a straight line will be traced out.

Table 6   Combining a Risk-Free and Risky Asset

Combination %		Expected Return %	Standard Deviation %
Risk-Free Asset	Risky Asset		
100	0	5.00	0.00
75	25	6.25	2.50
50	50	7.50	5.00
25	25	8.75	7.50
0	100	10.00	10.00

What happens in terms of the efficient frontier when we combine a risky portfolio with a risk-free asset? In Figure 4, three possible risky portfolios lying on the efficient frontier are combined with a risk-free asset. Portfolio R is a portfolio consisting of a risk-free asset. Portfolio A is a portfolio on the efficient frontier. The line connecting them represents various possible portfolios consisting of combinations of the risk-free asset and the risky portfolio. This set of portfolios dominates all the risky portfolios on the efficient frontier below portfolio A. Why? Because for every portfolio on the efficient frontier there is one on the line RA which has the same risk but a higher return or has the same return and a lower risk. If we look now at the line connecting portfolios R and B we see that it dominates all the portfolios on line RA. We can keep drawing new lines that dominate the others until we get to the line which is a tangent to the efficient frontier. This line produces a set of portfolios that dominates all portfolios below point M. Since no possible set of portfolios can be drawn to the north-west of line RM, once a risk-free asset is introduced, the new efficient frontier will be the straight line RM and then the curve MD.

In ordinary language, investing in a risk-free asset would be called lending. In effect line RM traces out different combinations of lending and a risky portfolio (M). What happens if investors can borrow, and can do so at the same rate as they can lend? If we go back to Table 6 and extend the table by entering a new line with −25% of the risk-free asset and 125% of the risky asset we can calculate the return and standard deviation of 11.25% and 12.5% respectively. What we are doing is continuing to extend the straight line relationship we have established. This means Figure 4 can be re-drawn as shown in Figure 5. The new straight line

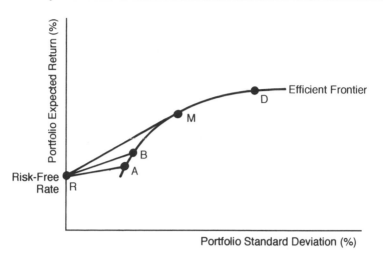

Figure 4   Feasible and Efficient Portfolios with a Risk-Free Asset

efficient frontier is called the Capital Market Line. It shows the risk/return relationship for efficient portfolios when borrowing and lending are possible at the
same rate of interest.

Figure 5 has a peculiar implication. All investors will want to invest in a portfolio on the efficient frontier: where they invest on the frontier will depend on their
attitude to risk. But notice that every point on our straight line efficient frontier
involves the same risky portfolio. Every investor will hold the same risky portfolio

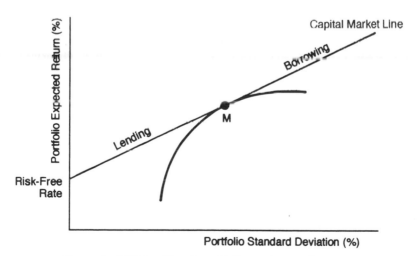

Figure 5   Efficient Frontier with Borrowing and Lending

but have a different amount of risk-free lending or borrowing, depending on their risk aversion. This result is known as the separation theorem, i.e., the selection of the optimal portfolio of risky assets is separate from an investor's attitude to risk and return. Can everyone invest in the same risky portfolio? Only if that portfolio is the market portfolio, i.e., all investors hold all stocks (or whatever assets are being considered) in proportion to their market capitalization. If we assume the FT-A All-Share Index represents the UK market, this would mean investors should hold the Index. This is a theoretical argument in favour of index funds, which are discussed in Chapter 35.

The arguments developed here, and in the next chapter, depend on a large number of assumptions (not all of which are needed for every argument). In general, it is assumed that there are no transaction costs, that assets are infinitely divisible, there are no taxes, investors think about risk and return in terms of means and standard deviations (the literature refers to means-variance analysis, but recall that variance and standard deviations are mathematically related), unlimited lending and borrowing at the risk-free rate is possible, there is homogeneity of expectations (i.e., investors have the exact same view of prospective returns, risks and correlations), information is freely and simultaneously available to investors, and so on.

We do not have to go through the reasons that all these assumptions are necessary. More to the point is whether they make the analysis useless. Economists would argue that no model is an exact description of reality and we can test the model in the real world to see whether it offers useful analysis. We will look at some tests in the next chapter. Another response is to change the assumptions one by one, making them increasingly more realistic, and see what happens. We'll do that for one assumption here.

In the real world investors do not face the same rate for borrowing and lending. Accordingly, Figure 5 can be re-drawn with a line for borrowing (i.e., a tangent line from a return that is higher than that from the risk-free asset to the original curved efficient frontier) and another for lending. This is done in Figure 6. The efficient frontier will consist of the straight line which involves lending up to its tangency point with the original curved efficient frontier, a section of the original frontier, and then the straight line efficient frontier which involves borrowing from its tangency point with the curved efficient frontier. The dotted parts of the lines are not available to the investor. (The investor cannot borrow at the lending rate, so the part of the line from the risk-free lending rate to the right of point L can be ignored. Similarly the investor cannot lend at the borrowing rate so that part of the line from the risk-free borrowing rate to the left of point B can be ignored.) Any portfolio on the curved segment will be an efficient portfolio. The argument that all investors should hold the same risky portfolio and vary their risk by borrowing or lending is now seen to be incorrect. The theoretical case for index funds will have to be made on practical rather than theoretical grounds.

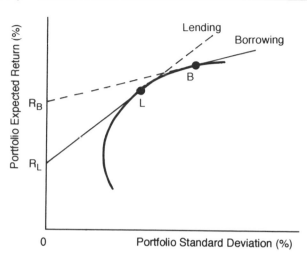

Figure 6 Efficient Frontier With Borrowing and Lending at Different Interest Rates

While the theoretical case for index funds may break down, there is a practical conclusion that can be drawn. Risk-averse investors should hold portfolios that are somewhere on the left side of the efficient frontier. Those who want portfolios with risks equivalent to, or less than, that of portfolio L in Figure 6, should hold portfolio L and adjust their risk by varying the amount of portfolio L and the risk-free asset that they hold. Most fund managers do not follow this approach for their more risk-averse clients. They increase the risk-free holding but also change the share portfolio—they buy "safe" stocks. Instead of buying slightly less of their "best" stocks and holding more cash, they buy stocks that they see as less attractive. Does this make sense?

FROM THEORY TO REALITY

A major practical problem with the notion of an efficient frontier is that once prices change, and they change every second the markets are open, all the calculations necessary to determine the efficient frontier must be redone. In practice, calculations would be made periodically but, whatever the frequency, there would still be a substantial computational burden. Moreover, the rebalanced portfolio may require substantial changes which involve heavy transaction costs. This suggests that this approach is impractical for a large share portfolio. The portfolio theory that we have been discussing, is largely due to Markowitz (1952 and 1959), with important contributions from Tobin (1958) and Sharpe (1963). It stimulated a substantial amount of research which resulted in the market model and the capital asset pricing model (usually abbreviated to CAPM, and pronounced CAP-M). The market model reduces the number of estimates and computations required to calculate an efficient frontier and is more readily applied to portfolios of stocks. However, while calculating a Markowitz efficient frontier demands numerous estimates and computations for a portfolio which can consist of hundreds or thousands of shares, the task is not too demanding if only a few broad asset classes are being considered. For overall asset allocation Markowitz efficient frontiers are used by some investors—usually without the borrowing and lending complication—and this is discussed in Chapter 30. In the next chapter, the market model and capital asset pricing model are examined. They originate from the work of Sharpe (1963 and 1964).

CONCLUDING COMMENTS

In this chapter we argued that investors are concerned with both risk and return. Investors are assumed to be risk-averse and they will bear more risk only for the prospect of extra returns. We argued that risk is the uncertainty that an asset will not deliver its expected return and can be measured by the variability of returns. The statistical measure of variability commonly used is the standard deviation, which is related to the variance. Combining securities into a portfolio reduces risk providing the securities' returns are not perfectly correlated.

Once securities are combined in a portfolio, the portfolio expected return will be the weighted average of the returns of the securities and the portfolio standard deviation will depend on the securities' standard deviations and the proportion held in each security as well as their covariances. From any group of securities, many portfolios can be formed, but some portfolios will dominate other portfolios, that is to say, they will offer more return for the same amount of risk or less risk for a given return. The combination of these dominant or efficient portfolios traces out an efficient frontier of portfolios. Which portfolio on the efficient frontier investors choose will depend on their degree of risk aversion.

When borrowing and lending are introduced, we find that a new efficient frontier becomes available which dominates the original frontier. If investors could all borrow and lend at the same rate, they should all hold the same portfolio of risky assets.

Calculating the Markowitz efficient frontier involves a large number of estimates and computations. In the next chapter we look at a model that relates each asset's return to only one other return, that of the market, and from this go on to look at asset pricing.

3
The Capital Asset Pricing Model

In the previous chapter we briefly mentioned why it is hard to get complete diversification of risks. We noted that while different companies will be affected by different factors, they will also be affected by broad movements of the economy. Further, we expect most of a stock's return to be determined by the return on the market. When we hear that the market is up 20 points, we expect that most of the stocks we hold will have gone up by some similar amount. This observation allows a simplification to be made to the Markowitz analysis in chapter 2, and points the way to explaining how stocks might be priced.

THE MARKET MODEL

In Figure 7 an individual security's returns have been plotted relative to the market's return. The latter is measured by a broad index such as the FT-A All-Share Index or the S&P 500. A line that best fits the observations shown in Figure 7 can be calculated using regression analysis. The resulting line shows the average tendency of how a stock's returns vary with the market's. The line is called the characteristic line.

The equation of the line estimated in Figure 7 can be written as follows:

$$R_i = \alpha_i + \beta_i R_m + \varepsilon_i$$

where

- R_i is the return on security i for some time period
- R_m is the market return for the same period
- β_i is beta, the slope of the line, i.e., an index of the sensitivity of the security's return to the market's return
- α_i is alpha, or the intercept term for security i
- ε_i is a random term for security i, on average equal to zero

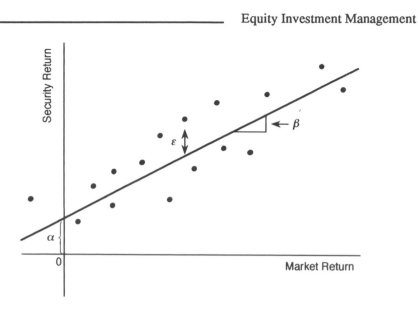

Figure 7 Characteristic Line

The above equation of returns is often referred to as the market model. It may be restated in words:

$$\begin{pmatrix} \text{security's} \\ \text{rate of return} \end{pmatrix} = (\text{alpha}) + (\text{beta}) \times \begin{pmatrix} \text{return from} \\ \text{market} \end{pmatrix} + (\text{unexplained residual})$$

The slope of the line is called beta and indicates how the security's returns vary with the market's returns. The market itself will have a beta of 1 and if a security has a beta equal to 1, the security's returns go up and down with the market's. If beta is greater than 1, the security exaggerates market moves and—assuming alpha is zero—returns more than the market when market returns are positive, and less when market returns are negative. If beta is less than 1 but greater than zero, the security's returns are less than the market's when market returns are positive and greater than the market's when the market returns are negative. If the beta is negative, security and market returns move in opposite directions. Alpha is the intercept of the fitted line and is the security's return when the market's return is zero. The term ε, is the unexplained return from factors not identified in the model. On average this term will have a value of zero.

In the previous chapter we saw that it was hard to calculate an efficient frontier because numerous estimates were required. If we accept that almost all securities' returns are highly correlated with the market as a whole, we can reduce the number of estimates required to find the efficient set of portfolios. Instead of calculating a huge number of covariances of every security with every other, all we need do is calculate the relationship of each security with the market. Using this approach, to calculate an efficient frontier we would need to know five types of information: the expected return and the standard deviation of the market, and the beta, intercept and standard deviation for the error term for every security. For a 1000 security portfolio, this would involve 3002 estimates. (The formula is 3N+2, where N is the number of securities.) Recall that the full Markowitz technique required 501 500 estimates. This simplification of portfolio theory is due to Sharpe (1963).

DIVERSIFICATION AND SYSTEMATIC AND UNSYSTEMATIC RISK

When thinking about stocks it is useful to think about their risk in terms of specific company risks that can be eliminated by diversification and market risk that cannot be escaped. The market risk is often called systematic risk and the specific risk is often called unsystematic risk. In Figure 8 the risk reduction effect of diversification is shown for UK and US stocks. Increasing the number of stocks held reduces risk, but only up to a point. After a while investors cannot escape from general market fluctuations. Figure 8(b) also shows the benefits of diversification if foreign stocks are included. Because the world's stock markets are not perfectly synchronized, some of the risk inherent in the fluctuations of one market can be diversified away by adding foreign stocks which, at least partially, march to the beat of a different drummer. Notice that you don't need many stocks—around 10 to 20, randomly selected—to achieve most of the benefits of diversification.

We can re-draw Figure 8 to show the risk reduction effect of diversification in terms of total, systematic and unsystematic risk and this is done in Figure 9. With a well diversified portfolio, investors bear only systematic risk.

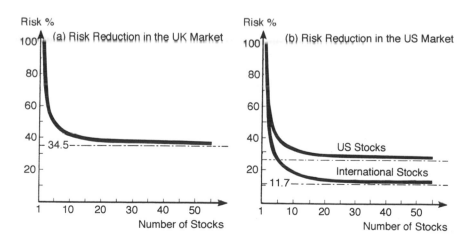

Figure 8 Risk Reduction by Diversification. Source: Solnik (1974, pp. 50–1). Reproduced by permission

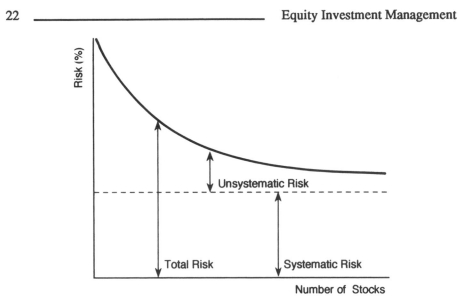

Figure 9 Types of Risk and Diversification

ONLY SYSTEMATIC RISK IS REWARDED

Diversification eliminates unsystematic risk. If investors do not like risk they can eliminate unsystematic risk by diversification. We saw in the last chapter that investors are likely to be risk-averse and will only bear extra risk for extra return. Should they be rewarded for bearing unsystematic risk? Presumably not, since they could so easily eliminate it by diversifying. Not all investors do diversify, but all could do so, even if they have quite modest means. Unit trusts and investment trusts offer diversified portfolios: many allow one-off purchases of around £250. Some offer savings plans that require investments of as little as £25 per month. Yet, by and large, private investors hold relatively undiversified portfolios while institutional investors hold diversified portfolios.

On first consideration it appears implausible that stocks with significant unsystematic risk do not get a reward for that risk. Consider, however, the matter from a different angle. Assume unsystematic risk is rewarded. All the big institutional investors who hold the bulk of all equities issued, and typically have portfolios of at least 50 stocks, would search for stocks with high unsystematic risk. Once an institution had put together a portfolio of 20 or so stocks, it would have diversified away the unsystematic risk. Yet it would be getting a reward for bearing the now non-existing unsystematic risk. This would be the investment equivalent of a free lunch. Presumably the institutions would scramble for these wonderful stocks with high unsystematic risk and their price would be bid up until any portfolio constructed from them achieved no extra return. From that point on, unsystematic risk would go unrewarded.

What this implies is that if investors expect a return for suffering risk, it must be the amount of systematic or market risk that a stock bears that is important in pricing the stock. How do we tell how much market risk a stock bears? We have already seen from the market model that a security beta tells us this: it measures the security's sensitivity to market moves.

We have now introduced two measures of risk. In Chapter 2 we discussed the standard deviation as a measure of *total* risk. In this chapter we have discussed beta, an index of *systematic* risk. Beta seems to be the better measure for pricing individual securities because we would expect security returns to be related to systematic risk rather than total risk. We now consider how beta relates to security prices.

CAPITAL ASSET PRICING MODEL

The capital asset pricing model seeks to specify the relationship between risk and return. It assumes that extra risk will only be borne for extra return and assets with the same risk will have the same return. If investors hold a security or portfolio that has the same risk as the market portfolio, i.e., it has a beta of 1, they will expect to get the market return. If investors hold a riskless security or portfolio, i.e., one with a beta of 0, they will expect to earn the riskless rate of return, the return from Treasury bills. Portfolios that are formed by a mixture of these two portfolios will have a return and risk that are the weighted averages of the return and risk of the two portfolios. In short, the returns and risks will trace out a straight line as shown in Figure 10. (Ignore assets A and B for now.)

Let's define R_i to be the expected return on security i, β_i as its beta, R_m as the expected return on the market and R_f as the return on a risk-free asset. The equation of the straight line in Figure 10 will have the form:

$$R_i = a + b\beta_i$$

One point on the line is the riskless asset with a beta of 0, i.e.,

$$R_f = a + b(0)$$

or

$$R_f = a$$

Another point on the line is the market portfolio with a beta of 1. Thus:

$$R_m = a + b(1)$$

or

$$R_m - a = b$$

If we now go back to the equation of the line and substitute for a and b, we have:

$$R_i = R_f + \beta_i (R_m - R_f)$$

This equation is called the security market line or capital asset pricing model and shows the expected return for any asset. In words:

$$\left(\begin{array}{c}\text{expected return}\\\text{from security}\end{array}\right) = \left(\begin{array}{c}\text{risk-free}\\\text{rate}\end{array}\right) + \left(\begin{array}{c}\text{security}\\\text{beta}\end{array}\right) \times \left(\begin{array}{c}\text{expected return from}\\\text{market} - \text{risk-free rate}\end{array}\right)$$

Notice that the risk-free rate and the market return appear in this equation and are not functions of the asset being priced. The only security specific measure is beta. The difference in return between any two assets will be solely related to the difference in their betas. All stocks will be priced on the security market line. The general relationship will be like that shown in Figure 10. Will risky assets always offer higher returns? The answer must be no, because if they did they could not be said to be risky. The *expected* return will be higher, but the *realized* return may turn out to be lower. (Remember the returns on UK gilts after the Second World War shown in Chapter 2?)

Notice assets A and B in Figure 10. Neither falls on the security market line. Can such assets exist? Yes, but not for long. Asset A offers an exceptional return

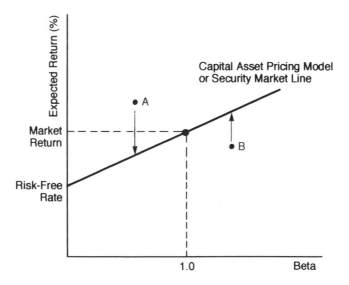

Figure 10   Capital Asset Pricing Model

for the amount of risk it bears. Investors will rush to buy such a security and their demand will push up its price. As this happens the prospective return will drop. The buying will carry on until the asset is priced onto the security market line. Asset B on the other hand will suffer a falling price until it too is priced on the line.

Let's look at a simple arithmetical application of the capital asset pricing model. We will calculate the expected return for a security using the security market equation given above. Imagine that the risk-free rate is 10%, the return from the market is 15% and a share has a beta of 1.2. If we substitute these numbers into the equation we get:

$$\text{expected rate of return } (\%) = 10 + 1.2 \times (15 - 10) = 16$$

Is this share cheap because it is expected to return more than the market? No: the share has a higher return than the market consistent with its higher risk. A share with an expected return of, say, 18% and a beta of 1.2 would be cheap. We would expect buyers to rush in and buy that share until its price had risen by enough to bring the expected return down to 16%.

If you refer back to Figure 5 and compare it with Figure 10 you will see that the diagrams are similar, but not identical. The capital market line is drawn using the standard deviation as the measure of risk, whereas the security market line uses beta. The capital market line is drawn to reflect total risk whereas the security market line is drawn to reflect only systematic risk. The capital market line tells us if a portfolio is efficient, whereas the security market line tells us if a stock or portfolio is properly priced.

USING THE CAPITAL ASSET PRICING MODEL

That's enough theory. How might betas and the capital asset pricing model be used? There are four main applications.

One use of the capital asset pricing model is in share selection and was implicitly discussed in regard to Figure 10. If we calculate a security market line, all stocks should lie along it. Stocks off the line are mispriced and stock A in Figure 10 should be bought, and stock B should be sold. The expected return for the stocks might have been calculated by techniques such the dividend discount model (which is discussed in Chapter 8) or the appropriate price-earnings ratio (see Chapter 9).

A second use of betas might be in overall market strategy. An investor who thought that the market was going to rise might wish to hold high beta stocks to earn an above market return. Note that this strategy relies on the investor having the ability both to call the market and have sufficient skill to overcome the transaction costs of adjusting the portfolio. If investors have no market timing skills and always holds high beta stocks, they might achieve a high return, but this would be purely a return for bearing risk.

Another use of the capital asset pricing model is to determine "the price of risk" (see Fouse, 1976). A security market line for the equity market may be relatively flat or rise steeply. In the first case the market is giving little extra reward for taking on risk whereas in the second it is offering a larger reward. Investors who calculate empirical security market lines at various times will see whether the market is offering a low or high degree of return for bearing risk. If the line is relatively flat, there is less attraction in having a high risk equity portfolio.

A fourth use of betas is in evaluating portfolio performance or a share selection scheme. A share selection scheme that earns an above market return is not necessarily a successful scheme if all it has done is to pick risky shares. Some adjustment for risk must be made. Recall our earlier example of a share with a beta of 1.2 being expected to earn 16% when the market was returning 15% and a risk-free asset was returning 10%. If a share selection scheme picked shares with an average beta of 1.2, it could only be said to be successful if they returned more than 16%. We can see if we have made an abnormal return by using betas to tell us what a normal return is. Notice the implication of this statement. Testing a share selection scheme always involves a test of a joint hypothesis: both the asset pricing model which is being used and the selection process are being simultaneously tested. When a share selection process, for example, is rejected as having no value, it could be that the selection process is valid but the asset pricing model is false.

One important reason for discussing the capital asset pricing model is that many tests of share selection schemes discussed elsewhere in this book have adjusted for risk on the basis of it being a valid model of asset pricing. The performance measure approach informally discussed in the above paragraph was suggested by Jensen. Two other measures that are frequently mentioned in the literature are the Sharpe index and the Treynor index. A complete discussion is unnecessary here. Suffice it to say both relate risk premiums to risk. The risk premium is the return from a portfolio less the riskless rate of interest. Sharpe divides this number by the standard deviation of the portfolio's returns, i.e., total risk, while Treynor divides by the portfolio beta, or systematic risk. Treynor's measure is better for well diversified portfolios, and Sharpe's for poorly diversified portfolios.

IS THE CAPITAL ASSET PRICING MODEL TRUE?

We have outlined the model and seen how it might be used. But is the model true, are securities priced the way the capital asset pricing model asserts? Well, yes and no.

Before we look at the results of tests, we have to note three practical problems that are encountered when testing the theory. First, how exactly should one measure beta? The idea is clear enough, but should one use weekly return data, monthly or some other frequency? And for how long a period: two years, five years or some other period? We find that different commercial measurement sources use different periods and produce different estimates of beta. Further, betas are unstable. Historical stock betas are not very good predictors of future betas. Various attempts have been made to improve the stability of betas by including fundamental accounting data, by allowing for the tendency of betas to drift over time towards one, and so forth. However, portfolios have much more stable betas than individual shares, so for most practical problems the stability of betas is not too important. Most academic tests of the capital asset pricing model have used portfolios rather than individual shares and most investors will be constructing a portfolio of shares.

The second problem we encounter is that investors act with regard to their expectations of risk and return. If we try to test the theory, what we will observe in the market when we measure historical betas and returns is what actually happened. All investors know there is often a wide gulf between their expectations and the outcome. The theory is *ex ante* and the tests are *ex post*.

The third problem is the most complex and a full discussion is beyond the scope of this book. Roll (1977 and 1978) has pointed out that tests of the theory usually use a broad index such as the S&P 500 Index. However the theory should apply to all assets and therefore the true market portfolio is one that holds all risky assets in proportion to market capitalization. It must include all stocks, bonds, property, and even human capital. A major point of Roll's critique is this: beta is not a characteristic of an asset alone—it is a characteristic of an asset in relation to an index. For every index, there will be a beta for every asset. These betas may or may not be the same. For every asset, an index can be found that will produce a beta of any size. Accordingly, for every asset, careful choice of the index will produce any desired performance against a security market line. Roll claims that the capital asset pricing model is not testable. Despite Roll's critique, studies relating beta and returns are still reported. Roll's arguments are not in dispute. What is disputed is their empirical relevance, that is to say, whether in practice tests are highly dependent on the index being used (see Stambaugh, 1982).

There have been many tests of the capital asset pricing model for the US market, but only a few for the UK. The findings may be summarized as follows:

1. The early major US studies (Black *et al.*, 1972 and Fama and MacBeth, 1973) found that in the short run, which can last as long as a decade, higher risk as measured by beta is not necessarily rewarded: higher risk and lower reward can go together. In the long run, higher risk and higher reward go together but the security market line is flatter than the theory suggests. The intercept of the security market line returns more than the risk-free rate, low risk stocks return a bit more than the theory says they should, and high risk stocks return a bit less. These points are illustrated in Figure 11.

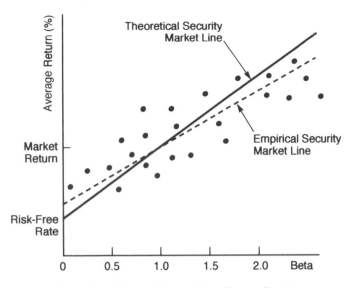

Figure 11   Risk and Return Over Various Periods

These findings have led to the suggestion that the risk-free rate should be replaced by the return from a zero beta portfolio, and the capital asset pricing model amended accordingly.

Fund managers may be more interested in a test that takes the form of simulated portfolio strategies. Sharpe and Cooper (1972) looked at a strategy of buying portfolios of stocks with different betas. They looked at all NYSE stocks for the period 1931–67. They calculated betas for stocks for every year by using the previous 60 months of data. They then ranked stocks by their betas, and split the stocks into deciles, i.e., the highest beta stocks were grouped in one portfolio, the next highest in another, and so on. Every year they constructed new portfolios in the same manner. They then looked at a strategy of buying the highest beta portfolio every year (Strategy 1), the next highest beta portfolio (Strategy 2), through to the lowest beta portfolio (Strategy 10). Finally they looked at the return from each strategy and the actual betas for each strategy. (Remember, they forecast each year's beta using past data, so what they thought would be the highest beta portfolio didn't necessarily turn out to be.) Their results are shown in Table 7. The results show a strong relationship between betas and arithmetic returns but a weak relationship between betas and geometric returns. Past betas appear useful, although not infallible, in constructing portfolios that have specified beta levels—i.e., the portfolio betas are not ranked perfectly in order but the ranking is broadly correct.

2. More recent studies have been less supportive of the capital asset pricing model. In the major recent paper on beta, Fama and French (1992) report finding no

Table 7 Returns to Beta Strategy: 1931–67

Strategy	Arithmetic Average Annual Returns (%)	Geometric Average Annual Returns (%)	Portfolio Betas
10	22.67	14.52	1.42
9	20.45	14.21	1.18
8	20.26	14.79	1.14
7	21.77	15.84	1.24
6	18.49	13.00	1.06
5	19.13	15.00	0.98
4	18.88	14.69	1.00
3	14.99	12.14	0.76
2	14.63	12.40	0.65
1	11.58	9.89	0.58

Source: Sharpe and Cooper (1972, derived from figures IVa, IVb and IVc by permission)

relationship in the US between beta and returns over the period 1963–90 and only a weak relationship over the 1941–90 period. No doubt this paper will lead to a flood of critical responses, for it is a stark rejection of the capital asset pricing model.

3. Corhay et al. (1987) found no relationship between beta and returns for the US, UK and Belgium for the period 1971–83. In France, investors were penalized for bearing risk. Other studies appear to show no relationship between beta and returns in the UK.

4. There have been studies which show that unsystematic risk and other forms of risk are rewarded in the US, e.g., Friend et al. (1978), Lakonishok and Shapiro (1984) and Fuller and Wong (1988). For the UK, Corhay et al. (1988), found a significant positive relationship between risk and return when risk was measured by either total risk (variance), unsystematic risk or skewness. (Skewness is a statistical term for a distribution of outcomes in which extreme values are more extensive on one side of the distribution than the other.) When fund managers are asked what they conceive risk to be they usually give a multidimensional response: e.g., Gooding (1978) found that US institutional fund managers' concept of risk included company risk, beta and standard deviation of return. All this suggests that, contrary to the theory, systematic risk is not the only risk which is rewarded. Recall that we noted that while private investors could diversify, many did not.

5. Finally, there are numerous studies, many of which are discussed in this book, which suggest that returns are related to size, book values and other variables which are not included in the capital asset pricing model. This suggests that the model is wrong, or at least omits relevant factors. It is worth developing this a little.

MULTIFACTOR CAPITAL ASSET PRICING MODEL

The original capital asset pricing model is a single index or single factor model. It states that return on an asset is linked to a single factor, the market, by the asset's beta. The theory assumes that the only reason two stocks' prices would move together is because they both are moving with the market. That is clearly not the case. It is quite clear that there are strong industry or sector effects as well. This naturally leads to the notion of multifactor models where returns depend on both a market factor and industry factors. These models were popular for a period although the evidence was somewhat mixed. Some researchers found the single factor model to be superior (e.g., Cohen and Pogue, 1967 and Elton and Gruber, 1978) while others found the multifactor models to be superior (e.g., Farrell, 1974).

We can think of factors other than sectors that might affect returns. The capital asset pricing model assumes that investors are only interested in returns and the variance of the returns. But investors may value liquidity, i.e., how quickly and easily they can convert their investment into cash (see Fouse, 1976 and Amihud and Mendelson, 1991). And taxes mean that there is a big difference between pre- and post-tax returns, and identical pre-tax returns can imply different post-tax returns depending on the mix of return from capital and income. This may affect the returns that investors demand from assets—high yield stocks may have to return more pre-tax than low yield stocks to compensate for the extra income tax the investor in the high yield stock will suffer.

We seem to have little difficulty in deducing broad general factors that may describe the return-generating process. We are not attempting to pick up every factor that may affect a stock but the broad factors that will affect stocks in general.

Table 8 Multifactor Model: NYSE 1931–79

Attribute	Annualized Values	% of Months in which Attribute was Significant
Beta	5.355	58.3
Yield	0.237	39.5
Size	−5.563	56.5
Bond Beta	−0.118	28.2
Alpha	−2.001	43.5
Basic Industries	1.653	32.5
Capital Goods	0.155	18.7
Construction	−1.589	15.3
Consumer Goods	−0.180	39.3
Energy	6.282	36.9
Finance	−1.478	16.3
Transportation	−0.570	43.9
Utilities	−2.622	35.0

Source: Sharpe (1982, pp. 8 and 10). This copyrighted material is reprinted with the permission of *The Journal of Portfolio Management*.

Let's look at an example of a multifactor model. Sharpe (1982) tried to identify the major factors that had generated returns on the NYSE, 1931–79. The factors or attributes he selected for study were chosen "more or less *ex cathedra*". He examined dividend yield, size of firm, S&P 500 market beta, alpha, an historical bond beta (i.e., the equivalent of the market beta but calculated against long-term bonds) and eight sector membership variables. His findings are summarized in Table 8.

What Table 8 shows is that the attributes did appear to be relevant. Chance alone would lead to some of the variables appearing to be significant in some months when they were not, but the third column shows that the variables appeared to be significant in many more months than chance alone could explain. As to the value of the attributes, one point of beta (e.g. 1.5 versus 0.5) was worth an extra 5% of return. For every 1% increase in yield, return increased by about a quarter of a percent. Small stocks returned much more than large stocks. Bond beta was not very important and stocks that had done well in the past (positive alpha) did poorly—returns reversed. The importance of sectors varied, but energy stocks did well over the entire period.

In Table 9 the extent to which the attributes explain an individual security's return is shown. What this shows is that beta alone "explained" less than 4% of the variation of a security's return. When the other attributes were added, this rose to about 8% for all attributes excluding sectors, and over 10% including sectors. This means that not much of the variation in returns was explained by the model, although it would be sufficient to add value to a stock selection process.

Table 9 Average Cross-Section Fits of Models: 1931–79

Model	Average R^2
Beta	0.037
Common Factors	0.079
Common and Sector Factors	0.104

Source: Sharpe (1982, p. 9). This copyrighted material is reprinted with the permission of *The Journal of Portfolio Management*.

ELEGANT THEORY, BUT WRONG

The single factor capital asset pricing model is clearly inadequate. It misses out factors that are relevant to pricing and assumes some factors are unimportant when they actually are important. Nonetheless, we haven't wasted our time in the past two chapters. The general arguments about expecting returns to be related to risk, the effects of diversification and the importance of the correlations of returns between assets are quite general. The concept of an efficient frontier is used in the real world. It is true that risk is a more complex concept than is assumed in the capital asset pricing model, and that investors may be concerned about other factors in addition to risk, but the simplicity of the model does help us to think about some difficult issues. Also, for at least some periods, beta has been a factor in determining returns.

The capital asset pricing model is part of the vocabulary of investment, and anybody who reads the academic and professional literature has to know the gist of the theory. We discussed performance measurement and the need to allow for risk. When share selection models are evaluated, some allowance must be made for risk. Academics have frequently done this in terms of the market model or the capital asset pricing model. Indeed, many professionals equate beta with risk. UK consulting actuaries organize most of the "beauty parades" that investment managers attend when they make presentations for new business. Before making their pitch, the managers have to fill in a questionnaire. Many actuaries ask how the manager measures risk. In a private communication, one of the largest actuaries admitted that a discussion of beta is the "correct" answer. It's an answer, but not the complete answer. Still, investment managers need to be able to think in terms of the capital asset pricing model.

While the capital asset pricing model provides a useful simple intellectual framework, we saw that a simple multifactor approach explained returns rather better. Part of our task in this book will be to examine in detail factors or attributes that are related to returns. How easy it will be to find attributes that relate to returns will depend in part on how efficient the market is. That's the topic of the next chapter.

CONCLUDING COMMENTS

In this chapter we outlined the market model which relates the return on a security to the return on the market plus a constant and an unexplained residual. The sensitivity between the market return and the security return is measured by beta, the slope of the security characteristic line. The total risk that a stock bears can be divided into market related or systematic risk and stock specific or unsystematic risk. Diversification of a portfolio into more than about 20 stocks will largely eliminate unsystematic risk. Since unsystematic risk can be eliminated, it seems unlikely that it should be rewarded. On this view, total risk is not the relevant concept for pricing securities, systematic risk is. A security beta measures a security's systematic risk relative to that of the market. The capital asset pricing model states that:

$$\begin{pmatrix} \text{expected security} \\ \text{return} \end{pmatrix} = \begin{pmatrix} \text{risk-free} \\ \text{rate} \end{pmatrix} + \text{beta} \times \begin{pmatrix} \text{expected market return} \\ -\text{ risk-free rate} \end{pmatrix}$$

Recent research shows that the US evidence supporting the capital asset pricing model is weak: international evidence is not very supportive either. Beta is probably relevant to security pricing, but returns appear to be determined by more than beta. Factors such as the market capitalization of a security and its yield are related to returns. Despite the weak empirical basis of the capital asset pricing model, it is still basic to much investment thought. The need to allow for risk in assessing share selection strategies is important. It is true that risk is a more complex concept than is assumed in the capital asset pricing model, and that investors may be concerned about other factors in addition to risk, but the simplicity of the model does help us to think about some difficult issues. The capital asset pricing model is part of the vocabulary of investment, and anybody who reads the academic and professional literature has to know the gist of the theory.

4
The Nearly Efficient Market

The efficient market theory states that security prices fully reflect all available information. This theory has been subjected to much research and analysis and has been a major source of disagreement between academics and practitioners. The practitioners have tended to resist the theory while the academics have forcefully promoted it. Before we see why the theory has been so divisive we should make a link with the last chapter.

For the capital asset pricing model to be true (and the multifactor arbitrage pricing theory which we discuss in Chapter 19) markets must be efficient. Recall points A and B in Figure 10 which were not on the security market line. We assumed that buyers and sellers would quickly step in to force the stocks onto the line. If that did not happen, the line would not describe the market trade-off between risk and return. There would in fact be no consistent relationship between risk and return. Asset pricing models need the efficient market theory. However, the notion of an efficient market is not affected by whether any particular asset pricing theory is true. If the market preferred stocks with high unsystematic risk, that would be fine, just as long as all information was immediately reflected in prices, the efficient market theory would be true.

EFFICIENT MARKET THEORY: TRUE OR FALSE, A PROBLEM FOR SOMEONE

Although the efficient market theory can be stated simply as in the first line of this chapter, there is a substantial academic debate about the exact specification of the theory (see, e.g., Ball, 1989). Nonetheless, for the purposes of this book, we need not get involved in the debate. The above definition will suffice, or the more operational version that says that all prices reflect all information up to the point where the benefits of acting on the information equal the costs of collecting it. Prior to the 1950s it was believed that traditional investment analysis could be used to outperform the stock market. In the 1950s studies began to appear (e.g., Kendall,

1953) that suggested that changes in security prices followed a random pattern. This generated a lot of theorizing and research which lead to the efficient market notion. (There had been earlier empirical studies pointing in the same direction, but these studies had been neglected.)

How could price changes have no pattern? The answer is obvious—once we have been told. If we assume that people who play the market are keen to make money we should expect them to grab every potentially profitable opportunity. The moment there is a chance to make money they will act, and prices will rise or fall in response to their purchases and sales, and stocks will then be priced so that there is no opportunity to make further profits. Stocks will be priced at their intrinsic value. This does not mean all stocks have to offer the same expected return—investors may well want additional returns for bearing extra risks—just that stocks will be priced at whatever seems the proper price allowing for risk.

For this model to work well, there will have to be an abundant flow of information, prices will have to respond quickly to changes in information, investors will have to make rational decisions, and it must be possible to deal easily, frequently and cheaply. Now we might argue exactly what "rational" means, but in general all these conditions seem to be met by the typical modern stockmarket.

As a result of all our assumptions it would seem that stock prices should fully reflect all available information. Of course when new information comes along, prices may well change. For news to be news it must be independent of earlier items. Thus, rational profit-maximizing investors will have driven all prices to a level which reflects available information, and they will also react to all pieces of news. Since the new information will arrive randomly, the percentage price changes should be random. Stock prices thus might be expected to take a random walk.

An interesting paradox in the concept of an efficient market was quickly noted. Analysts make the market efficient, but as a result there is no benefit from any piece of research because it is instantly reflected in market prices. It is not worth undertaking information gathering. Yet, if all the analysts left the profession, prices would become inefficient and there would be scope for research to add value. Slightly more formally, if markets are fully efficient, prices will adjust instantaneously to new information. As a result, no trades will take place and it will not be worth collecting information. Accordingly a market can only be efficient if some people (often described as noise traders) believe that it is not efficient and trade on something other than new information. Moreover the market must be sufficiently inefficient to allow informed traders to recover their costs of collecting information or none would be collected. (See especially Grossman and Stiglitz, 1980.)

In a famous review of the literature, Fama (1970) divided work on the efficient market into three increasingly wide categories depending on the information assumed to be impounded in prices. In the weak-form hypothesis, security prices reflect all security market information including all past prices, volumes, etc. In the semi-strong hypothesis, all publicly available information is reflected in security prices. In the strong-form hypothesis all public and private information (i.e., information not generally available, such as that company executives might possess about their companies) is impounded in prices.

Table 10   Three Versions of the Efficient Market Theory

Version of Theory	Information Impounded in Prices
Weak-form	Past prices of securities
Semi-strong form	All publicly available information
Strong-form	All public and private information

Most practitioners disputed the theory when it was first proposed. Chartists (see Chapter 18) look at past prices to deduce what will happen to future prices. This approach can have no value according to the weak-form efficient market theory. Fundamental research (i.e., research on economic and financial factors) fares no better if the semi-strong form hypothesis is correct. Now for the extremely well-paid security analysts, fund managers and brokers' salesmen, this is pretty threatening stuff. But it would be awkward for the academics if the efficient market theory were shown to be false. After all, the efficient market theory is little more than the spelling out of the consequences of the behaviour of a competitive market. As Marsh and Merton (1986, p. 484) have noted:

"To reject the Efficient Market Hypothesis for the whole stock market ... implies broadly that production decisions based on stock prices will lead to inefficient capital allocations. More generally, if the application of rational expectations theory to the virtually 'ideal' conditions provided by the stock market fails, then what confidence can economists have in its application to other areas of economics where there is not a large central market with continuously quoted prices, where entry to its use is not free, and where shortsales are not feasible transactions?"

STARTS WELL ...

At an empirical level, the efficient market school seemed to win the argument at first, not so much because their evidence was overpowering but more because there was persuasive evidence that went against the then prevailing belief that charts and sound fundamental analysis were self-evidently useful. The general academic view appeared to be that the weak-form hypothesis was true, the semi-strong form was mainly true and the strong-form probably was not.

The evidence was never quite as strong as it appeared. Some of the early evidence suggested inefficiencies, but not once transaction costs were allowed for. One problem with this is that transaction costs depend partly on the investor's circumstances. If investors have to buy equities, simply because they have new cash flow or because they have sold bonds to go into equities, they will suffer transaction costs. These are inescapable and would be involved if they bought the market as a whole. For such investors, pre-transaction cost outperformance is relevant. Of course, if a strategy involves endless turnover, then transaction costs will undermine the strategy. For market-makers, who have negligible dealing costs, even a strategy that required frequent transactions might be consistent with market inefficiency. Nonetheless, the economic value of the inefficiencies noted in early studies was usually modest.

With regard to the evidence relating to technical analysis, it is probably fair to say that technical analysis was not rejected by numerous specific tests. Rather the argument took the form that academics could not find patterns in past prices, technical analysts used past prices, therefore technical analysis was wrong. Further, technical analysts did not present any evidence to support their approach. However, not all studies found random price patterns. For example, an early UK study by Kemp and Reid, 1971, (p.47), concluded that "share price movements were conspicuously non-random over the period [studied, October 28, 1968 to January 10, 1969]".

With regard to the semi-strong version, the evidence seemed mainly persuasive except the academics seemed to find evidence of how the market reacted to events like stock splits to be interesting, while it is doubtful that practitioners did. These seem to be trivial technical matters that the market ought to get right, and is not the stuff of investment strategies. In any event, the evidence generally showed that a specific event was fully in the price and the market had anticipated the event over a period of some months or years. For example, Fama *et al.* (1969) found that abnormal returns accrued to stocks that had a split for a period of two years before the split, but returns were normal after the split. Stock splits probably follow good news and a rising share price, hence the rising returns prior to the split. By the time the split occurs, all the good news is in the price. But, one may ask, once the market latches onto something, why does it take a couple of years to be fully impounded in the price? Is such evidence for or against the theory?

Even though questions could be raised about the meaning of some of the studies, any reasonable person would have to have conceded that the evidence was sufficiently strong that the onus was now on investors to prove any claim that they could outperform the market. It appeared that the market was reasonably efficient, information was quickly incorporated into prices and there was little in the way of evidence that suggested that there were more fund managers with good records than chance alone might allow. Indeed, some academics gave the impression that about all that could be said for fund management was that it was an indoor job that paid well and involved no heavy lifting.

... SECOND THOUGHTS

From the late 1970s onwards, a spate of studies have appeared that suggest that the market is less than perfectly efficient. In 1991, Fama again reviewed the literature. He discussed the literature in three categories but he replaced weak-form efficiency with tests for return predictability, the semistrong-form with event studies and the strong-form with tests of private information. The biggest change over the twenty year period since his first review has been the research on return predictability. In particular there is now a huge literature on time-varying returns (e.g., are years of good returns likely to be followed by poor returns?) and cross-sectional returns (e.g., are stocks with low price-earnings ratios associated with high returns?). These studies appear to show that the market is much less efficient than the academics previously thought, although there is a problem of interpretation here.

To give an example, one finding that has been noted many times is that small market capitalization stocks have outperformed large over long periods, even after allowance for risk differences as measured by beta. One could say the studies refute the efficient market theory. However, the standard practice of scientists is not to let go of an old theory that has served well until a new theory is available to take its place. In the meantime the refuting evidence is labelled as an anomaly and is encompassed in rather *ad hoc* modifications to the old theory. It is hoped that the anomalies may be eventually shown to be mistaken or that a new theory will emerge. The process of *ad hoc* modifications seems an inevitable course in the case of the efficient market theory because all tests are tests of a joint hypothesis. They test an asset pricing theory at the same time as the efficient market hypothesis. How do we know that small stocks return "too much"? Only by knowing what the right return is, and we know this through the application of an asset pricing theory. It might turn out that many of the anomalies are not anomalies of the efficient market theory at all, but are a result of deficient asset pricing theories. For example, small stocks are more illiquid than large stocks. Maybe investors require an extra return for suffering illiquidity as well as bearing risk. In that case the efficient market theory need not be wrong but the simple one-factor capital asset pricing model would be.

How should we sum up on the state of the efficient market theory? The theory seems to have gone through three stages. There has been a swing from believing that the market was inefficient to a decade in which the academics believed that it was efficient, at least in the weak-form and semi-strong form. In the last 15 years there has been a steady stream of reported anomalies or exceptions to market efficiency. There has also been research suggesting that the entire market can be grossly mispriced as it overreacts to events or gets caught up in fads or speculative bubbles. Does all this mean we should abandon the efficient market notion? Probably not. If investors can make a quick profit, presumably they will—it still seems that the basic economic model of self-interest will force the market towards efficiency. There is still a lot of evidence of efficiency or near-efficiency. And the evidence of inefficiencies is tricky to interpret because of the joint hypothesis problem. Nonetheless, academics have become more aware of the circumstances under which the efficient market theory might not hold. As we shall see later, it may not hold where arbitrage is difficult. The evidence overall probably warrants the view that it is possible to beat the market but it will require some effort and organization to do so: possible, but hard.

IMPLICATIONS OF THE EFFICIENT MARKET THEORY FOR FUND MANAGEMENT

We now relate some of the above discussion and that of the last chapter to the task of fund management. We assume that investors try to price stocks in some rational way based on their intrinsic value (which we discuss in more detail in Chapter 8). How does the capital asset pricing model relate to that valuation? The capital asset pricing model asserts that investors demand a higher expected return for bearing risks. The relevant risk for pricing securities is systematic risk and this can be measured by beta. In the process of deriving a stock's intrinsic value, investors will allow for its level of risk. (We can introduce other notions of risk if we don't accept the capital asset pricing model.) The efficient market theory asserts that all relevant information is impounded in prices. Profit-orientated investors will ensure that stocks are priced at their intrinsic value.

The implications of the efficient market theory are that:

- investors can't use public information to earn abnormal returns
- new information that implies a change in intrinsic value will be acted upon quickly

How much faith investors have in the efficient market theory should determine their approach to managing investments. Funds may be managed passively or actively. A passive manager simply aims to match the return on some appropriate index whereas an active manager aims to purchase mispriced securities and assets and thereby earn a positive abnormal rate of return. Passive managers assume that:

- the market does not misprice securities or assets

or

- the market does misprice securities and assets but managers are not able to take advantage of the mispricing

Passive managers would adopt a strategy of determining the appropriate strategic asset class allocation and then broadly diversifying within each asset class. This might be achieved via index funds, which are discussed in Chapter 35.

Active managers assume that:

- the market misprices securities and/or assets

and

- managers are able to recognize the mispricing

Active managers may attempt to outperform by either or both of:

- security selection
- asset class selection

Active managers can make three kinds of bets:

- information bet: the active managers assume they have knowledge nobody else has—e.g., they have better company profit forecasts—or that they can respond faster to new information;
- valuation bet: the active managers assume that a security or asset class is mispriced on the basis of generally known information;
- factor bet: active managers assume they know something that others do not know and which will affect a group of stocks or assets. For example, an active manager might think that the price of oil or the rate of inflation will be higher than generally expected. This could be classified as an information bet, but it is useful to classify it separately as it relates especially to arbitrage pricing theory and sector strategy, which we discuss later.

The assumption of this book is that the market is not perfectly efficient and investors are interested in more than risk and return and it is possible to earn an abnormal return. Accordingly we look at various strategies based on information, valuation and factor bets. We concentrate on bets that have yielded abnormal returns, although some popular strategies that do not appear to work are also discussed.

Believing that there are exploitable inefficiencies does not mean that we think it is easy to make money. The efficient market theory does have a lot going for it in terms of theory and evidence. This suggests that if we are to base investment strategies on research findings that imply market inefficiency, we should always ask ourselves why a "sure thing" way of making money survives. Why have other investors not snapped up the opportunity? If we think we can satisfactorily explain the existence of the opportunity, we should be more confident about acting on it. Academics typically try to explain away anomalies as a problem with the capital asset pricing model—they say that risk is not being measured correctly or should be broadened to include other factors such as liquidity. Perhaps so, but investors should ask whether these factors matter to them. Even with the capital asset pricing model, there is no denying that an investor can earn more than the market, providing more risk is borne. If you don't mind risk, bear it, and expect to earn a higher return. Similarly, if small stocks enjoy a premium because of poor liquidity, and poor liquidity is not of concern to an investor, the poor liquidity should be borne for the prospect of extra return. Whether the extra returns are worth having, depend on what matters to an investor. Ibbotson (1989) explains the issue well.

Ibbotson points out that the capital asset pricing model assumes that investors are only interested in two attributes, risk and return, but assets have many more attributes such as information costs, taxes, transaction costs, constraints on marketability and so on. Investors will demand a high return from assets with lots of attributes that investors in general dislike. However for investors who don't mind the attributes that other investors dislike, such properly priced assets will appear to be a bargain. Ibbotson gives a useful analogy:

> "In assessing value, car buyers look first at the chronological age of a car, secondarily at its condition... Thus an owner of a two-year-old car with 5,000 miles would have a very hard time selling it as a nearly new car; it would be priced as a two-year-old car. Because of its low mileage, it might be priced at the high end of the range for two-year-old cars of that make and model, but it would be very cheap for a car with only 5,000 miles on it.
>
> A buyer might regard this offering as expensive (compared with other two-year-old cars) or cheap (compared with other 5,000 mile cars). When *most* buyers emphasize the car's age, then the clever buyer who appraises the car according to mileage gets a bargain. This example shows vividly that, depending on the scaling (age or mileage), the same good can be seen as cheap or expensive. Like our mispriced car, a stock might be seen as cheap on one scale and expensive on another....
>
> A simple generalization can be formulated to determine whether cheap assets are a bargain. If most investors (consumers, etc.) place too much emphasis on price and too little on other indicators of quality in appraising an asset class, then the cheap assets in that class are likely to be overpriced. If most investors place too much emphasis on indicators of quality other than price and too little emphasis on price in evaluating an asset class, then the cheap members of the class are likely to be underpriced: they are bargains" pp.10–11

This scaling problem is one reason why the market may offer bargains. Another reason might be that investors have systematic biases. For example, most investments are not managed by their owners but by agents (fund managers) who may be controlled by other agents (e.g., trustees) acting for the owners. It may be that these agents will act in a different way than the ultimate owners might, because the agents are mainly concerned with keeping their jobs. Performing well is part of that, but they may believe that they are less likely to be fired if they act in a way that conventional wisdom suggests is prudent. This may mean that they will be biased towards, for example, blue chip stocks rather than second line stocks, irrespective of their relative values. This could lead to a consistently higher return from small or neglected stocks.

Again, it is generally assumed that investors process information efficiently and are risk-averse. But what if human decision-making has some consistent biases, or people are not always risk-averse? For example, laboratory studies have shown that when confronted by losses, people tend to be risk-seeking. If faced with losing £8000 of a £10 000 investment with absolute certainty, or a 15% chance of retaining the whole £10 000 but an 85% chance of losing the lot, most people opt for the latter. The expected value of the options are £2000 and £1500: people opt for the lower expected return. This suggests that stocks that involve bad news may be treated differently, in some way, than other stocks.

Of course, in some cases we may note that anomalies have generated abnormal returns in the past but we cannot explain why. Some would argue that the anomalies may not be true and we should ignore them. Beware of quasi-academics bearing anomalies, as someone once put it. There is, however, an argument for acting on them anyway. If the anomalies are true one should be trading on them. If the anomalies are false, the market is efficient. If the market is efficient, the anomaly strategies will yield the risk-adjusted market rate of return. They cannot yield more but they cannot yield less either. If they did, they would give a negative signal and a consistent signal is not possible in an efficient market. Thus an anomaly-based strategy dominates a random one: "heads you win; tails you tie." (Joy and Jones, 1986, p. 53).

CONCLUDING COMMENTS

The efficient market theory states that security prices fully reflect all available information. The early evidence supported the theory, but evidence collected in the last 15 years has raised a number of doubts. There would appear to be a number of inefficiencies in markets that can be exploited to increase returns. These are discussed in this book. It is probably fair to describe security markets as nearly efficient. However one has to be careful when there appear to be market inefficiencies. There is a difficulty in assessing evidence because testing the efficient market hypothesis always involves a joint test with an asset pricing model. Often a seeming refutation of the efficient market hypothesis may instead be a refutation of the asset pricing model used in the analysis. A sensible precaution is to try and explain why an apparent inefficiency persists. Sometimes one will conclude that it is the asset pricing model that is at fault, but that is not without interest. Perhaps the factor that appears to be generating the extra return is not one that concerns the investor and so exposure to that factor should be accepted.

It makes sense for investors to try to outperform the market if they believe that markets are inefficient and that they can exploit the inefficiency. Most of this book is geared to such investors, who will make information, valuation or factor bets. Investors who believe either that the markets are efficient, or that they are inefficient but the investors are incapable of exploiting the inefficiency, should adopt a passive investment style. Chapter 35 discusses one aspect of this, equity indexation.

5
How Analysts Analyse and Fund Managers Manage

In this book we examine ways of managing money. All of the approaches discussed are used somewhere by someone. But how widely used are the approaches we describe? Is what we describe so commonplace that we are describing the knowledge possessed by every apprentice, or is it best practice, or, if you have contemplated the diagrams of Chapters 2 and 3, pure fantasy? To answer this we need to know how analysts and fund managers go about their job and that is what we shall consider here. There is a sort of Catch-22 with this chapter: you need to know what the techniques are before you can understand it. However, most readers will know enough and complete novices can postpone reading this chapter until they have finished the rest of the book.

We shall look at both analysts and fund managers. Although it is fund managers who make the investment decisions, analysts are important participants in the investment process. They are the major source of earnings estimates, company analysis and share recommendations. A number of studies of analysts have been made. Potentially the most useful and interesting is protocol analysis, which is the study of verbalizations of decision-making behaviour. Biggs (1984) and Bouwman *et al.* (1987) have used this technique to study how analysts assess financial and other information when screening prospective investments. Unfortunately, this work is somewhat limited to date and we are forced to concentrate on questionnaire surveys. These suffer from being rather old, and may be a little misleading given the rapid development of investment techniques in the last decade or so, but they are the best information we have.

STUDIES OF UK AND US ANALYSTS AND MANAGERS

Arnold and Moizer have published a series of papers looking at the appraisal techniques of UK analysts (Arnold and Moizer, 1984), the techniques of UK portfolio and non-portfolio managers (Moizer and Arnold, 1984) and the techniques of UK and US analysts (Arnold *et al.*, 1984). The data were drawn from a 1981 UK survey and a 1982 US survey. The authors sent questionnaires to a random sample of 465 members of the UK Society of Investment Analysts and to 40 non-members selected from the Continental Illinois survey of UK investment analysts. There was a 60% response rate and 202 of the respondents analysed UK ordinary shares. The US survey was sent to a random sample of 400 members of the Financial Analysts Federation. There was a 39% response rate and 102 of the respondents analysed equities.

Arnold *et al.* (1984) calculated the frequency of use of various methods of investment analysis. Their figures are shown in Table 11. The analytical methods were described in the questionnaire as: fundamental analysis—"the analysis of such fundamental factors as general business conditions, industry outlook, earnings, dividends, quality of management, etc."; technical analysis—"an analysis of market based factors such as stock price movements, charts, etc."; beta analysis/ modern portfolio theory (MPT)—"analysing the responsiveness of the price of a particular company's stock to changes in the value of some market average".

Table 11   Frequency of Use of Methods of Investment Appraisal (%)

	Almost always 96–100%	Usually 66–95%	Sometimes 36–65%	Seldom 6–35%	Hardly ever 0–5%
Technical analysis	12.5	13.9	25.1	23.4	25.1
Fundamental analysis					
● US	86.2	9.8	2.0	0.0	2.0
● UK	76.1	19.9	2.5	1.5	0.0
Beta analysis/MPT					
● US	4.9	15.7	22.6	18.6	38.2
● UK	2.0	4.5	18.4	24.4	50.7

Source: Arnold *et al.* (1984, p. 4). Reproduced by permission

In Tables 11 and 12, where separate US and UK responses are not shown, there was no significant difference between the two. Table 11 clearly shows that fundamental analysis is the dominant investment style with little use made of betas/MPT: UK analysts were especially reluctant users of betas/MPT. Turning to the usefulness of the techniques, it is not surprising that the perceived usefulness mirrors the frequency of use, although US analysts were no greater fans of betas/MPT than UK analysts. The fundamental factors analysts consider when evaluating shares are shown in Table 12.

Analysts presumably use various financial ratios in assessing the financial health of a company in terms of profitability ratios, liquidity ratios, gearing ratios and so forth. These are probably used as an input to valuation rather than as a valuation method *per se* (although they could be, as we discuss in Chapter 13). The price-earnings ratio appears to be the dominant appraisal method although the

Table 12 Factors Considered in Fundamental Analysis

	Almost always 96–100%	Usually 66–95%	Sometimes 36–65%	Seldom 6–35%	Hardly ever 0–5%
Company's net asset value	32.0	30.0	26.3	10.4	1.3
Estimate of "true" value of PE ratio	48.5	31.9	11.5	4.7	3.4
Estimate of market value by applying PE ratio to a forecast of next year's earnings	45.3	27.4	11.1	9.1	7.1
Various financial ratios					
• US	53.3	27.3	15.2	2.0	2.0
• UK	35.2	30.2	22.1	6.0	6.5
Estimate of future dividend yield					
• US	30.3	18.2	25.3	14.1	12.1
• UK	44.2	29.9	17.3	6.1	2.5
Estimate of NPV of future cash flows					
• US	25.3	18.2	22.2	13.1	21.2
• UK	8.2	7.7	21.5	25.1	37.5

Source: Arnold *et al.* (1984, p. 6). Reproduced by permission

dividend yield was seemingly important in the UK. About 80% of analysts "almost always" or "usually" estimated what they thought a company price-earnings ratio should be, and most then went on to use that to make a forecast share price using a forecast of earnings. The method favoured by academics, the dividend discount model (shown as NPV or net present value in Table 12) was far less popular, especially in the UK. It is surprising that analysts would "sometimes" use a dividend discount model. The approach is sufficiently technically demanding and requires such specific working practices that one would expect a firm that used a dividend discount model approach to require all analysts to use it. It seems unlikely that an individual analyst in a non-dividend discount model house would use the approach.

Arnold and Moizer (1984) discuss the unstructured interviews they had with six UK firms when they were drawing up their questionnaire. They comment on the price-earnings approach to share selection. Among UK analysts they note a common pattern for share appraisal which

"involved attempts to predict a company's share price at some time in the future, usually not more than one year ahead. Most frequently, this prediction involved estimating earnings for the current year and applying an 'appropriate' price-earnings ratio to the estimated earnings.... The main apparent differences between the approaches adopted by the six firms interviewed arose with respect to the procedures followed for estimating earnings. Most of the firms used the same broad approach to the selection of an appropriate price-earnings ratio.... The major similarity was that none of the analysts seemed to use a formal model to estimate the PE ratio." (p. 197)

The survey is more than a decade old and so one should be careful in drawing conclusions. Nonetheless, the data appear to show the US analysts to be better trained and more professional than UK analysts. US analysts find fundamental analysis more useful than do UK analysts, do more financial ratio analysis, and make more—albeit still limited—use of beta/MPT and dividend discount model analysis. Analysis of other data in Arnold *et al.*, and not discussed here, points in the same direction. The authors cite a study suggesting 85% of US analysts had a degree in a business-related area against 58% in the UK. More interesting, however, was an analysis made by the authors relating to Membership of the Institute of Chartered Financial Analysts. To become a CFA requires passing a series of tough exams—harder than the professional training available in the UK. Arnold *et al.* found that many of the differences in responses between UK and US analysts disappeared when US analysts who were members of the IFCA were excluded from the US sample.

Although the above discussion has referred to "analysts" Arnold and Moizer drew their sample from membership of a professional analyst association rather than from analysts *per se*. In fact 46% of their UK sample were fund managers. (This might explain the occasional use of the dividend discount model by some respondents—they were probably fund managers). Not surprisingly, the managers did rather less detailed work than the analysts, although they too were fundamentalists, and undertook their analysis in much the same way. Beta/MPT anal-ysis was used more by the managers than by the analysts, but was not used very much.

In another study, Chugh and Meador (1984) sent questionnaires to 1000 members of the Boston Security Analysts Society, and to 1000 US members of the Financial Analysts Federation outside the Boston Society. The questionnaires had a low response rate of 23% and 17% respectively and were presumably sent out in 1983 or earlier. Once again this survey is rather old. The questionnaire used was not published but seems to have been orientated towards strategic planning. It is difficult to determine whether analysts' answers were guided in their responses by the structure of the questionnaire. Chugh and Meador deduce from the questionnaire responses that analysts are essentially earnings orientated and do not rely very heavily on a dividend discount model approach. They believe that analysts develop an integrated prediction of financial performance:

> "The predictive process is based primarily on the quality and depth of management, market dominance, presence of a sound strategic plan and planning system, and the strategic credibility of a company. In assessing the quality and depth of management, analysts look at management's performance record, presentations, evidence of sound strategic planning, and ability to meet stated objectives. A sound strategic plan and planning system serve two functions—as independent variables in the prediction of financial performance and as media for evaluating the quality and depth of management. Presentations by management offer analysts an opportunity to learn about strategic plans and planning systems and to evaluate the quality and depth of management.
>   By processing all such information, along with assessments of the external economic and industry environments, analysts develop a systemic appraisal of the

firm. This evaluation becomes the foundation for a forecast of long term financial performance in terms of EPS [earnings per share] and ROE [return on equity], which determine the investment value analysts place on a stock." (p. 48)

Finally, let us end by looking at the findings of a study of techniques investment managers use. Carter and Van Auken (1990) sent questionnaires to a random sample of US investment managers in the investment, investment banker, investment management and bank trust industries. The questionnaire was mailed during September 1987 and May 1988. The response rates were 22% and 19%, and the sample size was 185.

The percentage of managers in this sample claiming to use various types of analysis and strategy are shown in Table 13 and the highest-ranked analysis and strategies for each broad type are shown in Table 14.

Table 13 Use of Analysis and Portfolio Management Techniques

Techniques	% Using
Fundamental Analysis	74
Portfolio Analysis	30
Technical Analysis	35
Options Strategy	24
Futures Strategy	19

Source: Carter and Van Auken (1990, p. 82). This copyrighted material is reprinted with the permission of *The Journal of Portfolio Management.*

Table 14 Highest Ranked Security Analysis and Portfolio Management Techniques

Category	Highest-Ranked Technique	Second-Ranked Technique
Fundamental Analysis (Firm)	Price/Earnings Analysis (3.78)	Ratio Analysis (3.19)
Fundamental Analysis (Industry)	Price/Earnings Analysis (3.51)	Business Cycle Analysis (3.37)
Fundamental Analysis (Market)	Monetary/Fiscal Analysis (3.66)	Price/Earnings Analysis (3.47)
Technical Analysis	Contrary Opinion Rules (2.86)	Bar and Point/Figure Charts (2.66)
Portfolio Analysis	Computer Simulation (2.11)	Return Mean-Variance Estimate (2.09)
Options Strategies	Hedging Market Changes (3.68)	Futures/Options (1.82)
Futures Strategies	Hedging Market Changes (3.69)	Hedging Interest Rates (2.69)

Respondent rating evaluated on a scale of 1 (not important) to 5 (very important). Computer simulation is the simulation of possible portfolio performance under varying scenarios. Source: Carter and Van Auken (1990, p. 83). This copyrighted material is reprinted with the permission of *The Journal of Portfolio Management.*

These results are similar to Arnold and Moizer's in as much as they again show the predominance of fundamental analysis and also show the wide use of relatively straightforward techniques such as use of price-earnings ratios and accounting ratios. Carter and Van Auken found that use of techniques was related to the size of the firm, with large firms more likely to employ all the techniques, with the exception of technical analysis.

CONCLUDING COMMENTS

The studies reviewed suggest that many techniques are being used to manage money. A fundamental approach is the most common, and relatively simple techniques predominate. The studies do not shed much light on how widespread is the use of anomaly-based strategies. One gets the feeling that the investment process is often not very disciplined, a feeling that would be confirmed by most practitioners. This does not prove that the market must be inefficient, but it does offer some hope that a disciplined approach to some of the factors discussed in this book may help add some value to investment decision processes.

PART TWO
Stock and Sector Selection

Part One dealt with both risk and return, but the major contribution for real world decisions is in terms of thinking about risk. Most practitioners turn to valuation models and other approaches to estimate returns. Part Two looks at various ways of estimating or ranking returns. The most general valuation method is the dividend discount model (Chapter 8) and the most widely used model is a short-cut version of the dividend discount model which involves estimating the appropriate price-earnings ratio for a stock (Chapter 9). Risk can be explicitly handled in these models either in a quantitative manner or subjectively. Both approaches give specific expected return numbers.

Many investors use approaches that select stocks on the basis of being more attractive than other stocks rather than by making explicit return estimates. These approaches include:

- forecasting earnings and relating them to the consensus forecast;
- reacting to earnings and dividend surprises and following earnings and dividend forecast revisions;
- buying stocks that are high on a factor that has been related to abnormal returns, e.g.,
  low price-earnings ratio
  low price-to-sales ratio
  low price
  small size
  high yield
  high book-to-market value
  net current assets less than price and other accounting attributes
  neglect
  new issues
  calendar-related factors
- following recommendations;
- using technical methods of share selection such as charts, relative strength, insiders' trades and contrary thinking.

We look at these methods in Chapters 7 and 10–18.

In Chapter 19 we discuss an asset pricing model, the multifactor arbitrage pricing theory. Usually this model is discussed after the capital asset pricing model and our location is somewhat idiosyncratic. However, there are two reasons for the location. First, putting even more theory at the start of the book would be overkill for many readers. The basic notions of the capital asset pricing model are sufficient for most of Part Two. Second, the various stock-related factors that seem to be associated with abnormal returns leads most investors to a pragmatic multifactor method of explaining stock returns. The arbitrage pricing theory is a formal multifactor equilibrium theory which uses mainly economic factors, rather than stock-related factors, to explain returns. It is used to manage money and to select shares and therefore we can justify its location in Part Two.

When constructing a share portfolio, most investors consider not only stocks but the sectors they are in. Sector strategy is briefly discussed in Chapter 20.

Finally, in Chapter 21 we discuss how a share portfolio might be constructed in practice, using either explicit return estimates or rankings. We discuss some quantitative approaches, but in an informal, algebra-free manner.

6
Assessing Investment Systems

There are numerous investment systems that have been put forward as a way of making money in the stock market. But do they work? In assessing investment systems there are a number of potential pitfalls that should be avoided. These pitfalls are worth reviewing before we look at any research. First, the pitfalls have not always been avoided in all published studies and due allowance must be made. Second, they are seldom avoided in the best-seller type of investment books. Third, many investment managers play around with data on systems such as Datastream and Bloomberg in the hope of spotting an investment system and are often unaware of the methodological problems. (This chapter draws on Alexander et al. 1993, pp. 347ff.)

POINTS TO LOOK FOR

Transactions costs

Many studies show good gross returns but neglect to consider transaction costs. This may be noted and dismissed with a casual "the profits indicated are so large that it is clear that the system would be profitable after transaction costs". Whether this is true or not depends on how much trading is required and on the type of stocks being traded. A few trades a year that cost 1–2% will soon consume abnormal profits, but often the cost is much higher—some small UK stocks have bid-ask spreads of 10%. With smaller companies the true cost may well be in excess of some notional calculation of commission, stamp duty and the usual spread. The stock may be so illiquid that either the deal cannot be effected, or can only be done over a period or at a huge discount or premium to the apparent price.

Omitting dividends

Some studies simply compare stock price performance with a price index. With this measure, any system that has a bias towards stocks with low yields, for example one involving "growth" stocks, will appear to be more successful than it is.

Ex-post-selection bias or survivor bias

If you have ever bought a stock that has gone bust you may have dreaded the end of the year newspapers which publish the ten best and worst performing shares. Who needs reminding that they have bought one of the worst performing shares in the market? But when you look at the list you find that the worst performing share has lost "only" 92% of its value, or some such number. What has happened is that the computer tape has removed stocks that have gone bust: they no longer exist and have no end-of-year price. This can pose a problem for researchers.

Consider a system of buying really awful stocks, measured perhaps in terms of very high gearing, or three consecutive years of declining sales, or whatever. One could search a database and test this investment system. There is a good chance that it will seem to work. Awful firms are probably more likely to go bust or get turned around than other firms, i.e., they are likely to generate more extreme results, but the computer tape will have systematically excluded all the firms that have gone bust. There is a bias in the test in favour of the hypothesis. Most of the recent academic studies have allowed for this problem and some computer tapes avoid this bias.

Look-ahead bias

Many systems effectively require knowledge of the future. One form of look-ahead bias is involved if, say, one relates contemporaneous changes in variables when in fact one is not actually known at the time. For example, one might believe that the money supply affects the stock market. Thus, February's money supply might affect February's stock market levels. But the February money supply numbers are not known until March, so the model is only useful if one can forecast February money supply numbers.

Look-ahead bias affected some of the early studies of the low price-earnings effect. Computing price-earnings ratios with year-end prices and earnings assumes earnings information that is not available to investors for some months. This can create a bias. Banz and Breen (1986, p. 780) give an example:

> "... the annual COMPUSTAT file reports earnings of $1.24 per share for Zenith for year end 1978. The 12-month earnings per share actually observed by the investor as of December 31, 1978 was $0.85 per share. At a December 31, 1978 price of $12.87, the earnings yield [i.e., earnings per share divided by price, times 100] computed using the COMPUSTAT data file was 9.6%, whereas the earnings yield using observed data was 6.6%. As might be expected, the price of Zenith went from the year-end price of $12.87 to a March ending price (when the new earnings were known to investors) of $15.00."

Failure to adjust for risk

As we have discussed, it is generally thought that investors will only bear extra risk for extra reward and risky assets are expected to produce higher returns than less risky assets. Accordingly, if an investment system selects risky assets it should only be considered a successful system if it produces returns greater than expected from a portfolio with an equivalent risk level. Recall that any test of an investment system that adjusts for risk is really a test of two things at once—(a) the investment system, and (b) the belief that risk is rewarded and the study is using the correct measure of risk. Academic studies have measured risk in a variety of ways such as total risk, beta risk and even unsystematic risk.

Misleading graphs

Many a fund manager will show clients a graph of the close relationship between two variables of interest. And the client, and fund manager, will believe what they think they see. But the relationship may be poor, for most of us cannot read a graph correctly. The graph in Figure 12 shows US Treasury yields and S&P 500 dividend yields. There appears to be a relationship as both trend down together. But could you make timing decisions based on this? Look closely. In four of the ten years the lines move in opposite directions: the relationship is less useful than it might have appeared. In general, it is changes that are of interest in forecasting returns and many graphs of levels should be converted to graphs of changes to see the value of the relationship for timing or selection purposes.

We also have to be careful with lead-lag relationships. If one series helps forecast another it should lead it (unless it is easier to forecast). Often graphs are produced to show how closely two series move together. Most people experience difficulty in spotting whether the lines are switching around so that sometimes the series being forecast is the leading series.

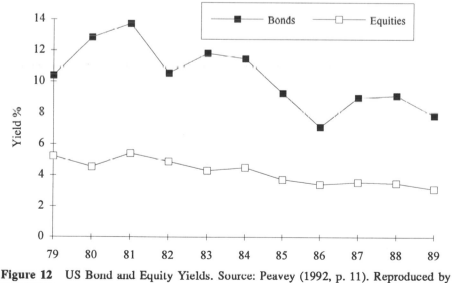

Figure 12 US Bond and Equity Yields. Source: Peavey (1992, p. 11). Reproduced by permission

Statistical and practical significance

Many academic investment studies report that their findings are statistically significant. What this means is that the finding is unlikely to be just a chance observation. For example, if we flip a coin ten times, we may find that we observe six heads. That doesn't mean the coin has a bias. Even with a fair coin there is a high probability that we will get six heads. In fact, the probability is so high that we would say that the finding was not statistically significant. It is usual to calculate the degree of statistical significance for research findings. Say we find two attributes of a stock are related to returns. The findings might be statistically significant at the 1% or 5% level. This means there is only a one in a hundred or a one in twenty chance of the findings being the result of chance rather than being true findings. Our findings are statistically significant in the sense of probably being true, but they might not be of practical significance. For example the finding might show us how to make an extra ¼% a year. This is not of much practical significance. If, however, we could make 5% extra a year, that would be of practical significance. It is important that findings are both statistically significant and of practical value.

Data-mining

It is often not difficult to find a statistical relationship that fits a set of data reasonably well. But if one has no theoretical reason for the relationship, it may just be a chance finding. If you go to a party and study the other guests you can probably find some odd feature about the group. Perhaps there are a large number of people whose names begin with B, or perhaps there are a disproportionate number of people with blue eyes. Because you've gone data-mining you've found a statistical relationship but it has no general validity. While the finding holds for this party, it won't necessarily hold for the next. Academic researchers don't intend to go on data-mining expeditions but they almost certainly do. American researchers frequently use two databases, COMPUSTAT and that of the Center for Research in Security Prices (CRSP). If 100 researchers each test the same database for different investment hypotheses, a few will appear to be statistically significant on the basis of chance. These findings may be published and the others will not. The problem is that we will never know how many other tested hypotheses failed. Nobody writes or publishes studies of the form "People attending parties in Mayfair, May 1979—February 1980, found not to have names mainly beginning with B". This sounds silly, but there is a large literature on which part of the year produces the best returns. With no prior theoretical expectations, this is a topic ripe for data-mining and spurious relationships.

Out-of-sample data

A more subtle form of data-mining is to take a well-accepted system and establish the decision rules for using it from one set of data and then calculate the returns from that system on the same data. It should work well—that's why the rule was chosen! One should always be sceptical of investment systems that are shown to work on the data that were used to construct the system. Accordingly, one should always look for an appraisal of a system made on data that was not used in the system's construction. This is usually called an out-of-sample or a holdout test.

Misleading predictive power

A predictive relationship may be true, but weak: it may not explain much of the variation in returns. If, however, one is selecting a small number of stocks from a large universe, one may get good results even with a weak relationship. It may be possible to select a high performance portfolio of 20 stocks from a universe of 1000. Quite a lot of studies use small portfolios. A fund manager who feels obliged to have a 50 stock portfolio and can only select from 400 blue chip stocks may find the relationship to be of no value.

Dating events

The academic literature often makes heroic dating assumptions. Often large statistical studies simply assume that the event of interest took place on the last day of a month. If you are running tests on 50 years of data with 1000 stocks, you can imagine why it is done. The effect on the results is unclear.

CONCLUDING COMMENTS

We have looked at a number of factors that should be taken into account when assessing claims of success for investment systems. It would be tedious to keep making these points every time we report a study so the reader should bear them in mind. We will, however, illustrate many of these problems in our discussion of some studies.

7
Earnings-Based Share Selection

Expectations about earnings lie at the heart of much investment analysis. Theoretical models of share appraisal usually require earnings estimates and investment analysts spend a great deal of time forecasting earnings. There are three main ways of utilizing earnings estimates. The first assumes that shares are correctly priced, based on consensus earnings, and that investors buy or sell depending on whether they think the consensus is too low or too high. This approach relies on superior earnings forecasting skills and it is discussed in this chapter. Variants of this approach rely on other investors reacting slowly to earnings surprises and to earnings revisions while reacting quickly oneself. These approaches are also discussed in this chapter.

The second approach involves calculating the present value of a stream of earnings or dividends (dividends are linked to earnings if one makes an assumption about the payout ratio). This approach is usually described as the dividend discount model and is discussed in Chapter 8. The third approach involves the price-earnings ratio, i.e., the price of a share divided by earnings per share. In this approach one calculates what price-earnings ratio a share should stand on and compares it with the current price-earnings ratio and buys or sells accordingly. This is discussed in Chapter 9. A variant is to buy stocks on low price-earnings ratios which is discussed in Chapter 10.

Given the importance of earnings in investment decisions, it seems worth spending a few paragraphs discussing some aspects of earnings forecasts.

HOW GOOD ARE EARNINGS FORECASTS?

An obvious issue is whether analysts' forecasts are any good. This answer must depend on what is meant by "good" and also what the comparison benchmark is. We shall begin by looking at the US evidence before turning to the UK. It is worth looking at the US studies not only because they are more numerous than the UK studies (which tend to follow along the lines set out in the US), but the bulk of the studies reported in this book relate to the US and it is therefore necessary to know a bit about US analysts. (A useful review of US evidence is Givoly and Lakonishok, 1984.)

One of the first questions one might have about analysts' forecasts are whether they are accurate or, more usefully, whether they are more accurate than some cheaply constructed "naive" forecast. Such a forecast could be that there will be no change from period to period, or whatever percentage change occurred in the previous period will recur, or perhaps the absolute change will recur. In fact most research has used rather sophisticated time series models such as exponential smoothing as a naive model! The key point about the naive approaches is that they rely solely on statistical manipulation of past data.

Some of the early studies of forecast accuracy found that the naive models did about as well as the analysts (e.g., Cragg and Malkiel, 1968 and Elton and Gruber, 1972). However these studies used small samples and short time periods. Later studies (e.g., Brown and Rozeff, 1978, Collins and Hopwood, 1980 and Fried and Givoly, 1982) used more refined techniques and longer test periods and concluded that the analysts outperformed the naive models.

One might imagine that managers would produce better forecasts than analysts. The evidence is somewhat mixed but does slightly favour managers (see e.g., Bartley and Cameron, 1991). The problem for investors is that managers do not usually, or consistently, make forecasts. Most forecasts may be unplanned and simply be the result of the CEO wanting to share some good news with shareholders. Occasionally, however, a management will wish to correct market perceptions when these are significantly in error. If there is a marked divergence between a company's forecast and analysts', it would seem to be sensible to go with the company's.

Despite the above point, analysts appear to be the best consistently available source of earnings forecasts even though they do not generate perfect forecasts. Elton et al. (1984) examined the nature of their errors using a sample of 414 firms for each of the years 1976, 1977, and 1978. Their findings were interesting:

- Analysts' forecasts improved in accuracy during the course of the year and, perhaps surprisingly, they improved at a more or less constant rate through the year. Analysts systematically overestimated growth for high growth companies and underestimated growth for low growth companies.
- By partitioning the sources of error to economy, industry and company it was possible to look more closely at the sources of error. It appeared that analysts made relatively little error in forecasting the average growth rate of earnings per share for the economy, made larger errors for the industry and the largest for the company. As the year progressed, forecast accuracy grew in general, but relatively more so for industry performance relative to company.
- Some firms are harder to forecast than others—firms for which analysts produced poor forecasts tended to be the same from year to year.
- Analysts' forecasts tended to have the greatest divergence of opinion over the first four months of the year. There tended to be greater divergence in some

industries relative to other industries every year, i.e., some industries are harder to forecast than others. Finally, analysts tended to make the greatest forecast errors for the companies with the greatest divergence of analysts' forecasts. Divergence of forecasts is therefore a measure of uncertainty.

Turning now to the UK, the major study is by Bhaskar and Morris (1984) (but see also Cooper and Taylor, 1983; Cooper, 1984; Taylor and Ward, 1985; and O'Hanlon and Whiddett, 1991). Bhaskar and Morris developed three samples. The first consisted of brokers' circulars from 58 firms providing profits forecasts for the period 1970–74. The second sample was the first sample but with an average forecast substituted for individual broker forecasts when there was more than one forecast for a company. The third sample comprised the profit forecasts of a single broking firm in August 1975.

Bhaskar and Morris found that analysts outperformed three simple naive models. However the forecasts were biased—there was a tendency to underestimate profits. Somewhat oddly, forecasts made 9–12 months before the year-end were more accurate than those made 3–9 months ahead, although those made within three months of the year-end were the most accurate. Forecast errors tended to be greatest for the smallest and the largest firms. It was not clear whether some industries were more difficult to forecast than others: the first sample suggested this was the case, but the third rather undermined this conclusion. Most US evidence suggests that there is little difference in forecasting ability amongst analysts. The UK evidence suggested there was a difference, but the authors said the results could be explained away: the better forecasters were forecasting less than a year ahead, or specialised in a few easy-to-forecast industries, etc. The above conclusions are based on looking at each issue separately: when the issues were examined simultaneously, the results were less clear-cut.

Although analysts outperform naive methods, the forecasts are not necessarily very good. Cooper (1984) reported that at the pre-interim stage, over half of all out-turns were outside the total range of UK broker's forecasts and even after the interims, one-third of out-turns were outside the total range of forecasts.

We have reviewed some of the evidence relating to analysts' forecasts. It is important to note that while UK analysts' forecasts have some features in common with US analysts', there may also be differences and some caution should be exercised before assuming that US earnings based studies necessarily apply to the UK.

THE BIG PAY-OFF FROM ACCURATE EARNINGS ESTIMATES

This section discusses the first method of share selection based on earnings estimates that was mentioned above, i.e., attempting to produce accurate earnings forecasts.

The simplest approach to selecting shares is to assume that earnings are self evidently "a good thing" and that investors should buy shares with the highest consensus earnings growth. If many investors take this view, however, it is likely that shares will be priced to reflect consensus earnings estimates: as a result there may be no relationship between returns and consensus estimates. A slightly more complex approach would be to assume that shares are correctly priced based on consensus forecasts and to try to make a more accurate forecast than the consensus. Investors with forecasting skills might assume that if their forecast is, say, 10% higher than the market's, then the share price should be 10% higher than it currently is.

Elton *et al*. (1981) examined the above issues. They studied US data consisting of a monthly file of one and two year earnings forecasts prepared in 1973, 1974 and 1975. They examined December year-end companies and looked at forecasts available in March and September. They felt that March was the first date a forecast could be made for the current year with the previous year's figures known, and September was far enough into the year for substantial evidence to be available about companies' prospects but for the full year figure not to be known with certainty. Only firms followed by at least three analysts were studied. The total sample of firms varied between 700 and 900.

Elton *et al*. analysed actual growth rates of earnings, consensus forecast growth rates of earnings and the forecast error. In their calculations of excess rates of return they used the market model to adjust for risk.

Do earnings matter? They certainly do. Elton *et al*. divided stocks into deciles on the basis of the next year's *actual* growth of earnings. In practice this could only be done by an investor with perfect forecasting ability. Elton *et al*. then looked at the excess returns that would have been earned if each decile had been purchased and held until actual earnings were announced. Stocks with the highest growth produced the highest returns. The returns were both statistically significant and economically significant. Over a 13 month period, the three deciles with the fastest growth returned 7.48% versus −4.93% for the three deciles with the slowest growth. Perfect forecasting ability is a desirable skill.

Can investors achieve excess returns by buying the stocks with the highest consensus *forecast* growth of earnings? Unfortunately they cannot. Elton *et al*. divided stocks into deciles based on forecast growth. There was no difference in returns between deciles: it seems consensus expected earnings are reflected in stock prices. This suggests that a growth stock selection strategy will not be profitable.

Of course there is a gap between actual earnings and forecasts: analysts make forecasting errors. What is the relationship between forecasting errors and returns? Firms which produced results above expectations generated excess returns and firms with results below expectations generated poor returns.

These results taken together show that earnings affect returns, consensus earnings are discounted and differences between consensus and actual earnings affect returns. Good forecasters would be able to generate excess returns from their skills.

(Klemkosky and Miller, 1984, reach a similar conclusion). But exactly how good do forecasters have to be? Elton *et al.* provided a useful table, shown here as Table 15.

Table 15 Excess Annual Returns (%) from Avoiding Firms that had the Largest Overstated Earnings Errors

Percentage of Firms Eliminated	Excess Return if Completely Accurate	Excess Return if 50% Error	Excess Return if 90% Error
0%	0.00	0.00	0.00
10%	1.56	0.78	0.16
20%	2.88	1.44	0.29
30%	3.07	1.53	0.31
40%	4.32	2.16	0.43
50%	5.77	2.88	0.58
60%	7.35	3.67	0.74
70%	9.08	4.54	0.91
80%	9.90	4.95	0.99
90%	10.42	5.21	1.04

Source: Elton *et al.* (1981, p. 986). Reproduced by permission of The Institute of Management Science

Consider the third row of the data. This shows that if forecasters could have eliminated the 20% of stocks that would most disappoint by reporting earnings below consensus expectations, they would have earned 2.88% more than normal, allowing for the risk of the stocks. If, however, of the stocks chosen, half were in the worst 20% but half were average stocks, an excess return of 1.44% would have been earned. From the Figure we can see that really good forecasting would have earned over 10% but even quite modest forecasting ability was worth something.

Accurate forecasting of earnings can lead to superior share selection. Investors should assess their own forecasting ability, irrespective of whether this takes the form of forecasts produced *ab initio*, or from adjusting consensus forecasts for their own non-consensus views (for example, on the economic outlook) or simply from selecting brokers who appear to have skills in specific sectors.

In the UK, many young fund managers have never had to make a forecast themselves and have little feel for the variables that affect forecasts or the magnitude of any effects. This suggests many will neither be able to generate their own forecasts nor judge the plausibility of analysts' forecasts. Given the pay-off from good forecasting this seems an unnecessary handicap. These comments apply, of course, to analysts using forecast-based share selection methods. As we shall see in subsequent chapters, it is perfectly possible to use non-forecast based methods.

EARNINGS SURPRISES AND REVISIONS

As we noted above, Elton *et al.* (1981) commented on earnings surprises and we now look at these in more detail. Benesh and Peterson (1986) took samples of 380 and 384 US firms for 1980 and 1981 respectively. They then split each of their samples into three parts consisting of the 50 firms with the highest returns during the year, the 50 with the lowest returns and finally all the rest. The January consensus earnings per share as reported by Institutional Broker Estimates Service (IBES) for the coming year and the actual earnings per share for that year were noted for all stocks. Table 16 shows the average projected rate of growth of earnings per share versus the actual rate for the 50 highest and 50 lowest return shares. Clearly the best performing shares benefited from positive earnings surprises whereas the worst suffered from negative earnings surprises.

Table 16   Projected vs. Actual Earnings Growth Rates (%)

	1980		1981	
	Best	Worst	Best	Worst
Average projected rate of growth in EPS	9.1	13.5	19.5	21.3
Average actual growth in EPS	27.1	−15.3	35.4	−5.3

Source: Benesh and Peterson (1986, p. 34). Reproduced by permission

If earnings surprises lead to large changes in prices, is it necessary to forecast earnings surprises, or can investors earn abnormal returns simply by responding to the surprises? Let's see. Rendleman *et al.* (1982) studied a large sample of US stocks for most of the 1970s. They categorized earnings surprises by size into ten groups on the basis of standardized unexpected earnings. These were calculated by first estimating earnings on the basis of past earnings using a simple regression model and then calculating surprises in terms of the divergence of actual earnings from forecast earnings (which they standardized by the standard error of estimate of the regression model). They examined excess returns for 20 days prior to earnings announcements and 90 days after. They found perfect ranking of their ten groups by size of surprise and excess returns; i.e., the group with the largest positive surprise earned the largest excess return, the next largest surprise group earned the next largest return, and so on. In the 20 days prior to earnings announcements share prices correctly anticipated the surprise, but continued to respond to the announcement for the next 90 days. These results were largely unaffected if an adjustment for differences in risk (measured by beta) was made for each group. This study implies that investors who respond quickly to earnings surprises will perform well. Of course, they would do even better if they could achieve some of the excess return earned prior to the earnings announcement. So, can "surprises" be forecast?

The key issue here is whether earnings surprises come as a bolt out of the blue or whether analysts have some inkling that their forecasts are off the mark. We have already seen from the research by Elton *et al.* (1984) that analysts steadily revise their forecasts which get better the closer they are made to the end of the financial year. Benesh and Peterson, in the study cited above, looked at the course of analysts' forecasts over the year for their top and bottom 50 stocks. They found a gradual reduction in forecast errors through the course of the year as analysts revised their forecasts and became more optimistic for the top performers and less optimistic for the worst performers.

Benesh and Peterson then asked whether it was possible to make excess returns if one bought or sold stocks that had significant earnings revisions in the first half of the year. They tried two rules—buying or selling after an earnings revision from the previous month of 5% and 2%. Excess returns were achieved for 7 out of the 10 holding periods for the purchases, and for all 10 periods for the sales. Unfortunately the study does not really show what returns might be achieved by a real portfolio that has to hold a specific number of stocks, bear transaction costs, etc.

Hawkins *et al.* (1984) also studied earnings revisions using earnings per share expectations data collected by IBES, and they formed portfolios of the 20 stocks whose earnings estimates had the largest increase. They formed portfolios every quarter over the period March 1975 to December 1980. The portfolios were formed at the end of the appropriate months from data available mid-month. The portfolios had holding periods of 3, 6, 9 or 12 months. Table 17 shows annual rates of return for the top 20 earnings revision stocks portfolio and the IBES universe.

Table 17 Earnings Revision Portfolios and IBES Universe: Annual Rates of Return, 1975–80

Holding Period (months)	No. of Linked Portfolios	Top 20 Earnings Revision Stocks (%)	IBES Universe (%)
3	24	27.7	20.1
6	12	30.0	18.4
9	8	26.6	17.8
12	6	25.9	17.6

Source: Hawkins *et al.* (1984, p. 31). Reproduced by permission

The earnings revision portfolios had higher betas than the IBES universe. Allowing for this reduced the excess return, but it was still substantial. For the three month holding period portfolios, the annual risk-adjusted excess return was 7.1%.

A more recent study by Dowen and Bauman (1991) asked whether the above studies (and other studies not outlined here) were picking up a smaller stock effect (see Chapter 11) or a neglected stock effect (see Chapter 15). They studied the period 1977–86. Their conclusion was that the earnings revision effect is real and has persisted despite its disclosure in earlier articles.

"Based on the results of this and earlier studies, it appears that analysts' early revisions of their EPS estimates tend to be too small, and that investors continue to be slow to respond to the useful indicators provided by analysts' consensus revisions to EPS estimates." (p. 90)

To return to our earlier question as to whether surprises can be forecast, the answer appears to be that they can if you watch analysts' earnings revisions.

The fact that investors react slowly to revisions and surprises might suggest that Wall Street is not interested in earnings revisions. This is not the case at all. For example, the US brokerage and fund management firm Sanford C. Bernstein has integrated earnings revision research with its dividend discount model approach to share selection. Other brokerage houses such as Prudential Securities, have produced regular quantitative comments on earnings surprises.

In the UK, the earnings revision effect appears to be less researched (but see O'Hanlon *et al.*, 1992) although it will surely be given increased attention. UK data have been available for a long time, but machine readable data, with data provided by a broad sample of brokers, have not been available for very long.

CONCLUDING COMMENTS

If you can forecast more accurately than the consensus, you can achieve superior returns. Unfortunately this insight does not help you to forecast better. Stocks that produce favourable earnings surprises perform well, and stocks that produce unfavourable surprises perform poorly. The abnormal returns both precede and follow the announcement. It is possible to earn abnormal returns by reacting quickly to surprises. Finally, analysts tend to be cautious in their earnings revisions and trends in earnings revisions can be used to earn abnormal returns.

The market is inefficient in its response to earnings surprises and revisions. It is possible to base a share selection strategy on these findings. But since these findings have been known for many years, one must wonder why the market does not seem to learn. It is easy to think of possible causes. Many of us have held a stock that has suffered an adverse earnings surprise and watched the price slump. We then found it hard to admit we had made an error and we rationalized no action by saying that the fall in earnings was now in the price, the earnings disappointment was a one-off, and so forth. Again, some institutional investment organizations have share selection committees that must meet before decisions to change a stance on a stock are made and that may make responses to surprises somewhat drawn-out. However, these are just *ad hoc* explanations. For the time, being no satisfactory explanation exists for the phenomena we have described, but the surprise/revision strategy still seems worth following, as long as one recognizes that it might eventually be discounted.

8
Dividend Discount Models

In Chapter 7 we saw that accurate forecasts of earnings are useful. The strategy adopted was to accept the market's valuation of a share and use better forecasts, or changes to forecasts. But should investors accept the market's valuation of a share, or can they add value to share selection by following a formal valuation process? In this chapter the dividend discount model (DDM) of valuation is examined, and in the next chapter the price-earnings ratio approach is examined. Both these approaches provide a means of developing explicit return estimates for individual shares, sectors or the market as a whole. The model builder is forced to specify those factors believed to be of relevance and to systematically forecast them.

The discounted dividend approach requires a knowledge of the concepts of the time value of money and discounting. Readers familiar with these concepts should skip the next section.

THE TIME VALUE OF MONEY AND THE ARITHMETIC OF DISCOUNTING

Would you rather have £100 now or next year? Most people would take the money now. As a result, money is said to have a time value—money is preferred sooner rather than later. There are three reasons for this: utility, risk and opportunity cost. Let's take each in turn.

Money is usually wanted for what it will buy, for its ability to provide goods that give satisfaction or utility. Most people would prefer to have that utility now rather than some time in the future. Second, having money now rather than in the future also would seem to be less risky. The chances of not getting a promised sum of money seem likely to rise the further into the future is the payment date. Finally, if one has money now, it can be placed on deposit and earn interest. Thus, a £100 now, may be worth £110 in one year's time. The £10 difference would be the opportunity cost of getting the money in a year rather than now.

Of course, while money now is worth more than money in the future, there will be some sum of future money which, if we were offered, would make us indifferent between that sum and some smaller sum today. For example, we might be indifferent between £100 today and £110 in one year. With this background, we can now move on to discounting.

The concepts that we will discuss here are compound interest, future value, present value and a discount rate. We begin with compound interest or compound growth, with which everyone is familiar. If we leave money in our bank account we benefit from compound interest. If we deposit £100 and earn interest at 10% on the balance, after one year we will have £110 (i.e., £100 x 1.10), after two years we will have £121 (i.e., £110 x 1.10), and after three years £133.10 (i.e., £121 x 1.10). The increase is larger every year because we get interest both on the original investment and on the interest added in the previous periods.

Future value is the value in the future of some quantity subject to compound interest. Present value is the value of that quantity today. Thus the future value of £100 in three years earning 10% per annum is £133.10. More generally, if P_0 is the starting principal, or present value, i is the rate of interest earned, and t is the period, the future value is:

$$P_t = P_0(1+i)^t$$

for our example it is:

$$P_3 = 100(1+0.10)^3$$

i.e., the future value in year three is:

$$£100 \times 1.10 \times 1.10 \times 1.10 = £133.10$$

The formula for future value can be rearranged to give an expression for present value:

$$P_0 = \frac{P_t}{(1+i)^t}$$

The present value of £133.10 received in three years with a discount rate of 10% is:

$$\frac{£133.10}{1.10 \times 1.10 \times 1.10} = £100$$

What we did above was to assume a discount rate and a future value and calculate a present value. We could assume a future value and present value and find the discount rate that makes them equal. For example, we could ask what discount rate would make £133.10 received in three years time equal to a present value of £100. We already know the answer, it is 10%. This discount rate is the return from the investment. Depending on the context, the discount rate is described as the required return or the expected return.

With this as background we can turn to the dividend discount model.

AN INTRODUCTION TO DIVIDEND DISCOUNT MODELS

What is the value of a share held for one year? It is the value of the dividend and the value of the share when sold in one year's time. And what is the value of the share in one year's time? It is the value of the dividend in the second year and the value of the share at the end of that year. This argument can be extended indefinitely so that the value of a share is simply the value of all the dividends for eternity. We know that money has a time value so the present value of a share (i.e., the current price) will be the sum of all the dividends, each one discounted. This can be shown as:

$$\text{Current price of share} = \frac{\text{Dividend in Year One}}{(1 + \text{discount rate})} + \frac{\text{Dividend in Year Two}}{(1 + \text{discount rate})^2} + \frac{\text{Dividend in Year Three}}{(1 + \text{discount rate})^3} + \ldots + \frac{\text{Dividend in Year n}}{(1 + \text{discount rate})^n}$$

or, using symbols:

$$P_0 = \frac{D_1}{(1 + k)^1} + \frac{D_2}{(1 + k)^2} + \frac{D_3}{(1 + k)^3} + \ldots + \frac{D_n}{(1 + k)^n}$$

where P_0 is the current price of the share, D is the dividend and k is the discount rate.

The reader might wonder what has happened to earnings. Earnings are still implicitly in this model because dividends are simply earnings multiplied by a payout ratio. Thus if a firm usually pays out 60% of earnings as a dividend there is a direct link between earnings and dividends. It is natural to ask why we only value part of earnings, i.e., the amount paid out as a dividend. The answer is that earnings not paid out as dividends are retained in the firm and invested in the maintenance or growth of the business and should result in higher dividends in the future than could otherwise be attained.

The above equation requires us to forecast each dividend until eternity. Since this is an impossible task, some simplifying assumptions are made in practice. Three common models and their assumptions are:

- a one-stage model which takes the current dividend and assumes it grows at the same rate for ever;
- a two-stage model which either makes specific forecasts for each year of the first period or assumes that growth at the same rate occurs each year, and which then assumes in the second stage the same growth rate as the average firm;
- a three-stage model which is the same as the two-stage model with an extra middle stage during which the two different growth rates converge. One version of such a model is shown in Figure 13.

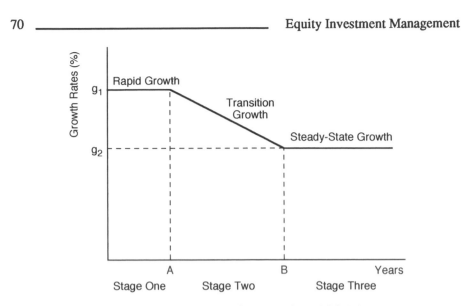

Figure 13   Three-Stage Dividend Growth Model

Most users don't go beyond a three-stage model although UK stockbrokers Kleinwort Benson use a four-stage model. Stage one is forecast dividend growth for the next two years; stage two forecasts normalized growth for years three to five; stage three assumes dividends move in a hyperbolic fashion to the market rate; and stage four assumes all dividends grow at the market rate.

These various stage models greatly simplify the dividend forecasts required. Consider first the least realistic model, the one-stage constant growth rate model. By assuming a constant growth rate, g, it can be shown that on the assumption that k is greater than g, the dividend discount model can be simplified to the following (in which we have also dropped the subscripts):

$$P = \frac{D}{k - g}$$

i.e., price = current dividend/(the discount rate − the dividend growth rate)

Alternatively, if we swap terms around:

$$k = \frac{D}{P} + g,$$

i.e., expected return = dividend yield + dividend growth rate

These last two equations are simplified dividend discount models for a firm growing at a constant rate, expressed in slightly different ways.

In the US, some investors restate the dividend discount model by considering the retention rate, payout rate and earnings. The retention rate is the percentage of earnings retained by the firm and not paid out as dividends. If $(1-b)$ represents the payout rate, b is the retention rate. If E represents year ahead earnings, then:

$$D = (1 - b)E$$

If r represents the return on equity, the growth rate of the dividend will be a function of the return on equity and the retention rate:

$$g = br$$

The constant growth model equation can now be restated as:

$$k = \frac{(1 - b)E}{P} + br$$

This is a simplified form of the dividend discount model used by US stockbrokers Goldman Sachs.

So far we have just looked at the constant growth model. The mathematics of two- and three-stage dividend discount models are more complex than the one-stage model, but these may be readily solved by computer programmes. Fuller and Hsia (1984) have suggested a simplified approach for a three-stage model. Referring back to Figure 13, we assumed a rapid growth rate g_1 that lasts for A years and a steady growth rate g_2 that begins in year B. Growth in the transition period declines at a linear rate from g_1 to g_2. The Fuller-Hsia formula is:

$$P = \frac{D}{k - g_2} \left[(1 + g_2) + \frac{A + B}{2}(g_1 - g_2) \right]$$

This is useful for rough and ready calculations, although most dividend discount adherents do not use such shortcuts.

SELECTING SHARES

How would the dividend discount method be used to select shares? There are two basic ways. For simplicity we will discuss the constant growth version of the dividend discount model. With this model, if we know the dividend of a share and the expected growth rate, we can use the market price to calculate the share's expected return. Alternatively, we can assume a discount rate and deduce what the share price should be. Deciding what discount rate to use is a tricky process and as a result most investors deduce a return from the share price. An example will be helpful. Table 18 shows data for two shares. We can take market data for the price and dividend and we must forecast the growth rate. Given this data we can calculate the expected return from each share.

Table 18   Data For Two Shares

Data	Share A	Share B
Current Price	100p	120p
Current Dividend	5p or 5%	9.6p or 8%
Forecast Dividend Growth	5%	3%

Recalling our earlier analysis:

expected return = dividend yield + dividend growth rate

The expected return for share A is 5% + 5% = 10%. For share B it is 8% + 3% = 11%. On this basis we would prefer share B. Had we decided to use the required discount rate approach we would have had to assume a discount rate. We will assume that it is 10% for both shares. Recall the constant growth formula for the price of a share:

$$P = \frac{D}{k - g}$$

For share A the data in Table 18 gives us a price of $(5/(0.10 - 0.05)) = 100$p. For share B the price is $(9.6/(0.10 - 0.03)) = 137$p. These are the prices the shares must trade at if we are to get our required return of 10%. Note that share A does trade at 100p, it is correctly priced. Share B, however, trades at 120p, i.e., it is selling below its correct value. Share B is more attractive than share A. Notice that both approaches have given us the same answer.

Let's assume that we have decided to approach the dividend discount model approach by accepting the market price of each share and calculating the implicit return that each is offering, and we do this for all the shares in the market. We can then rank all shares by their expected return. Shares at the top of the expected return list are buys, and those at the bottom are sells. This, however, ignores risk. Individual stocks may be more or less risky than the market. In our example above, share B might have been very risky and in that case a 1% higher expected return might not be enough to compensate for the extra risk. Risk should be brought into the calculation and there are many ways of doing this. Risk can be measured using beta or other measures such as the dispersion of analysts' forecasts (the wider the dispersion, the greater the uncertainty, or risk, associated with a share) or by some subjective measure provided by an analyst. Beta provides a readily available quantitative measure of risk which some firms have used, but we have seen that there are some doubts as to its value. An investor might prefer to use some more traditional measure of risk. For example, an analyst might score a share's risk in terms of financial strength, the uncertainty attached to earnings forecasts and political or regulatory risk. The share could then be put into one of, say, five categories of risk. This approach has been used by US stockbroker Kidder Peabody. We will adopt it here. Imagine that the expected rates of return for 15 shares have been calculated and these have been assigned a risk category. A graph of the data might look like that shown in Figure 14.

Each point in Figure 14 represents a stock and, using regression analysis, a line can be calculated which is the best fitting line for the data. It is an estimated security market line and shows the expected market return for each level of risk. Stocks above the line offer above average return for a given level of risk whereas stocks below the line offer a lower return. Stocks above the line are therefore relatively attractive.

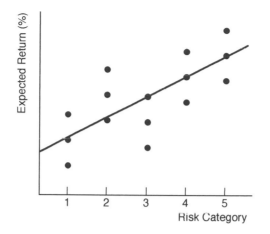

Figure 14 Expected Return and Risk for 15 Stocks

Inevitably, the discussion here has a somewhat artificial air given the constraints of space and a desire to minimize the use of mathematics. Useful descriptions of real models are contained in Lanstein and Jahnke (1979), describing the Wells Fargo system, and Donnelly (1985). Institutional investors will be able to obtain detailed papers from US stockbrokers setting out their dividend discount model approach (e.g., Einhorn, 1978) to get a feel of real models in action. For readers without access to such work, the following short description of money manager and broker Sanford C. Bernstein's approach may be helpful.

Bernstein uses a three-phase dividend discount model and applies it to S&P 500 stocks.

"An explicit five-year earnings and dividend forecast is created by an analyst for each stock in the model....Earnings estimates for the next two calendar years are monitored versus the IBES consensus. A second phase transition growth rate is also specified for a subsequent period of two to six years. The default value for the second growth phase is 7%, with a specified range of 4.5% to 15%. In the third phase of growth, all companies are assumed to grow at 7%." (Goldstein *et al.* 1991, pp. 7 and 12)

From this data the expected return for each stock is calculated. Forecasts for cyclical companies are made on a slightly different basis using the concept of normalized earnings, i.e., the earnings achieved at the midpoint of the economic cycle.

Of course, analysts can get any result they want for a stock by entering extreme forecasts. To make sure analysts' estimates are sensible, some data control elements are included in the Bernstein process. Forecast returns on equity and growth rates are checked against historical experience to see that they are plausible. As well as company controls, all analysts use the same macroeconomic assumptions. Errors in these assumptions are not too damaging as they affect all companies and the objective of the dividend discount model is to produce relative rankings rather than correct absolute values. Bernstein adjusts the required return for risk, but does not use betas to do this. Instead it uses duration, which measures the timing of investors' return on their investment, as a proxy for risk.

Bernstein's model has tended to rank most highly stocks that offer good value in the sense of having above average yields and price-to-book and price-earnings ratios at a discount to the market. The advantage of a dividend discount model, claims Bernstein, is its flexibility. Depending on growth prospects and how stocks are priced, high yield stocks are not necessarily attractive, and the price-to-book discount can sometimes be quite small.

PROBLEMS WITH DIVIDEND DISCOUNT MODELS

Despite the flexibility that Bernstein notes, dividend discount models do tend to favour stocks with high yields and low price-earnings ratios. Many critics see this as a problem and there has been a lively debate as to whether this is a consequence of how the market values stocks or whether there is some fatal flaw in the structure of the dividend discount model.

There are, in fact, many difficult issues that have to be faced with dividend discount models (see, e.g., Nagorniak, 1985) but three are worth mentioning here. First there is the question of the sensitivity of the model to changes in assumptions. Slightly different assumptions lead to dramatically different answers. To see this, assume a share has a dividend of 10, a discount rate of 10% and a growth rate of 5%. The share price should be 200. Change the growth rate to 6% and the price changes to 250. Quite a difference. Yet it is easy to see the scope for disagreements about assumptions.

A second problem is that of the quality of the inputs. If the forecasts are poor, so too will be the model's results. We have seen above how Bernstein processes its analysts' forecasts to get consistent and plausible inputs. This forecasting problem, however, is not unique to dividend discount models, it applies equally to attempts to forecast the appropriate price-earnings ratio for a share. In fact, one might expect the dividend discount model approach to lead to improved forecasts. There is a tendency for investors to categorize some stocks as growth stocks, as though this were a permanent condition. In reality, periods of rapid growth seldom last for very long. The structure of the typical dividend discount model of a major user of the approach will tend to force forecasters to be realistic. Most models in use have a third stage that pushes growth down to the average market level.

A third problem for dividend discount models is that there are periods when the market changes its trade-off between value and safety. In a recessionary period there may be a scramble for "safe" companies which promise to continue to increase earnings. These companies may be bid up to high prices and offer poor value on a dividend discount model analysis. Over time this will unwind, but any institutional investor slavishly following a model's output will have awful performance for a period and may lose a substantial part of its client base. Most types of investment style suffer poor periods and the dividend discount model is not unique in this. (For the recent trials and tribulations of value managers and some dividend discount managers in the US, see Rohrer, 1991.)

It may strike the reader that the prospects for a dividend discount based approach being successful do not look promising. An approach that forecasts dividends to eternity, even if only approximately, is not easy to accept. But intellectually the approach makes sense and is only the equity equivalent of how bonds are valued, i.e., by discounting the value of a stream of interest payments and the principal. Moreover some of the other valuation models available have to handle the variables required by a dividend discount model.

IS THE DIVIDEND DISCOUNT MODEL USEFUL?

The acid test is whether dividend discount models are used and whether they pick out undervalued stocks. In the UK, such models are not in widespread use. In the US, the major brokers (e.g., Goldman Sachs, Salomon, and Merrill Lynch) produce data generated by some form of dividend discount model, a number of money management firms use this output and some have produced their own models. A few firms manage money largely or exclusively by dividend discount models. Two trade press articles which give a good feel for the use of these models in the US are by Donnelly (1985) and Rohrer (1989).

Although investment textbooks usually discuss dividend discount models at length, scant evidence is provided that they work. Indeed, there have been surprisingly few studies published in the academic and professional journals assessing dividend discount models. One is by Sorensen and Williamson (1985) who tested four models; a price-earnings ratio approach, a constant growth model, a two-period growth model, and a three-period growth model. Their price-earnings ratio model simply ranked stocks from low price-earnings ratios to high. The other models were similar to those discussed in this chapter. They took a random sample of 150 firms from the S&P 400 at January 1981. They took data necessary for model estimation at that date from IBES (which provides industry concensus estimates) and Merrill Lynch. They used each model to rank the 150 stocks by degree of undervaluation. Stocks ranked by each model were then split into quintiles, i.e., the 30 most undervalued companies, the 30 next most undervalued companies, etc. They calculated a one year holding return for January 1981–January 1982, a two year holding return for January 1981–January 1983, and a one year holding return for January 1982–January 1983 which used data available in January 1982.

The results were excellent, all systems ordered the quintiles correctly in terms of returns, and the more complex the system, the better the results. Table 19 shows the results for the two year holding period. The returns shown have been rounded to two figures and are not risk-adjusted—risk adjustment strengthened the results.

Various US brokers, e.g., Salomon and Goldman Sachs, have periodically reported on the value of dividend discount models and claim that they are successful at ranking shares. No real world managers appear to produce results anywhere

Table 19 Rates of Return (%) by Quintile for Four Models S&P 400: January 1981–83

Quintile	Three period	Two period	Constant growth	PER
1 undervalued	30	29	27	27
2	28	25	23	22
3	18	14	15	14
4	6	11	9	10
5 overvalued	−5	−2	3	5

Source: Sorensen and Williamson (1985, p. 65). Reproduced by permission

close to the results claimed in the Sorensen and Williamson study or by most brokers, and quite different results were reported by Michaud and Davis (1982). They examined four samples utilizing different numbers of stocks, data sources and sample periods (specifically 1973–80, 1973–76, 1977–88 and 1979–80). They concluded that the dividend discount model had positive, but statistically insignificant, forecasting performance. The forecasting performance disappeared once the low price-earnings ratio and high dividend yield bias of their model was controlled for. Jacobs and Levy, 1988b, also found positive but insignificant returns for the period mid-1982 to mid-1987.

The record of fund management firms that use dividend discount models can be examined, but few use solely these models. One of the most rigorous users, Sanford C. Bernstein, claims that

> "In the long term, the dividend discount model yields outperformance. The top quintile of the model has outperformed the market by about 3% a year on average since 1980. Using a longer 20-year period the premium is about 4%." (Goldstein *et al.*, 1991, p. 14)

Other firms claim that the model works, although it should also be noted that some former supporters have now abandoned the approach.

We noted at the beginning of the chapter that good forecasting (i.e., information) was useful and asked whether processing of information by a dividend discount model was useful, i.e., could a dividend discount model identify valuation errors. Looking at the results of real firms confounds the information and valuation effects. Note, however, that Sorensen and Williamson used some consensus data in their test—in that case the dividend discount model worked mainly as a valuation tool. If most investors do not use rigorous valuation tools, it might not be surprising if the dividend discount model were to prove useful. We'll discuss this again in the next chapter.

CONCLUDING COMMENTS

The evidence suggests that there is probably merit in dividend discount models. The logic and evidence in favour of these models is greater than that supporting many investment approaches that have adherents, so it is perhaps a little surprising that there are relatively few fund management firms committed to the approach. Perhaps this can be explained by the discipline and commitment that is required. Significant expenditure is required to set up the analytical capability, and a major cultural shift is required. Research has to be processed in a specific way and analysts and fund managers lose their independence. Flair is played down and egotistical fund managers have to become good team players. Chief executives have to be modestly numerate. The major US brokers have invested in developing models, but smaller brokers have generally not done so, presumably because they do not follow a large enough universe of stocks to make the ranking exercise worthwhile. One gets the impression that brokers' institutional salesmen are not in love with the dividend discount model. Sexy stock stories are easy enough to peddle, but selling revisions of computer ranking lists is hard work.

Dividend discount models have not made much headway in the UK; some brokers have experimented with them and then shelved them—for example, James Capel toyed with a model more than a decade ago but gave up. The UK has generally invested less in research technology than the US; UK fund managers are not as well trained as US managers and disciplined investment styles have only recently been accepted by some UK fund management firms. The UK financial culture has not been right for dividend discount models, but the author expects that culture to be transformed in the next few years with a move to more quantitative investment styles.

9
Price-Earnings Ratio Models

We saw in Chapter 5 that few analysts use the dividend discount model and most use a price-earnings ratio model for selecting stocks or analysing market levels. We also noted that analysts typically approach price-earnings ratios in an informal manner. In this chapter we look at both the theory and the practice of selecting shares by assessing their appropriate price-earnings ratio.

WHAT DETERMINES PRICE-EARNINGS RATIOS? THE THEORY

The theoretical background to determining the appropriate price-earnings ratio is straightforward. Recall from the previous chapter the simplest form of the dividend discount model:

$$P = \frac{D}{k - g}$$

where P is the price of the share, D is the current dividend, k is the discount rate and g is the rate of dividend growth.

We can use this to derive some information about what affects price-earnings ratios. If we divide both sides by E, we get:

$$\frac{P}{E} = \frac{\frac{D}{E}}{k - g}$$

This tells us that a price-earnings ratio will be higher the greater is g, the growth rate, the larger is the payout ratio D/E, and the lower is k, the discount rate. If we assume that a company has a 50% payout ratio, a 7% growth rate and a 12% discount rate, we can calculate the price-earnings ratio as follows:

$$\frac{P}{E} = \frac{\frac{D}{E}}{k - g} = \frac{0.5}{0.12 - 0.07} = 10$$

Similar calculations can be made for other discount rates and rates of growth. Such calculations are brought together in Table 20.

Table 20 The Price-Earnings Ratio as a Function of Growth and the Discount Rate

Discount Rate (%)	Rate of Growth (%)			
	5	6	7	8
9	12.5	16.7	25.0	50.0
10	10.0	12.5	16.7	25.0
11	8.3	10.0	12.5	16.7
12	7.1	8.3	10.0	12.5

Notice that the impact of a rising discount rate varies with the growth rate. As the discount rate rises from 9% to 12%, the price-earnings ratio for a share with a growth rate of 6% would halve, but for a share with a growth rate of 8% it would fall to a quarter of its previous level. Notice also that at the lowest discount rate shown, 9%, extra growth has a dramatic effect on the price-earnings ratio which quadruples as we read across Table 20. However, with a 12% discount rate, the effect of the same increase in growth is only a 76% increase in the price-earnings ratio.

Table 20 is illustrative only. It assumes that the specified growth rates are maintained for ever, but we know that fast growth stocks, for example, eventually have more normal growth rates. Accordingly, the effects shown in the table will be more muted in the real world. Further, our simple calculations assume that when one variable is changed, the others remain constant. No allowance is made for interdependence among variables. For example, if growth prospects are good, a firm might increase its gearing. The net effect will depend on a balance between a higher g and a possibly higher k, if increased gearing is thought to increase risk. Again, a firm that increases its payout may reduce its growth prospects.

Despite the shortcomings of Table 20, it does illustrate why some investors like growth stocks and some do not. A little extra growth generates a big increase in the price-earnings ratio, or a lot of multiple expansion in the market's jargon, and a big increase in a share's price. But when things go wrong—interest rates rise or the growth does not materialize—the scope for a share price collapse is equally obvious.

ASSESSING THE APPROPRIATE PRICE-EARNINGS RATIO

Real investors tend not to use the algebraic approach shown above. The usual approach is to go through the following steps:

1. Data is examined for a number of years. Although UK analysts will look at a number of past years in their analysis, in the summary data they present in their share evaluation conclusion they are likely to show one year's historical

figure and two forecast years' figures. These will be the next financial year to be reported and the following year. The "next" year will thus be the current year or even a year that has ended but not yet been reported.

2. For these three years, earnings per share data will be presented and this will necessitate forecasts for two years. Given that one of these years will be wholly or partly finished, the forecasts do not go very far into the future.

3. A price-earnings ratio will be calculated for each year. To do this the *current* price will be used for each year.

4. A price-earnings ratio relative will be presented for each year, either relative to the market or the appropriate sector. For example, if the market, stock and sector are selling on price-earnings ratios of 12, 10 and 8 respectively, the stock is selling on a discount to the market (i.e., 10/12 or 83% of the market rating) and a premium to its sector (i.e., 10/8 or 125% of its sector's rating).

5. An analyst may then decide the appropriate price-earnings ratio or price-earnings ratio relative for the stock on the basis of experience. The factors that are likely to be considered are growth rate of earnings, both past and present, past sales growth, profitability, stability of past earnings, financial strength, quality of management, as well as the nature and prospects of the industry, competitive position of the company and so forth.

6. The appropriate price-earnings ratio or price-earnings ratio relative derived from step 5, is compared to the current ratio: If appropriate exceeds current, the stock is a buy, and a sell if current exceeds appropriate. Comparison will also be made based on forecast earnings.

7. As an alternative to the blending of factors and derivation of the appropriate price-earnings ratio of step 5, the current price-earnings ratio may be compared to the historical sector or market price-earnings ratio relative ranges for the past 10 years. Thus a stock that has traded in a sector relative range of 120–150 and is selling on a current relative of 125, would appear cheap. Steps 5 and 7 can be brought together. For example, if some deterioration in the company's prospects had occurred, or are expected to occur, it might seem that the future sector relative range should be somewhat lower, say 100–130, in which case a stock with a current relative of 125 would be unattractive.

8. Analysts sometimes utilize a concept of normalized earnings in their price-earnings ratio assessment. In cyclical sectors, a high price-earnings ratio may not signify growth prospects but the collapse of earnings and the market's assessment that they will recover. Accordingly some analysts will assess a price-earnings ratio on the basis of what it would be using normalized earnings. An alternative would be to use the current rating but, when making the comparison against the market or sector relative range, to bear in mind that the stock should be assessed not against the full range, but that part appropriate to the prevailing stage of the economic cycle.

This approach certainly seems more straightforward than the dividend discount model discussed earlier. This is misleading, however, because the approach is driven by earnings forecasts and the determination of the appropriate price-earnings ratio and the analyst should consider similar factors to those which go into the dividend discount model. The price-earnings ratio approach seems simple because the factors that go into the assessment and how they are weighted and processed is skipped over in an outline such as that shown above.

The textbooks do not skip over the factors that must be considered, but they are not very helpful in explaining how the investor handles them. In determining the appropriate price-earnings ratio investors are advised to analyse company accounts, review corporate strategy, appraise industry prospects, assess management and so forth. Now the problem with all of this is that it is not clear how one makes the assessment, or pulls it together. For example, if a company has the conventional levels of liquidity and gearing, what does that imply for the price-earnings ratio? Again, few investors will have much idea as to how to assess corporate strategy and industry prospects: one suspects they will largely extrapolate recent experience. We shall show some evidence for this in Chapter 10. Many investors place great store by the quality of management, but how does one assess this and reflect it in the appropriate price-earnings ratio? There is some evidence relating to quality of management and stock returns which is worth reviewing here, both because it is interesting in itself, and because it illustrates the sort of problems that have to be faced with the appropriate price-earnings ratio approach.

QUALITY OF MANAGEMENT

One might expect excellently-managed companies to perform well and investment analysts often write about the quality of the management of the company they are appraising, and justify a higher rating when they perceive high quality management. Nonetheless, it is still worth asking whether excellent management really does offer investors the prospects of abnormal returns.

There are three reasons why one might suspect that high quality management does not lead to abnormal returns. First, good management should already be reflected in earnings, sales, etc. Second, even if good management is a separate factor (because today's earnings represent yesterday's management whereas today's management will generate tomorrow's earnings) why is this not already reflected in a share's price? Third, what is good management, and who would recognize it? Before making some general comments let's look at some empirical studies.

Granatelli and Martin (1984) analysed the performance of a portfolio of US stocks headed by award-winning CEOs in the period 1975–80. *Financial World* magazine published annually a list of 10 CEOs selected for gold and silver awards by panels of security analysts. One panel selected and ranked the three top CEOs in each of 53 industries. A second panel chose from these the top CEOs in broader industry groups. Granatelli and Martin constructed their portfolios by investing in the firms of the top ten CEOs and changing the portfolio each year when the new award winners were announced. They constructed a control portfolio by selecting ten firms in the same industries as the well-managed firms. (They simply took the next firm on their database tape after the well-managed firm.) They then calculated the returns and standard deviations for the well-managed portfolio, the control portfolio and the market. Their results are shown below in Table 21.

Table 21 Annual Holding Period Return and Standard Deviation (%) 1975–80

	Well-Managed	Control	Market
Average Return	21.8	23.4	16.4
Standard Deviation	24.0	19.2	15.9

Source: Granatelli and Martin (1984, p. 73). Reproduced by permission

The well-managed firm portfolio beat the market—albeit with more risk—but randomly-selected firms in the same industries as the well-managed firms offered the highest return, and with less risk than the well-managed firms.

The first detailed empirical study on management and the market was by Clayman (1987). This draws on the best-seller by Peters and Waterman (1982) *In Search of Excellence: Lessons From America's Best Run Companies*. Peters and Waterman began with a list of 62 companies considered to be innovative and excellent by "informed observers". The companies were screened for six measures of long-term financial superiority. From the list of 43 companies (36 of which were publicly-traded) that passed all the criteria, Peters and Waterman deduced the behavioural attributes that contributed to excellence. There were eight, which they described as: a bias towards action; close relations with customers; autonomy and entrepreneurship; productivity through people; hands-on and value-driven; stick to the knitting; simple form, lean staff; and simultaneous loose-tight properties.

Clayman (p. 56) notes that "The list of excellent companies compiled in 1981, however, makes curious reading in 1987." Clayman gives some examples of companies that had encountered difficulties. More importantly, she studied 29 companies of the original 36 publicly-traded excellent companies for which complete data was available. Data on the six financial attributes used as selection criteria for these 29 companies for the period 1976–80 is presented as well as the same data for the period 1981–85. Of the 29 companies, 86% experienced declines in asset growth rates over the two periods: 93% had declines in equity growth rates; 69% had a drop in market-to-book ratios; 83% had lower average returns on capital employed; 79% had lower average returns on equity; and 83% had lower average returns on sales. These figures suggest regression to the mean, although no data is given for what was happening to the average firm over the same periods. In terms of investment results, over the period 1981–85, 11 of the 29 companies outperformed the S&P 500, and 18 underperformed. Because the companies that outperformed did especially well, an equally-weighted portfolio of all 29 companies outperformed the S&P 500 by 1.1% per annum over the five years.

Clayman then looked at companies that were not excellent, or dogs as they are usually called in the market. Companies in the S&P 500 were ranked on the six financial variables used in the excellent companies selection process. A portfolio was constructed that consisted of companies that ranked in the bottom third on every variable. The portfolio consisted of 39 companies. These companies showed improving ratios for two financial variables for 1981–85 compared to 1976–80, and deteriorating values for four variables. More interesting was the performance of the dogs: 25 outperformed the S&P 500 and 14 underperformed. An equally-weighted portfolio of dogs outperformed the S&P 500 by 12.4% per annum. The betas and standard deviations of returns of the excellent and dog portfolios were approximately the same, but the study probably suffers from a survivorship bias (recall our comments in Chapter 6).

A later, more detailed study, by Kolodny et al. (1989), using the Peters and Waterman framework, came to the conclusion that ex ante knowledge of excellent firm characteristics cannot be used to produce superior returns. Bannister (1990) extended Clayman's study over a longer time period and came to a similar conclusion.

What is one to conclude from these studies? Well, one might question whether Peters and Waterman truly capture the essence of excellent management. Some writers would see excellence of management as situationally-specific. Thus, excellence would always be relative to changing economic circumstances and to the type of configuration an organization has—e.g. entrepreneurial, mature, diversified, professional and innovative to use Mintzberg's (1979 and 1992) terms. Nonetheless, Peters and Waterman's analysis is much more sophisticated than the typical broker's shallow comments on management. It is doubtful that most analysts have much idea how to assess management quality. They probably just interpret recent good performance as good management.

Irrespective of one's reaction to these views, the evidence suggests that whether good management is selected on the basis of analysts' votes or detailed studies, there is no pay-off to investors from good management. This is not really surprising. Not only will the market tend to discount any obvious factors, it should always be borne in mind that economic forces tend to eliminate both good and bad margins: new firms enter attractive areas and some firms exit from unattractive areas. And, as we discuss in Chapter 10, there is a large random element in economic life. It is hard to see how one will establish an appropriate price-earnings ratio by adding in a quality factor. We could make similar points about many of the factors that go into judging an appropriate price-earnings ratio. This is not to say the judgement cannot be made, just that it is not easy.

OTHER APPROACHES TO PRICE-EARNINGS RATIOS

A rather different approach to that of looking at accounts, management quality etc., has been to go back to theory (such as that at the start of this chapter) and specify some factors that should affect price-earnings ratios and then try to find, by multiple regression analysis, the equation that best fits the real world data. This approach was popular in the 1960s and early 1970s and one of the best known studies is for the US market by Whitbeck and Kisor (1963). They used a sample of 135 NYSE stocks to estimate the relationship between the price-earnings ratio, historical growth, historical dividend payout ratio and risk—which they measured as the volatility of past earnings around the earnings trend (they were writing in the pre-beta days). The equation they estimated was:

price-earnings ratio = 8.2 + (1.5 × earnings growth) + (6.7 × the payout ratio) − (0.2 × the standard deviation of earnings)

The equation gives us an estimate of the simultaneous impact of three factors on the level of the price-earnings ratio for the period studied. The signs tell us the direction of the impact. The equation tells us that the price-earnings ratio increased as a company's earnings growth increased and the greater was the payout ratio. The price-earnings ratio fell as risk increased.

The above equation could be used for share selection in the following manner: for any share calculate the values of the three variables and then use the equation to estimate the "appropriate" price-earnings ratio. Compare the forecast with the current ratio and then sell if the forecast is below the current ratio and buy if it is above. Whitbeck and Kisor claimed that their model was successful in picking shares. This led to a spate of studies for the US and some for the UK. These studies, however, have fallen out of fashion. To see why, a study by Malkiel and Cragg (1970) will be examined.

Malkiel and Cragg collected data for 178 US corporations and studied the period 1961–65. In an attempt to explain price-earnings ratio differences, they collected data on forecasts of long-term growth rates of earnings, estimates of "normal" earnings for the preceding year ("normal" earnings in this case assumed that the economy was operating at a normal level and were adjusted for one-off events such as strikes), forecasts of the next year's earnings, and expectations about the future variability of earnings. This expectations data came from 17 investment firms.

For each year Malkiel and Cragg calculated a regression equation. They used six different models and obtained high R^2 for every model. The results for one are shown in Table 22, which shows that the four variables used in the analysis have the expected signs: price-earnings ratios increase with increases in long-term growth, short-term growth and the payout ratio. The price-earnings ratio is negatively related to risk. Long-term growth has the greatest impact on the price-earnings

Table 22 Normalized Price-Earnings Ratios Estimated Using Expectations Data US: 1961–1965

Year	Constant	Forecast long-term growth	Forecast short-term growth	Dividend payout ratio	Instability of earnings	R^2
1961	−27.96	2.91	31.78	4.57	−0.58	0.77
1962	3.42	1.61	6.88	3.21	−2.20	0.79
1963	−11.33	2.29	15.11	8.11	−1.14	0.80
1964	−9.29	1.87	15.20	7.03	−1.13	0.78
1965	−11.15	2.42	13.78	4.22	−0.81	0.83

Source: Malkiel and Cragg (1970, p. 612). Reproduced by permission of the American Economic Association

ratio. The growth variables are always statistically significant and the payout ratio and risk are usually significant. The R^2 show the amount of variation of price-earnings ratios explained by the four variables. For example, in 1961, 77% of the variation is explained. The equations do seem to have captured variables that are important in determining a price-earnings ratio. But could investors have made money from the findings?

Malkiel and Cragg used their equations to pick undervalued shares and measured returns over one year. The results were poor. There were several reasons for this:

- the valuation relationship changes over time. An inspection of the table reveals that the coefficient of each variable changes from year to year. For example growth, both long- and short-term, had its biggest weighting in 1961 and its smallest in the following year, 1962. In 1962, risk had its most negative effect, and its smallest effect in the previous year.
- analysts' forecasts are not accurate—every time a forecast changes, so too does the appropriate price-earnings ratio for a share.
- the model is too general and misses specific firm variables. For example, Malkiel and Cragg noted that Reynolds Tobacco always appeared mispriced and it was clear that the risk of government intervention was important but was not picked up in the equation.

Malkiel and Cragg concluded that while they could explain a large part of the variability of price-earnings ratios with a few variables, their findings were not useful in selecting undervalued shares. (For a discussion of unstable coefficients in the UK, see Bomford, 1968.) Notice, however, that neither Whitbeck and Kisor nor Malkiel and Cragg are really using the price-earnings model. Neither has a discount rate in their equation and both use linear additive relationships whereas the simple model at the start of the chapter is not of that form.

IS THE PRICE-EARNINGS RATIO MODEL WORTHWHILE?

We have seen that whether we treat price-earnings ratios informally or formally (via regression analysis) there are some difficulties. This does not mean that some investors are not able to use the method successfully: but we seem to be looking at a craft rather than a science. Moreover it is easy to believe that other approaches are more attractive. For the price-earnings ratio model to be useful, investors must be able to forecast profits accurately (or, at worst use consensus estimates) and be able to assess the appropriate price-earnings ratio. If an investor can forecast profits accurately, that alone is sufficient to earn abnormal profits (see Chapter 7) and it is not necessary to go on to try to find valuation errors as well. Of course, if they can be found, they will add extra value. Faulty judgements, however, might undermine the value of accurate forecasts.

If investors wish to process information, the dividend discount model seems a better model. It too will suffer from changes in how investors value growth and so forth (although dividend discount model adherents tend to have longer time horizons than other investors and be willing to wait for valuations to return to "normal"), but is a better approach because it properly allows for the time value of returns. It also forces investors to accept that above-average growth does not continue for ever. The structure of the price-earnings ratio approach does not encourage, but nor does it discourage, any psychological bias investors may have towards emphasizing recent experience. If this occurs, it is likely that highly-rated "appropriately valued" stocks will in fact be overvalued. There is evidence that low price-earnings ratio stocks outperform. Since most investors use an appropriate price-earnings approach, this suggests that investors are not capable of determining "appropriate" price-earnings ratios and have a systematic bias. Rather than try to find mispriced securities on the basis of appropriate price-earnings ratios, many investors might be better advised to buy low-rated stocks. All of this suggests that for many investors the most widely used technique may not be very useful. That is a comforting conclusion. It suggests that there is scope to beat the market by using other techniques.

CONCLUDING COMMENTS

We know from Chapter 5 that analysts and investors prefer a price-earnings approach to that of a dividend discount approach. The above analysis and evidence suggests that price-earnings models require much the same sort of long-term forecasts as dividend discount models. It is possible to quantify factors which are influencing price-earnings ratios at any particular time. Unfortunately the importance of these factors varies from year to year.

Investors with superior forecasting and analytical skills might be able to use the appropriate price-earnings ratio approach successfully, but it may be doubted that most investors can. Most investors who subjectively focus on growth, quality, and so forth, probably rate stocks more on the basis of what the companies have achieved than what they will achieve. We saw an illustration of this in our examination of management quality.

In the next few chapters we abandon the difficult notion of appropriate ratings and select shares simply on the basis of the extent they posess certain attributes.

──────── 10 ────────
└ Low PER and Low PSR Stocks ┘

In Chapters 10–13 we look at six attributes that have been found to be related to abnormal returns: low price-earnings ratio stocks, low price-to-sales stocks, low price stocks, small stocks, high yield stocks and high book-to-market value. There is a degree of artificiality in looking at each attribute individually because many studies treat several attributes together and the attributes appear to be related to each other. This is not surprising—the six attributes are calculated using a common variable, price per share. If we rank stocks into deciles based on one attribute, we find that we will also have roughly ranked the stocks by the other attributes too. Nonetheless, we will treat each attribute separately and, to keep chapter lengths manageable, we have spread our discussion over several chapters. As a practical matter, investors would wish to untangle the interrelationships so that they know whether to pick stocks by one attribute or use several, and also which attributes deliver the highest risk-adjusted returns. We also would like to think about each attribute separately to see if we can work out why it is rewarded and if we are happy accepting exposure to that attribute. Selecting stocks on the basis of low price-earnings ratio, low price-to-sales ratio, high book-to-market and high yield is usually described as a value-based strategy, sometimes as a contrarian strategy. The assumption is that the market makes a systematic valuation error.

Before we begin our discussion of the six attributes we must say a bit about January and a bit about experimental design. January is a special month—as is discussed in Chapter 17—because many US studies have shown that a number of reported relationships apply only to January or especially to January. For example, we might find that attribute X is related to annual returns, but when we look at monthly data we find the annual relationship is based on a very strong relationship in January and a weak relationship for the rest of the year. We mention this effect now because it crops up in a number of studies we will discuss before we get to Chapter 17.

Experimental design is trickier. As we have noted, if we pick a portfolio of low price-earnings stocks we may also have picked a portfolio of small stocks. So, how can we tell which attribute is driving returns? A number of studies have tried to get round this problem by splitting the available sample into a number of portfolios which combine attributes in a controlled manner. These portfolios are constructed on "within-groups" only and "within-groups" plus randomization methods. This sounds awful, but it is easy to understand, if we take it in stages.

Imagine we are interested in size and low price-earnings ratios and we want to find the effect of each attribute alone and the interaction between the two. We need to find a way of stopping size varying with the price-earnings ratio and also to control the variation of each attribute. Here's how we could do it.

1. We begin by arraying the sample by size from the largest to smallest stock and then splitting it into quintiles, i.e., five groups ranging from large stocks through to small. (Different studies use different numbers of groups.)
2. Now we take the smallest quintile and array all the stocks in it by price-earnings ratio.
3. Next we split this smallest size quintile into price-earnings ratio quintiles.
4. If we repeat steps 2 and 3 for every size quintile we will have 25 groups.

So, we arrange our data by size and then sort each size quintile into price-earnings ratio quintiles. This will show us what happens as we vary either size or price-earnings ratio. Table 23, which we'll come to shortly, gives an example.

The next step is slightly more complex and involves re-grouping our data.

1. From every size quintile we can take the lowest price-earnings ratio group and use them to form one new group. What does it consist of? All the stocks have low price-earnings ratios, but they were drawn from every size quintile so they are random with respect to size.
2. Next we can pull out the second lowest price-earnings ratio group from every size quintile and form our second group. And so on.
3. At the end of the process we will have five portfolios ranked by price-earnings ratio but random with respect to size.

If we start with our sample arranged by price-earnings ratio we can allow size to vary and randomize with respect to price-earnings ratio. If we think other variables move together, for example, dividend yield and low price-earnings ratio, we have to go through the whole randomization procedure again.

With this as background we can look at some studies.

LOW PRICE-EARNINGS RATIO STOCKS

The Evidence

Every investor probably accepts that a company's price-earnings ratio should vary with its growth prospects and perhaps with some measure of "quality" or safety. Although price-earnings ratios should be forward looking, it would not be surprising if views about the future were formed at least partly on the basis of the past. Thus one might expect that price-earnings ratios would be related to past earnings and sales growth, profitability, stability of past earnings, financial strength, quality of management, as well as the nature and prospects of the industry, competitive position of the company and so forth (see, e.g., Cottle *et al.*, 1988). But does the market do a good job in judging the "appropriate" price-earnings ratio for shares using this historical data plus forecasts, or can abnormal returns be made by purchasing portfolios of high or low price-earnings ratio stocks?

There are two camps in the investment community—one advocates low price-earnings ratio stocks, whereas the other advocates growth stocks. Famous investors can be found in each camp, for example Templeton in the first and T. Rowe Price in the second. Graham and Dodd's famous textbook, first published in 1934, (current edition by Cottle *et al.*) recommended stocks with modest price-earnings ratios. What is the evidence?

Since Nicholson (1960), there has been a steady stream of articles reviewing the US evidence and this has generally pointed to low price-earnings ratio stocks generating abnormal returns. This literature has been reviewed in a number of books and articles (e.g., Melnikoff, 1988). Amongst the most influential articles in the investment community have been those by Basu (1975), (1977) and (1983). However the academic evidence is somewhat mixed. While it is generally agreed that low price-earnings ratio stocks produce abnormal returns, there have been disputes as to whether the effect vanishes when firm size is allowed for (e.g., Reinganum, 1981, and Banz and Breen, 1986) or whether it subsumes the size effect (e.g., Basu, 1983) or whether both variables have independent effects (e.g., Cook and Rozeff, 1984, Jaffe *et al.*, 1989, and Keim, 1990). The study by Jaffe *et al.* will be outlined here after first making a technical point.

Although this section is about price-earnings ratios, the research literature often looks at the earnings-price ratio, the reciprocal of the price-earnings ratio. There are two advantages of using earnings-price ratios. First, companies with negative earnings are automatically ranked as having the lowest earnings-price ratios, whereas they are not automatically ranked as the highest price-earnings ratios. (Most studies have simply ignored companies with negative earnings.) Second, price-earnings ratios "blow up" when earnings approach zero and this can cause statistical problems: this does not happen with earnings-price ratios. While this switch is statistically convenient it means the reader has to do some mental gymnastics. To avoid this, we will often discuss results in terms of price-earnings ratios even when the study being discussed used earnings-price ratios. However, when we don't, remember that a positive relationship between earnings-price ratio and abnormal returns (i.e., the higher the earnings-price ratio, the greater the abnormal profit) is the same as a negative relationship between price-earnings ratios and abnormal returns (i.e., low price-earnings ratios offer high abnormal returns).

Reverting now to the study by Jaffe *et al.*, this used a substantially longer sample period, 1951–86, than previous studies and examined size, price-earnings ratio, month-of-year effect and share price. Jaffe *et al.* drew their data from databases which included NYSE and AMEX firms. Firms for which relevant data were available ranged from 352 in 1950 to 1,309 in 1974. Portfolios were constructed by the following ranking procedure. Firms were ranked by earnings-price ratio and placed into one of six groups. Group 0 included all securities with negative earnings and groups 1 to 5 contained securities with positive earnings. Stocks with the lowest earnings-price ratio were placed in group 1 and the highest in group 5. Next, the stocks in each earnings-price ratio group were ranked by market value into five sub-groups with the smallest stocks in sub-group 1 and the largest in 5. This procedure resulted in 30 portfolios, each of which was updated annually.

To avoid look-ahead bias (see Chapter 6) the authors used year-end earnings and the end of March price to calculate earnings-price ratios. They also used end March values for the size variable and they calculated monthly equally-weighted returns starting on April 1 and ending on the following March 31. Table 23 shows some of their findings.

In section A we can see that if we ignore the negative earnings-price ratio stocks, returns rise with higher earnings-price ratios (i.e., lower price-earnings ratios). We can also see that returns rise as market capitalization decreases. In section B we see that the higher earnings-price ratio shares tend to be smaller stocks. We can also see that the negative earnings-price ratio shares, which seem to earn more than might be expected from the rest of the pattern shown in section A, are especially small. This data poses the question as to whether there are two independent effects or one.

Table 23 Average Monthly Returns (%), and Market Value of Equity (Size) for 30 Portfolios of NYSE and AMEX Firms ranked First by E/P Ratio and then Size over the Period April 1951 to December 1986.

A: Average Monthly Returns

Size	Earnings-to-Price Ratio					
	Negative	Lowest	2	3	4	Highest
Smallest	1.52	1.62	1.36	1.52	1.68	1.90
2	1.08	1.14	1.15	1.13	1.42	1.62
3	1.13	1.12	0.99	1.09	1.44	1.52
4	0.72	1.02	1.01	1.10	1.43	1.47
Largest	1.21	0.89	0.90	0.97	1.24	1.43

B: Mean Market Value of Equity*

Size	Earnings-to-Price Ratio					
	Negative	Lowest	2	3	4	Highest
Smallest	5	20	25	25	20	16
2	10	74	84	77	57	47
3	20	211	205	175	136	107
4	44	539	467	420	333	259
Largest	262	3095	2455	2306	1897	1464

* Millions of dollars. Data shown has been rounded. Source: Jaffe *et al.* (1989, p. 139)

Jaffe *et al.* tried to disentangle the earnings-price ratio and size effects by use of statistical technique called Seemingly Unrelated Regression, a particular form of regression analysis. They found that for the overall period 1951–86 there was a size and earnings-price ratio effect across all months. They also found that there was a difference between January and the rest of the year. The earnings-price ratio effect applied to January and also to February–December whereas the small size effect only held in January. They calculated that moving from earnings-price ratio quintile 1 to quintile 5, while holding the effect of size constant, led to a 3.2% increase in returns. The effect of moving from size quintile 5 to 1 while holding earnings-price ratio constant was to increase returns by 3.4%.

A recent large-scale US study involving price-earnings ratios and size, by Fama and French (1992), suggested that although low price-earnings ratios were related to returns, once one had controlled for size and price-to-book, picking low price-earnings ratio stocks offered no extra return.

The evidence can be summarized as follows. Many careful US studies have shown that low price-earnings stocks outperform over long periods, although not necessarily over short periods. Some studies suggest low price-earnings ratios are more important than small size, whereas others suggest the reverse or that other variables taken together are more important. Because this conclusion is so dependent on the period and the variables used, and the experimental design, one might argue that low price-earnings ratios are worth seeking, but so too are other variables. There is no point in making a one attribute bet. Further, because of the overlap of low price-earnings ratio strategies with small size and other strategies, low price-earnings ratio investors might wish to be sure they understand why other value strategies or small size strategies are associated with higher returns.

We now turn to studies for the UK by Levis. Levis (1985 and 1989) conducted studies using data from the London Share Price Database. In this section we discuss Levis (1989) which reports results for the period 1961–85 for price-earnings ratios, price, size and dividend yield. Levis used three different methods of calculating abnormal returns and he used "within-groups" only and "within-groups" plus randomization, all of which resulted in an enormous number of findings, far too many to be reported here. However, we can give the flavour of some of his findings. The excess returns we report will be simply the return from an attribute, less the return from the market, as beta appeared to be irrelevant to an explanation of returns.

In Figure 15 we show the monthly excess returns from investing in portfolios with varying price-earnings ratios and also the returns from portfolios with varying price-earnings ratios but randomized with respect to each of size, yield and price. Here's how to read the chart. The PER column shows that the lowest quintile of price-earnings ratio stocks returned about 0.4% excess return per month. If, however, we randomize for size, so that we look at the lowest price-earnings ratio stocks from each size quintile, the excess return is shown by the PER/Size column, and is about 0.3%. For all four ways of looking at the data, low price-earnings stocks offer excess returns. Controlling for size does not eliminate the low price-earnings effect, in fact, controlling for yield has the greatest effect.

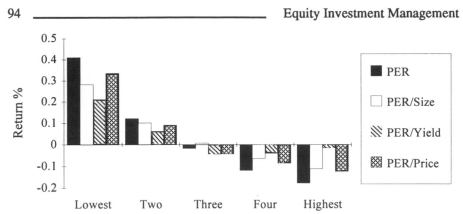

Figure 15 Monthly Excess Returns: Price-Earnings Ratio Quintiles UK: 1961–85. Source: Drawn from data in Levis (1989, p. 687). Reproduced by permission of the author and Elsevier Science Publishers BV

Is there an interaction between price-earnings ratios and other attributes? If size and price-earnings ratios are independent, there may be additional returns from combining low price-earnings ratios with low size. Levis found that the size effect was concentrated mainly in the lowest price-earnings ratio quintile and the price-earnings effect was greatest in the lowest size quintile. Readers interested in more interrelationships should refer to Levis. Suffice it to say he thought low price-earnings ratios were a source of excess returns.

Possible Reasons for the Findings

Why do low price-earnings ratio stocks outperform? One explanation is that they are riskier, but if risk is measured by betas, standard deviations or most other measures, risk does not explain the abnormal return. Another explanation, associated mainly with Dreman (1982), is based on a mixture of economic facts and human psychology. A number of studies in both the UK and US have suggested that corporate earnings growth rates are essentially random. (The studies are cited by Fuller *et al.*, 1992, who produce somewhat different results.) If one looks at the number of firms that increase their profits by more than the corporate average in one, two, three, etc. years in succession, one finds a distribution that is approximately the same as that for flipping a head in one, two, three, etc. times in succession. This should not be surprising.

To say that profit increases follow a random, or near random, pattern is not to say that business life is random. Far from it. When firms make large profits they are likely to begin to suffer increasing competition and when firms do badly they are likely to be under pressure to improve. Firms are also affected by the unintended consequences of other firms' actions. For example not all UK property firms participated in the development frenzy of the late 1980s but most will have suffered the consequences of the weak property market that followed. Firms can be affected by genuinely random factors such as the weather. A good or bad summer can make a lot of difference to a clothes retailer; in the UK, the restaurant trade is adversely affected by both very hot weather and by snow; the UK composite insurance sector has suffered from large domestic claims for house subsidence, a result of several consecutive very dry years. There are good reasons for believing that firms have less control over their profits than is often thought.

The market price of a share will be a function of both its earnings and the appropriate price-earnings ratio. We have seen that analysts have some skills in forecasting earnings, but that they often make large mistakes. We have also seen in the first paragraph of this section the sort of historical factors that probably go into assessing a stock's appropriate price-earnings ratio. The essential argument for low price-earnings ratio stocks is that the ratings reflect the fact that investors rely too much on historical data and give insufficient weight to the large random element in profits.

If a share sells on a high price-earnings ratio, investors expect good things of the company. If it has better than expected earnings it will probably rise in price to reflect the extra earnings, but its price-earnings ratio may not change. If it has poor earnings, the price may well fall to reflect the lower earnings and additionally to reflect a re-assessment of the appropriate price-earnings ratio. For low price-earnings ratio stocks one would expect the same asymmetric response, but this time in a favourable direction. Notice that with this argument, analysts might generally be able to forecast which stocks will grow fastest in the next year. It is simply that given the frequent errors analysts will make, investors pay too much for growth. (Recall, however, that Elton *et al.*, 1984, found that analysts systematically overestimated growth for high growth companies and underestimated growth for low growth companies.)

This general line of argument has recently received empirical support from an important article by Lakonishok *et al.* (1993). They looked at various value-based versus glamour-based strategies, including for example, low (i.e., value) versus high (i.e., glamour) price-earnings ratio stocks, high versus low book-to-market and high versus low cash flow to price. We shall discuss the price-earnings ratio section here, as well as the general argument of the paper. Lakonishok *et al.* studied portfolios of stocks from 1968 to 1990 and their universe was the NYSE and AMEX. Their holding period was five years with annual re-balancing. They found that low price-earnings ratio stocks substantially outperformed high price-earnings ratio stocks. They actually worked with earnings-price ratios and they found for the average of all five-year holding-periods, that the highest decile high earnings-price ratio stocks returned a cumulative 139% and the lowest returned 72%. Adjusting for size, they still found that high earnings-price stocks performed best.

They then looked at the five-year average growth of earnings, cash flow, sales and operating income for each decile of the attribute being studied, i.e., earnings-price, book-to-market, etc., *prior* to portfolio formation. For most value-based strategies there was a strong relationship between past growth and the attribute studied—for example high market-to-book stocks (value) had low past growth and low book-to-market stocks (glamour) had high past growth. The relationship was broadly the same for stocks ranked by earnings-price ratio, although the highest decile of earnings-price ratio stocks had fast growth and the lowest decile had slow growth. This is probably because earnings are more variable than measures such as book value. For example, a cyclical company's earnings will collapse in a recession, and although the price will react, the price-earnings ratio may soar if the market believes that earnings will recover eventually. This means that stocks at the ends of the earnings-price ratio decile distribution may have somewhat different characteristics than stocks at less extreme deciles—the extremes will include temporary winners and losers.

Based on these findings we might argue that past performance leads to stocks being seen as glamour or value stocks and that the value stocks have the better stock market performance. A refinement is to distinguish true glamour and value stocks from those that are temporarily rated as glamour or value. A true glamour stock would have both a high rating and fast past growth whereas a true value stock would have both a low rating and slow past growth. Lakonishok *et al.* found such stocks by placing all stocks into one of three earnings-price ratio categories (i.e., high, medium and low) and one of three growth categories. The cumulative five year return for true value stocks was 172%, and for true glamour stocks it was 67%. Picking value on this basis outperforms simply picking low price-earnings ratio stocks.

Why do value strategies work and glamour strategies fail? For just the reasons we suggested earlier—the market prices glamour stocks on the basis of extrapolating past growth but, sometimes in the short run, certainly in the long run, the growth rates of glamour and value stocks converge or overshoot.

Lakonishok *et al.* looked at the riskiness of the value-based strategies in a number of ways. They looked at how the strategies performed in poor economic conditions, poor stock markets and also at risk as measured by the standard deviation of returns and beta. The value strategies turned out to be *less* risky.

The writer finds the low price-earnings approach plausible because it does seem that investors systematically overstate the likelihood of past earnings patterns being repeated and many trustees view "glamour" stocks as less risky and more prudent. Some investors reject a price-earnings ratio strategy on the grounds that it involves buying the same old stocks in the same old sectors. This is not in fact true, although there is a bias at any time to certain industries. What happens is that these sectors change over time, albeit sometimes only slowly. Some managers perceive a risk of being concentrated in a few sectors: the risk is volatile short-term performance, rather than poor long-term performance, but clients are often lost on the short-term results. This risk can be offset by seeking greater diversification by buying shares that are cheap relative to their sector. Stocks cheap on an intra-sector price-earnings ratio basis tend to outperform (see, e.g., Goodman and Peavey, 1983, and Jones, 1989) and diversifying in this way will reduce a portfolio's volatility relative to the market, although it will also reduce its abnormal returns.

LOW PRICE-TO-SALES RATIO STOCKS

Buying stocks with a low price-to-sales ratio is sometimes recommended in the US as a worthwhile investment strategy but is seldom discussed in the UK. Perhaps the higher profile in the US is due to Kenneth Fisher, a columnist on the influential US magazine *Forbes*, being a proponent of the technique. He has discussed the technique in his column and elsewhere—see, for example, Fisher (1984a and 1984b).

Fisher claims that the reason for purchasing low price-to-sales ratio stocks is essentially contrarian. High price-to-sales ratio stocks are popular and discount too much of the future. Fisher argues that profits growth often comes from margin expansion and investors then form excessive expectations. "Few companies can sustain significantly above-average profits margins for long. Even fewer analysts can tell which companies will maintain profitability." (1984a, p.14). A stock with a low price-to-sales ratio will have low sales margins and might be thought to be a candidate for recovery or improvement.

Dividing a firm's price-to-earnings ratio by its net, after-tax profit margin, produces its price-to-sales ratio, so there is a relation between low price-to-sales ratios and low price-earnings ratios. Why would one use a price-to-sales ratio approach rather than a price-earnings ratio approach if they are related, especially as earnings might be thought to be more important to investors than sales? Proponents of the price-to-sales ratio approach argue:

● sales are more stable and less subject to accounting manipulation than earnings;
● a price-to-sales ratio is meaningful for a firm losing money, whereas a price-earnings ratio is not (although an earnings-price ratio would be meaningful);
● a low price-earnings ratio strategy faces problems with cyclical and turnaround stocks. Both will have high price-earnings ratios before their profits soar, and low price-earnings ratios before their profits decline.

Senchack and Martin (1987) examined the relative performance of low price-to-sales ratio and low price-earnings ratio strategies. They studied approximately 400–450 randomly selected firms quoted on the NYSE and AMEX. They excluded financial services such as banks and insurance companies which do not generate sales in the usual accounting sense. They drew their data from COMPUSTAT tapes for the period 1975–84.

The results of this study suggested that low price-to-sales ratio stocks produced positive abnormal returns. They were subject to greater risk, but still produced a higher risk-adjusted return than high price-to-sales ratio stocks and an equally-weighted market portfolio of comparable risk. The price-to-sales ratio screen worked even with companies losing money. Low price-earnings ratio stocks in the study, however, dominated low price-to-sales ratio stocks on both an absolute and risk-adjusted return basis. The relative performance of the low price-earnings ratio stocks was more consistent than that of low price-to-sales ratio stocks. Low price-earnings ratio stocks outperformed low price-to-sales ratio stocks in more than two thirds of the quarters studied.

Senchack and Martin ranked their universe by price-to-sales ratio quintiles and calculated for each quintile the price-earnings ratio, median market value, median price per share and median number of shares outstanding. For each variable there was a monotonically increasing relationship, i.e., the lowest price-to-sales ratio stocks had the lowest price-earnings ratio, lowest share price and lowest shares outstanding, while the next lowest price-to-sales ratio stocks had the next lowest price-earnings ratio, etc. When the universe was ranked by price-earnings ratio quintiles, the price-earnings ratio/price-to-sales ratio relationship was monotonically increasing. For other variables, however, the relationship was increasing then decreasing. From these findings one concludes that the price-to-sales ratio and price-earnings ratio relationships are related, but there are differences. A price-to-sales ratio strategy is more likely to be confounded by small size and low price effects than is a price-earnings ratio strategy.

Turning to implementation of a low price-to-sales ratio strategy, Fisher does not recommend simply buying the cheapest price-to-sales ratio stocks. He notes that the technique is not applicable to every sector, not to banks for example, and that the definition of a low ratio varies with the type of sector. He empirically derived the classifications shown in Table 24. Once an investor has screened some low price-to-sales ratio stocks, Fisher recommends traditional fundamental analysis to identify quality amongst the possible purchases.

Table 24   The Popularity Monitor

	very unpopular, with P/Ss less than	accepted, with P/Ss over	very popular, with P/Ss over
Small, growth-oriented or technology:	0.75	1.50	3.00
Multi-billion dollar sales sized, or without growth attributes:	0.20	0.40	0.80
Inherently thin margin, such as supermarkets:	0.03	0.06	0.12

Source: Fisher (1984a, p. 14)

CONCLUDING COMMENTS

Low price-earnings stocks have outperformed in both the US and UK over long periods of time. This outperformance does not appear to be a reward for high risk, if risk is measured by beta or any other popular statistical measure. Although there is less evidence, it seems that low price-to-sales ratio stocks outperform, at least in the US. Based on the single research study cited here that compares low price-earnings ratio stocks and low price-to-sales ratio stocks, if investors were to use a single attribute to guide investment strategy it would be low price-earnings ratios because such stocks produce better risk-adjusted returns. The two approaches are related, but not identical, so an investor might wish to consider using low price-to-sales ratio in a multi-attribute approach.

Before we rush off to buy low price-earnings ratio stocks, we have to face the fact that it may seem implausible that a low risk-high reward strategy has survived for so long. Why hasn't it been discounted? There is a danger that it has been. Certainly there have been some poor years recently for low price-earning stocks. Lakonishok *et al.* offer three explanations for the strategy working that suggest it might continue to work in the long-term.

The first explanation depends on the psychological basis of human decision-making. There is some psychological evidence that suggests that people focus on vivid, concrete case material and find it harder to focus on abstract statistical material (the "availability heuristic"). Information presented by the media (and perhaps investment analysts) focuses on the vivid. People also overemphasize the characteristics of specific cases. This is called the "representativeness heuristic" and can be illustrated with a quiz. In a small British city it is discovered that there are 1000 engineers and 50 librarians: John Smith is 37, slim, quiet and bookish. Is he a librarian or an engineer? Most people think John is a librarian. People tend to focus on the case data, which is the data about the specific case (John) and ignore the base rate data which is the data about the distribution of the relevant events (i.e., the percentage of engineers and librarians). John fits our stereotype of a librarian, and we tend to ignore the information that there are 20 times as many engineers as librarians. The odds favour John being an engineer. Now, if investors are subject to these psychological mechanisms, is it not plausible that they will focus on recent vivid news about companies and ignore the inevitable randomness and eventual decline that the statistics suggest affect all companies?

The second reason why investors might favour glamour stocks is that both institutional managers and fund trustees prefer to act "prudently" and not make mistakes. There is less criticism when a fund holds a glamour stock that underperforms than when an unattractive stock is held and underperforms. Managers and trustees are less likely to be replaced for being wrong with the crowd than if they act alone. Moreover, many funds are instructed to buy only blue-chip stocks, i.e., yesterday's heroes.

The third reason that Lakonishok *et al.* suggest for value continuing to work as a strategy is that value strategies work over many years but do not work every year and so managers risk losing their clients in the short run. However, this is true of all investment strategies and most must fail more frequently than value strategies seem to, so this seems an implausible point.

11

Low Price and Small Stocks

In this chapter we continue our examination of price-related attributes and consider low price stocks and small capitalization stocks. Since market capitalization is calculated by multiplying price per share by the number of shares in issue, it is inevitable that low price stocks will tend to be small stocks too. However, as before, we shall consider each attribute separately.

LOW PRICE STOCKS

Very low price or "penny" stocks seem to have attractions for many private investors. Perhaps this is because they can buy a lot of shares for a given sum of money; or perhaps it is thought that a low price has more scope to rise than a higher price. Many sophisticated investors scoff at such "reasons", and they are probably right, yet low price stocks have been studied for more than 50 years and most studies have concluded that low price stocks outperform.

The first scientific study of low priced stocks was probably by Fritzemeier (1936). He noted that low price stocks were more volatile than high price stocks and

> "In a 'bull' market the low price stocks tend to go up relatively more than high-price stocks, and they do not lose these superior gains in the recessions which follow."
> (p. 153)

He concluded that low price stocks offer greater prospects for speculative profit and if two shares seemed to offer equal profits the low price share should be bought. More recent studies of low price stocks include Blume and Husic (1973), Edmister and Greene (1980), Kross (1985), Tseng (1988), Jaffe *et al.* (1989) (who found the price effect to be wholly a January effect) and Levis (1989). We will look briefly at Edmister and Greene's study and Levis', i.e., a US and a UK study.

Edmister and Greene used monthly data taken from COMPUSTAT tapes for February 1967 through to the end of 1979. Observations were separated into 61 price groups based on the beginning of period price. The groups had an interval width of $1, except for the 61st group which included all stocks priced over $60.

Table 25 Return and Risk Summary Statistics for Price Groups. US: 1967–79

Price Group	Monthly Return %—Average	Monthly Return %—Standard Deviation	Beta
1	11.0	21.6	1.2
2	4.6	11.4	1.1
3	2.6	10.6	1.2
4	2.0	10.0	1.2
5	1.4	9.7	1.3
6	1.5	9.3	1.4
7	1.3	8.5	1.4
8	1.2	8.3	1.3
9	1.3	7.9	1.3
10	1.4	7.8	1.3
11–15	1.0	7.1	1.3
16–20	0.9	6.1	1.2
21–25	0.7	5.9	1.2
26–30	0.6	5.5	1.1
31–35	0.6	5.7	1.2
36–40	0.5	5.4	1.1
41–45	0.7	5.5	1.1
46–50	0.6	5.6	1.1
51–55	0.7	6.3	1.2
56–60	0.3	5.9	1.1

Source: Edmister and Greene (1980, p. 38). This copyrighted material is reprinted with the permission of *The Journal of Portfolio Management*.

For example, a stock priced at the beginning of a month at $10.625 was assigned to group 11. Table 25 highlights some of the study's findings.

Table 25 shows that risk and return are related to price. Edmister and Greene calculated Sharpe, Treynor and Jensen risk measures and concluded that risk-adjusted returns were superior for the low price and super-low price stocks. Other US studies have used different methods, different periods, included other attributes and used different intervals for rebalancing the portfolios. The results all point to low price stocks outperforming; some researchers claim that the size or price-earnings effect is essentially a price effect.

Levis (1989), in the UK study discussed in Chapter 10, also found that low price stocks outperform. His results are shown in Figure 16, for price alone and after randomization for other attributes. However, low price stocks have a remarkably similar return pattern to small stocks (see Figure 18) and the return pattern is significantly affected if size is controlled.

Some Possible Reasons for the Findings

One can surmise why low price stocks outperform. First, low price stocks will be essentially small stocks and the reasons for small stocks outperforming

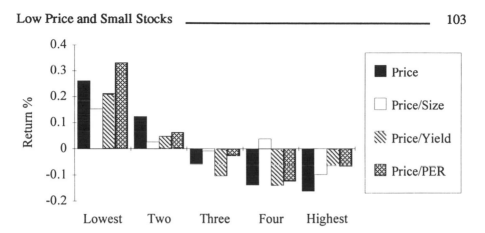

Figure 16 Monthly Excess Returns: Price Quintiles UK: 1961–85. Source: Drawn from data in Levis (1989, p. 687) by permission of the author and Elsevier Science Publishers BV

(discussed below) will apply to low price stocks too. Second, low price stocks are probably more illiquid than small stocks and, if investors like liquidity, this will warrant a premium return. Third, low price stocks will have out-of-date prices. This is because the market generally moves only a small amount each day. Even a penny move for a 20p stock would be a 5% move. Low price stocks will tend not to move for a period and then make a large percentage move to reflect past market moves. Investors may require a premium to bear this uncertainty about the value of their stock. Fourth, Elton et al. (1983, p. 142) note that many institutional investors will not hold stocks priced at less than $5 and

> "Stocks which sell for less than $5 are not considered as appropriate collateral for margin....Therefore, an investor who borrows or uses margin would find these stocks less attractive unless they offered a higher return."

Finally, one must wonder whether the estimated abnormal returns the studies report are overstated, because price spreads are greater for low price stocks and this would make portfolio rebalancing expensive.

Notice that all the arguments just made relate mainly to super low price stocks although the relationship with return holds throughout the price range. Low price seems to be a genuine effect but probably should not be used as a share selection variable if size is also being used.

SMALL CAPITALIZATION STOCKS

The size of a firm may be measured by the market value or capitalization of its ordinary shares. Over long periods of time, and in many countries (e.g., Australia, Belgium, Canada, Finland, France, Japan, Netherlands, UK, US and the former West Germany) small companies have produced higher returns than large companies.

The Evidence

We will present evidence for the US and UK. Reinganum (1992) has calculated average annual returns from NYSE stocks ranked by size. He assigned the smallest 10% to decile 1, the next smallest 10% to decile 2, and so on. The portfolio compositions were revised annually. The return data includes reinvested dividends and is shown in Table 26.

Table 26   Average Annual Returns for Portfolios Ranked by Size. NYSE: 1926–89

Deciles	Average Annual Returns %
1 Smallest	23.96
2	18.83
3	16.78
4	16.66
5	15.32
6	15.74
7	15.18
8	13.31
9	13.51
10 Largest	11.10

Source: Reinganum (1992, p. 56). This copyrighted material is reprinted with the permission of *The Journal of Portfolio Management*.

Because the data consist of arithmetic returns, and smaller stock returns are more variable, the geometric return difference between the largest and the smallest portfolios would be much smaller than the average return differences shown here. For example, for the period 1926–80, Banz' data (as analysed by Ibbotson and Brinson, 1987, p. 92) found a geometric annual return difference of 3.2% between the lowest and highest quintiles. This is still important: a dollar invested in the highest quintile stocks at the end of December 1925 would have grown to $109 at the end of 1980, while a dollar invested in the smallest quintile would have grown to $524.

Turning to the UK, the Hoare Govett Smaller Companies Index (HGSCI) comprises the lowest 10% by capitalization of the main UK equity market. At the start of 1992, the HGSCI consisted of 1213 companies, representing over two-thirds of all listed companies. The largest company in the index was valued at £216 million. The HGSCI has a history since 1955 and since that date (to end-1991) it has outperformed the FT-A All-Share index by 4.4% per annum on a geometric mean basis. Figure 17 shows the record of the HGSCI relative to the FT-A All-Share.

As we have seen, Levis looked at small size in his studies cited above and when he ranked his data in quintiles by size he found a consistent increase in returns as size decreased. His results are shown in Figure 18.

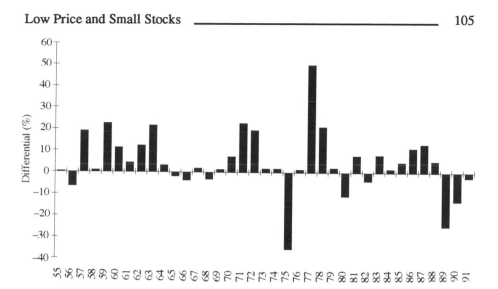

Figure 17 Return Differential: HGSCI Minus FT-A All-Share Index 1955–91. Source: Drawn from data in Dimson and Marsh (1992, p. 41) by permission

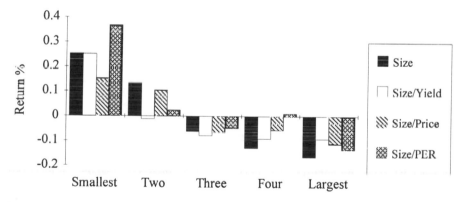

Figure 18 Monthly Excess Returns: Size Quintiles UK: 1961–85. Source: Drawn from data in Levis (1989, p. 686) by permission of the author and Elsevier Science Publishers BV

Recently small stocks have performed poorly in the US and the UK and there has been some concern that the small company effect has run its course. This seems unlikely. In the US small stocks have produced higher returns than large stocks over long periods, but not in every year, or even in every period consisting of several years. According to Reinganum, when small stocks have performed poorly over a period of four or five years, they have usually outperformed over the next four or five years. He looked at the period 1926–89 and calculated the degree of correlation between past and current returns for portfolios of various sizes and for various lengths of period. He found that for periods of three years or more, there was negative autocorrelation, that is to say good periods followed bad periods and vice versa. A specific illustration may be helpful.

The period 1926–89 has 56 overlapping five-year periods that could be used in the study. In ten of the five-year periods, the smallest decile stocks returned less than the largest decile stocks. For each of these cases, in the following five years, the smallest stocks outperformed the largest. In fact, for the smallest decile of stocks, for holding periods of four, five, six and seven years, there were 14, 10, 10 and 9 periods respectively when the small size effect did not hold and in only a single case (for the six-year holding period) did the small size effect not reassert itself in the following holding period. Reinganum put his neck on the line:

> "Given the abysmal performance of small-cap stocks [in the US] in the latter half of the 1980s, history would suggest that the first half of the 1990s should be a boom period for small-cap stocks. Far from being dead, small-firm performance could revive in the first half of the 1990s." (p. 62)

Smaller stocks have performed better in the US since late in 1990.

For the UK, Figure 17 shows that small stocks have underperformed large stocks in many years. Over five-year periods, the HGSCI has underperformed the FT-A All-Share in the periods ending 1968, 1969, 1990, 1991 and 1992. At this stage, all we can say is that smaller companies have bounced back in the past.

Some Possible Reasons for the Size Effect

Why do smaller companies generally outperform larger companies? (This section partly follows Dimson and Marsh, 1989.) Many fund managers would argue that small companies are more likely to double in size than large companies, and it is superior growth prospects that explain the better performance. Smaller companies as measured by the HGSCI have generated faster earnings growth than larger companies. However, one would expect faster growth to be discounted and reflected in the share price so that smaller stocks do not keep on outperforming. After all, among the larger stocks it is normal for "growth" stocks to have high price-earnings ratios reflecting their anticipated growth.

Another explanation might be that small stocks have a different sector or industry distribution than large stocks. This is in fact the case, but the small firm effect tends to apply within each industry and it is size rather than industry which generates performance.

A different approach would be to explain the higher return as a reward for greater risk. In the capital asset pricing model framework we might expect smaller stocks to have higher betas than larger stocks. In the US the evidence is a little mixed but to the extent that small stock portfolio betas are higher, they are not sufficiently high to explain much of the higher return. In the UK the HGSCI has almost always had a lower beta than the FT-A All-Share Index and a lower standard deviation of returns (Dimson and Marsh, 1992). Levis found that betas increased with increasing size for his quintiles. Small stocks, however, trade less frequently and as a result of this nonsynchronous trading it can be shown that there is a downward bias in small firms' betas. Allowing for this bias Levis found that beta rose with increasing size and then declined. In other words, small firms still did not appear risky. This is another example of a test of a joint hypothesis—that small firms are risky and that betas measure risk.

Beta is not the only measure of risk, or the capital asset pricing theory the only asset pricing theory. Chan *et al.* (1985) and Chen (1988) attempt to explain the size effect in terms of arbitrage pricing theory (which is discussed in Chapter 19). They claim considerable success and explain the extra return from small firms as a reward for risk. Specifically, they note that there is a relationship between small firm returns and the difference between the returns on a low grade bond portfolio and a government bond portfolio (this will widen during a recession) and also with net business formation. It is argued that smaller firms suffer disproportionately during recessions and smaller stock shareholders are rewarded for this risk. If we look at the differential return of the HGSCI less the FT-A All-Share against the Central Statistical Office's profit series (ex-North Sea Oil), we find a useful relationship. Specifically, when profits are declining or increasing modestly, i.e., less than 5%, smaller stocks tend to underperform. When profits are rising strongly, smaller stocks tend to outperform handsomely. These observations are the result of data-mining but fit in with the risk/recession argument. Optimists will see this as a suggestion that investors can really strike it rich in small stocks, if they have good economic forecasting skills.

There is another risk argument. Most investors probably believe small firms are dynamic and tomorrow's winners. Chan and Chen (1991), however, argue that, at least for the US, the small firms studied by the academics are marginal firms.

> "They have lost market value because of poor performance, they are inefficient producers, and they are likely to have financial leverage and cash flow problems. They are marginal in the sense that their prices tend to be more sensitive to changes in the economy, and they are less likely to survive adverse economic conditions.... Furthermore, firms that suffer from past misfortunes tend to be smaller in size. If they do not change their capital structure accordingly, they have higher financial leverage." (p. 1468)

Analysis of firms listed on the NYSE supports this argument. Firms in the smallest quintile tend to have fallen from higher quintiles. Newly-listed firms tend to be successful and do not enter the bottom quintile. The financial characteristics of the bottom quintile firms tend to support the Chan and Chen argument. If one turns to NASDAQ firms, because these are typically smaller than NYSE listed stocks, firms the same size as the bottom quintile of NYSE firms are less likely to be "fallen angels". Sure enough, they have different financial characteristics. In short, Chan and Chen speculate that the small firms that have been studied earn higher returns because they are genuinely risky.

A different explanation for the small firm effect is the higher costs (bid/ask spread and commission) associated with dealing in small stocks, e.g., Stoll and Whaley (1983) and Loeb (1991). Stoll and Whaley used US data for 1960–79 and found a small company effect. However, when transaction costs were allowed for, and portfolios rebalanced every month, the small stock portfolio did not generate abnormal returns. Of course, as the holding period is extended, the profitability of the small stock portfolio improves (or becomes less negative). At about a four-month holding period the small firms start to generate abnormal returns. Institutional investors turn stocks over less frequently than every four months. Moreover, any investor willing to take a relatively or totally passive approach would achieve exceptional returns (see, e.g., Sinquefield, 1991). Thus, transactions costs may diminish the small firm effect but they do not explain it away.

Another explanation for the small company effect might be neglect. Neglected companies—i.e. those neglected by analysts or institutional investors—tend to outperform (see Chapter 15). Carvell and Strebel (1987) claim that the small firm effect is a proxy for the neglected firm effect and there is no underlying small firm effect. Small firms are certainly neglected. The bottom line for brokers' investment research is the value of the buy/sell orders generated by the research and clearly the economics of investment research do not justify spending as much time and money researching a £1 million company, or even a £50 million company as one capitalized at £1 billion. The research costs for smaller stocks are disproportionately high and this would justify a higher apparent return from smaller stocks. Investors willing to buy stocks about which they have little detailed information will buy a smaller companies index fund to diversify some of the specific company risk.

One peculiarity of the size effect is that the bulk of the abnormal return in the US occurs in January (Keim, 1983)—if one adds in the last day of December, most of this occurs in five days, the last day of December and the first four days of January. The January effect is discussed in Chapter 17. Dimson and Marsh (1992) report that for the UK the picture is different. January and April (the start of the fiscal year), have provided the worst relative performance for the HGSCI.

CONCLUDING COMMENTS

It is clear that low price and small capitalization stocks have outperformed in many countries over long periods. Academics and fund managers have tended to concentrate on small stocks rather than low price stocks. Small stocks do not outperform every year, but if they underperform for periods of five or more years, the following period will probably show outperformance. Small stocks are more risky in some senses, but not all. They are more expensive to deal in, there is less information available on small stocks and it is disproportionately expensive to collect information. Investors willing to live with this information deficiency and willing to buy and hold an index fund will achieve abnormal returns—if the future is like the past. The small capitalization effect interacts with other stock attributes such as low price, neglect, low price-earnings ratio and seasonal effects. Most of the above comments also apply to low price stocks. Small stocks are risky in the sense of being especially vulnerable to recessions. Some investors will be willing to be widely diversified in small stocks and ride out recessions, believing that a full economic cycle will produce abnormal returns, others may wish to try and forecast recessions so that they can switch between small and large stocks.

12
Dividend Matters

Whether high-yielding stocks offer higher returns has been a subject of considerable debate for a long time. In many countries income has been taxed at a higher rate than capital gains. Even when the tax rates have been the same, capital gains tax has not been paid until the gains were realized and thus the tax could be postponed in a way that income tax could not. If investors are interested in after-tax income they will presumably only purchase high-yielding stocks if they offer the same after-tax income as low-yielding stocks, i.e., offer higher returns than low-yielding assets on a pre-tax basis. Another argument suggesting high-yielding stocks will offer higher returns is the belief that investors demand a high yield in compensation for poor growth prospects. If investors are poor at assessing growth prospects—see the arguments in the section on low price-earnings ratio stocks in Chapter 10—high yield may be related to high return. On the other hand some private investors may require high income and may prefer high-yielding stocks, otherwise they would have to continually sell small parcels of shares to generate income from capital gains or even consume capital. Both tax-paying and tax-exempt investors might prefer high-yielding stocks on the grounds that a dividend is more certain than a capital gain.

HIGH YIELD: EVIDENCE

Faced with these conflicting arguments there is a temptation to simply ask whether there is evidence that high yields are associated with high returns. A major US study by Black and Scholes (1974) found no effect but this study has been criticized on statistical grounds. While there have been other studies pointing in the same direction, most major studies have suggested that high yields and high returns go together, e.g., Litzenberger and Ramaswamy (1979), and Elton *et al.* (1983). We shall outline the latter study before turning to UK evidence.

Elton *et al.* examined whether dividend yield has an impact on return above that explained by the zero beta capital asset pricing model. They used data for the period 1927–76 but, because of their estimation procedure for betas, which involved 10 years of data, they estimated yield and return relationships for 40 yearly periods from 1937 to 1976.

Stocks were grouped by their dividend yield in year t-2, i.e., two years prior to each year studied. All stocks paying dividends were ordered from highest to lowest and split into 19 equally-sized groups. Group 20 consisted of all stocks not paying a dividend in year t-2. As a forecast of dividends in year t, Elton *et al.* used actual dividends in year t-1. They felt that if this procedure produced a bias, it would be against observing a yield/return relationship.

Figure 19 shows the average portfolio dividend yields (–□–) and average excess returns (–■–) over the period 1937–76. As can be seen, excess returns rise with dividend yields except for group 20, which was formed from stocks not paying a dividend in year t-2. Other studies, e.g., Blume (1980), have also found excess returns from zero dividend stocks. Elton *et al.* looked at five-year non-overlapping sub-periods. While, as we have seen, high yields and excess returns were related over the entire period, this did not hold for every sub-period; it failed for 1937–41 and 1957–61.

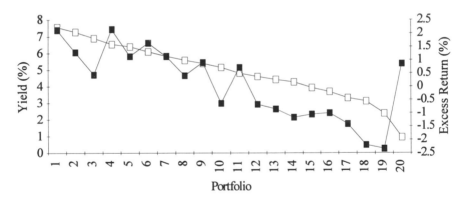

Figure 19 Portfolio Dividend Yield and Excess Return US: 1937–76. Source: Elton *et al.* (1983, p. 141). Reproduced by permission of the author and Elsevier Science Publishers BV

Why do stocks paying no dividends earn higher returns? Elton *et al.* note that small stocks and low price stocks make up a higher proportion of zero dividend stocks than of other groups. To see if they were picking up a small stock/low price effect, they re-estimated returns omitting all stocks under $5 in price. The same general relationship shown in Figure 19 appeared, although group 20 stocks earned a smaller excess return.

The above study can be summed up as follows. Except for stocks which had previously not paid a dividend, over a long period, the higher the yield, the higher the excess return. This relationship, however, did not hold every year or even for periods of as long as five years. Stocks which had previously not paid dividends offered excess returns, even after allowing for a low price effect.

Turning to the UK, Levis (1989), in the study discussed in Chapters 10 and 11, looked at the relationship between yields and return. In Figure 20 we show the excess returns related to dividend quintiles. Using Levis' calculations for excess return, the difference between quintile one and quintile five returns was 0.828% per month. Randomizing the yield portfolios for size, price and price-earnings ratio had little impact on the return/yield relationship. In general, relative to size, price-earnings ratio, and share price, the yield effect was the strongest relationship Levis found.

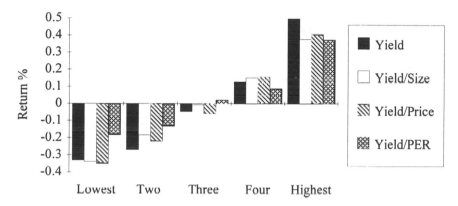

Figure 20 Monthly Excess Returns: Yield Quintiles UK: 1961–85. Source: Levis (1989, p. 686). Reproduced by permission of the author and Elsevier Science Publishers BV

Two detailed studies look specifically at tax effects and UK dividends. Both Poterba and Summers (1984) and Chui *et al.* (1992) found significant tax effects. However as Poterba and Summers (p. 1398) note:

> "The finding that dividend taxes are recognized by investors and affect the ex ante returns which they demand only deepens the puzzle of why firms pay dividends."

Perhaps part of the reason is that dividends convey information and investors are interested in that. This suggests we should be looking at changes in dividends as well as dividend levels. We do that in the next section. However, it is worth noting that taxes cannot be a complete explanation of why high-yield stocks produce an excess return. Keim (1985 and 1986) found a similar relationship between dividend yield and abnormal return in the US as did Elton *et al.* but also examined the relationship in the month of January and in the rest of the year. The return was essentially a January effect only. How does this fit into an explanation based on pre- and post-tax returns? Note also that zero dividend stocks have high returns too, which does not fit a tax explanation.

Given the above evidence from both the US and UK, should high yield be an attribute investors seek? Presumably it should for tax exempt investors. Tax payers will wonder whether they would make excess returns after paying more income tax. Based on Levis' findings, they would have. Like most attributes, high yield is not always beneficial—recall the two five-year periods reported by Elton *et al.* where it was not beneficial. Given the current low cover for UK dividends and the widespread belief that economic recovery may be relatively modest, one might wonder whether, at least in the UK, we have entered a lean period for high-yield stocks, many of which will either cut their dividends or offer little dividend growth for some time.

DIVIDEND CHANGES

Research in the US and UK suggests that companies relate dividend changes to earnings changes but they try to smooth the dividend changes. Thus dividend changes tend to follow changes in sustainable earnings and transitory changes in income do not affect dividends. It follows from this that dividends have some information content and reflect management's assessment of the earning power of a company. There is a particularly strong reluctance to cut dividends. There is a large US literature which finds that announcements of dividend increases (decreases) are related to stock price increases (decreases). This suggests dividends are seen by investors as providing information.

Marsh (1992) has conducted a large UK study on the effect of dividend announcements. He analysed stock price reactions to nearly 6000 dividend announcements, including 754 dividend reductions, over the period January 1989–April 1992. During the period studied, small firms underperformed large firms by very large amounts so Marsh controlled for firm size in calculating abnormal returns. He did not control for beta, arguing that there was considerable evidence that beta adjustments make little difference to UK findings.

Some of Marsh's key findings are shown in Table 27 which shows that the bigger the dividend announced, the greater are the abnormal returns at the time of the announcement, and vice versa. Table 27 also shows that the market has anticipated the direction of the dividend announcement in the month prior to the announcement, but still reacts to the actual announcement. The same picture applies for dividend cuts. Further, the same basic story is repeated for a period of one year prior to and post the dividend announcement. Clearly, good dividend forecasting skills would provide abnormal returns. There was not much evidence to support the notion that it was possible to make money simply by reacting to dividend changes.

Marsh's paper contains much more of interest than is shown here. For example the anticipation of dividend cuts is shown to take place two years ahead of the cut. On this latter point Marsh (p. 50) argues that the market was responding to information about deteriorating company prospects rather than specifically anticipating

Table 27 Announcement Period Abnormal Returns. UK: January 1989–April 1992

Dividend Announcement	Abnormal Returns (%, size-adjusted) during:			
	Days −20 to −1	Days −1 to 1	Days 1 to 20	Days −20 to 20
Increases of more than 25%	1.1	1.7	1.8	4.6
Increases of less than 25%	0.6	0.9	1.9	3.4
Maintained	−0.3	−0.1	2.4	2.0
Cuts	−2.7	−4.3	2.2	−4.8
Omissions	−5.3	−7.4	1.4	−11.1

Source: Marsh (1992, p. 23). Unpublished material; reproduced by permission of the author

the dividend cut. Of course this leaves open the question whether dividends actually contain any new information that is not included in earnings and other information. Dividend announcements usually are made at the same time as earnings announcements. Further, while analysts forecast dividends, the bulk of their effort and attention goes into forecasting earnings.

In a US study, Aharony and Swary (1980) looked at dividend announcements that were at least 11 trading days apart from earnings announcements. Sometimes the dividend announcements led the earnings announcements and sometimes they lagged. Aharony and Swary found abnormal returns around both announcements, suggesting both conveyed information.

DIVIDEND SURPRISES

If dividends convey additional information from that contained in earnings, it might follow that abnormal returns can be earned by reacting to dividend surprises and dividend forecast revisions. (Earnings "surprises" were discussed at some length in Chapter 7). Marsh showed there was a relation between returns and the size of dividend changes but this is not the same thing. He briefly discusses the effect of prior expectations, and does argue that they are important, but his evidence is based on a few newspaper reports of what the market was expecting in a few cases. Aharony and Swary's study used dividend surprises, but we shall detail a study by Cole (1984) here as it is of more interest to investors. Cole used a sample drawn from NYSE firms in the period 1970–78. He formed two extreme portfolios, one based on earnings surprises and one based on dividend surprises. He defined surprises not in terms of analysts' expectations, but in relation to forecasts from models. He forecast earnings using the most recent 20 quarters earnings data, adjusted for seasonality. He assumed dividends would be the same as in the last quarter, adjusted by any change made in the corresponding quarter a year ago. To calculate surprises, he related actual earnings and dividends to forecast earnings and dividends.

Using specified definitions of high (positive) and low (negative) surprises he formed four surprise portfolios of high dividend, low dividend, high earnings and low earnings. The portfolios formed had different characteristics, i.e., the high dividend surprise portfolios were not replicating the high earnings surprise portfolios. Cole calculated the various holding period returns shown in Table 28.

Table 28 Averages of Differences in Holding Period Returns.

Period	HD-LD	HE-LE	HD-HE
1 month	0.5%	0.6%	0.6%
2 months	3.0%	1.4%	1.1%
3 months	4.3%	2.4%	1.9%
4 months	4.9%	2.6%	2.3%
5 months	5.9%	6.2%	1.8%
6 months	7.3%	6.9%	2.9%

HD = high dividend surprise; LD = low dividend surprise; HE = high earnings surprise; LE = low earnings surprise. Source: Cole (1984, p. 48). This copyrighted material is reprinted with the permission of *The Journal of Portfolio Management*.

Table 28 shows that stocks offering favourable earnings or dividends surprises earned higher returns. The high dividend surprise stocks outperformed the high earnings surprise stocks. And what is the relevance of this? According to Cole

"The relevance for security analysts and portfolio managers is that they may use unexpected current quarterly dividends to augment portfolios determined exclusively on the basis of earnings." (p. 49)

Notice that even if an investor reacted a month after the surprise, superior returns could have been achieved.

CONCLUDING COMMENTS

It would seem that high-yield stocks produce higher returns, dividend changes are related to returns, and dividend surprises are related to returns. Given the size of the difference in returns which Marsh reports, given studies such as Aharony and Swary which point to dividends having separate information value, and given Cole's study, it is surprising that so much work has been carried out on earnings revisions and surprises and so little, by comparison, on dividend revisions and surprises. To benefit from the relationship between dividend changes and returns, an investor would need forecasting skills. But the high yield/high return finding is a valuation anomaly and the dividend surprise finding suggests the market reacts slowly to some types of information.

13
Book-to-Market and Other Accounting Ratios

Accounting data is an important source of information about firms and accounting ratios are a useful means of summarizing accounting data. They help the analyst to ask the right questions. There are many accounting ratios and it is useful to group them into four categories:

- liquidity ratios—measures of how easily a firm can meet its short-run obligations. Examples include current asset ratio, and quick ratio.
- gearing or leverage ratios—measures of how heavily in debt a company is. Examples include debt ratio, debt-equity ratio and times interest covered.
- profitability ratios—measures of the efficiency of a firm. Examples include return on equity, return on total assets, net profit margin and sales to total assets.
- market ratios measures of how a company is rated in the stock market. Examples include price-earnings ratio, dividend yield, and book-to-market equity or net asset value.

We have already looked at some of the stock market ratios, for example, the price-earnings ratio, price-to-sales ratio and dividend yield, and most investors seem to see them as stock market ratios. They seem to see the book-to-market ratio in a slightly different light, and so we'll treat it in this more general accounting chapter. First we will make some general comments, then we will discuss book-to-market and finally look at some accounting ratio screens.

Accounting information has a somewhat odd status in most textbooks. Accounting ratios are often discussed at length in relation to assessing a company's financial soundness. But after acquiring the junior accountant's tool kit, readers are left to do what they will with their knowledge. The information is usually provided as part of the package of determining an appropriate price-earnings ratio. But say the current asset ratio of a company is two, which is generally regarded as acceptable, what does that imply for the price-earnings ratio? Well, perhaps what one should be looking at is not a single ratio, but the total picture. Now the total picture for a firm such as Unilever is that the finances are sound. But what does that imply? Unilever has usually traded at a discount to the market. Since the writer has no great insights on accounting information as applied to individual companies to determine appropriate price-earnings ratios, we will look at using accounting information on its own as a way of sorting companies into attractive and unattractive. We assume readers know their way around the basic ratios.

ASSET VALUES

Many modern textbooks give asset values short shrift, although the commercial providers of share and accounting information (e.g., Extel and Standard and Poor's) will usually provide asset values and, as we saw in Chapter 5, many analysts look at asset values (although a reader of their reports often will be hard pressed to see how this affects their share recommendation). Clearly there are conflicting views on the merits of looking at the value of assets and it worth saying a few words on this before looking at some studies.

Investors who consider asset values to be important calculate the net asset value (ordinary shareholders' funds divided by number of ordinary shares in issue) and relate it to the price per share. This can be done either by calculating a premium or discount to net asset value, or the ratio of price to net asset value, or net asset value to price. In the US the equivalent concept to the price to net asset value ratio is the book-to-market ratio. (Most studies have been carried out using this term, so that is the one we've used in the chapter title.) The range of values the price to net asset ratio can take is very wide: at the time of writing, British Steel and many property companies are selling at around two-fifths of historical net asset value while many insurance companies are selling at ten times historical net asset value.

Interest in net asset value seems to wax and wane, although there is always some interest. Private businesses are often purchased or sold primarily with reference to net asset value. The courts, when forced to be involved in valuing companies, will include net asset value as one of the determining factors. Corporate raiders will certainly have regard to net asset value. If a company is selling at a discount to net asset value, the acquirer will obtain assets at less than their replacement cost, plus sales and personnel. Finally investors always have regard to asset value for some categories of company. Companies which invest in property or shares (e.g., investment trusts) are always appraised partly (often mainly) by their discount or premium to asset value. Asset values are relevant for public utilities in the US and Hong Kong because of the regulatory structures in those countries. Banks, which hold mainly assets whose stated net worth should be close to their liquidating or sale value, are often valued in the US with regard to asset value, although this seems less common in the UK.

If the market looks at net asset value in some sectors as the main appraisal technique and raiders use it elsewhere, surely the case for valuing stocks with regard to net asset value is established. Well, not necessarily. If a company is worth its dividend stream (see Chapter 8) why should there be any direct connection between share price and asset value? To take an extreme example, service companies may have few assets other than their people and these do not appear on the balance sheet or enter net asset value calculations. What merit would a net asset value calculation have in these circumstances? Clearly prices can exceed net asset value for sensible reasons. One might be tempted to accept that the presence of corporate raiders will stop share prices being below net asset value, but even this is uncertain. The problem is that a net asset value sum is not necessarily a very reliable guide to "value".

The stated net asset value will depend on a number of accounting conventions with regard to the treatment of intangibles, depreciation policy and the accuracy of property valuations. Did anyone in late-1992 believe 1991 year-end balance sheet UK property values? Further, however sensible the accounting treatment, there may be little economic rationale for the net asset value. Consider, for example, the case of British Sugar, the UK's monopoly processor of sugar beet into sugar. What is the value of its processing plants? It seems perfectly sensible for the balance sheet to show the value of a new plant less some sum to reflect wear and tear, obsolescence, etc. But say the EC decides to impose a quota on the amount of sugar beet that can be grown in the UK at around half the current amount, or alternatively that there is some technical innovation that makes sugar cane much cheaper: what then is the value of a beet processing plant? In general, very specific assets may not be worth to an investor or raider their depreciated value, while more general assets such as cars, may be.

Finally, it was mentioned earlier that along with the physical assets a raider might acquire some staff. If the raider has to lay off the staff, it may face large redundancy costs so that net asset value on a break-up basis may well be below net asset value calculated on a going concern basis. The conclusion must be that net asset values will be relevant to a corporate raider, but published net asset values may be little guide to how a raider values assets and need not therefore be a prop to share prices.

The conclusion one might draw from the above discussion is that in some industries net asset value is a vital tool but, for the stock market as a whole, it is an empirical issue as to whether shares selling on a low price relative to net asset value will offer excess returns. Indeed the empirical evidence may produce variable results, depending on the degree of merger activity, which varies over time. Let us turn to the evidence.

Rosenberg *et al.* (1985) looked at returns to a strategy of purchasing low price-to-book stocks. They constructed a retrospective test on a database of monthly stock data from January 1973 through to March 1980 and a prospective study from April 1980 to September 1984. The universe of stocks consisted of 1,400 of the largest companies in the COMPUSTAT database. The stocks were mainly NYSE stocks, with a few from the ASE, regional exchanges or NASDAQ.

The study was constructed as a hedge study, that is to say buying stocks with a low price-to-book and selling stocks with a high price-to-book. The return to the strategy is thus the return that might be achieved by adjusting an existing portfolio to be consistent with a low price-to-book strategy. The prospective study showed an excess return of 0.32% per month with positive returns in 38 out of 54 months. Because book values do not change frequently, this is not a strategy likely to involve high transactions costs, although any transactions costs would reduce the returns.

In Chapters 3 and 10, a study by Fama and French (1992) which relates betas ans other attributes and returns was cited. They found betas were not related to returns during the period July 1963 to December 1990. They also related returns to price-earnings ratios, size, book-to-market equity and leverage. Relating each variable to returns they found the results we would expect based on studies cited in earlier chapters. For leverage, which has not been discussed, one would expect increased leverage to be associated with increased risk and returns. Bhandari (1988) found this relationship for US stocks for the period 1948–79. When Fama and French looked at their five variables together in a multivariate analysis, only size and book-to-market equity were related to returns with book-to-market equity being the stronger variable. Figure 21 shows returns for equally-weighted portfolios arrayed by book-to-market ratios.

In the study by Lakonishok *et al.* (1993), discussed in Chapter 10 in relation to low price-earnings ratios, book-to-market was also examined. Their sample period was 1968–90, i.e., substantially the same as Fama and French's. They too found that investing in high book-to-market stocks produced significant returns.

Capaul *et al.* (1993) examined the returns from a price-to-book strategy for

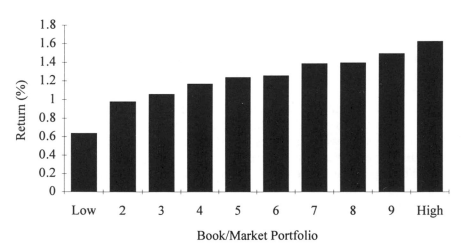

Figure 21 Average Monthly Returns by Book-to-Market Equity Quintiles. US: July 1963 to December 1990. Source: Drawn from data in Fama and French (1992, p. 446)

France, Germany, Switzerland, the UK and Japan over the period January 1981 to June 1992 and concluded that low price-to-book ratio stocks (i.e., high book-to-market) provided superior risk-adjusted performance to high price-to-book stocks.

We have now reviewed a number of studies which suggest that net asset value or book-to-market is related to returns. Given the arguments put forward earlier as to why there might not be a relationship we might still wonder what exactly we are measuring. Fama and French wonder if there is some systematic difference between high and low price-to-book firms, for example in their economic prospects. They felt that the results must show that there is a relationship between book value and risk. As we saw in Chapter 10, Lakonishok et al. seem to effectively refute that argument. They looked at how the value strategies, including book-to-market, performed in poor economic conditions, poor stock markets and also at risk as measured by the standard deviation of returns and beta. The value strategies were less risky.

NET CURRENT ASSETS

Buying stocks that are cheap in relation to assets is usually seen as a value strategy and thought to be conservative. An even more conservative accounting measure, net current asset value applicable to ordinary shareholders, has been suggested as a basis for share selection. Benjamin Graham defined this as current assets less current liabilities less long-term debt. In effect, a minimum liquidating value is being calculated. If stocks can be purchased for less than liquidating value then "the results should be quite satisfactory" according to Graham, who developed this stock selection criterion between 1930 and 1932 and used it extensively in his money management business. Cottle et al. (1988, pp. 604–605*) note that as a practical matter, most such companies could be disposed of for not less than their working capital and comment:

> "Before the 1920s, common stocks selling under current asset value were practically unknown. During the twenties, when prime emphasis was placed on prospects, to the exclusion of other factors, a few issues in *depressed* industries sold below their working capital. In the Great Depression of the early 1930s, this phenomenon became widespread....At the top of the ensuing bull market, in 1937, this situation had all but disappeared, but, in the following recession about 20 percent of all industrials sold on a 'sub-current-asset' basis....In 1947–1950, however, we witnessed a new and more extraordinary phase of the phenomenon. Sustained high earnings built up working capital for many companies at a rapid rate, but the prevailingly cautious attitude toward the future prevented stock prices from moving up in the same proportion. The result was not only that many issues persistently sold in those years at less than their working capital, but, more strangely, that this relationship was largely due to the very fact that the companies had been showing such large earnings. In earlier years a low price in relation to current assets almost always indicated unsatisfactory

* Cottle, S., Murray, R.F. & Block, F.E. (1988) *Graham and Dodd's Security Analysis*, 5th edn. New York, McGraw-Hill. Reproduced by permission.

current earnings....A characteristic of depressed markets is an abundance of stocks which can be purchased for less than their working capital....Even in average markets a diversified portfolio can be constructed. As this is written, in early 1987 with the Dow at 2400, few such stocks can be found. From the vantage (or disadvantage) point of our experience we are inclined to regard the drying up of these bargain opportunities as an indication that the general market has reached a hazardous level."

That is the background—but does net current asset really work as a selection criterion? Oppenheimer (1986) tested it for the period 1970–82. The stock universe was taken from a December issue of the *Security Owner's Stock Guide* which includes all NYSE and AMEX stocks as well as a large number of OTC and regional exchange stocks. The entire sample of stocks selling below net current assets outperformed, as did the AMEX and OTC stocks although the NYSE stocks did not. The outperformance—omitting transaction costs and dividends—of the entire sample was impressive: $10 000 invested in the net current asset portfolio on December 31, 1970 would have grown to $254 973 by December 31, 1983. The comparable figures for the NYSE-AMEX and small-firm indexes were $37 296 and $101 992 respectively.

The biggest difficulty with this study is that the number of stocks meeting the criterion each year ranged from only 18 to 89. In fact 1983 was eliminated from the study because only four stocks met the criterion. In only 4 of the 13 years, 1970–1982, did the number of qualifying NYSE stocks reach double figures. Vu (1988) also tested the criterion and used the *Value Line Investment Survey* for his data source for the period April 1977–December 1984. Again he found it to be a profitable strategy but again found few stocks met the criterion. They were also very small. As a result an institution which invests significant sums in a diversified portfolio could not put together a portfolio in many years. This is not to deny that the criterion is worth looking at, but it is unlikely to be the sole basis for constructing a portfolio. This presumably applies with even more force in the smaller UK market. Of course the rule could be extended so that stocks are ranked by net current assets and the cheapest stocks purchased whether or not they sell at less than net current asset value. But that is a different criterion.

ACCOUNTING RATIOS: A BROAD BRUSH APPROACH

Instead of examining specific ratios, what happens if we consider several at the same time? We turn now to a more general set of Benjamin Graham selection criteria. In his book *The Intelligent Investor*, Graham (1973) gave a list of stock selection criteria. These may briefly be summarized as: medium to large firms; strong financial condition; earnings stability; dividend continuity; significant earnings growth; moderate to low price-earnings ratio; and low price-to-book ratio. In the last years of his life, Graham, with his colleague Rea, assembled a new list of stock selection criteria and these are discussed in Rea (1977). Seven of the criteria were Graham's and three were Rea's. The criteria were:

1. An earnings yield (i.e. the reciprocal of the price-earnings ratio) of at least twice the AAA bond yield.
2. A price-earnings ratio less than 40% of the highest average price-earnings ratio over the previous five years.
3. A dividend yield of at least two-thirds the AAA bond yield.
4. A stock price less than two-thirds of the tangible book value per share.
5. A stock price less than two-thirds net current asset value.
6. Total debt less than tangible book value.
7. A current ratio greater than two.
8. Total debt no greater than twice net current asset value.
9. Compound ten-year annual growth of at least 7%.
10. Two or fewer annual earnings declines of 5% or more in the last ten years.

The first five criteria deal with "rewards" and the second five with "risks". It is not necessary for a stock to meet all the criteria; Graham and Rea stressed criteria (1), (3), (5) and (6). Sell signals were if a stock:

1. appreciated by more than 50%;
2. had been held for more than two years;
3. stopped paying dividends;
4. its earnings dropped sufficiently to make it overpriced by 50% or more relative to buy criterion (1).

Oppenheimer (1984) tested the Graham and Rea rules. He tested three strategies, forming portfolios meeting buy criteria (1) and (6), (3) and (6) and (1), (3) and (6) with stocks sold after either a 50% price rise or two years. The COMPUSTAT tapes were screened for all NYSE and AMEX securities satisfying any of the three sets of criteria on December 31st of each year between 1973 and 1980. In half of the years, there were less than 30 shares meeting criteria (1), (3) and (6) and in one of the years, not a single share met the criteria. In 1980 only five shares satisfied criteria (1) and (6) and 14 satisfied criteria (3) and (6). The other years provided at least 49 stocks satisfying either pair of criteria.

The returns available from these strategies are shown in Table 29. The superior performance was not due to systematic risk or size. The performance was much

Table 29 Graham and Rea Criteria: Mean Annual Returns 1974–81

NYSE-AMEX Index	14%
Criteria (1) and (6)	38%
Criteria (3) and (6)	26%
Criteria (1), (3) and (6)	29%

Source: Oppenheimer (1984, p. 72)

better prior to publication of the criteria (in 1977) but still offered excess returns after publication. The decline in excess returns post-publication is not necessarily related to publication although most commentators have assumed that it is.

The Graham–Rea approach appears to be worth considering and has been used in the US by the Rea–Graham, Sequoia, and Pacific Funds. How useful it would be in the UK is unclear. Some modification would probably be needed, but because this sort of approach is not as common in the UK as in the US it may well be profitable. Whether enough stocks would meet the criteria to form a portfolio is a cause for concern. It is worth noting that long lists of criteria, (e.g. the full Graham and Rea list of ten) are quite impractical. Even for the large US market, Oppenheimer found very few eligible stocks when he used a screen of four criteria—(1), (3), (6) and (9). In his eight year sample the number of stocks selected ranged from 38 to none. Once again, this approach would appear to be a supplement to stock selection rather than a method in its own right unless one uses only a few of the criteria so that a wider list is generated. That would have been Graham's recommendation, because he was keen to have a wide list to allow broad diversification.

CONCLUDING COMMENTS

It would appear that measures of asset value and stock market ratios are related to returns. Book-to-market, net current asset value and some of Benjamin Graham's other criteria seem to be related to returns. Book-to-market may be a general strategy, but the other two sets of ratios may not always provide enough stocks for a diversified portfolio. Notice that the accounting analysis we carried out was not of the sort most analysts carry out. We compared various ratios across firms without discussing the underlying firms. Most analysts study individual companies and consider accounting ratios in relation to some notion they have as to what are proper values for the ratios. This is one way of using accounting information, but not necessarily the best way.

14

Creative Accountancy and Bankruptcy

The chapter heading signifies two topics and is not meant to imply that creative accounting and bankruptcy are inevitably linked. However, some spectacular cases of bankruptcy in recent years have also involved creative accounting, so perhaps the heading is not too misleading. (Strictly speaking, only individuals or partnerships become bankrupt in the UK; companies go into liquidation.)

The previous chapter's approach may have given the impression that it is not worth getting to grips with an individual company's set of accounts. That's not the case at all. It may be difficult to decide if a set of accounts rates as "above average" rather than "good", and it may be difficult to go on to use this to decide an appropriate price-earnings ratio. But it may be well worth screening out companies that have really bad accounts, and as we shall see, this may involve a great deal of attention to detail.

SSAPS, GAAP, CREATIVE ACCOUNTING AND FRED

In the UK there are Statements of Standard Accounting Practice (SSAPs), in the US there are Generally Accepted Accounting Principles (GAAP) and in both countries there are what Professor Abraham Briloff has called Cleverly Rigged Accounting Ploys (CRAP), more usually referred to as creative accounting in the UK. There was a new accounting standards setting structure introduced in the UK in 1990 and there are now FRSs (Financial Reporting Standards) and FREDs (Financial Reporting Exposure Drafts), but these ruin the alliteration. A useful review of the new structure and the likely effects is Gray and Walton (1992).

Accounting principles are not rigid and unambiguous. They are rightly flexible, to a degree, and honest men can disagree as to how a particular issue should be treated. But this flexibility and inevitable uncertainty give scope for creative accounting, which ranges from putting the best face on a situation to misrepresentation. Naser and Pendelbury (1992) found that UK auditors think that creative accounting is widespread. This section is about creative accounting and may seem a bit out of place in this book. The reason for including it is that we discuss at some length a number of strategies which do not involve detailed analysis of accounts. It is all too easy to select shares by various value attributes and end up with a large number of companies with dubious accounts.

This is not an accounting text, and not the place to discuss at length the details of creative accounting practices, although some examples will be listed to give some background to the discussion. A simple introduction to creative accounting is Jameson (1988), a general discussion with numerous examples is Smith and Hannah (1991) and Holmes and Sugden (1990) cover the topic in their excellent textbook. Some of the practices that have so upset investors and regulators will soon be prohibited by the new FRSs. But not immediately and not all, and new standards will probably just shift the abuses to new areas rather than eliminate abuses altogether. New uncertainties will be introduced by the increased volatility of earnings that will be introduced by new rules on the treatment of one-off items.

Creative accounting means that published accounts cannot be taken at face value and the numbers must be reworked. To give a flavour of some of the issues that investors should have been thinking about in recent years, consider the following:

(a) firms with accounting policies that are different from the industry standard;

(b) changes in the year end reporting date—this makes it difficult to make comparisons and an extended reporting period may include two peak trading periods;

(c) changes in divisional splits—e.g., from a pre-interest to pre-tax basis which gives scope for notional internal interest allocation and concealing the trading situation;

(d) switching from using year-end exchange rates to average, or vice versa, when this benefits the current year;

(e) transferring assets between current and fixed assets—e.g., a property company may hold development profits as work in progress. If property prices fall, a write-off should be taken in the profit and loss account but the company could transfer the property into an investment category and take the loss against the revaluation reserve;

(f) the treatment of extraordinary and exceptional items. Some companies seem to have routinely treated non-trading profits as exceptional and non-trading losses as extraordinary. Some have treated on-going trading costs such as redundancies as extraordinary.

(g) contingent liabilities—especially where this takes the form of a guarantee of the debt of associated companies or third parties (e.g., management buyouts from the parent) and is large in relation to shareholders' funds. Large contingent liabilities result in the balance sheet giving a misleading picture;

(h) changes in depreciation policy—e.g., stopping depreciating freehold and long leasehold buildings or extending the estimated useful life of assets, both of which boost profits;

(i) unrealistic depreciation policies—e.g., excessively high residual values on computer leases which do not allow for obsolescence;

(j) capitalizing expenses—e.g., start-up costs of an overseas venture might be capitalized and written off over several years instead of charged to the profit and loss account as incurred. Another example is capitalizing the interest charges involved in constructing buildings. The interest gets added to the value of the assets rather than charged to the profit and loss account. Capitalized expenses pose no problems when everything is going well, but come a set-back there can be a startling difference between profits and cash flow;

(k) Writing off direct to reserves. An example of this practice involves currency mismatching where it is possible to generate a net interest credit even if in overall debt. For example if a company lends in a soft currency (such as Turkish Lira) and borrows in a hard currency (such as Deutschmarks) it will generate a positive interest rate differential. Unfortunately it will probably suffer exchange losses—these can escape a profit and loss impact if written off direct to reserves;

(l) Making marginal adjustments in shareholdings to turn associated companies into subsidiaries or vice versa depending on trading profitability.

Well, we are half way through the alphabet and have not got to merger accounting, deferred consideration (earn-outs), premature income recognition, pension funding and so forth. But we will call a halt—let's face it, published accounts need careful analysis.

Yet, since it is so easy to list creative accounting techniques, one may reasonably wonder whether they really mislead the professionals. Accounts are commented on in the press and investment analysts and investors scrutinize them. Publications such as *Company Reporting* draw attention to how companies report key items in their accounts. Those who believe in efficient markets argue that creative accounting doesn't fool the markets. Two arguments are put forward (see e.g., Watts, 1986). The first relates to earnings changes. Stock prices respond to earnings changes and this gives a reason to cheat. If this happens and investors do not see through it, then stocks with good earnings figures should contain many which are misrepresented. Unless the market never sees through creative accounting, then the companies with good earnings numbers should perform poorly in the future. This does not happen. The second argument relates to studies of a number of accounting policy changes which affected stated earnings but did not have real economic effects. The evidence suggests that stock prices were not affected, on average. Although these findings are often stated as though they were conclusive, there are in fact few such findings and there are others which suggest that the markets do get fixated on the reported numbers. (See, e.g., Biddle and Lindahl, 1982; Elliott and Philbrick, 1990; Hand, 1990; Harris and Ohlson, 1990; Kaplan and Roll, 1972; Ricks, 1982; and Saunders, 1975.)

We shall outline just one study. Briloff, mentioned earlier, is a noted US critic of accounting standards. He has published a number of books and various articles in magazines such as *Barron's* criticizing companies' financial reports. Watts describes Briloff as a demagogue and his work as a curiosity and a relic of a past age of scholarship. The evidence suggests otherwise. Foster (1979) looked at 15 of Briloff's articles and calculated the abnormal return (based on a version of the capital asset pricing model) suffered by 28 companies criticized in his articles. He looked at the abnormal returns for 30 days before and after publication. On average the companies suffered an immediate 8% fall in their share price. This fall was maintained for the 30 day period following the articles. Foster looked at a number of possible explanations for the price reaction—e.g., Briloff had access to new information, other information was released at the time, and Briloff's exposé might prompt Government regulation, but Foster ruled these out. One is left to wonder whether this study shows how quickly new information is incorporated into prices (although one cannot say whether the price reaction is too little or too much) or whether it shows how little skilled accounting analysis is in fact incorporated into prices and how much scope there must be to earn abnormal returns from a modest application of accounting skills. Most practitioners believe the latter.

Most studies cited in this area are American and it is worth remembering that it is possible that the US studies of the effect of accounting changes tend to attribute more skills to investors than is warranted in the UK, where analysts' technical skills seem to be lower. Consider some of the disasters of the UK stock market in recent years—e.g. Coloroll, MCC (Maxwell), Polly Peck, Burton, Trafalgar House. All had been subjected to accounting criticisms for a long period, but in each case the share price collapsed after a longish period of poor share performance. Were the accounting issues fully discounted and the collapses in share prices, when they happened, attributable to new information, e.g., poorer economic prospects than expected (Coloroll and Trafalgar House), or fraud (MCC)? Or is it reasonable to believe that when the inevitable happened, the price collapse reflected the fact that many investors were fooled for a long time by creative accounting?

We can argue in the following manner. The typical institutional investor would be delighted to beat the market by 1% a year. Not much, but over the years it would mount up. If an institutional portfolio holds, say, 50 shares, each share might represent two per cent of the portfolio. If just one share has a precipitous decline in value the typical institutional investor would not expect to outperform in the year that happened: it is important to avoid the dogs. If one employs an attribute style of investing, say combining low price-earnings ratio and good earnings growth, it is easy for fund managers to skip over some of the boring aspects of fund management—like getting to grips with accounts. Most creative accounting problems seem to be noted by brokers' analysts or the press. Sometimes they may be a bit slow in noting the problem, but they still often do it before a precipitous share price decline. However many investment managers simply lack the accounting skills to appraise the accounting problem when alerted to it and to make a sensible investment judgement. If the market does not fully discount creative accounting, some effort in improving accounting skills will be valuable. This is not to deny that much creative accounting is discounted by the market, just that sufficient is not discounted for it to be worth spending some time studying accounts.

Further, even if the market does fully discount creative accounting, it is important for analysts to understand what the market is discounting so that sensible decisions can be made. For example, Coloroll was lowly rated partly because of its contingent liabilities. A low price-earnings ratio investor who fully understood this would be in a better position to make decisions than one who did not. A pure low price-earnings ratio investor, i.e., one who looked at nothing but the level of the relative price-earnings ratio would have believed the shares were cheap. Investors who applied fundamental analysis to a low price-earnings ratio universe would have had varying views. Those who understood the accounting issues and believed the economy would be strong, might also have thought the shares were cheap, but those who understood the accounting issues and thought consumer expenditure was going to fall, might have thought the company was vulnerable, and selected a different share from the low price-earnings ratio universe.

Even if nobody is fooled by creative accounting, the need for companies to undertake such activities suggests poor prospects. A recent working paper by Lev and Thingarajan, cited in *The Economist* (1992), apparently found that US firms that introduced accounting ploys to boost earnings, underperformed the market by 20–25% over a five year period. If you spot a company cheating, avoid it.

The author thinks creative accounting does fool many investors but even if it does not, investors would probably benefit from spending some time taking accounts apart, especially if their basic investment style is some form of attribute screening. These comments will be most relevant when the economy is heading into recession and may be less relevant if the world moves out of recession in 1993. But there will be recessions in the future. The arguments here are not meant to suggest that accounting analysis be used to determine the correct price for shares. Rather, the analysis should be more broad brush and used to screen out some stocks that might otherwise appear cheap.

AVOIDING BANKRUPTCY CANDIDATES

While some companies engaged in creative accounting became bankrupt, so too do other firms. Detailed accounting and economic analysis may identify these companies, but investors focusing on certain attributes may miss the signs. Some form of accounting screen for bankruptcy candidates would be useful.

Some early US work on this issue was undertaken by Beaver (1966) who analysed trends of seven financial ratios for five years prior to the failure of 79 firms.

He compared these firms to 79 others which were matched for industry and size. He found some clear trends: for example the mean cash flow/total debt ratio for the non-failed firms was a little under a half in each year whereas, for the failed firms, five years before failure it was around one quarter and it fell to minus one quarter one year before failure.

If financial ratios can distinguish between failing and non-failing firms, combining the ratios into an equation might lead to useful predictions. There are a number of US models and the best known have been developed by Altman. The original Altman (1968) model utilizes five financial ratios which are combined and analysed within a statistical procedure called discriminant analysis. An overall discriminant score, or Z score, is produced for a company from the following equation:

Z = (0.012 × working capital/total assets) + (0.014 × retained earnings/total assets) + (0.033 × earnings before interest and taxes/total assets) + (0.006 × market value of equity/book value of total debt) + (0.1 × sales/total assets).

Equations such as that shown above have limited accuracy. Some firms that are expected to survive will fail, and some firms expected to fail will survive. The higher the Z score, the less the likelihood of failing. Above a certain cut-off score firms are expected to survive and below that to fail. If the cut-off Z score is set at a very low number there will not be many firms expected to fail which in fact survive. On the other hand a lot of the eventual failures will be classified as survivors. If the cut-off Z score is set at a high number the opposite type of error will occur. Where the Z score cut-off is set depends on which type of error is most important: Altman chose a cut-off Z score of 2.675—firms scoring below that were expected to fail. Naturally this score gave good results on the sample Altman used to select his number. On a second sample, biased to financially weak firms, the numbers were poorer, but still useful, as Table 30 shows.

Table 30   Z Score Classification Accuracy

	Predicted	
	Bankrupt	Non-Bankrupt
Actual		
Bankrupt	24	1
Non-Bankrupt	14	52

Source: Altman (1968, pp. 601-02)

All but one of a sample of bankrupt firms were correctly classified, whereas about one fifth of a sample of firms that survived were incorrectly classified. The data shown is for a one year prediction horizon; a two year horizon produced more classification errors and beyond that the Z score had no real power.

Altman *et al.* (1977) subsequently extended Altman's work to develop a Zeta model. This combined readily available financial statement data adjusted to reflect current accounting standards. The variables used measured overall profitability, size, debt service, liquidity, cumulative profitability, capitalization and stability of earnings over a 10 year period. Looking at 73 bankruptcies that occurred after the model's development, it correctly identified 68 of the 73 using data from one statement prior to failure and 62 out of 71 using data from two statements prior to failure. There is a high correlation between Zeta scores and Value Line's Relative Financial Strength Measure (see Altman and Spivack, 1983).

Z score models have been developed for the UK and are sold by commercial organizations. These models are reviewed by Taffler (1984) and his own model is discussed in Taffler (1983). Taffler uses an approach similar to Altman, and the variables he uses are: profit before tax/average current liabilities, current assets/total liabilities, current liabilities/total assets and the no-credit interval (i.e., the number of days a company can continue to trade if it generates no revenues). Taffler claims that his model has true predictive ability: the probability of a firm classified as "at risk" by his model subsequently failing within a year was six times greater than for a firm selected at random. One problem is that his model on average classifies about one sixth of all firms as at risk. This is much lower than some other models, but still a large number.

Z scores are ordinal, but non-linear. What this means is that a Z score of, for example, 2 is better than a Z score of 1, but it is not necessarily twice as good. However if all companies' Z scores are ranked and then transformed into a scale of 0-100 this problem is overcome. This procedure allows a company's Z score to be tracked over the years to see both whether the company is at risk and whether it is deteriorating or improving relative to other companies. The statistical validity of this approach has been challenged.

Z score models have been criticized frequently. There is no accounting theory behind the variables used—the whole procedure is basically an exercise in data-mining. However, at a pragmatic level, Z scores seem to have some value in as much as they seem to lead to better decisions. Moreover, investors could use Z scores as a supplement, rather than as a strategy *per se*. But, even if Z scores have predictive value, would they be useful for investors? That depends on how information about deteriorating companies is incorporated into stock prices. There is ample US evidence (e.g. Clark and Weinstein, 1983 and Aharony *et al.*, 1980) that firms entering bankruptcy generate abnormal losses for shareholders from around five years prior to bankruptcy. Despite the long-term decline, significant losses take place on the days surrounding the bankruptcy. The studies imply that abnormal profits can be earned if bankruptcy is predicted.

Altman and Brenner (1981) utilized the original Altman Z model and examined a sample of companies that went from Z scores greater than 2.675 to scores less than 2.675, i.e., had a deteriorating financial condition. Unfortunately their sample was drawn from COMPUSTAT tapes and contained no companies that actually became bankrupt. This could inject a bias against finding abnormal performance.

In fact their results were ambiguous. When they used one risk adjustment they found persistent large abnormal returns up to a year after the release of the accounting data. Using another model there were no abnormal returns.

A study by Katz et al. (1985) produced rather more clear-cut results. They too used COMPUSTAT tapes to form their sample which was for NYSE stocks for the period 1968-76. They used the Z score cut-off of 2.675 and looked for firms that went from above 2.675 to below, and vice versa, and they called their two groups a distress group and a recovery group. Katz et al. found that in the 15 months preceding the issuance of the annual report that lead to the change in state as classified by the Z score, significant positive abnormal returns accrued to the recovery group and vice versa for the distress group. Both groups produced abnormal returns in the expected direction over the following nine months. This study's results held whether the market model or capital asset pricing model was used to adjust for risk. Against this study should be set that by Zavgren et al. (1988) who have produced results which they claim support a view that it is difficult to achieve abnormal returns from bankruptcy prediction models.

What should one conclude? Clearly one does not want to hold stocks that go bust. But many stocks in poor financial health will recover and could produce spectacular returns: indeed some US fund managers specialise in "phoenix" stocks and there are books recommending such a strategy (e.g., Grace, 1985). Ignoring all stocks that are "at risk" could eliminate a big part of the market and eliminate some big winners. Perhaps one might reason much as we did for creative accounting. If an investor follows a strategy of picking low price-earnings ratio stocks or neglected stocks or any approach which will select some stocks which may be "cheap" for a good reason, it makes sense to scan the selected stocks to see if they might be heading towards bankruptcy. This scan can be made on the basis of general "experience" and standard accounting skills, but it could also be by a Z score model.

CONCLUDING COMMENTS

Creative accounting is widespread; managers often have an incentive to put their best face forward. It seems likely that accounting regulators will always be one step behind. There are mixed views as to whether creative accounting fools many investors, but investors who select stocks on the basis of attributes seem especially vulnerable. It seems worthwhile to put in some effort to try to untangle creative accounting. The ultimate disaster is bankruptcy. Investors who select shares on the basis of attributes might find Z score models a useful supplement to try and ensure that they do not hold stocks that are apparently cheap, but actually lemons.

15
Neglected and New Stocks

In this chapter we look at two groups of stocks about which, relative to other stocks, there is limited information, neglected stocks and new issues. Areas of limited information seem a good place to look for market inefficiencies although as we shall see, it is not lack of information that causes new issues to earn abnormal returns.

NEGLECTED STOCKS

For most institutional investors, stockbrokers' analysts are a major source of information. But analysts do not follow all the stocks in the S&P 500 or the FT-A All-Share Index, let alone all the smaller stocks. There are around 7000 stocks in the US NYSE, AMEX and OTC markets and around 2500 quoted stocks in London. What are the prospects for stocks followed by few analysts, or not followed at all, i.e., neglected stocks? Arbel, Strebel and Carvell have examined this in a number of papers and books (e.g., Arbel, 1985a; Arbel 1985b; Arbel *et al.*, 1983; Arbel and Strebel, 1983; Carvell and Strebel, 1987; and Strebel and Carvell, 1988).

Analyst Neglect

Arbel and Strebel (1983) focused on stocks in the S&P 500 Index in the period 1970–79. They measured analyst neglect by a ranking system based on two indicators: the number of analysts regularly following a stock, as measured by Drexel Burnham Lambert surveys, and the number of analysts reporting earnings forecasts as compiled in the Standard and Poor's *Earnings Forecaster*. They classified firms as highly followed, moderately followed or neglected, depending upon whether they were followed by four or more analysts, two or three analysts and one or no analysts respectively. They found that degree of neglect and average annual return were related, as shown in Table 31.

Table 31 Average Annual Rate of Return by Degree of Neglect.
S&P 500: 1970–79

Highly Followed	Moderately Followed	Neglected
9.4%	12.7%	16.4%

Source: Arbel and Strebel (1983, p. 38). This copyrighted material is reprinted
with the permission of *The Journal of Portfolio Management.*

Neglected stocks outperformed highly followed stocks by 7% per annum on average. Is this finding a result of neglected stocks being riskier or being smaller
stocks? Using three measures of risk (systematic risk, unsystematic risk and total
risk) neglected stocks did not appear to be significantly riskier. They were smaller,
so Arbel and Strebel looked at analyst neglect by size category. They found that
smaller stocks did generate higher returns than larger stocks but within each of
three size categories, as shown in Table 32, neglected stocks produced higher
returns. After adjusting for total risk, the smaller company effect disappeared.

Table 32 Return by Degree of Analyst Neglect and Company Size (%)
Average 1970–79

	Small Company	Medium Company	Large Company
Highly Followed	5.0	7.4	8.4
Moderately Followed	13.2	11.0	10.2
Neglected	15.8	13.9	15.3

Source: Arbel and Strebel (1983, p. 39). This copyrighted material is reprinted with
the permission of *The Journal of Portfolio Management.*

Institutional Neglect

So far only one aspect of neglect has been examined. What if neglect is measured
in terms of actual investment by institutions rather than analyst neglect?

Arbel *et al.* (1983) studied a random sample of 510 companies drawn in equal
numbers from the NYSE, AMEX and OTC, over the period 1971–80. They
divided firms into three categories based on the number of institutional holders
according to data published by Standard and Poor's. One of their findings is shown
in Figure 33: neglected stocks outperformed. Risk was examined in a number of
ways but did not seem to be the explanation of the higher returns.

Table 33 Average Annual Returns by Degree of Institutional Neglect 1971–80

Number of Institutional Holders	Return (%)
More than 12	10.4
2 to 12	16.9
1 or none	20.8

Source: Arbel *et al.* (1983, p. 59). Reproduced by permission

Abnormal Returns or Reward For Risk?

Before we conclude that neglected stocks offer abnormal returns, we should question whether the correct notion of risk is being applied to neglected stocks. Investors' knowledge of neglected stocks is limited—estimates of returns and standard deviations and correlations of returns with other stocks must be subject to greater uncertainty than for other stocks. This means that if investors attempt to use the Markowitz approach to portfolio construction that we discussed in Chapter 2, incorporation of neglected stocks will make the whole estimation much more uncertain. Unless investors receive higher returns for holding neglected stocks, they would rationally omit them from their portfolio construction. Individual neglected stocks may bear greater unsystematic risk than other stocks but this can be diversified away by holding a basket of neglected stocks. However, the estimation uncertainty cannot be diversified away, it is a source of undiversifiable risk (see e.g., Klein and Bawa, 1977 and Barry and Brown, 1986).

Private investors are more important in the neglected stock universe than in the blue chip universe. Given the limited diversification of private investors, the extra return from neglected stocks may be a reward for both unsystematic risk and systematic estimation risk. Investors who buy a basket of neglected stocks will eliminate unsystematic risk and will get an investment free-lunch. Investors must decide whether undiversifiable estimation risk is worth bearing. For many who do not approach their stock portfolio construction in the manner suggested by Markowitz, it may well be.

One distinct attraction of neglected stocks is that some stocks will always be relatively neglected, so this does not seem to be a strategy that automatically self-destructs if it becomes popular. Arbel, Carvell and Strebel go further. They claim that the size effect and the low price-earnings effect disappear once neglect is allowed for. Arbel also claims to be able to explain the January effect (see Chapter 17) which is stronger for neglected firms. Part of his explanation seems implausible to this writer, and part relates to the increase of corporate information that occurs as the financial year ends. This is more valuable for neglected firms than large. But does this really suddenly happen on a few days at the turn of the year?

What does happen at the turn of the year is that lists of the year's winning stocks appear and these will contain many neglected stocks. This may stimulate interest in them, leading to high January returns. Well, whatever one might think of these explanations and claims, neglected stocks have historically produced higher returns.

NEW ISSUES

When the owners of a firm wish the firm to be quoted on the exchanges they will make a new issue or an initial public offering (IPO). In the UK, new issues which were to be quoted on the London Stock Exchange or USM, have been made by introduction, placing, offer for sale by subscription, offer for sale by tender and offer for sale at a fixed price. This latter route has been the most popular, although the tender offer has been used for some of the larger issues in the last few years.

The Underpricing of New Issues

Would buying all new issues be a profitable investment strategy? Table 34 and 35 suggest it would.

Table 34   New Issue Returns: UK

Study	Sample Period	Duration	Return
Levis (1990)	1985–88#	First day	8.6%
Levis (1993)	1980–88#*	First day	14.3%
Keasey and Short (1992)	1984–88*	First week	14.0%

Main market; #* Main market and USM;* USM

Table 35   New Issue Returns: US

Study	Sample Period	Sample Size	Initial Returns: one week	Initial Returns: one month
Reilly/				
Hatfield	1963–65	53	9.9%	8.7%
McDonald/Fisher	1969–70	142	28.5%	34.6%
Logue	1965–69	250		41.7%
Reilly	1966	62	9.9%	
Neuberger/Hammond	1965–69	816	17.1%	19.1%
Ibbotson	1960–71	128		11.4%
Ibbotson/Jaffe	1960–70	2,650	16.8%	
Reilly	1972–75	486	10.9%	11.6%

Table 35 (*continued*)

Study	Sample Period	Sample Size	Initial Returns: one week	Initial Returns: one month
Block/Stanley	1974–78	102	5.9%	3.3%
Neuberger/LaChapelle	1975–80	118	27.7%	33.6%
Ibbotson	1971–81	N/A		2.9%
Ritter	1960–82	5,162	18.8%	
	1977–82	1,028	26.5%	
	1980–81	325	48.4%	
Giddy	1976–83	604	10.2%	
John/Saunders	1976–82	78		8.5%
Beatty/Ritter	1981–82	545	14.1%	
Chalk/Peavy	1974–82	440	13.8%	
Ritter	1977–82			
• Firm commitment		664	14.8%	
• Best efforts		364	47.8%	
Miller/Reilly	1982–83	510	9.9%	
Muscarella/Vetsuypens	1983–87	1,184		7.6%

Source: Extracted by permission from Saunders (1990, p. 10).

Saunders, from whose article Table 35 is taken, states "Although the time periods, sample, sizes and ways of calculating initial returns (especially raw versus market-adjusted) differs widely across these studies, each finds underpricing on average" (p. 5). The same can be said of the UK studies although, on average, the returns have been lower than in the US.

Why are new issues underpriced? There have been a number of suggestions put forward, none of which is very well supported by evidence. One argument is that the merchant banks know more about the correct price than the issuer and it is in the banks' interest to underprice so as to be sure they are not left bearing the underwriting. Moreover, ensuring good on-going relationships with institutional investors is more important than with a client, who may make only one new issue. Another argument, especially relevant to the US, is that underpricing is safer for a bank required to exercise due diligence with regard to prospectus information offered to investors. If an issue performs poorly there is a danger that a dissatisfied investor will seek, and find, misleading or incomplete information in the prospectus. These arguments suggest that an investor who buys a spread of new issues will earn abnormal returns.

The explanation for underpricing that has attracted most academic attention is due to Rock (1986). Rock assumes that the new issue market is composed of two groups—a small informed group and a larger uninformed group. The informed group is assumed to be too small to purchase all of an issue. Rock also assumes that there are good and bad new issues. The uninformed investors will bid for all issues and the informed will only bid for good issues. Because of the demand for good issues, the informed investors will get scaled down allocations as will the uninformed investor. For the poor issues, only the uninformed investor will be allocated stock. The uninformed investor will thus get a large allotment of bad issues and a smaller allotment of good issues. As a result of this effect—the winner's curse—new issues have to be underpriced on average so as to produce an acceptable expected return for the uninformed investor. You may or may not find this explanation plausible—this writer doesn't. However, if Rock is right, even although new issues are underpriced on average, uninformed investors won't make excess returns by buying them. The UK evidence does not seem to bear this out, as we shall see in the next section.

Before we look at that, it is worth noting that new issues come in waves: for several years new issues are hot and returns high. Ritter (1984) examined these waves in the US and it seems that returns peak before the value of new issues peak. Anybody thinking of investing in new issues should be aware of the feast or famine nature of the new issue market. One implication of these waves may be that "investors are irrationally over-optimistic about the future potential of certain industries" (Ritter, 1991, p. 4) and that the high return from new issues is not the result of intentional underpricing.

The Pay-Off From Buying New Issues

Levis (1990) studied UK new issues in the period 1985–88. He looked at 123 new issues. He notes that the first day price rise gives a misleading impression of returns because of the interest costs involved in applying for a new issue (from having to put up cash with the application) and the limited allocation of shares that may be obtained. Allocation of shares is at an issuing house's discretion—it can ballot or scale down applications. Sometimes small shareholders are favoured, sometimes large. Interest charges will be borne on the value of the full application of shares, no matter how many are received. (It should be remembered that issuing houses did not always present the cheques of unsuccessful investors—a practice not allowed for in Levis' calculations, which therefore bias returns downwards.) In Table 36 some market data is shown for Levis' sample.

Table 36   UK First Day Returns (%) 1985–88

	Absolute opening return	Absolute closing return	Market adjusted return
All issues	9.14	8.77	8.64
Issues opening at or above offer	14.80	15.30	15.88
Issues with negative first day returns	−10.09	−9.04	−7.54

Source: Levis, (1990, p. 83). Reproduced by permission of the author and publisher

The first column shows the first day returns based on the opening price, the second shows the return based on closing price and the final column adjusts the second column for general market movements. Levis calculated the amount of stock allocated for 13 application levels (using the actual allocation details) and, allowing for loss of interest, he produced a table of effective returns for various values of application. This is partially reproduced as Table 37.

Table 37   UK New Issue Effective Returns: 1985–88

Value of Application (£)	Net Expected Return (%)
500	1.67
1000	2.09
2000	2.69
4000	3.24
8000	4.18
16000	5.20
32000	5.16
64000	5.11
128000	4.31
256000	4.31
512000	3.89
1024000	3.33
2048000	1.44

Source: Levis (1990, p. 84). Reproduced by permission of the author and publisher

Table 37 assumes an application was made for every issue but obviously well informed investors might earn a better return. The returns improve if under-subscribed issues are not applied for—all under-subscribed issues generated negative returns (as did 18% of oversubscribed issues). Thus investors who can predict under-subscription will make additional profits.

For the US market, Ibbotson et al. (1988) have suggested that it is possible to predict which new issues will offer the best returns

"by comparing the final offering price with the offering price range listed on the front page of the preliminary prospectus of a firm commitment offering. The preliminary prospectus is generally issued about three weeks prior to the offering date, and during this interval the underwriters conduct pre-selling activities, achieving better knowledge about the demand for an issue in the process."(p. 45)

Ibbotson et al. claim that investment bankers only partially adjust prices in response to demand. If demand is high they raise the offer price, but not by enough, and vice versa for low demand. The advice from Ibbotson et al. is to watch the direction of price change when deciding whether to purchase.

Is buying all new issues a worthwhile strategy? From Table 37 we can deduce that private clients investing less than £4000 probably would not have made a profit if they sold their shares at the end of the first day. Commission charges and half the bid-offer spread would consume their price gains. Other investors, except perhaps the largest, would have made money. The sums are not enormous, but the returns would appear attractive for being involved in a process that takes about one Stock Exchange account. During the four year period under review, there were perhaps 150 opportunities to make 3 or 4%. The chance to make 3 or 4% per account seems attractive, especially as Levis' 1990 study is based on initial returns that are among the lowest produced by any UK or US study. It would seem that institutional investors probably should purchase all new issues likely to be oversubscribed or, if they lack prediction skills, all new issues.

Buy ... But Remember To Sell

The evidence cited above suggests that for all but the smallest private clients and the largest institutional investors, it is worth buying new issues. New issues are even more attractive if investors have some special knowledge of which issues are likely to be oversubscribed. It is important to note that this is a trading view and not a long-term investment view. The findings of two recent studies are worth bearing in mind. They suggest investors should buy new issues and then sell them immediately.

Ritter (1991), in the US, found an initial positive return of 14.32% from purchasing IPOs but there was then more or less steady underperformance by these shares over the following three years. Ritter notes that

> "A strategy of investing in IPOs at the end of the first day of public trading and holding them for 3 years would have left the investor with only 83 cents relative to each dollar from investing in a group of matching firms listed on the American and New York stock exchanges. Younger companies and companies going public in heavy volume years did even worse than average .... firms go public near the peak of industry-specific fads." (p. 23)

Ritter makes an interesting point:

> "It has always been somewhat of a mystery why IPOs are priced in a manner that results in such large positive average initial returns. This paper's evidence indicates that the offering price is not too low, but that the aftermarket price is too high. [But this].... is even more of a mystery..." (p. 24)

Levis (1993) looked at new issues listed in the UK in the period 1980–88. He found a first day return of 14.3% and then underperformance over the next 36 months. There was evidence that this continued even after 36 months. There was also evidence that the issues with the highest initial returns had the worst long-run performance. Are new issues deliberately underpriced? Levis (p. 41) felt that

> "The emerging evidence is more consistent with the proposition that while a certain level of first day returns is the result of intentional underpricing, marked deviations from this baseline represent some form of market overreaction."

CONCLUDING COMMENTS

Both neglected stocks and new issues appear to offer high returns. Neglected stocks appear not to be especially risky in terms of the usual forms of risk, but they do suffer from greater estimation uncertainty. Whether the reward for that uncertainty is attractive is something that each investor must decide.

New issues offer high returns, although the first day returns somewhat exaggerate the achievable returns because investors will not normally get as much of an issue as they would wish. New issues are probably intentionally underpriced to some extent but there is also an element of investor over-reaction. New issues tend to be made when stocks or particular industries are in favour. Investors price the new issues too high on the first day and the typical issue then underperforms for some years. New issues should be bought and then sold immediately.

16
Following Recommendations

Many investors buy shares on the basis of other people's recommendations. In this chapter we look at three different types of recommendation, those of brokers, the press and commercial services. The likely performance gains seem rather modest, so we shall just give a flavour of the research in this area.

STOCKBROKERS

Stockbrokers produce a large proportion of the research carried out on the equity and bond markets. There is no reason to believe that brokers have any advantages in producing this research. They produce it to make money for themselves, rather than as a service to the community, or even to fund managers. Brokers around the world have preached the virtues of competition but formed cartels for themselves, which have established high fixed commission rates. A consequence of these rates has been excess profits (often concealed by high staff remuneration) and competition has taken the form of service competition—principally research services for institutional clients. Normally one would expect competition to force prices down towards costs. With prices fixed, however, service competition has meant costs have tended to move up towards prices (Kahn, 1971). Thus, the amount of research provided has had very little to do with the optimal amount of information required by fund managers. In the past two decades, fixed commission rates have been abolished in most countries as a result of government initiatives. Nevertheless, brokers have gone on producing research and resisted de-bundling—i.e., selling execution and research services separately.

In recent years, integrated houses have developed in the UK; these combine a brokerage firm and a market-maker in one operation. Not only can one question the amount and type of research produced (presumably that which favours dealing activity will be the most profitable for the broker) but one can wonder whether the views of the analysts and the timing of the release of their research is affected by the state of their market-makers' books.

Institutional investors vary in their attitude to brokers' research. Some use it as their major source of research (supplemented by the press, Datastream, etc.); some have in-house research capabilities which largely ignore outside research; some have modest in-house research capabilities which essentially processes the outside research in some way; some largely ignore the views of analysts but use their forecasts and company analysis; and so on. In Chapter 7 we looked at analysts' forecasts, we turn now to analysts' recommendations.

There have been a large number of studies of analysts' recommendations and we shall discuss here two large-scale studies, one for the UK and one for the US. We begin with the UK study which, unfortunately, was undertaken before the development of integrated houses.

UK BROKERS' RECOMMENDATIONS

Dimson and Marsh (1984 and 1985) begin their analysis by reviewing other studies of the value of published and unpublished investment advice (e.g., privately circulated brokers' studies). Most studies find that the advice is helpful but, on average, it only produces one per cent or so of abnormal return. Another type of study has calculated the correlation between forecast returns and subsequent outcomes, usually called information coefficients. These have typically been about 0.1. This is small, but potentially useful.

In Dimson and Marsh's study they sought the assistance of "one of the City's largest investment institutions". Over a two year period, 1980–81, the institution collected 4187 specific return forecasts for 206 UK shares. These accounted for 75% of the value of the FT-A All-Share Index. Of the forecasts, 3364 were made by 35 different UK stockbrokers and the remaining 823 were provided by the institution's internal analysts. All forecasts were of specific returns relative to the FT-A All-Share Index. (Actually matters were more complicated than that but the details can be ignored here.) The forecast period was typically a year.

Notice that this study is not a test of the typical output of brokers' analysts. Analysts typically grade a stock buy, sell or hold (some use a five point scale) rather than forecast specific returns. In reality, buy and hold recommendations predominate with few sell recommendations. The forecasts Dimson and Marsh studied were made solely for the fund and not sent to all institutional clients—this eliminated the possibility that a share price rose solely because of the forecast and the marketing effort of the broker.

Dimson and Marsh calculated an information coefficient between forecast returns and outcomes of 0.077, which is lower than most previous studies, but still may be of some value. Interestingly, the coefficient for the brokers was 0.086 and for the fund's internal analysts 0.042. This lower number for the latter group was because they followed more small stocks—where they forecast the same stocks as the brokers, the coefficient was similar.

Dimson and Marsh claim that the forecasts had demonstrable value. In the two year study period the fund generated 2950 transactions in the 206 stocks studied. The transaction value-weighted specific return achieved on the 2950 transactions over the year following the trade was 2.2%, or 1.7% after non-avoidable transaction expenses were deducted. (These costs are very modest, biased by the fund's enormous positive cash flow and unlikely to be attainable by other investors.) The authors state that the forecasts had real commercial value. This seems a brave conclusion. Did the fund managers make decisions solely on the advice studied or on the usual flood of data from numerous brokers giving buy/sell/hold recommendations that the fund would have been receiving daily? Brokers' research nonetheless, albeit not the subject of the study. Did the fund managers have any sector weighting criteria that might have affected share selections? However, if one takes the authors' view, brokers' research has a real, but modest, value.

Are some brokers better at forecasting than others? Possibly, but the authors concluded "for practical purposes, our best assumption is probably that all brokers have about the same degree of share price forecasting ability". (1985, p. 33).

What we have been looking at is brokers' written research. This has a bias towards buy recommendations. Over the telephone an institutional salesman might add something which in effect says: "the report carries a hold recommendation but we are brokers to the company and actually the analyst thinks the stock is a sell". Some companies are very uncooperative with analysts who give sell recommendations, whether or not there is a corporate brokerage relationship. There appears to be no substantial research on telephone recommendations. (But see Dimson and Fraletti, 1986.)

US BROKERS' RECOMMENDATIONS

We turn now to a major US study. Elton et al. (1986) used data compiled by the investment group at Banker's Trust. Starting in March 1981 and continuing for 33 months, forecast data was collected from 34 brokerage firms. The data was generated by an average of 720 analysts, producing over 10 000 forecasts per month. The authors claimed that the database was three times larger than the total of the data used in all prior studies. Stocks were ranked on a five point scale, with 1 the most attractive, 3 neutral and 5 the least attractive. The usual broker bias to "buy" or "hold" was apparent; only 13% of the recommendations were rated as 4 or 5. About 11% of the recommendations were changed every month.

Do changes in recommendations have value? Elton et al. tackled this in an interesting way. We shall explain their methods by a specific example. For a particular month they collected all stocks upgraded to 1 or 2, and all stocks downgraded to 4 or 5. They calculated the betas for all stocks and arranged the stocks for each group from highest to lowest beta. They then calculated the beta for each group. If the betas differed by more than 0.01, they deleted stocks with betas at the extreme from the group with the largest number of stocks. For example, if the largest group had the higher beta, they dropped the stock in that group with the highest beta and so on down the line until the two groups had similar betas. This process hopefully controlled for risk, without having to specify a particular asset pricing model. Analysts do not follow all sectors or as many small stocks as large, and this procedure obviated a need to make allowance for this. What were the findings? Table 38 shows the performance of a portfolio of newly-recommended 1s and 4s compared to a portfolio of new 3s. Table 39 shows results for all possible changes in recommendations in less detail. Month zero is the month of recommendation.

Table 38 Return in Per cent

Month	Up to 1 compared to 3		Down to 4 compared to 3	
	Monthly Returns	Cumulative Returns	Monthly Returns	Cumulative Returns
0	1.91	1.91	−0.56	−0.56
1	1.24	3.15	−0.74	−1.30
2	0.28	3.43	−0.08	−1.38
3	−0.11	3.32	0.04	−1.34
4	0.37	3.69	0.17	−1.17
5	0.06	3.75	0.00	−1.17
6	0.28	4.03	−0.14	−1.31
7	0.04	4.07	−0.07	−1.38
8	−0.04	4.03	0.22	−1.16
9	−0.05	3.98	0.13	−1.03
10	−0.11	3.87	0.13	−0.90
11	−0.34	3.53	−0.33	−1.23
12	−0.34	3.19	0.53	−0.70

Source: Calculated from Elton *et al*. (1986, p. 705)

Table 39 Excess Portfolio Return Comparisons

Change in Class	Comparison	Month of Recom -mendation	1 Month After	2 Months After	Total
Up to 1 or 2	Down to 4 and 5	2.43	1.86	0.37	4.66
Up to 1	3	1.91	1.24	0.28	3.43
Up to 2	3	1.65	0.84	0.20	2.69
Up to 4	3	0.68	0.09	−0.80	−0.03
Down to 2	3	0.29	-0.37	−0.09	−0.17
Down to 4	3	−0.56	−0.74	−0.08	−1.38
Down to 5	3	−0.38	−1.48	−0.40	−2.26

Source: Elton *et al*. (1986, p. 706)

What do these exhibits tell us? First, following brokerage recommendations has some value. Stocks that have been upgraded do better than stocks that have been downgraded. Second, most of the excess return takes place in the first three months. Third, these effects are not enormous. Finally, notice that we have been examining changes in recommendations—we have not examined the value of the recommendations *per se*. Elton *et al.* looked at recommendations and concluded that there is evidence of analysts possessing some skills. However the changes in recommendations are more valuable. Finally, the authors tried to find if there was a best buy amongst the brokerage firms: they thought not.

PRESS RECOMMENDATIONS

Financial journalists usually receive brokers' research and may have their own contacts with companies. Is it worth following press tips? The answer is complex.

The major UK study is by Dimson and Marsh (1986). They examined 862 recommendations from 11 national publications drawn from the period 1975–82. Half of the recommendations came from the *Investors Chronicle*. The tips outperformed the market as measured by the FT-A All-Share Index by about 3% over the year from the end of the recommendation month. The level of outperformance increased further over the next year and eight of the publications achieved outperformance while three did not.

This seems to suggest that it is worth following press tips. However, against an equally-weighted index, the recommendations underperformed in the following year by about 6%. The problem is that there was a size effect (small firms outperformed large) and it is difficult to know which is the correct benchmark. The problem can be illustrated as follows. All UK stocks were ordered by their capitalization and then split into deciles. There was a bias in the recommendations towards large stocks, with 36% coming from the top decile. But this decile accounted for 83% of market capitalization. The tipped stocks were four times the size of the typical UK stock but the probability of a large stock being tipped was less than proportional to its capitalization. The recommended stocks were typical of neither an equally weighted-index, nor a capitalization-weighted index.

When the recommendations were measured against a set of diversified control portfolios in different capitalization classes, it turned out that the recommendations offered neutral performance over a year. The recommendations did offer outperformance of about 4% from the date of the recommendation to the end of the recommendation month. Unfortunately there was a lag between a recommendation being made and it being published. For the source of one-third of the recommendations studied, two-thirds of the performance occurred prior to public distribution. No information is given for the pre-publication performance of the other recommendations.

Immediately after mentioning the 4% abnormal return, Dimson and Marsh state:

"The magnitude of the abnormal performance is, however, relatively small, and any potential short-term profits from following tipsters' recommendations would be more than consumed by UK transaction costs." (p. 126)

This conclusion seems at odds with the much more favourable comments (and assumed costs) made by the same authors with regard to their study of brokers' recommendations which was discussed earlier. One could argue that the journalists seem to be better stock pickers than the analysts (based on the 4% return figure for the journalists), yet readers of both groups' published output would make slightly better returns from following the analysts because a substantial part of the journalists' ability is lost due to a publication lag. Both groups, incidentally, choose stocks that have performed well in the previous year: both are trend followers.

VALUE LINE

There are many commercial advisory services, but we shall look at the merits of following the recommendations of only one, that of Value Line. The *Value Line Investment Survey* is an independent, weekly, investment advisory service covering US stocks. It claims to be the largest advisory service in the world measured in terms of revenues and numbers of subscribers. Value Line covers 1700 stocks which it ranks weekly for "timeliness" and "safety". It reviews all stocks every three months and produces an information-packed page on every stock. Although a US service, even investment managers who do not invest in the US should be interested in Value Line's record and the research undertaken on the service.

The emphasis here will be on Value Line's timeliness rankings although it should be noted that its safety rankings were found in one study (Fuller and Wong, 1988) to correlate with subsequent returns better than either beta or standard deviation measures of risk. A component of the safety rank—relative financial strength—is highly correlated with Altman's Zeta score.

Value Line ranks the 1700 stocks it covers on the basis of expected performance over the next 12 months. Stocks with a timeliness rank 1 are expected to perform the best. The number of stocks in each category is, by design, as shown in Table 40.

Table 40 Value Line Timeliness Rank Distribution

Timeliness Rank	Number of Stocks
1	100
2	300
3	900
4	300
5	100

For obvious commercial reasons, the exact details of how the timeliness ranks are determined is not published, but the key elements have been, e.g., Bernhard (n. d.) and Gerstein (1986) and these are:

- a value position based on three factors: relative earnings rank, relative price rank and relative price momentum. The first two factors are calculated in a similar way. The objective is to know where earnings and price stand compared to where they have stood for the same company in the past 10 years. Relative earnings and relative prices are defined as the stock's latest 12 months earnings and price divided by an index of earnings and prices of all Value Line stocks for the same period. Thus a stock whose relative earnings are currently the highest in the last 10 years would be highly valued. The price momentum factor is determined by dividing the stock's latest 10 week average relative price by its 52 week average relative price;
- an earnings momentum factor determined by a stock's latest quarter's earnings change, compared to a year ago, relative to that of all other stocks;
- an earnings surprise factor, where the most recent quarter's earnings are compared with the Value Line security analyst's forecast.

Interestingly, Value Line used to include its analysts' views but dropped them in mid-1979 because they did not add any value.

Value Line has published graphs of its record based on portfolios drawn up under two different assumptions. The "frozen" basis, shown in Figure 22, assumes an equal amount of money is invested in each stock in every group at the beginning of each year. Each stock is then held for 12 months without any allowance for

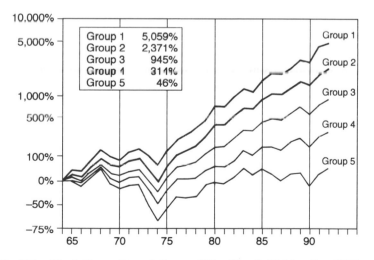

Figure 22   Value Line's Frozen Record. Source: Value Line Publishing, Inc. (1993, p. 9605). Copyright Value Line Publishing, Inc. Reprinted by permission

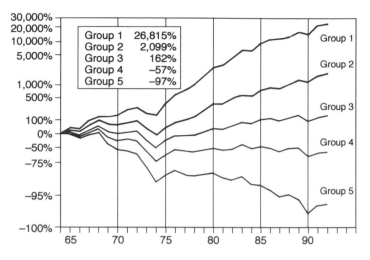

Figure 23 Value Line's Total Conformance Record. Source: Value Line Publishing, Inc. (1993, p. 9604). Copyright Value Line Publishing, Inc. Reprinted by permission

subsequent changes in ranking. The "total conformance" basis, shown in Figure 23 takes into account every ranking change as it occurs. The results—pre-transactions costs—are, apparently, fabulous. Moreover, the timeliness ranks as a group show perfect discrimination, i.e., rank 1 beats rank 2, which beats rank 3, etc.

Although many people noted Value Line's record, it was probably Black's (1973) "Yes Virginia..." article which gave the record academic respectability. Subsequent studies have been less positive. Holloway (1981) examined Value Line's record and allowed for transaction costs. It turned out that a total conformance portfolio of stocks ranked 1 required so many trades that transaction costs overwhelmed the Value Line system and abnormal returns were not achieved. (Recall the comments in Chapter 6 about the need to include transaction costs when evaluating an investment system—few systems that claim success can have pre-transaction cost records as spectacular as Figures 22 and 23.) However, the buy and hold Value Line rank 1 portfolio did produce annual abnormal returns of 8.6%, even after transaction costs.

Copeland and Mayers (1982) also found abnormal returns pre-transaction costs, but very little after. However, if investors had to trade, Value Line would offer scope for abnormal returns. Most of the abnormal performance appeared in rank 5 stocks. They looked at returns to both ranks and changes of ranks. For the latter they found that pre-transaction cost abnormal returns were concentrated in the two weeks following a rank change. A later study by Stickel (1985) found most of the abnormal returns were concentrated in the three-day period around a rank change. Stickel found the rank change from 2 to 1 to have the biggest impact on returns and the significant three-day period includes the Thursday preceding the official

Value Line issue date. Value Line attempts to mail its weekly survey so that all subscribers receive it on the same day, Friday. In fact some subscribers are thought sometimes to receive their copy on Thursday. Hall and Tsay (1988) corrected for what they saw as deficiencies in previous studies and found that after transaction costs, neither active nor passive investors in rank 1 stocks outperformed random portfolios.

A number of academics have tried to explain how Value Line produces its good pre-transaction cost forecasts, e.g., Huberman and Kandel (1990) and Affleck-Graves and Mendenhall (1992). We will discuss the latter here. They note that there are many studies that show that abnormal positive returns accrue to firms reporting earnings which exceed expectations and vice versa for poor earnings (see Chapter 7). Affleck-Graves and Mendenhall note that Value Line timeliness ranks are based on, amongst other things, earnings momentum and earnings surprises. Is Value Line's ranking success due solely to "post-earnings-announcement drift"? The authors note that over half of all Value Line rank changes follow earnings announcements by eight days or less. They partition their sample into two roughly equal-sized groups based on the lag between earnings announcement and the rank change and then examine the difference in abnormal returns between firms moving into rank 1 and those moving into rank 5. Abnormal returns only exist when the rank change follows closely an earnings announcement. This suggests that post-earnings-announcement drift explains Value Line's results. The authors undertook further statistical tests which supported this.

The above results are not too surprising. One of the author's former colleagues used to try to guess each week which new firms would be ranked 1 by Value Line. He based his guesses on recently reported earnings surprises. It might be reasonable to assume that part of the abnormal return generated by stocks on the day prior to their Value Line rank change is a result of investors guessing rankings rather than an abnormally speedy US postal service.

Value Line is an excellent product. For a low cost it provides an enormous amount of useful historical information, and its safety and timeliness ranks have some value. The timeliness rankings show perfect discrimination, rank 1 stocks beat rank 2, and so forth. The rankings have produced abnormal returns before transaction costs but it is less clear if they have after costs. If an investor has to trade, for example when setting up a new portfolio, the rankings would be useful. There is evidence that over the years the abnormal returns have been earned in a shorter and shorter period; indeed it may be that returns are concentrated in three days around the weekly issue date. The major factor leading to Value Line's good timeliness ranking ability may be its emphasis on earnings surprises. Value Line may be better at identifying losers than at identifying winners (e.g., Copeland and Mayers, 1982 and Lacey and Phillips-Patrick, 1992). And yet, despite all this evidence, it is not clear that investors can make money from using Value Line. Value Line manages a fund on the basis of its published recommendations. Over long periods, it has not consistently beaten the average growth and income fund (according to Lipper's statistics). This is perhaps an unfair comparison because Value Line's fund holds cash and bonds, but clearly, there is more to good fund management than good share recommendations. Investment organizations should subscribe to Value Line—but this will not necessarily lead to outperformance and the added value for investors already using earnings surprise models may be limited.

CONCLUDING COMMENTS

Should an investor follow recommendations? Pulling together the two studies of brokers' recommendations discussed above and other literature (see the survey by Dimson and Marsh, 1984), it would appear that brokers' recommendations are worth something: but not a lot. It is important to note that the studies do not typically assess buy, hold and sell recommendations. The bias of brokers' research to buy and hold recommendations would probably produce poor results if the recommendations were slavishly followed. A private client who does not have access to brokers' research need not despair, but institutions should not ignore it—although to get value they may have to process the information and they should probably concentrate on changes in recommendations. They might integrate this with monitoring changes in earnings and dividend forecasts. The size of outperformance achievable by following brokers' views is modest in relation to some of the outperformance offered by other strategies in this book. Indeed, since analysts' recommendations will be partly based on their profit forecasts and changes, it is reasonable to ask whether their recommendations have any value over and above that contained in their profits forecasts. Since earnings surprises and revisions seem to lead to higher returns than recommendations, one might argue that analysts' views are actually a negative if one is already looking at their forecasts. Recall that Value Line dropped its analysts' views from its model. Further, investors should ask whether they are getting good value by paying enormous sums to brokers in bundled research/execution fees. Switching some of the budget towards databases, specialist subscription services, quantitative analytical software etc., would seem to make good sense.

Press recommendations may offer a modest pay-off, but this conclusion must be a little uncertain because of the problems in determining the appropriate performance benchmarks.

Few commercial advice services have been evaluated in a rigorous manner. Value Line is an exception, and its record suggests that its timeliness recommendations contain useful information. Whether it would add much value for an investor who already monitors earnings revisions and surprises is unclear. Value Line's safety ranks also contain useful information.

The market seems to be reasonably—but not perfectly—efficient with regard to published advice.

17
Calendar Effects

Mark Twain's view on stock market timing is well known: "October. This is one of the peculiarly dangerous months to speculate in stocks. The others are July, January, September, April, November, May, March, June, December, August and February." But is there a best time to buy stocks, a favourable season? The evidence is that returns are related to many calendar events and in this chapter we look at a number of them.

Researchers have examined returns in relation to weekends, holidays, turn-of-the-month, part-of-the-month, January and December as well as intraday. This type of research is usually described as being concerned with seasonal effects, but calendar effects is a more accurate description.

Some commentators have found the notion of regular calendar effects slightly implausible—they imply that if you have a calendar and a watch that you can make money—and one certainly has to beware of data-mining. It is all too easy to trawl through computer banks of data and discover, say, that for a 20 year period stocks have typically risen on the third Tuesday of every month or some such bizarre occurrence. However, such a finding is likely to be just a chance finding and unlikely to hold true in the next sample period. We should have more confidence in calendar effects if they are found in samples from different periods, especially if they apply to various sub-periods within the sample periods, and if the effects can be found in a number of different international markets. Ideally a theory would precede the data, but there have been few academic theories about calendar effects that have preceded the empirical findings. Failing this, a plausible theory produced after the empirical discovery would be useful, especially if it could be tested independently of the data it purports to explain. With these cautionary words we will move on to a brief review of the various calendar effects.

THE JANUARY EFFECT

January, it seems, is a very special month. Rozeff and Kinney (1976), using an equally-weighted equity index (i.e., one in which a small firm has as much weight as a large one), found that for the US for the period 1904–74, the average return per month was about 0.5% whereas for January it was 3.5%. Subsequent research has shown that the January effect is essentially a small firm phenomenon. Keim (1983) found that small firms earned half their abnormal returns in January. Lakonishok and Smidt (1988) using a 90 year sample (1897–1986) for the Dow Jones Industrial Average (DJIA) found no January effect. The DJIA is essentially a large stock index: the 30 stocks account for about 25% of the market capitalization of the NYSE. A standard explanation for the January effect is that it has been tax-related. The US has a calendar tax year and it has been argued that poorly performing shares will be sold late in the year to realize capital losses and then investors will buy the shares back in the New Year, pushing up prices.

Gultekin and Gultekin (1983) looked for a January effect in 16 countries and found it in 15. A January effect was observed in countries which did not have capital gains tax for all or part of the period studied (e.g., Japan and Canada). The UK and Australia also had a January effect, but the UK's tax year starts on April 6, and Australia's on July 1. However, the UK and Australia also had high returns in April and July. Recalling that it is the small firm effect that is a January phenomenon in the US, it should be noted that in the UK the small firm effect is largest in May, not in April, (e.g., Corhay et al., 1988 and Levis, 1985). We noted earlier that Dimson and Marsh report that the HGSCI's performance relative to the FT-A All-Share Index is poorest in January and April. So does a tax explanation underlie the January effect? Perhaps a bit, but not exclusively.

It is not just small firms that behave differently in January. High-yielding and zero-yielding stocks do. The overreaction effect, the tendency for extreme performance stocks over various periods to reverse their performance in the following period, (see e.g., De Bondt and Thaler, 1985 and 1989) occurs mainly in January. Finally, risk, as well as return, behaves differently in January (Rogalski and Tinic, 1986). Jacobs and Levy (1988a) (see Chapter 21) claim that after disentangling all the effects that are at work, it is the rebound for stocks with embedded tax losses and zero- and high-yielding stocks that account for most of the January effect. They claim that other January seasonals, such as small size, are merely proxies for these two effects.

With regard to the UK, it is worth noting that Gultekin and Gultekin's data for 1959–79 shows a strong seasonal pattern in returns. Although January was the best single month, the period December to April consisted of months which on average produced positive returns. December through April produced more than the annual return, and the other seven months produced a negative return. The traditional advice of "Sell in May and go away" would have been a profitable strategy.

THE WEEKEND EFFECT

Fields (1931) made the earliest study of day-of-the-week effects. He found the US market tended to rise on Saturdays (the market used to open for a couple of hours on Saturday). Cross (1973) found that the market tended to rise on Fridays and fall on Mondays and this finding has generated a flood of research, all reporting the same "Blue Monday" effect with rates of return tending to be high at the end of the trading week. Where Friday was not the last trading day it still has tended to produce high returns (see, e.g., Lakonishok and Smidt). The fall in prices on Monday seems to take place between the close on Friday and the first 45 minutes of opening on Monday. As a result, the Monday effect is often called the Weekend effect.

Jaffe and Westerfield (1985), Condoyanni *et al.* (1987) and O'Hanlon and Papaspirou (1988) and others have examined the weekend effect for countries other than the US. It exists, but perhaps it should once again be called the day-of-the-week effect because, in countries whose market's trading hours overlap with the US market's, Monday tends to be a down day (e.g., the UK and Canada) but where, because of time zone differences, the closing market value is computed before Wall Street opens for Monday trading, Tuesday is the down day (e.g., Australia, Japan, Singapore and France).

Turning specifically to the case of the UK, Choy and O'Hanlon (1989) report a strong day-of-the-week effect and it appears to be stronger in larger, frequently traded stocks, than smaller—the opposite of the US finding. Choy and O'Hanlon rejected the effect of stocks going ex-dividend on Mondays as the explanation of the UK day-of-the-week effect. Board and Sutcliffe (1988) found evidence of a weekend effect in the UK over the period 1962–86 with the significance diminishing over time. They found returns on Mondays which were the first day of a trading account were positive, while returns on other Mondays were significantly negative, leading to an overall negative Monday effect.

THE HOLIDAY EFFECT

If stocks rise before weekends, do they rise before other trading breaks caused by holidays? In the US there have been a number of studies looking at this, e.g., Fields (1934), Ariel (1987 and 1990) and Lakonishok and Smidt (1988). Lakonishok and Smidt found a pre-holiday rate of return of 0.22% for their 90 year sample compared to the regular daily rate of return of 0.0094%. This gain is 23 times the regular daily rate and means that the approximately 10 days preceding holidays each year accounted for about 50% of the price increase of the DJIA.

Cadsby and Ratner (1992) looked at turn-of-the-month and pre-holiday effects on stock returns in various international markets. They examined returns in relation to both local and US holidays. The periods examined varied for the markets; for the UK the period was 16/8/1983–13/6/88. They concluded:

> "Pre-holiday effects are significant for the United States, Canada, Japan, Hong Kong and Australia but not for any of the European countries in the sample [the UK, Italy, Switzerland, West Germany and France]. All countries exhibiting pre-holiday effects do so with reference to their own local holidays. The only country which also

exhibits a significant US pre-holiday effect is Hong Kong, though in all countries the highest returns seem to be earned on days just prior to joint local-US holidays." (p. 508)

WITHIN-THE-MONTH EFFECT

Ariel (1987) found that from 1963–81, positive rates of return only occur in the first half of the month, which he defined to include the last day of the previous month. In their longer sample period, Lakonishok and Smidt, defining the first half of the month in the usual way, found only mild support for Ariel's results (the results were in the right direction but not statistically significant). Jaffe and Westerfield (1989) did find a positive first half effect in Australia, but a second half effect in Japan, and no real effect in the UK and Canada.

TURN-OF-THE-MONTH EFFECT

Lakonishok and Smidt followed up Ariel's work on turn-of-the-month returns. For their 90 year period they found that the four days at the turn-of-the-month—the last day of one month and the first three of the next—averaged a cumulative rate of increase of 0.473% (versus 0.0612% for an average four days). The average monthly increase was 0.349%—i.e., the DJIA goes down during the non-turn-of-the-month period. This result was consistent across sub-periods.

Cadsby and Ratner found a turn-of-the-month effect in the US, UK, Canada, Australia, Switzerland and West Germany. They did not find the effect in Japan, Hong Kong, Italy or France. For the UK the turn-of-the-month return was four and a half times the rest of the month's return.

THE DECEMBER EFFECT

Lakonishok and Smidt note that the second half of December has the highest rate of return of the 24 half months. For their 90 year period the average rate of return in the second half of December for the DJIA was 1.54%. This period includes two pre-holiday dates and the return is concentrated from the pre-Christmas trading day to the New Year trading day. The DJIA is a large stock index and Lakonishok and Smidt note that:

"If the importance of an anomalous rate of return is evaluated in terms of its impact on a dollar-weighted portfolio, then the high average end-of-December rate of return is far more important than the high average rate of return for small companies in January." (p. 409)

THE INTRADAY EFFECT

Harris (1986) studied intraday effects by examining a time-ordered tape of every transaction in every common stock traded on the NYSE for the period December 1, 1981 to January 31, 1983. There were 15 million transactions. Harris found that prices fell on average on Mondays and rose by increasing amounts during the rest of the week. The negative Monday effect took place mainly in the first 45 minutes of trading. The pattern of returns for the rest of Monday was similar to other days. On other days of the week prices rose significantly in the first 45 minutes. On all weekdays, i.e., including Monday, the market tended to rally between 12.30 p.m. and 1.30 p.m. and to fall between 2.15 p.m. and 3.30 p.m. The market rallied at the close and prices rose on the last transaction of the day. These results were pervasive over the period studied (i.e., one or two months did not dominate the results) and applied to all market value groups.

Harris suggested some trading strategies based on his findings:

"Although trading strategies based only on these patterns would not be profitable because of transactions costs, portfolio managers can increase profits when they have other reasons to trade:

- Purchasers of stock should avoid purchasing stock early in the morning on Monday. On the other weekdays, they should purchase as early as possible.
- Sellers of stocks should try to sell late on Friday. If they must sell on Monday, they should do so as early as possible. On the other weekdays, if they must sell early, they should try to wait at least until 45 minutes after the open.
- On all weekdays a 'limit sell order' at a price just above the market price and submitted shortly before the market closes may yield the best price." (p. 64)

CONCLUDING COMMENTS

Most investors will find calendar anomalies interesting and rather good fun compared to some of the topics discussed in other chapters, which call for a lot of effort if the investor is to make money. Many of the calendar anomalies seem real enough as they occur in several markets and have been discovered in time periods that had not been examined when the effects were first found. But what causes calendar effects? There may be tax effects at work; the flow of institutional funds may be related to the calendar; private clients tend to get offered buy recommendations by their advisers and may be left to work out their own selling strategy, which they are likely to do on the weekend; good news and bad news may be released at different times, bad news may come after the markets have closed on Friday; psychological factors may be at work—for example most people may prefer Friday to Monday; and so on.

Whether or not these explanations have merit will be debated for years but investors should be cautious and keep matters in perspective. As Lakonishok and Smidt note for the US:

"It is useful to relate the magnitude of the anomalies with the size of a tick (the smallest price change), which is 12.5 cents. Because the average price per share on the NYSE is about $40, a movement of one tick corresponds to a price change of 0.313 percent or more, which is much larger than most seasonal anomalies discussed... [in their paper]. For example, the average Monday price decrease of −0.144 percent is well within one tick." (p. 417)

If investors wanted to trade the turn-of-the-month effect, for example, they would have to turn their portfolio over 1000% in a year. But for anyone who has to trade, it makes sense to play the odds and time the trades to take account of the calendar effects. The effects discussed in this chapter seem more the basis of trading tactics than investment strategy. The only exception to this might be the UK's seasonal pattern which suggests being in cash from May until December and then in equities. Fund managers should get their traders to read this chapter.

18

Technical Analysis and Contrary Opinion

Technical analysts arc often seen, at least in the UK, as chartists, pure and simple, but most of them nowadays are more than that. Technical analysts certainly look at past prices, believing that future trends can be deduced from the past, and so may seek head and shoulders, descending triangles, flags and other exotic charts patterns, but they also look at the behaviour of various types of market participants, company directors and other insiders, sentiment and contrary opinion, liquidity levels and so on. Recall Table 14 of Chapter 5: contrary opinion was the most frequently cited technical tool.

WHAT'S TECHNICAL AND WHAT'S FUNDAMENTAL?

Technical analysts are contrasted with fundamental analysts who try to calculate the true underlying value of a stock by analysing dividends, growth, interest rates and other factors. The problem with this contrast is that it seems artificial. Of course a dividend discount model adherent and a chartist have different beliefs but what about everybody else? Is an investor who simply buys small stocks really a fundamentalist? And what of a low price-earnings ratio investor? The notion of neglected stocks sounds folksy enough to be a technician's tool—or is it fundamental because statistically-orientated professors elaborated the concept? Why is insider trading a technical tool? Are calendar effects technical, fundamental or astrological?

The great bulk of the interesting research findings seem to be just that interesting, and it does not really matter how they are classified. Accordingly, in this book various topics the author finds interesting are discussed and, in general, no attempt has been made to classify them as fundamental or technical. In this chapter we shall comment briefly on chartist analysis, relative strength, insiders' trades and contrary opinion. There is more to technical analysis than this and contrarians may not wish to be labelled technicians. No matter, it is the ideas that are important, not the labels.

CHARTIST ANALYSIS

Chartists are the people the academics love to hate. It is beyond the scope of this book to outline chartist theories; the interested reader should refer to the standard book by Edwards and Magee (1984) or a long article by Shaw (1988). An old, but still worthwhile review of the evidence, was made by Pinches (1970). Most readers will have sufficient chartist background for the comments here. It should be noted that US technical analysts often look at volume statistics and price and volume patterns together. UK chartists generally seem to omit volume. It is beyond the scope of this book to review the volume literature: interested readers should refer to Karpoff (1987), who reviews the academic literature on the relation between price changes and trading volume, although he does not tie it to specific technical rules.

There are at least four grounds for being suspicious of the validity of chartist analysis:

1. early academic research claimed that share prices took a random walk, i.e., the next price for a stock is not predictable from past prices and therefore a method based on past prices was bound to be flawed;
2. there are many different methods of chartist analysis and two chartists will often come to different conclusions about whether a stock is a buy or a sell;
3. chartist analysis is often non-scientific because it is not refutable. For example one leading textbook quotes a leading technician as writing

    "If the Industrials close below 1247.35, then a fully fledged secondary downside reaction à la Dow Theory, would be in force. This, plus many of our negative sentiment indicators, would imply further weakness for the entire market. However, if the 1247.35 level holds, it is called positive divergence."

    Well, yes, if it goes up it goes up, and if it goes down it goes down. Unfortunately a lot of chartist comment is like this. Often the level being described is so far away that investors could lose 10–15% of their assets before the chartist would conclude that the market is going down.
4. chartists often point out that fundamental analysis is suspect because it is hard to tell what fundamental information is discounted in prices. This invites the question as to why chartist analysis is not also discounted in prices.

Point 2 above does not seem especially telling, for the same could be said of fundamental analysts. Points 3 and 4 do seem telling. With regard to point 1, there has been some wavering on this, as there is evidence that there is a short-run return-reversal effect, that relative strength may persist and that there is a longer term return-reversal effect. Sad to say, most of these findings have not been as a result of chartist research and they are discussed elsewhere in this book. Only the relative strength findings seem in the mainstream of chartist tradition and they will be discussed in the next sub-section.

Although the writer is sceptical of the merits of chartist analysis, it is worth noting that investors still buy charts and chartist analysis is important in some markets—especially the foreign exchange markets (see Frankel and Froot, 1990)—where it may be more successful than other techniques (see, e.g., Goodman, 1980).

RELATIVE STRENGTH

Relative strength is calculated for a stock to show how it has been performing relative to its sector or to the market as a whole. Relative strength can also be calculated for a sector relative to the market.

An early test of relative strength was by Levy (1967) who concluded that relative strength was a useful technique. He looked at 68 different trading rules and his study is open to the charge of data-mining. It was also subject to other criticisms by Jensen and Bennington (1970) who did not find relative strength useful. Subsequent studies have suggested relative strength does have some validity, e.g., Akemann and Keller (1977), Bohan (1981), Brush (1986), Pruitt and White (1988) in the context of a three screen model, and Jacobs and Levy (1988a) in the context of a multi-attribute model discussed in Chapter 21. A study by Reinganum (1988) supporting relative strength is discussed in Chapter 34. Arnott (1979) did not support relative strength. We will take a brief look at these studies.

Akemann and Keller used relative strength over a 13 week period to forecast the next 52 weeks for industry groups for the period 1968–77. The highest ranked group outperformed the market significantly (in fact the top four groups outperformed). Bohan also used industry groups but used relative strength over a year to predict relative strength the following year. His sample period was 1969–80. He found a strong correlation between the performance of the strongest and weakest quintiles from one year to another but no predictive strength for the middle quintiles. Notice that both these studies use groups and not stocks. They do not, therefore, tell us anything about relative strength and stocks. This does not diminish interest in the findings, however, because many investors find picking sectors harder than picking stocks.

Arnott argued that the relative strength model should be revised to incorporate beta coefficients. If the market is rising, a stock with a high beta may appear to have high relative strength but in fact could have neutral or even weak relative strength on a beta-adjusted basis. Arnott studied the period January 1968 to September 1977 and examined individual stocks. He found a negative correlation between past relative strength and future performance. He noted previous studies had found positive results and by way of reconciliation he pointed out that his study did not rule out the possibility that extremes of relative strength did work, that relative strength did work for some of the years in his sample, and finally he had studied stocks and not sectors.

Pruitt and White tested relative strength in a multi-component technical model they called CRISMA, based on cumulative volume, relative strength and moving average. To be purchased a stock had to meet three criteria. First, the 50 day price moving average for a stock had to intersect the 200 day moving average from below when the slope of the latter was greater than or equal to zero. Second, the relative strength graph (relative to the S&P 500) from beginning to end over the previous four weeks had to have a slope greater or equal to zero. Finally, the cumulative transaction volume graph over the previous four weeks had to have a slope greater than zero. These three rules required a stock's price to be rising, performing at least as well as the market and have increasing trading volume. To avoid "whipsaws" even when the three criteria were met, a purchase was only made when the price reached 110% of the level established by the intersection of the 50 and 200 day moving average.

Pruitt and White examined all stocks that were covered in the O'Neil *Datagraph* series and were on the CRSP tape for the period 1976–85. This system generated excess returns even after assuming 2% trading costs. Unfortunately, it is not clear how useful the system would be in practice. Only 204 stocks were selected and trading was rapid—stocks were held for a mean of 24.4 days. The portfolio was almost always in cash.

Irrespective of the practicality of the CRISMA system, note that it uses a one month relative strength model whereas Bohan, for example, used a one year model. These studies are not really support for each other as they are testing quite different relative strength models. Brush reported on eight models but tested many more. He noted various restrictions—don't use the relative strength models in November and December because they don't work, use extreme quintiles because the relative strength relationship is non-linear and so forth. Despite the evidence in favour of relative strength (see also Chapters 21 and 35), one is left with an uneasy feeling of too many models, too much data-mining and so forth.

INSIDERS' TRADING

Insider trading which, loosely speaking, is the use of non-public information in connection with a share transaction, is illegal in the US and the UK. Illegal insider trading can be remarkably profitable, as Levine and Hoffer (1992) demonstrate. (Levine was convicted for insider trading, so it was profitable only up to a point.) In the US, even legal trades made by "insiders" are usually referred to as insiders' or insider trading. By insider trading we will mean legal trading by insiders.

US Federal law requires directors, officers and shareholders owning 10% or more of a share traded on an organized exchange, i.e., insiders, to report their transaction within 10 days of the end of the month in which the transaction was made to the Securities and Exchange Commission (SEC). The SEC should publish details of trades by insiders in its *Official Summary* in the following month. Thus information about insider trading should be available within about two months of a trade taking place.

Insiders have been described as "America's most knowledgeable investors". Can these investors make abnormal returns and, more importantly, can the rest of us make money by following their trades? Many books written by practitioners answer these questions affirmatively, but the evidence is less clear cut, although it is true that many of the early studies did suggest that following the insiders was a winning strategy (e.g., Pratt and DeVere, 1968; Jaffe, 1974; and Finnerty, 1976).

A major recent US study is by Seyhun (1986), who studied the period 1975–81. His sample comprised all firms listed on option exchanges plus a stratified random sample, based on the size of firms' equity of all publicly held firms. He analysed 769 firms and a total of 59 148 open market sales and purchases.

Insiders trade for many reasons: they may be using their specific knowledge, but they may be taking up stock options, they may be selling to raise cash for family reasons, and so forth. It is therefore not unusual to observe both purchases and sales being made by different insiders at the same time. If the number of insider buyers exceeded the number of insider sellers in a month, Seyhun considered this to be an insider purchase (and vice versa); if the number of purchasers and sellers was equal, the month was ignored. Seyhun used the market model to measure the expected return to securities. He found that during the 300 days following the insider trading day, stock prices rose abnormally by 4.3% for purchases and fell abnormally by 2.2% for sales.

These are not enormous numbers, but if the SEC is tough about insiders acting illegally, it would be surprising if insiders acted in advance of very noticeable events affecting their company. Accordingly, one might expect modest returns. But what of the earlier studies that suggested much bigger returns? There are a number of possible explanations. First, the studies used samples of insider trades and there may simply be large sampling errors. Second, the differences in results may be a result of the methodologies employed—for example the definition of an insider trade, the dating of the event day and the method of measuring abnormal returns. In particular Seyhun argues that some previous studies using the capital asset pricing model may have had a smaller company bias. Seyhun's sample showed that small firm insiders are far more likely to be buyers than large firm insiders. If small firms produce higher returns than large firms, other studies may really have been picking up a small firm effect.

Seyhun further analysed his data in terms of looking for relationships with regard to particular types of insiders. He reported

> "it appears that insider information arises as a result of insiders' association with the firm, since insiders who are closer to day-to-day decision-making [e.g. officer-directors] trade on more valuable information. Second ... [the] most profitable insider trading occurs in small firms. Third, insiders can distinguish the differences in the value of their information and trade a larger volume of stock when they have more valuable information." (p. 206)

The first point is demonstrated in Table 41.

Table 41 Abnormal Returns from Stock
Purchases by Insider Type: 1975–81

Insider	Abnormal Return (%)*
Chairman	3.3
Officer-Director	3.3
Director	2.3
Shareholder	1.9
Officer	1.5

* Earned in 100 days following insider trade. Source:
Seyhun (1986, p. 205). Reproduced by permission of
Elsevier Science Publishers BV

Turning to outsiders (i.e., ordinary investors) trading on the back of insiders' reported deals, the findings were not encouraging. The *Official Summary* does not report insider trades as fast as it might. The delay between the insider trading day and the availability of the *Official Summary* exceeds 90 days for 31% of transactions and 60 days for 84%. Various commercial organizations produce insider trade information on a more timely basis by collecting the relevant data from the SEC offices rather than waiting for the *Official Summary*. Seyhun reports that

"if an outsider trades on the basis of insiders' transactions as soon as insiders' reports are received by the SEC, he can earn 1.4% [abnormal return] after 100 days and 1.9% after 300 days. If the outsider waits until after the *Official Summary* is available, the gross abnormal return is only 1.1% during the next 300 days." (p. 208)

Once one allows for transaction costs, the abnormal returns disappear. This conclusion was not affected by using more selective rules based on the identity of insiders, the dollar volume of trading and so forth.

Seyhun's study can be summarized simply: insiders can make modest abnormal profits—outsiders copying them make very little indeed. As was noted above these findings are somewhat at odds with most studies. Apart from the points noted earlier about differences in sample and methodology, what other reasons might account for the finding of an absence of abnormal returns to outsiders? Following insiders has become a popular strategy in recent years with a number of commercial services providing up-to-date information, the *Wall Street Journal* publishes a monthly "Inside Track" column and so forth. One might be tempted to conclude that insider actions are now instantaneously compounded in stock prices. However, that does not seem correct—in Seyhun's study the failure of the strategy is primarily caused by the modest returns to the insiders and by part of the abnormal return being earned in the period before the insider trades are published.

Some years ago, Finnerty (1976) had noted that insiders who bought shares were buying companies that were smaller, had larger earnings and larger dividends compared to those companies insiders were selling. What if allowance is made for the abnormal returns likely from small size and low price-earnings ratio? Zaman (1988) examined this issue and studied the period 1973–82, a period that substantially overlaps Seyhun's. His key findings were as follows. On the basis of the market model, insiders earned abnormal profits over 1, 3, 6 and 12 month holding periods: if 2% transaction costs were assumed they earned abnormal profits of around 0.5% per month over the 3, 6 and 12 month holding periods. Outsiders also earned abnormal returns over all holding periods if no transaction costs were allowed for, but only over 6 and 12 months after costs. They earned about 3.7% over 12 months. When Zaman allowed for size and price-earnings ratio effects, insiders still made abnormal returns after 2% costs, although returns were more than halved. Outsiders, however, made no abnormal returns.

Before drawing all this together, one other study is worth mentioning. Seyhun reported that insiders can tell the value of their information. A rather different finding was reported by Oppenheimer and Deilman (1988). They looked at insiders' profits in relation to two specific information releases—the announcement of the resumption of dividend payments after at least two years of non-payment and the announcement of the omission of dividend payments after at least two years of steady payment. The results were startling:

> "insiders as a group seem to exhibit little timing ability. Some insiders (for example, insiders buying shares of firms omitting dividends) exhibit terrible timing ability. Officers, however, perform better than insiders as a whole. It is suggested that the book on insider trading is still open; it is not clear that insiders as a group always utilize insider information to achieve profits." (p. 539)

We would appear to know the following about insider trading in the US. A number of studies have shown that insiders and the outsiders who follow them have made abnormal returns. Recent studies show lower returns than the early studies and possibly no abnormal returns, but these returns are calculated after making adjustments for small size and low price-earnings ratio effects. These adjustments are debatable. They may explain why following insiders is profitable, but they do not remove the profit. If insiders tip small firms, and small firms outperform, so be it. Following insiders would be a profitable investment strategy, even if it is really just a small firm strategy. Further, transaction cost adjustments would not apply to investors who had to deal anyway.

Nonetheless, investors should be aware of the insider/size/price-earnings interrelationships. If investors adopt an investment strategy of following insiders they might outperform. Part of that outperformance probably can be attributed to buying small and low price-earnings ratio stocks. If, however, investors already invest in small and low price-earnings ratio stocks, the addition of an insider trading strategy may add very little. Note too that some insiders are not very intelligent in their investment actions so it is not clear what returns would be available from selecting just a few insider trades to follow, rather than following all of them. Investors could be subject to large sampling error. On the other hand, some classes of insiders (e.g. chief executive officers) are better guides than others (Nunn et al., 1983; Seyhun, 1986), so an investor might be able to improve on the overall return reported by various studies.

Regan (1991) provides food for thought. He reports that Mark Hulbert, who monitors the performance of US investment newsletters' stock recommendations, found that for the period January 1985 to September 1990, *The Insiders*, a major newsletter issuing stock recommendations based on insider trades, underperformed the US market by about 9%. During this period, small stocks and low price-earnings stocks performed poorly. Pratt, co-author of one of the early studies, and owner of a newsletter, performed so poorly that he sold the newsletter.

Turning to the UK, insider trading has been much less thoroughly studied. UK directors must notify their company as soon as possible of any share transaction for their personal account and the company must notify the Stock Exchange immediately. The Stock Exchange will then release the information through its Regulatory News Service which appears on Topic screens. The information will also be published on a weekly basis. Two UK studies of insider trading will be outlined here.

King and Roell (1988) took a sample of insider transactions reported in a weekly "share stakes" column in the *Financial Times* from January 1986 to August 1987. They point out that this is far from a complete set of disclosed transactions:

> "each week, the journalists composing the news item review all such transactions and include only those they judge particularly interesting or significant, subject to column space constraints." (p. 16)

Thus, King and Roell actually appear to be testing not insider trades *per se*, but the share selection skills of *Financial Times* journalists drawing stocks from a universe consisting of stocks involved in insider trades. They found that both insider buys and sells outperformed over one, three and twelve months following publication, although the sell figures were not statistically significant. Although there was a small firm bias, this effect would not have been sufficient to explain away the over 50% outperformance by the insider purchases.

Quite different results were reported by Pope *et al.* (1990), who estimated returns from following directors' trades as reported in the Stock Exchange's *Weekly Official Intelligence*. They studied the period April 1977 to December 1984; they looked at returns for six-month holding periods for three sub-periods as well as the overall period. Outsider purchases generated a positive abnormal return, but this was not statistically significant for two of the sub-periods and the whole period. For the entire period outsider sells produced abnormal returns of 6.7% before costs. This was statistically significant and the returns for two of the sub-periods were also significant.

Based on the conflicting results from two UK studies it is hard to know what to conclude. The King and Roell paper is not really a study of insider trading and the findings are implausible: sales outperform (albeit not at a statistically significant level) and buys outperform by more than 50%. Based on Pope *et al.* one might argue that investors should construct a portfolio by whatever strategy they wish but should guide their selling decisions by following insider sales. Note, however, how long ago the sample period was. Insider trades are now printed in regular newspaper features. On the other hand, the insider effect, before size and price-earnings ratio adjustment, has persisted for a long period in the US.

CONTRARY OPINION

Going against the crowd is often described as contrary thinking or contrarian investment strategy. Going against the crowd just for the sake of it does not seem sensible but when emotions run strongly and one can see how the crowd could be wrong, a contrarian bet may be warranted. Now there are two potential problems with this line of argument. First, is it really true that the market loses touch with reality and second, how does one know when this has happened?

There is little doubt that investors look at the fundamentals of earnings, dividends, future prospects and so forth. It also seems from the rating that groups of stocks and the market sometime sell on, that how these fundamentals are valued varies—this is discussed further in Chapter 23. The fundamentals are subjected to waves of optimism and pessimism and, occasionally, mania. The first of our two potential problems can probably be answered in favour of the contrarians. Knowing when the crowd has got out of touch with reality is, in a sense, the justification for low price-earnings ratio and some other value-based share strategies, and also is the basis of value-based tactical asset allocation. Some contrarians base their view on some measure of intrinsic value but more of them probably act on a view that price trends reverse, i.e., they believe prices display negative serial correlation—as discussed in Chapter 23. Most investors, however, when they talk of contrarian strategies have something much more folksy in mind than negative serial correlation. So, just for a change, let's get off the research treadmill and look at some more subjective indicators.

Anyone who has read the investment columns for a period will have seen articles with titles such as "how to tell if it's the top" or "how to spot a company going bust." These articles consist of lists of serious and jokey points and usually most investors would agree there is some sense in the lists. But the lists are soon buried in the waste-bin. Since there are some sound observations in the lists, we'll resurrect a few here.

Let's begin by looking at the characteristics of a market top. The following points are quoted from Band (1989, p. 34) describing a market top:

- A breathtaking parabolic rise in prices...
- A widespread rejection of old standards of value...[it is often said that the four most expensive words in investment are "this time it's different".]
- A proliferation of dubious investment schemes promising huge returns in an inordinately short time.
- Intense and—for a time—successful speculation by uninformed members of the public...
- Popular fascination with leveraged investments...
- Heavy selling by corporate "insiders" and other investors with a long-term orientation.
- Extremely high trading volume that enriches brokers and snarls ... back offices...

We can find similar lists for specific areas. The following quotes are from Band (pp. 198–200) who is discussing the top in the property market:

- Glowing news reports about the booming real estate market, perhaps tempered by worries about rising mortgage rates.
- A peak in housing starts … followed by several declines.
- Low vacancy rates in apartments and office buildings, sparking a construction spree. When you see construction crews working on every vacant lot in town, you should think about selling.
- A multi-year low for the local unemployment rate, followed by two or three seemingly innocuous upturns.
- Rude, hard-nosed brokers (i.e., estate agents).… The universal hard sell will tip you off that the market is about to go bust.

Now nobody would claim that all these signs apply to every peak and trough but many of them will apply to very over-heated markets. Putting a scientific hat on one would have to say this is a little vague. But maybe a little subjectivity is worth bearing if it helps avoid being the last buyer. Let's relate these ideas to the UK property market of 1987–89.

House prices had been rising rapidly and commercial rents, especially in the City of London, were rising rapidly. The ratio of house prices to income reached new heights. London's Docklands had a forest of construction cranes and new office buildings were going up in the City of London. There were no estimates of demand that suggested the on-stream supply of office buildings could find tenants. Two tax avoidance opportunities flourished: Enterprise Zone property schemes and Business Expansion Schemes, which focused on real assets, mainly property. At first the Enterprise Zone schemes sold mainly buildings that had tenants, but soon there was a move to unlet properties and sometimes properties not yet built, backed by rent "guarantees". Unfortunately tenants can go bust and so too can the property developers involved: many of the tenants and Enterprise Zone developers have. A very large number of Business Expansion Scheme property developers have gone into liquidation.

The Business Expansion Scheme companies often geared up for investors. The Enterprise Zone schemes encouraged the investors to gear up. For every £1000 invested, the Inland Revenue gave tax relief to higher rate tax-payers of approximately £350, so the net cost was £650. A yield of 6% on the property produced an income of £60. If the investor borrowed £650 at 9%, the interest would equal the income: so why not borrow the £650, and have an investment for no down-payment? When the building is eventually sold, investors can pay off their borrowings and pocket the profit. This was the story in the promotional literature. Of course, when interest rates soar and when the tenant or developer defaults in a falling property market, the investor has a negative income stream and an asset with declining value.

Anybody who owns a house in the UK knows what has happened to property prices since 1988. Office rents in Docklands (outside of Canary Wharf) have fallen from £20 in 1988 to probably £5 (after incentives) in 1993. Even at £5, 55% of Docklands' commercial property is unlet. This story is a contrarian's dream! Greed, gearing and the top of the market.

Sticking with major moves, many investors believe that one can get a good clue to big market moves by looking at the covers of the news magazines. If *Business Week*, *Time* or *Newsweek* run a cover story such as "The Death of the Dollar", then that is the time to buy the dollar, according to this contrarian approach. Regan (1981) gives some examples. On June 1, 1962, *Time's* cover story picture was of a large black bear mauling a red bull. The Dow had fallen 21% from December 1961 to May 1962. After the story the Dow fell another 6% to 536 and then began a four year climb to 1000 in January 1966. The market then fell to 767 by August. *Time's* August 19 cover was "Wall Street: The Nervous Market". Six weeks later the Dow bottomed at 744 and then rallied to 943.

Band reports (p. 39) that Montgomery reviewed *Time* covers back to 1924. He claimed that in four out of five financial cover stories, the outcome within a year was the opposite of what the editors foresaw. This suggests that while not a perfect contrary indicator, cover stories are worth bearing in mind when forming a market view. Some readers may feel uncomfortable with this type of indicator since it seems to be based on someone else's incompetence. But there is a more charitable and comforting explanation. As Regan (1981, p. 13) notes:

> "The cover story syndrome applies to all journalists—media as well as print. The only time the television camera crews visit the stock exchange or interview leading analysts is when volume and price fluctuations are unusually large. Because the articles and interviews are fostered by extremes in market psychology, they are often ill-timed."

Turning to companies, there have been many lists published of things that make a contrarian squirm. For example a list relating to companies likely to go bust has been provided by Costello (1992). He gives ten warning signs of candidates for bankruptcy (although his article actually covers more points). The following list combines some of his points and some others, and should be seen in terms of possibly overvalued stocks rather than bankruptcy candidates:

- Reliance on creative accounting. (Polly Peck, Parkfield, Coloroll, British and Commonwealth).
- Resignation of directors.
- Changing financial advisers.
- Chairman or managing directors with bow ties, gold bracelets, toupees and sun tans. All these are signs of vain management. (e.g., Roger Levitt, the disgraced financial salesman and Peter Goldie of British and Commonwealth, both wore bow ties).

- Moves to new headquarters or sumptuous headquarters buildings (e.g., Saatchi and Saatchi). Before they were common in the UK, this point was often expressed as "company with atrium".
- Bullies holding the position of chairman and chief executive (Maxwell and Ashcroft at Coloroll—Ashcroft asked an analyst who had criticized the company to leave a meeting).
- Changing the year end (Maxwell) or company name (Systems Reliability).
- Bear squeezes and profits warnings. Bear squeezes often do have some basis in reality (Lonrho) and one company profit downgrade is frequently followed by another.
- Substantial director share sales (Yellowhammer, Hodgson, Shandwick).
- The research file on a company is full up.

A tough minded approach would be to say these lists are worthless because they apply when they apply and don't when they don't and this makes good copy for journalists but is not the stuff of professional investment. A kindlier view is that most investors will recognize some truth in these lists and they simply remind one that many investment disasters could be avoided if investors showed a bit of common sense and scepticism. The market appears to get carried away by emotion from time to time. Shares that collapse wreak havoc on investment performance. There are thousands of shares in the world that one can invest in: it doesn't seem necessary to gamble in shares, sectors or markets that common sense or a bit of contrary thinking would make one cautious of.

CONCLUDING COMMENTS

A distinction is frequently drawn between fundamental and technical analysis. The distinction is sensible in theory but more problematic in practice. A number of approaches could be viewed as either technical or fundamental. Four topics were discussed in this chapter—chartist analysis, relative strength, insider trades and contrary opinion. There are a number of reasons to be suspicious of chartist analysis: little evidence has been put forward by chartists to support their work; the form of chartist statements is often not refutable, i.e., it is unscientific; it is not clear why, if chartist analysis has merits, it is not already largely discounted in prices. According to some studies, buying stocks or sectors with relative strength is worthwhile, but this is an area ripe for data-mining and some scepticism may be warranted.

Following the investment decisions of insiders may be more promising. Recent US studies, however, have not reported the large returns that earlier studies claimed, indeed, investment newsletters making recommendations based on following insiders have underperformed massively since the mid-1980s. Investors following insiders should be aware that in the US there is an overlap with small stock and low price-earnings ratio strategies. In the UK there is less research, and the studies give conflicting findings. Insider trades might provide an additional variable in a share selection model, but on the basis of the evidence there is no case for giving insider transactions a key role. More research would be helpful.

Contrary opinion inevitably appeals to anybody who believes that markets overreact. The problem, at least for the more popular versions of contrary opinion, is getting testable hypotheses to examine. Nonetheless, combining a bit of contrary thinking with some more rigorous techniques does have some attraction, at least to the writer.

19
Arbitrage Pricing Theory

In previous chapters we have seen that various attributes of shares seem to be related to returns. If the findings are true, either the efficient market theory is false or the capital asset pricing theory is. Most commentators have assumed that the problem lies with the capital asset pricing theory. It does seem as though there are a number of factors or attributes involved in the return generating process. The capital asset pricing model has only a single factor, the market. It seems that a multifactor theory might be helpful. Indeed, there are some multifactor theories which are extensions of the capital asset pricing theory. Some are formal and some rather ad hoc as was the one we outlined in Chapter 3. The most general multifactor theory is the arbitrage pricing theory, which is discussed in this chapter.

THE THEORY

Arbitrage pricing theory was propounded by Ross (1976), and has been described as a mixture of common sense and algebra. As Ross (1985, p. 73) explains:

> "The APT is based on the notion that the market prices risk by looking at central systematic risks such as inflation and the business cycle. That is about as close to common sense as economics gets."

Arbitrage pricing theory is an equilibrium theory, like the capital asset pricing model. Both seek to explain how investors will behave and, as a result, how asset prices will be set and the relationship between risk and return that will prevail in the market. Arbitrage pricing theory asserts that a few systematic factors affect the long-term average returns of assets. It accepts that daily price movements of individual assets are affected by many factors, but focuses on the major factors. These major factors affect all securities and are unlikely to be diversified away. Accordingly they will affect the expected return from a security. The unsystematic factors, or idiosyncratic influences, that affect individual stocks or some sectors can be diversified away, and it is unlikely that they will be priced.

Some of the events that affect stocks will be anticipated and some not. Anticipated events will be incorporated into asset prices. We know that industrial production, for example, fluctuates, and we can measure the sensitivity of asset returns to industrial production. What happens if industrial production is unexpectedly low? Companies with a high sensitivity to changes in industrial production will probably do poorly and this will affect the return earned on their stocks. The capital asset pricing model views risk in terms of an asset's sensitivity to market returns. The arbitrage pricing theory views risk in terms of sensitivity to unanticipated changes in major factors. We would expect assets that are highly sensitive to unanticipated changes in major economic factors to offer high returns.

Arbitrage pricing theory relates the expected return from an asset to the return from a risk-free asset and a series of systematic common factors. Thus:

$$\text{Expected return} = \text{risk-free return} + \beta_1(\text{factor 1}) + \beta_2(\text{factor 2}) + \ldots + \beta_n(\text{factor n})$$

The betas measure the sensitivity of the asset to each systematic factor. Arbitrage pricing theory does not detail the systematic factors, nor the signs or sizes of the betas. Different stocks and portfolios will have different exposures to these factors. How can we be sure that returns and risks really will be related? The theory makes no assumptions about investors making mean-variance decisions. The theory does, however, assume arbitrage is possible and this will ensure a linear relationship between factor risks and rewards. The theory simply assumes that two stocks with the same sensitivity to economic factors will offer the same return. If this were not the case, an investor could earn a risk-free profit. Let's consider this in more detail.

We will assume four assets and also that there are only two factors, and that the expected returns and factor sensitivities are as shown in Table 42.

Table 42   Characteristics of Four Stocks: Disequilibrium

Stock	Expected Return %	Production Sensitivity	Inflation Sensitivity
1	13	0.2	2.0
2	27	3.0	0.2
3	16	1.0	1.0
4	20	2.0	2.0

Source: Bower *et al.* (1984, p. 33). Reproduced by permission of Stern Stewart Management Services, Inc.

A risk-free arbitrage return can be earned if it is possible to buy and sell the four stocks in a combination that will eliminate exposure to the two factors and yet give a positive return. In Table 43, we see that an arbitrage profit is available if stocks 1 and 2 are purchased and 3 and 4 are sold short. The purchases and sales must be made in the proportions shown (these proportions are derived via some algebraic manipulation that we can skip here). If this is done, we can see in the portfolio row that there is no net investment, no net exposure to either factor and an expected return of 2.129%. The theory assumes that arbitrage activities like this will drive stock prices to levels that eliminate such riskless returns. It follows that all stocks will be priced to produce a return that reflects their exposure to systematic factors.

Table 43 Arbitrage Portfolio

Stock	Investment	Expected Return %	Production Sensitivity	Inflation Sensitivity
1	+1.000	+13.000	+0.200	+2.000
2	+0.643	+17.361	+1.929	+0.129
3	−1.157	−18.512	−1.157	−1.157
4	−0.486	−9.720	−0.972	−0.972
Portfolio	0	2.129	0	0

Source: Bower *et al.* (1984, p. 34). Reproduced by permission of Stern Stewart Management Services, Inc.

MAKING THE THEORY OPERATIONAL

Since the theory does not specify the systematic factors that are priced, there remains the task of identifying them. There have been two approaches. One is purely empirical, the other uses explicitly defined factors. We can call these "unspecified factor tests" and "specified factor tests" respectively.

Unspecified factor tests use a group of statistical techniques known as factor analysis. These techniques have been used a lot in psychology and market research and have been used relatively infrequently in economics and finance. There are many versions of factor analysis and all are complex and beyond the scope of this book. The basic procedure is to take many observations of returns for many securities and then find groups of stocks whose returns are highly correlated with each other but not with stocks outside the group. This procedure should identify a few underlying factors that explain returns. (A simple introduction is Kritzman, 1993.) Once a set of factors has been obtained, a cross-sectional regression is performed for each stock and returns are related to the factors. Those factors with statistically significant coefficients are "priced", i.e., affect returns. Roll and Ross (1980) studied the period July 3, 1962 to December 1972. Because the mathematics of factor analysis is too complex to handle more than a small number of stocks at a time, they split their sample into 42 sub-samples of 30 stocks each. The number of factors varied with each sub-sample but they concluded that there were at least three but no more than four common factors affecting returns.

There are many problems with the above approach. One is that the number of factors discovered may be dependent on the sample size. That would not really be surprising—presumably there are industry- and firm-specific factors and, as the sample size increases, more of these will be included. But that is not the same as saying these factors are priced. The number of factors that actually affect returns may not be sample size dependent. This topic is the subject of a lively debate.

Another problem with the factor analytical approach is that the factors are simply statistical groupings—they are not identified as real economic variables, although the pattern of correlations may suggest which economic variables the factors represent. A way of avoiding this problem is to use the second approach to identifying factors and pre-specify economic factors that are likely to be relevant and see if they are rewarded.

How might one pre-specify likely common factors? One approach might be to go on a data-mining trip looking at every conceivable factor. A preferable approach would be to deduce some factors from economic and financial theory. Taking this tack, an obvious starting point is the dividend discount model. Chen *et al.* (1986) specified a number of variables that would appear relevant on this basis, i.e., factors that could affect the discount rate or expected cash flows. For the period 1958–84 they found, for the US, that the following variables were priced: changes in industrial production, changes in the risk premium (the difference between long-term government bond yields and corporate bonds rated Baa and under), changes in the term structure (i.e., the difference between long-term and short-term government bond yields) and measures of unanticipated inflation and changes in expected inflation. Chen *et al.* specifically tested for whether the market portfolio was priced: it wasn't.

TESTING THE THEORY

A major problem with arbitrage pricing theory is that it has few rejectable hypotheses. The theory does not specify factors, neither the number nor their identity. There are two ways of testing the theory. First, one can estimate the return relationship and consider the appropriateness of the factors, but this does not seem very scientific. Alternatively, one can see if arbitrage pricing theory can account for the anomalies that cannot be explained by the capital asset pricing model. A short summing up of the US results of such tests is that arbitrage pricing theory shows promise, but needs more work. In the UK, the position is a little less promising.

Diacogiannis (1986), for the period late-1956 to 1981, found that the number of factors he identified varied as the size of the security group examined changed, and that for the same groups, examined at different periods, the number of factors changed. He felt that arbitrage pricing theory could not be used for making predictions. Abeysekera and Mahajan (1987) found that over the period 1971–82 the risk premia for the factors they identified were not significantly different from zero. Beenstock and Chan (1986 and 1988) published studies measuring UK common factors by both the unspecified and pre-specified approaches. In their factor analysis they found 20 factors. In their pre-specified analysis they used only 11 variables and found that the data (October 1977–December 1983) suggested a four factor model. The risk factors were an interest rate, fuel and materials costs, the money supply and inflation. Poon and Taylor (1991) attempted to test the applicability of the Chen *et al.* (1986) study to the UK. For the period 1965–84, Poon and Taylor concluded that the macroeconomic factors which Chen *et al.* claim affect returns in the US, did not affect UK returns in the same way.

At the end of 1992, stockbroker Hoare Govett had an arbitrage pricing model in development. It used 11 factors: debenture yield, debt/equity yield ratio, oil prices, the retail price index, the dollar/sterling rate, the term structure, the current account balance, retail sales, bank lending, the deutschmark/sterling rate and a measure of market sentiment. Because it is surprises in these variables that should affect returns, the factors used were transformations of the everyday variables.

Let's step back and think about all of this. There is no doubt that unexpected fluctuations in the economy, inflation and such like are the things that most investors would conceive as being fundamental risks and would expect to affect security returns. And there is no reason why different analysts should find exactly the same factors. We can, for example, relate weight to height (tall people weigh more than short) or sex (men weigh more than women). Height and sex are different factors, but both models appear to be valid descriptions. Nonetheless, one can still be a little disconcerted by claims that there are none, four, eleven or twenty factors in the UK market. At the very least this suggests that practical applications of arbitrage pricing theory should be used with caution. Let's briefly look at how the theory could be used.

APPLYING THE THEORY

There are a number of ways of applying the theory. One is to calculate the estimated return for a stock. In the same way as an expected return for a stock can be calculated based on a security market line and the stock's beta, a return for a stock can be calculated based on its exposure to various factors. It's harder to draw a diagram because several factors are involved. But the basic idea is the same. If the stock appears to offer more than the theory says it should, it is a buy, and if less, it is a sell.

It is important to note that the capital asset pricing model and the arbitrage pricing model can produce quite different expected returns. An example of this is shown in Table 44, based on estimates derived from an 815 US stock sample for the period 1970–79 which was then used to forecast returns for a 17 stock hold-out sample.

Arbitrage pricing theory is normally used with the emphasis on factor weightings rather than individual stock selection. There are two tactical approaches and

Table 44 CAPM and APT Estimates of Expected Return

Company	CAPM	APT
American Broadcasting Company	21.5%	14.3%
American Hospital Supply	22.9	12.8
Baxter Travenol Laboratories	21.0	11.6
CBS	18.2	13.9
Chris Craft Industries	22.2	17.1
Cook International	16.7	20.2
Ipco Corporation	29.3	32.7
Matrix Corporation	24.7	25.3
Metromedia	22.9	19.2
Napco Industries	22.6	16.4
Parker Pen	21.7	22.6
Rollins	24.3	16.2
SBS Technologies	21.7	22.3
Storer Broadcasting	20.4	15.4
Taft Broadcasting	25.2	21.1
Teleprompter	36.0	28.4
Western Union	19.1	10.8
Average	23.0	18.8
Standard Deviation	4.43	6.05

Source: Bower (1984, p. 38). Reproduced by permission of Stern Stewart Management Services, Inc.

one strategic that might be used. One would be to take an active tactical bet. If investors thought they could forecast a surprise in a particular factor, for example better than expected industrial production, they could construct a portfolio that had high exposure to that one factor and a market exposure to the other factors. In this use of the model the investors are not buying mispriced stocks. The stocks should be properly priced for their exposure to a particular risk. What the investors are doing is attempting to be rewarded for their ability to forecast which risks are worth bearing.

A second tactical factor approach is based on the fact that the market index may not be an efficient portfolio with regard to factor risks and returns. The strategy would be to calculate the return per unit of risk for each factor and construct a portfolio that is loaded up relative to the index on higher return factors. It is debatable that this approach can be said to be genuinely producing superior performance. All that is happening is that bigger risks are being borne for bigger returns. The arbitrage pricing theory is an equilibrium theory—this means that investors get paid returns commensurate with the risks they bear—there are no free lunches. This strategy seems to be based on performance measurement deficiencies.

The strategic way of using factor bets would be to ask whether the institution owning the portfolio is itself affected by any of the factor risks. If it is, it could be worth tilting the portfolio exposure to those factors to have an appropriate offsetting effect. For example, a pension fund may require its income to rise when inflation is high. It should hold a portfolio that has a high sensitivity to inflation. It may or may not earn more than the market but, if inflation soars, it will achieve its strategic objective.

CONCLUDING COMMENTS

The capital asset pricing theory is a single factor theory. The arbitrage pricing theory assumes that a number of factors determine returns. Despite the academic origins and claims that arbitrage pricing theory is an equilibrium theory, unlike the pragmatic factor approaches that might result from the evidence described in previous chapters (e.g., load up on stocks with earnings surprises, small size, etc.), it is difficult to see arbitrage pricing theory as very different in practice. The major difference is that the factors tend to be economic ones rather than the company or market valuation factors we have discussed in earlier chapters. Arbitrage pricing theory involves a large computational burden. This is not an approach that can really be run as another model on-the-side, unless a third-party supplier's product is adopted. Commercial use of the theory has been limited, although Roll and Ross appear to have been successful as money managers (Clark, 1991), both in the US and Japan. How successful arbitrage pricing theory will be in the UK remains to be seen.

20
Sector Strategy

Investment organizations vary in the amount of time they devote to sector strategy and in their approaches. Some take the pragmatic view that it is too difficult to add value at the sector level and simply set their sector weightings equal to those of an appropriate index or take very modest sector bets. Other managers take a more aggressive stance.

Some managers make stock and sector decisions at the same time—for example a dividend discount model might show that all bank shares offer exceptional value and this will automatically lead to an overweight position in the bank sector. This would be a bottom-up approach to sector strategy. Other managers form sector views based on macroeconomic views: a top-down approach. This may be criticized on the grounds that the macroeconomic insights should be already reflected in earnings forecasts. Looking at the macroeconomy as a separate input is double counting the same factors. This would be true if analysts' forecasts were always up-to-date or were based on the same macroeconomic view as the investment manager's, but this may not be the case. In the UK, the market has been periodically convulsed by big interest rate or currency moves and managers must act before analysts revise and circulate their individual stock earnings estimates and views. A broad view of sector strategy related to the macroeconomy may be necessary. Again, fund managers may rely on external analysts for company forecasts and may take the view that their forecasts for the economy may differ from analysts' and they must therefore adjust analysts' forecasts in some broad-brush way and derive a sector strategy based on their top-down view.

In this chapter we will comment briefly on these various approaches and we begin with some broad aspects of sector strategy.

WHAT IS A SECTOR?

Sectors are groups of stocks that have some features in common in terms of the industry in which they operate. In both the US and the UK the major indexes used for portfolio evaluation consist of a number of sectors, but the sectors are aggregated in different ways. In the UK, investment managers will typically look at the FT-A All-Share Index sectors aggregated in terms of the type of industry involved—e.g., industrial, consumer and financial. US investment managers are more likely to aggregate sectors in a way that reflects their response to the economy and the business cycle—e.g., cyclical, growth and stable. Table 45 shows the FT-A All-Share Index by sector with the typical aggregation that UK investment managers tend to think in terms of, and the S&P 500 by sector and the sort of aggregation that might be used by a US investment manager.

Table 45   Sector Classifications

UK Sectors Classified by FT-A All-Share Index	US Sectors Classified by Type*
Capital Goods	*Growth*
Building Materials	Hospital Management
Contracting, Construction	Pollution Control
Electricals	Cosmetics
Electronics	Drugs
Engineering-Aerospace	Hospital Supplies
Engineering-General	Electronics
Metals and Metal Forming	Entertainment
Motors	Hotels and Restaurants
Other Industrials	Computers
Consumer Group	Oil Service
Brewers and Distillers	Newspapers and Broadcasters
Food Manufacturing	Speciality Chemicals
Food Retailing	Growth Retailers
Health and Household	*Stable*
Hotels and Leisure	Food Processors
Media	Beverage
Packaging, Paper and Printing	Tobacco
Stores	Household Products
Textiles	Retailers
Other Groups	Utilities
Business Services	Telephones
Chemicals	Banks
Conglomerates	Insurance
Transport	Finance
Electricity	*Cyclical*
Telephone Networks	Aluminum
Water	Copper
Miscellaneous	Miscellaneous Metals
Industrial Group	Autos
Oil and Gas	Auto Parts and Trucks
500 Share Index	Building Materials
Financial Group	Chemicals
Banks	Containers

Table 45   Sector Classifications   (*continued*)

UK Sectors Classified by FT-A All-Share Index	US Sectors Classified by Type*
Insurance (Life)	Textiles
Insurance (Composite)	Tires
Insurance Brokers	Electrical Equipment
Merchant Banks	Machinery
Property	Forest Products and Paper
Other Financial	Steel
Investment Trusts	Railroads
All-Share Index	*Energy*
	Coal
	Domestic Oil
	International Oil
	Crude-oil Producers

*Adapted from Farrell, (1983)

US fund managers in practice use a few more categories than shown in Table 45 but this classification is shown because it was used in an interesting study by Farrell (1974 and 1983, chapter 8: for a related study see Arnott, 1980). Farrell (1983, p. 206) explained his sector groupings as follows:

Growth:

> "Earnings of these companies are expected to show a faster rate of secular expansion than the average company"

Cyclical:

> "These companies have an above-average exposure to the economic cycle. Earnings would be expected to be down more than the average in a recession and up more than the average during the expansion phase of the business cycle."

Stable:

> "These companies have a below-average exposure to the economic cycle.... Earnings of these companies are the most adversely impacted by inflation but fare relatively the best during periods of decelerating inflation, or disinflation."

Energy:

> "The earnings of these companies are affected by the economic cycle but, most importantly, by trends in the relative price of energy."

Farrell wondered whether the classification shown above really consisted of homogeneous stock groups. Since stocks tend to move with the market as a whole, Farrell stripped out this market effect and then examined monthly returns for 100 stocks over the period 1961–69. If the aggregate sectors had any meaning, stock returns should be highly correlated within sectors, but not between sectors. That is what he found. This suggests that the approach to sector aggregation sometimes used in the US and which puts disparate industries into the same broad group, is worthwhile, and UK managers might find it profitable to think about similar classifications. Further, Farrell's findings suggest that there may be scope to add value by an active sector strategy, although this is not to say managers will realize the potential.

FOR EVERY SECTOR THERE IS A SEASON

Many managers think in terms of a stylized economic cycle with different sectors performing at different stages of the cycle. Figure 24 shows one version of when different US sectors show their best relative performance. Figures like this have to come with a wealth warning; no two cycles are exactly the same and the research basis of such exhibits is unclear.

It is the writer's impression that US managers are more inclined to think in terms of an economic cycle than UK managers. Perhaps because of the openness of the UK economy and more dramatic interest rate moves, UK managers seem to be at least as much interested in questions such as which sectors gain from a rise/fall in sterling and which sectors are interest rate sensitive. These questions seem to be approached in a manner that divorces them from the economic cycle, presumably a consequence of the crisis nature of much UK economic policy.

Let us take as an example interest rates. Wadhwani (1991a) examined the

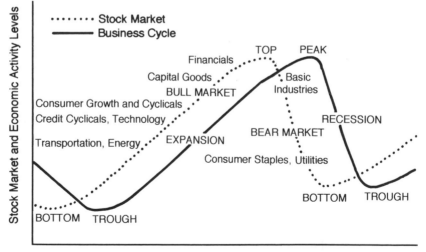

Figure 24 Business Cycle and Relative Sector Performance Source: Markese (1986, p. 31)

interest sensitivity of stocks based on a multiple regression equation for the period 1970–91. He found that about a quarter of the variation in interest sensitivity could be explained by the sector a stock belonged to. The most interest rate sensitive sectors were, most responsive first, telephone networks (–), merchant banks (–), oil and gas (+), property (–), composite insurance (–), brewers and distillers (–) and chemicals (+). The stock market as a whole benefits from lower interest rates: responsiveness is measured here as the additional effect on a sector over and above the market impact. The signs behind each sector show the response relative to a rise in interest rates, i.e., telephone networks perform relatively poorly and oil and gas relatively well.

These findings are interesting, but how useful are they? First, can we be confident that the historical relationship will apply in the future? Sectors change their economic structure over time, and the composition of the stock market continually evolves. Second, the amount of variation explained is low, although not to be ignored, and high in comparison to many relationships in investment research. Third, to use the historical relationship, we must make interest rate forecasts. These may be just as hard to make as sector forecasts. Alternatively, we may wait for an interest change to take place, and then react quickly. However, big changes in interest rates or sterling often lead to a sharp movement in markets the day they happen and the bulk of any relationship may be quickly discounted. This catalogue of problems leads many managers to place more reliance on sector valuations than macroeconomic themes as a way of deciding sector weightings.

SECTOR VALUATIONS

Sector valuations can be approached in several ways. One would be to look solely at company valuations and then derive sector weights as a result of stock decisions. Thus, if a manager selects shares with low price-earnings ratios, then sectors that possess many such shares will be overweighted automatically. A variation on this would be to select sectors on the basis of the attribute used for selecting shares—thus a low price-earnings manager might select sectors on the basis of the sector price-earnings ratio. While these two approaches would normally lead to similar results, they might not. A sector might have a two-tier rating—many high and low price-earnings ratio stocks. The sector price-earnings ratio rating might be average, although many low price-earnings ratio stocks could be selected.

A different approach is to buy sectors that are cheap in relation to their own past history on some valuation measure. For example, a sector may have sold at a price-earnings ratio premium to the market over the past 20 years of, say, 20%, with a range of –5% (i.e., a discount) to 45%. If the sector currently stands at a premium of say, 10%, the sector might be deemed to be cheap. Of course, low price-earnings stock pickers would not follow such a strategy, although they might weight sectors selling at a discount to the market on this basis.

Jones (1989) looked at the two approaches of buying sectors that are absolutely cheap and those that are cheap relative to their own history. He used US data for the period 1969–87 and he measured cheapness in terms of 12 measures (e.g., dividend discount model, earnings yield, small capitalization, etc.) and a multifactor model combining these measures. Unfortunately, the two approaches appeared to be unreliable guides to sector strategy.

Wadhwani (1992) looked at sector selection strategies for the UK based on buying: (a) sectors trading at a price-earnings ratio discount to their historical average; and (b) sectors with a dividend yield above their historical average. His dividend strategy results will be outlined here. His buy signal was that the relative dividend yield should exceed its average by more than one-half its standard deviation. Over the period 1974–91 this strategy led to a 4.4% per annum outperformance by the purchased sectors over the residual sectors. The portfolio was rebalanced quarterly. It was not stated how diversified the portfolio was, nor the returns after costs.

Of course, many stocks sell on high historical dividend yields when the market anticipates a dividend cut. Wadhwani tested an alternative strategy of holding high yield sectors when GNP growth was not expected to be negative and to hold the other sectors when it was. Outperformance increased to 5.5% per annum. This outperformance increased further if high-yielding sectors could only be purchased if they also had earnings growth above average. Again one wonders how diversified such a portfolio was.

Wadhwani claimed that both low price-earnings ratio and high dividend yield relative to history are useful signals. Generally he found the dividend signal to be the more powerful, but for some sectors the price-earnings relative was more important, for example, construction, electricals, electronics, food retailing, health and household and insurance brokers.

CONCLUDING COMMENTS

We have reviewed evidence relating to how an investor might set sector strategy. We have discussed the way sectors might be aggregated into economically meaningful categories. We reviewed some material on approaching sector strategy in terms of economic themes, and on a valuation basis. If investors think they have information nobody else has (e.g., information that sterling will be devalued) or there are valuation errors (e.g., sectors with a high yield relative to their own history) they may wish to make, what we called in Chapter 4, an information or a valuation bet respectively. You may not have found the evidence discussed in this chapter compelling. If you didn't, you will understand why some investors set their sector weights equal to those of an index.

There is a general point to be made here. Many investors are embarrassed to admit they do not know how to add value on some issue. This is foolish. Warren Buffett argues that independent investors have a great advantage: they can stand at the baseball plate and wait forever until they get the perfect pitch (see Train, 1981, p. 15). Investment is one of the few games where you get to choose exactly how and when you will play. If you can pick stocks, do so, and if you can't, then index. And ditto for sectors. If you can pick markets, do so, and if you can't, then just adhere to your strategic asset weights. In investment, knowing what you don't know is valuable.

— 21 —
Constructing A Share Portfolio

Having discussed a number of techniques for valuing stocks and various findings which relate stock attributes to returns, we now turn to forming a portfolio of stocks. We could put together a portfolio that treated all UK stocks, for example, as one group. Alternatively we could divide the UK market into sub-groups and form portfolios from each sub-group and then make a decision as to how to weight the sub-groups. This latter approach is the one usually adopted in practice, and the sub-groups are typically sectors of the market (which are loosely based on industries) or groupings of sectors of the market—for example capital goods or cyclical sectors. The sector weights may be the same as those of an appropriate index or over- or underweighted relative to the index. Constructing a portfolio in this way ensures diversification across industries. It is also usual to specify some additional constraints such as the number of stocks to be purchased (often in the range 50–90 for the UK market, but possibly many more for a small capitalization stock portfolio where there may be marketability problems). The maximum size of holding is often specified (typically 5–7½% of the fund) and sometimes a minimum size too (perhaps ½%).

Given these constraints, there are a number of ways of forming a portfolio. One way would be to calculate an efficient frontier subject to various constraints of the sort just outlined, and then select the appropriate efficient portfolio given the investor's risk level. As we discussed in Chapters 2 and 3, this could be done on the basis of a Markowitz optimization calculation or, more likely, a Sharpe optimization. However, in practice, these methods are not widely used for constructing a portfolio of shares, although they are used by some investors, and could easily be used for small markets with few stocks, such as Botswana, Ireland or New Zealand. Nonetheless, optimization is more often used for selecting optimal portfolios of different asset classes and most commercial optimization software ("Optimizers") is mainly concerned with asset allocation. Accordingly, we shall not discuss Markowitz and Sharpe optimization here, but will discuss it in the context of tactical asset allocation in Chapter 30.

The traditional methods of portfolio construction are based on either buying the "best" shares in each sector on a single share valuation method—for example, those with the highest returns generated by a dividend discount model—or based on a combination of selection methods. These can be combined intuitively, by a composite method or by multiple cut-offs. Before we discuss these methods, we should make some general points.

THE KEY QUESTIONS OF RELIABILITY AND STABILITY

Previous chapters have suggested a number of ways of appraising shares that might lead to high returns. There are at least three problems with basing a share selection strategy on one of the techniques or empirical findings that have been discussed:

- the studies cited may be wrong because of inappropriate statistical methods or inadequate allowance for cost and risk;
- findings that were true when they were made may now be fully discounted;
- the predictive relationship may work only intermittently.

Some investors are sceptical as to whether all the studies supporting various strategies are correct. Professor Richard Roll is a well known academic and co-proprietor of a consulting firm selling investment strategies based on arbitrage pricing theory. But, judging by the following comments, he is also an unsuccessful anomaly-based investor:

"I have personally tried to invest money, my clients' money and my own, in every single anomaly and predictive device that academics have dreamed up .... And I have yet to make a nickel on any of these supposed market inefficiencies." (Roll, 1992, p. 30)

For example:

"I read all this literature on the January effect, even wrote a paper on it, and then I tried to make money from it. On December 27th, 1988, I bought the 25 stocks that went down the most in the preceding 18 months and I held those stocks for the next six months.[This strategy is based on over-reaction, see, e.g., De Bondt and Thaler, 1985.] In the first six months of the next year, 14 of the 25 stocks went bankrupt. But the rest of them made money. My suspicion, of course, is that academic studies may have somehow failed to account for those companies that went bankrupt or were delisted for other reasons." (p. 34)

There are other grounds for suspicion of many studies. Have the proper costs been built into the study, especially the true bid-ask spread? Could a transaction actually be made or is the market illiquid? And so on. Even if a study is correct, it may suggest a strategy that is not very practical. Sometimes studies note effects that are statistically but not economically significant—e.g., some of the calendar effects. Sometimes the strategy in many years will generate far too few stocks—e.g., the net current asset value strategy—either to form a portfolio, or to form a portfolio diversified by sectors in the manner an institutional investor might require.

Some of the studies may not have properly accounted for risk. This means that both findings that are false will have been accepted as true and true relationships will have been rejected as false. Investors should assess the nature of the risk associated with a particular strategy and decide whether the risk is relevant to them.

Even if a strategy is valid when discovered, it may be rapidly discounted. It is hard to say how significant this effect is. It is claimed that around 30% of US fund managers follow a low price-earnings ratio strategy. Does that mean that the strategy is fully discounted in market prices or does the fact that 70% of managers do not follow this strategy imply that there is still a rich seam of value to be mined? Consider neglected stocks. Since analysts do not follow all stocks, some stocks will always be neglected. So can a neglected stock strategy ever be discounted? Well, investors could buy a basket of such stocks and, at least in the US, they are easy enough to find: Nelson Publications produces a volume called *Neglected Stock Opportunities*. Another example: earnings revisions are readily available in the US via Nelson, IBES or Zacks. In the UK, IBES and other services are available. Investors devising share selection strategies must make allowance for the possibility that the approach will use factors that have become fully discounted.

Another problem that share selection strategies suffer from is that they are seldom strategies for all seasons. We have seen that strategies such as buying small stocks or high-yield stocks can suffer lean periods. Moreover there is more than one concept of value. To some, value may be a high return from a dividend discount model, but charities may be more concerned with immediate high yield. Lord Hanson may focus on break-up value and leveraged buy-out investors will focus on free cash flow to service debt. Measures of value vary with sector: net asset value is less important for a people business, and price-earnings ratios are not the usual measure for a life insurance or property company. It should be clear that no one method of share selection is likely to work across all sectors and at all stages of market cycles. Arnott and Copeland (1985, p. 26) have put the matter well:

> "All systematic investment strategies are vulnerable to the dynamics of the marketplace. The market may reward a value-orientated strategy one year, a growth strategy the next .... The low-P/E strategy, for example, has a demonstrated and significant long-term track record. Yet some practitioners failed to survive the long dry spell from 1969 through mid-1973. In our industry, consistency is as important as performance."

It may be that it is possible to forecast which model will work at which time. Arnott and Copeland (1985) related a number of share selection models to economic conditions and concluded that those which focused on past growth, profitability or low price-earnings ratio were rewarded in a strong economy. Jacobs and Levy (1988b) found that dividend discount models work best in up-markets. With both studies it is unclear whether the results are general or just apply to the period examined. Moreover, even if the relationships are general, to be useful they require that the investor has an ability to forecast the economy. Back in 1985, Citicorp was reported to be experimenting with share selection models which reflected macro views (see Gropper, 1985). It was reported as having three sets of screens which identified aggressive stocks, defensive stocks and stocks with good earnings momentum. The aggregate ranking used varying screen weights, depending on their expected relative performance which was forecast on the basis of economic and market variables. The rationale was that different strategies worked at different times and varying styles should outperform a constant style.

Jones (1990) looked at whether investors should use different factors or combinations of factors in different sectors. He found evidence that different factor models could be constructed for different sectors but argued that the added benefits from using specific models were less than from the original decision to use a factor model.

To make clear some of the difficulties that have to be faced in a share selection model, and to provide a useful reminder of some of the variables that we have looked at in earlier chapters, we shall introduce some findings by Jacobs and Levy (1988a).

Most of the studies that have been examined in previous chapters look at returns in relation to one, or at most a few factors at a time. We have seen that some relationships become muted or disappear if other factors are introduced. Jacobs and Levy tried to explain returns to specific factors when a very large number of other factors were simultaneously having an effect. They carried out their analysis on a universe of 1500 of the largest US capitalization stocks on data from January 1978 through to December 1986. They estimated monthly regression equations and averaged the results. They carried out univariate (one variable or factor) and multivariate (several variables) regressions. That is to say they looked, for example, first at the relationship of low price-earnings ratios with abnormal returns and then second at the relationship of low price-earnings ratios with abnormal returns but specifically controlling for small size, neglect, low price-to-book and so forth. These variables were held at their average market value. Jacobs and Levy explain that their multivariate regressions measure all effects jointly, thereby "purifying" each effect so that it is independent of other effects whereas univariate regressions "naively" measure only one anomaly at a time, with no effort to control for other related effects. Table 46 shows their pure and naive effects for various anomalies. Most of the anomalies listed will be clear enough given the discussion in earlier chapters. Comments on a few are, however, necessary.

Although the capital asset pricing theory argues that only systematic risk should be rewarded, some studies have found that unsystematic risk is also rewarded, so Jacobs and Levy included unsystematic risk—or sigma—in their study. Some authors have claimed that investors may value stocks with returns which exhibit positive skewness (i.e., a higher probability of large gains than large losses). The evidence is mixed, but coskewness—a measure of this—was included. Earnings uncertainty, or unusual disagreement amongst analysts with regard to future profits for a company, was included because of the argument that such stocks produce higher returns, either as a reward for information deficiency or as a proxy for systematic risk.

Table 46   Monthly Average Returns to Anomalies 1978–86

Anomaly	Naive anomaly: monthly average return (%)	Pure anomaly: monthly average return (%)
Low PER	0.59**	0.46**
Small size	0.15*	0.12**
Yield	−0.01	0.03
Zero yield	0.00	0.15
Neglect	0.14*	0.10*
Low price	−0.01	0.01
Book/price	0.17	0.09
Sales/price	0.17	0.17**
Cash/price	0.36**	0.04
Sigma	0.16	0.07
Beta	−0.01	0.04
Coskewness	0.09	0.04
Earnings uncertainty	−0.33*	−0.05
Trend in estimates (−1)[†]	0.48**	0.51**
Trend in estimates (−2)[†]	0.40**	0.28**
Trend in estimates (−3)[†]	0.29**	0.19**
Earnings surprise (−1)[†]	0.44*	0.48**
Earnings surprise (−2)[†]	0.47*	0.18
Earnings surprise (−3)[†]	−0.03	−0.21
Earnings torpedo	−0.00	−0.10*
Relative strength	0.30	0.34**
Residual reversal (−1)[†]	−0.54**	−1.08**
Residual reversal (−2)[†]	−0.13	−0.37**
Short-term tax	−0.08	−0.04
Long-term tax	−0.29	−0.00

**Significant at the 1% level
*Significant at the 10% level
[†]Numbers in brackets refer to months of lagged response.
Source: Jacobs and Levy (1988, p. 25). Reproduced by permission

The earnings torpedo effect is the belief that stocks expected to have high future earnings growth are more susceptible to negative surprises (i.e., torpedoes). Residual reversal is more complex. Based on the regression equations, we can forecast a stock's return. Sometimes it will earn more than forecast and sometimes less; there is an unexplained residual. If a stock returns too much in one month, residual reversal implies that it will subsequently return less. Finally, Jacobs and Levy try to capture the January effect by using separate proprietary measures of potential long-term and short-term tax loss selling pressure for each stock. The January effect was the only seasonal effect included in the study because the use of monthly data meant that time-of-day, day-of-the-week and week-of-the-month effects had to be excluded.

If the value shown in Table 46 for any factor were zero, this would mean that there was no relationship between the factor and returns. It is possible for factors to appear to affect returns when they do not, simply because of sampling error. It is therefore important to ask what are the chances of observing a relationship when none really exists. Some returns in Table 46 are labelled as significant at the 1% level and some at the 10% level. This means that there is only a probability of one in a 100, or one in 10 respectively, that the observed relationship occurred by chance alone.

It is worth recalling the difference between statistical and practical investment significance. A monthly average abnormal return of 0.1% may be statistically significant but at just over 1% a year it is of less investment significance. This should be borne in mind when considering Table 46. Also, the transactions costs will differ between strategies. For example, small size is a relatively stable characteristic and would not require much trading, but residual reversal would require a lot of trading and the returns after costs would be much smaller than the regression estimate might appear to suggest.

The most statistically significant relationships in pure form are low price-earnings ratio, small size, low price-to-sales ratio, favourable trend in estimates, earnings surprise (lagged one month), relative strength and residual reversal. Neglect and the torpedo effect were significant at the 10% level. Cash flow was significant in naive form but not in pure form: it appeared to act as a surrogate for low price-earnings ratio in the univariate regression.

Now the important point to make here is that many of the variables we found to be relevant in earlier chapters do not appear relevant in this study (i.e., yield, zero yield, low price, book/price). Is this study wrong?—one might suspect it is handling too many variables that have some overlap for the data to be able to sort out true effects. Were the other studies wrong? Are the variables unstable? These problems should make investors cautious about adopting a single variable selection strategy or putting too much weight on the findings of a single study.

COMBINING SEVERAL SHARE SELECTION APPROACHES

If all models fail at the same time—as they seemed to in the US in the second-half of the 1980s—there is little one can do, but if they simply have the occasional dry spell it will make sense to use more than a single selection approach. Providing there is less than perfect correlation between the forecasts, multiple predictive approaches will improve forecasting power. It would be reasonable, following the catalogue of concerns that has been presented, to wonder whether it is worth bringing together several distinctly imperfect selection approaches. The answer is that providing selection methods are used efficiently, even quite modest amounts of forecasting ability can be profitable.

Although all investment organizations should seek approaches with a high correlation with returns and low correlation with each other, it is unlikely that this will mean every investor uses the same factors. Investors with a large research staff and also high forecasting accuracy will inevitably have a different selection technique from those that do not. Some investors will have the capability or desire to build a dividend discount model—others will not. Some investors, because they have large amounts of funds under management, will not be able to invest very easily in small stocks. Others will have a client base that will only be happy in blue chips and so neglected stocks will be ruled out. Some fund management companies may have a staff that is unwilling to accept certain approaches. If the team has a good record, it would be a risky business decision to impose changes on the team. In short, the share selection model will be a function of perceived statistical relationships, client attitudes and staff interests.

If an approach's share picks are ranked and then related to subsequent returns, a correlation or information coefficient of only 0.15 will be sufficient to outperform an index fund—if the information is used efficiently. If several share selection techniques are combined, even lower individual correlations can be useful. For example, two techniques, each uncorrelated, and each with an individual correlation to returns of 0.10 will, when combined, have a correlation with returns of 0.14. Combining more and more approaches runs into diminishing returns in terms of increased selection ability. About four approaches will usually suffice.

How can different share selection approaches be brought together? There are two main ways—some form of weighted composite or some form of multiple cut-off. The latter approach is usually referred to in the investment literature as screening. In broad terms the composite weighting approach gives a stock points for the possession of desirable attributes; the more of an attribute possessed, the greater the number of points. The more points a stock scores, the more attractive it is. The screening approach is all or nothing: it's more like a hurdle race—a stock has to clear the hurdle or it's out. If low price-earnings ratios are deemed to be desirable, all stocks with multiples above, say, 80% of the market's multiple will be eliminated from further consideration. The two methods will select some of the same shares but there will be differences. The composite method allows a poor score on one attribute to be offset by good scores on other attributes. The screening approach does not—in the case just mentioned, if a stock has a high price-earnings ratio, it will not be selected, irrespective of the fact that it may score highly on every other attribute. Because the screening approach imposes a series of hurdles, each one of which will eliminate stocks, setting many hurdles, or high hurdles (e.g., setting a hurdle at 50% of the market price-earnings ratio), soon diminishes the population of eligible stocks to a very small number. To avoid this, one has to limit the number of screens, and adjust the hurdle height, to allow enough stocks to survive to allow a diversified portfolio to be constructed.

Although there are some problems with the screening approach, most non-quantitative managers are likely to feel more at home with the screening approach than the composite. There are many articles describing screening but, for a practical discussion, Arbel (1985b, pp. 90–115) is useful. Using neglected stocks as the basic screen, Arbel tries to screen out stocks that might become bankrupt. Next he tries to screen out overpriced stocks and finally stocks that are correctly priced but cannot be expected to perform in the foreseeable future. Arbel's discussion is too long to be summarized here, but is a useful practical guide.

Screening approaches do not systematically control for risk. Risk control tends to be informal, based on ensuring broad diversification. This usually involves sector weightings but can be more complex, depending on the manager's experience. Many managers will look to see if they are taking hidden and unwanted bets. For example, a fund will have exposure to property from its property sector weighting but it will also get exposure through the hotel and brewers and distillers sectors, and it may wish to control this exposure. Or a fund might look to see if it is selecting the more highly geared shares in each sector. A few years ago, a low price-earnings approach would have pointed to Trafalgar House, Maxwell Communications, Polly Peck, ADT and Coloroll as potential purchases. These companies were in different industries but each was dominated by one individual and all had interesting accounting practices. These stocks might all have been seen as involving the same sort of risk. A fund manager might be willing to hold one of them, but not all. This sort of approach gives a role to the traditional fundamental research usually employed in the appropriate price-earnings ratio approach. However, the fundamental research is used to discriminate amongst a universe of shares that have been selected by a less subjective, and more quantitative, approach.

Let's now look at the weighted composite approach. After choosing the relevant attributes, the next stage is to weight them by forecasting power. This may be done formally or an investor may simply use several variables and give them equal weight, or weight them on the basis of prior beliefs. It is not our intention to produce a recommended model, or go through possible mathematical techniques for combining variables. Instead the discussion will be illustrated by looking at a couple of share selection models—without any judgement as to whether they are good or bad. They will give the non-quantitative manager a feel for the sort of model that might be built on the basis of the research reported in this book.

A model used by Harris Investment Management has been described by Kirscher (1990). Harris selects shares on the basis of a five component model. The components are low price-earnings ratio, dividend discount model, earnings momentum, analyst revisions and price momentum. The weights for each component are not stated but, judging from a pie graph included in the description, they are roughly 35%, 25%, 10%, 15% and 15%. The first two components are measures of value, to determine if a stock is cheap, and the remaining components are measures of momentum, to discern if the cheapness is being recognized by other investors.

Harris appears to monitor a list of only 175 stocks and each stock is ranked on each component. The overall ranking for a stock is simply its ranking on each component times that component's weighting. The stocks are re-ranked by their overall score. The top stocks are not the buy list because they could be excessively risky and poorly diversified. A second programme is used to balance risk against return.

Kirscher reports that use of a computer model allows more time to be spent developing client relationships. He notes that research on enhancing the value of the model can be undertaken and, very important from a client perspective,

"the model can be gradually re-engineered without introducing drastic and unsettling change in investment style." (p. 56)

For the eight years for which data is presented, the model (plus risk/return trade-off) has beaten the S&P 500 by about 3% per annum, although it took "a bath" in 1987, underperforming by 8.1%. Notice that the small number of shares monitored suggests a large capitalization bias: during many of the years for which performance data are provided, small shares performed poorly.

The most detailed series of publications that use forecasts on stock over- or under-valuation, assessments of correlations of forecasts and returns, and then goes on to build a composite forecasting model is by Ambachtsheer and Farrell (see Ambachtsheer 1974 and 1977, Ambachtsheer and Farrell, 1979, and Farrell, 1982 and 1983). These publications discuss the calculation of expected alphas, which will be omitted here—see especially Farrell (1983)—but the gist of the model described by Farrell will be given.

Ambachtsheer and Farrell (1979) report work using the Wells Fargo Market Line approach (i.e., a dividend discount model) in conjunction with the Value Line Timeliness measure. They describe the former as long-term fundamental and the latter as short-term fundamental. Farrell (1982 and 1983) describes managing money with this approach using models identical in spirit although different in detail. In addition to the two variables noted, he includes a measure of trading fundamentals (which includes information provided by share repurchase programmes or insider trading patterns) and a measure of analyst judgement (which monitors buy and sell recommendations of security analysts). The four variables are said to be attractive because all have demonstrated predictive content and statistical measures suggest that they are mutually independent. These share predictors are then combined to produce a composite forecast for 800 shares. Specifically, Farrell estimates an alpha for each share, the amount it should deviate from the market's return. A portfolio is then constructed along the following lines:

1. the portfolio beta is kept between 0.95 and 1.05, i.e., risk, to the extent that beta is a measure of risk, is explicitly controlled;
2. investments are spread over sectors in line with the S&P 500;
3. 60–90 companies are held;
4. no large positions are held in individual stocks.

Over the period 1974–81, this strategy outperformed the S&P 500 every year by amounts varying from 1.7% to 9.7%.

BEFORE WE LEAVE STOCKS ... AN ASIDE

Good stock selection is always helpful but often when one reads a broker's report which expects the market as a whole to go nowhere there is a rider that "It's all down to stock selection for performance this year". The writer undertook some casual analysis some years ago for the UK and it seemed that differences in stock performance were greater in bull markets. McEnally and Todd (1992) have recently more formally studied the cross-sectional variation in returns for NYSE stocks. The inter-quartile range of stock returns is a useful measure of cross-sectional variability: if all stocks are ordered by return and then split into quartiles, the difference between the return that separates the top two quartiles and the return that separates the bottom two quartiles is the inter-quartile range. The variation in stock returns in the US since World War II has been reasonably stable. For the 31 post-war years with positive returns the inter-quartile range was 37.5% and only 30.5% for the 13 years with negative returns. In short, the scope for outstanding stock selection to add to returns is greater in bull markets.

CONCLUDING COMMENTS

Earlier chapters appear to offer many opportunities for outperforming. Some of the returns available seem extraordinary. It is doubtful that, in practice, these returns will be easily obtained. Some of the studies probably make statistical mistakes, some probably under-estimate costs, some anomalies hold generally but not in every year and some findings will get discounted in the market. Still, there do appear to be information and valuation opportunities for investors.

Given the points just made, it seems sensible to use several approaches/anomalies in stock selection and to blend these together in some formal way. This can be done by an optimizer, screening or a composite score method. The latter may be done in a mathematically sophisticated way or a more pragmatic manner. The selection criteria should, ideally, have low correlations with each other, i.e., they should be contributing new information as far as possible and not be duplicating each other.

Different organizations are likely to produce different share selection models depending on their perception of the statistical relationships between attributes and returns, their own skills and interests and the perceptions and attitudes of their existing and anticipated clients.

PART THREE
Strategic and Tactical Asset Allocation

In this part we examine:

1. the setting of strategic targets for a fund, i.e., the allocation between asset classes that is thought appropriate for a fund over the long-term;

and

2. short term tactical asset allocation, i.e., the short-term deviations from the strategic allocation based on a view of short-term risk and return prospects.

Chapter 22 discusses strategic asset allocation and Chapter 23 gives an overview of tactical asset allocation—the approaches that are used and whether tactical asset allocation is likely to add value to investment management. Tactical asset allocation techniques fall into five types: business cycle anticipation, valuation measures, liquidity approaches, technical analysis and bottom-up stock driven approaches. Tactical asset allocation does not necessarily involve economic forecasts, but often does.

Chapter 24 provides background information on the different sorts of economic forecasts available to investors and their likely value. While there is an extensive academic literature on share selection, there is relatively little on tactical asset allocation. Much of the work done in this area is by US fund management organizations and is not published. Most textbooks omit the topic or give a treatment that is technically correct but not very useful. The treatment here, by way of contrast, does discuss methods actually used. The level of sophistication varies dramatically, and there are no rigorous studies to support the value of some of the approaches. Many studies use the same data to derive a decision rule and to test its effectiveness. Nonetheless, the discussion does give a feel for some of the approaches in use. Chapter 25 discusses business cycle anticipation and scenario forecasting. Chapters 26 and 27 examine valuation-based tactical asset allocation. Chapter 28 gives a brief treatment of liquidity and technical approaches. Chapter 29 looks at international tactical asset allocation.

When constructing a tactical asset allocation model, it is sensible to combine various approaches, providing they contribute new information and do not just duplicate each other. The combination used will depend on an investor's knowledge and skills: for example, some will be drawn to use methods that involve economic forecasting whereas others will avoid such methods. Chapter 30 discusses the optimization approach to tactical asset allocation as well as less formal approaches.

22
Setting Strategic Weights

In Chapter 1, the four broad issues that must be addressed in managing a portfolio were outlined. In this chapter, the second item, the strategic weights, will be examined. There are four ways of tackling this issue:

- use the proportions of assets in the world portfolio as the benchmark;
- use risk/return optimization;
- relate asset distribution to liabilities;
- do what other funds are doing.

CAPITALIZATION-BASED STRATEGIC WEIGHTS

The first approach of basing strategic weights on a capitalization-weighted world portfolio of assets can be justified in terms of some of the models discussed in Part 1. Recall the argument that all investors should hold the same risky portfolio—the market portfolio—and should vary their holding of a risk-free asset to obtain the risk/return trade-off that they desire. Although most investors think of risky assets in terms of a broad domestic index, strictly speaking the argument applies to all assets, including all international markets. We saw that the market portfolio notion was not quite right once we allowed for different borrowing and lending costs, but the world market portfolio might seem a useful starting point. Yet most investors would find this approach a little bizarre as both Japanese and British investors, for example, would hold identical risky portfolios which would be dominated by US dollar assets. Portfolios are not normally managed with regard to a world portfolio of assets benchmark, but it may be appropriate for some funds and appropriate, in part, for all.

For countries such as Kuwait and Saudi Arabia, with few domestic financial assets available for investment and with a US dollar-based economy (because oil is priced in dollars), a world index may well be an appropriate starting point. Further, to the extent that any institutional fund invests in, for example, overseas equity markets, the weights of the world equity index, ex-the domestic market, may be considered to provide a benchmark for strategic policy weights for the international portion of the fund, although there is no theoretical argument to support this. Thus, UK pension funds might consider the distribution of a world equity index ex-UK as providing the appropriate strategic weights for their international equities. In fact, most of them do not appear to have taken this approach (or the permitted range of deviation from the strategic weight has been exceptionally broad). In recent years most funds have been massively overweight in Continental Europe. Funds with a global equity brief run by the same managers have usually had a quite different Continental European weight. One suspects that UK investment houses follow a strategy of having weights close to their competitors in each distinct fund management market.

MEAN-VARIANCE OPTIMIZATION

A second approach to setting strategic asset weights is to use a mean-variance optimization model, i.e., to calculate an efficient frontier, as was discussed in Chapter 2, and then choose an efficient portfolio. The difficulties with this approach for setting strategic weights are that it is essentially a one-period model and also no explicit attention is paid to the liabilities of the investor. These problems can be overcome but one is then moving close to asset-liability modelling which we discuss below. We will omit discussion of optimization here, although we will discuss it in Chapter 30, in the context of tactical asset allocation.

ASSET-LIABILITY MODELLING

A third approach to setting strategic asset weights is to relate the asset distribution to the tax position, liabilities and time horizon of the fund. This approach, often described as asset-liability modelling, requires complex computer simulations. A simplified discussion will be given here.

It is widely accepted that different funds have different objectives and liabilities and that funds should be invested with regard to these. The fund of a life office has obligations to its policy holders and a pension fund has obligations to its members. These are generally thought of as long-term funds although a pension fund, for example, might be for employees of a firm that had gone out of business and all the members might be at or near retirement age. Such a fund would be relatively short-term. Charities may have long run objectives but may also be subject to substantial immediate income requirements.

How does one go about ensuring that liabilities can be met, and at least cost in terms of contributions? One approach is asset-liability modelling which gives a picture of how the assets and liabilities of a fund might develop over time, the resulting surplus or deficit and the risks involved. Assets and liabilities should both be modelled, but this is complex. For example, to do this properly for a pension fund we would need to know:

- expected returns for each asset class;
- standard deviations for each asset class;
- correlation coefficients between each asset class;
- expected level of pension payments each year;
- standard deviation of pension payments;
- correlation coefficients between asset class returns and changes in pension payments.

There are probably no computer models that develop a totally integrated asset-liability model. Most simulate asset behaviour and then relate this in some way to critical return requirements, the probability of shortfalls, etc. Even these simpler models are mathematically complex and beyond the scope of this book. To give a flavour of a typical approach, we will model assets here and then relate them to liabilities in an intuitive manner.

We know that equities have historically produced better returns than bonds over long periods of time, but with greater risk, i.e., greater variability of returns. So that we can draw on some calculations made in an article by Fielitz and Muller (1983), let us assume that for a particular period stocks are expected to have a return of 17% with a standard deviation of 15% and bonds have an expected return of 13% with a standard deviation of 3%. Assume also that stocks and bond returns have a 0.1 correlation, i.e., there is a very weak tendency for returns for stocks and bonds to move in the same direction. What is the pattern of returns likely to be as we vary the equity/bond mix?

One way of approaching this is by simulation. Imagine a huge bag of billiard balls, each with a return value written on it. The values would be set to be consistent with a distribution of returns with a mean of 17% and a standard deviation of 15%. A lot of billiard balls will have a value of 17%, rather less will have a value of 16%, and so on down to a few extreme values. Now if we shake the billiard balls up in a bag and then dip in and pull out a ball, we can read off a simulated return for the equity market. If we do this twice more we have simulated a three year return for the equity market. We can repeat this hundreds of times and we will produce a distribution of possible three year equity market returns. At the same time we can also simulate returns for the bond market. Things are a little trickier here because the returns have to be slightly related to the equity returns (recall the small positive correlation) but it doesn't take a computer too long to do the sums. Two sets of computer calculations are shown in Tables 47 and 48.

In Table 47 the distribution of terminal wealth for three years is shown for various asset mixes. The mixes range from 0% in stocks through to 100% in stocks. Let us focus on the bottom row, the 100% in stocks row. Remember that we made

_____ Equity Investment Management

many simulations so that we have a whole range of possible outcomes. If we order these outcomes we can observe the return at various percentiles. In Table 47 we see that a terminal value of 90 (i.e., over three years the investor has lost 10) was observed at the 1 percentile level. At the other end of the spectrum we see at the 99 percentile a terminal value of 264. For the all bond portfolio we see that the corresponding terminal values are 129 and 160.

Table 47 Distribution of Terminal Wealth in Three Years (Per £100 Initial Investment for Various Bond-Stock Combinations)

Bond-Stock Mix (% Stocks)	Distribution Percentiles										
	1	10	20	30	40	50	60	70	80	90	99
0	129	135	138	140	142	143	145	147	149	152	160
10	129	136	139	141	143	145	147	149	151	154	163
20	127	135	139	142	144	146	148	151	154	158	169
30	123	133	138	141	145	147	150	154	158	163	177
40	118	131	137	141	145	149	152	156	161	169	187
50	113	128	135	141	145	150	154	159	166	175	198
60	108	126	134	140	145	151	156	162	170	181	209
70	104	123	132	139	146	152	158	165	174	187	222
80	99	120	130	138	146	153	160	168	178	194	235
90	94	117	129	137	145	153	162	171	183	200	249
100	90	114	127	136	145	154	163	174	187	207	264

Source: Fielitz and Muller (1983, p. 47). Reproduced by permission

In Table 48, the data is presented in a slightly different way. The annualized mean and standard deviation for the three year period is shown for every stock/bond mix and the probability of achieving a given or greater annual compound return for each mix. If we focus on the all bond portfolio, we see that there is a 95% chance the portfolio will return at least 10% and a 5% chance that it will return at least 15.9%.

At this point the fund's trustees or sponsors must decide what their liabilities are and also their attitude to risk. Imagine that the liabilities require a 10% annual compound return. How does one make the risk return trade-off? Fielitz and Muller provide an expected utility analysis based on power functions. Normally some form of quantitative analysis would be made but we will approach the matter in a more intuitive manner. Note that an all equity portfolio gives the best expected return. There is a 50% chance it will beat the all bond portfolio by at least 2.7%, (i.e., 15.6%–12.9%, from the last and first rows of Table 48) and a 5% chance it will beat it by at least 15.4% (i.e., 31.3%–15.9%). The possible rewards from an aggressive equity stance are high. On the other hand there is a 25% chance that the all equity portfolio will fail to produce a 10% return. There is a 5% chance an all equity portfolio will fail to produce even a 2% return. If 10% is the minimum required, an all equity approach seems too risky. As we introduce bonds (i.e., moving

Table 48 Average Annual Compound Return (Summary Statistics and Associated Probabilities of Achieving Given Returns or Greater for Various Bond-Stock Distributions)

Bond-Stock Mix (% Stocks)	Mean	Standard Deviation	Probability Level (per cent)				
			95	75	50	25	5
0	12.9	1.6	10.0	11.7	12.9	14.1	15.9
10	13.3	1.7	10.3	12.0	13.3	14.5	16.4
20	13.6	2.1	9.9	12.1	13.6	15.2	17.5
30	13.9	2.7	9.1	11.9	13.9	16.0	18.9
40	14.2	3.3	8.2	11.7	14.2	16.8	20.6
50	14.5	4.1	7.3	11.5	14.5	17.6	22.3
60	14.8	4.8	6.2	11.2	14.8	18.5	24.0
70	15.0	5.6	5.2	10.9	15.0	19.3	25.8
80	15.2	6.4	4.1	10.5	15.2	20.2	27.6
90	15.4	7.2	3.0	10.2	15.4	21.0	29.4
100	15.6	8.0	1.8	9.8	15.6	21.8	31.3

Source: Fielitz and Muller (1983, p. 47). Reproduced by permission

up Table 48 from the bottom) matters improve, but only at the 20% equity/80% bond mix do we get within a whisker of achieving 10% with a 95% probability. If we look at Table 47 we see the 1 percentile returns from the 20/80, 10/90, and 0/100 mixes are similar. Given the higher expected returns from the 20/80 mix, that would be the one the writer would recommend.

Now this analysis is plausible if we are analysing a medical charity paying, say, research academics' wages. But what if we are analysing a pension fund? Here the company might reason a little differently. If the required 10% is not achieved by the investments that may not be the end of the world: the company may simply top-up the scheme out of current profits. A 100% equity strategy might involve a lot of topping up if a return of 1.8% is achieved, but look at the 50/50 split. At the 75% probability level the returns from this strategy are not very different from strategies with more bonds. At the 50%, 25% and 5% probability levels, the returns are distinctly better. At the 95% level the return is smaller than for more bond-orientated strategies but perhaps this risk is bearable for the expectation that the returns will be superior.

Would all firms reason in this way? Probably not. A highly cyclical, poorly financed company should be more risk-averse. A well financed, well diversified company might be willing to take larger risks.

The example used here produced a pro-bond strategic asset allocation. In general the equity weighting will be a function of a number of factors.

1. The greater the return difference in favour of equities, the greater the equity weighting.
2. The greater the correlation between equity and gilts, the greater the equity weighting. The example used in Tables 47 and 48 had an equity risk premium

of 4%, yet in the UK it has been around 6 to 7%. This would produce a larger equity weighting.
3. The lower the volatility of equities, the greater the equity weight.
4. Most practitioners assume that it is self-evident that the longer the investment time horizon, the greater the equity weighting that will be appropriate. This is because it is thought that equity risk declines over time—time diversification as it is sometimes called. In the professional journals there is, however, a lively debate as to whether equity risk does decrease over time. (See, e.g., Lee, 1990, Leibowitz and Langetieg, 1990; Lloyd and Modani, 1983; McEnally, 1985; and Samuelson, 1989.)

To understand the time diversification issues let's imagine that equities only offer two returns, with equal probability, either +24% or –2%, i.e., an average of 11%. In year one, what is the likely outcome? Well, it will not be 11%, because it can only be +24% or –2%. If risk is uncertainty, equities are very uncertain over a one-year holding period. It's a bit like flipping a coin: we cannot sensibly forecast the outcome of one flip. With 20 flips, though, we can be reasonably confident that there will be close to 10 heads and 10 tails. The outcome is much less uncertain, or risky, over a long run of flips. Similarly, it seems likely that over 20 years, equities are going to average out at around an 11% return. There is more scope for good and bad years to average out. This is time diversification, and equity risks are reduced over time. Note, however, that it is possible for 20 tails to turn up in a row and it is possible for 20 bad years for equities to turn up, each yielding –2% in our example. If that happened, as each year went by, the losses would increase. Now the odds of 20 consecutive bad years are small, but the outcome would be terrible. That seems risky. So, the odds of getting close to the average return increase with time, but the adverse consequences of numerous bad outcomes, albeit unlikely, increase. The range of possible returns gets larger with the passage of time. If you focus on this, risks increase with time. So, are equities less risky over long periods? It depends on which risk you focus on.

But this is not the whole story. There may be two aspects of risk to focus on, but whoever heard of twenty consecutive bad years? Annual equity returns may not be independent as assumed in the simulation. As we shall see in Chapter 23, over periods of several years, bad returns tend to be followed by good returns and vice versa. This means the wide range of equity returns that are possible in a simulation based on each period's return being independent of the previous period's returns are unlikely to be realized. Actual returns are more likely to be bunched around the mean than the simulation suggests. Equities over long periods are less risky in practice than they seem to be based on variability of returns. Thus, not only are equities more likely to achieve their average expected return over a long period, but the greater the negative serial correlation of returns, the smaller the chance of a bad outcome. (Many computer simulations now allow for negative serial correlation.) Providing there is negative serial correlation of returns, the traditional fund manager view of time diversification does seem sensible, so the longer the time horizon the greater should be the equity weighting.

It is common for investment texts to discuss only an equity/bond split in asset/liability modelling. This is easier to handle and anyway made good sense in the UK in the past and still does in the US. But in the UK nowadays, international equities take up a bigger proportion of portfolios than bonds. Property, too, remains not insignificant. Clearly an asset allocation simulation should include these assets too. The effect of adding these categories will be to decrease the weighting of bonds. Although domestic equities, international equities and property may all be riskier than bonds, because their returns are not perfectly correlated, it will be possible to increase the proportion of risky assets if all three categories are included.

Asset-liability modelling is a sensible way of setting strategic weights, but there is no ducking the fact that it is complex. Few UK actuaries seem willing to provide models for their clients, and few clients seem to want to grapple with the problem.

FOLLOWING THE MEDIAN MANAGER

We turn now to the fourth possible strategic asset allocation method—doing what other funds are doing or, as it is usually called in the markets, following the median manager.

In the writer's view, the strategic asset allocation (plus a permitted range of deviations for tactical asset allocation) should be set by plan sponsors and their actuaries, and fund managers should operate within those parameters. Only the plan sponsors and their advisers are in a position to assess the plan sponsors' liabilities and attitude to risk. Currently in the UK, many fund managers tend to set their strategic asset allocation on the basis of the median institutional asset distribution, plus some notion of their own competitive interests. Strategic asset allocation in the UK often seems more designed to maximize fund managers' utility than that of the funds they manage. This is a crazy situation, but the fund managers can hardly be blamed for following their commercial interests. While the correct approach is complex, even rough and ready calculations relevant to the fund seem more appropriate than following the crowd.

CONCLUDING COMMENTS

There are four major ways of setting strategic asset weights: matching a world index, mean-variance optimization, asset-liability modelling, and doing what other funds are doing.

The most widely used method is probably the last, which maximizes the manager's utility, rather than the client's. Matching a world index seems appropriate for only a few funds. Asset-liability modelling is an appropriate approach for many funds but it is complex, requiring return estimates, variances, and so forth, plus a liability model and a clear understanding of the client's attitude to risk. The discussion of this approach given in this chapter is but a bare outline of what is necessary to determine the appropriate strategic weights. It is essentially a task that trustees and their actuarial advisers should undertake.

23
Tactical Asset Allocation: Background

The tactical asset allocation decision determines what departure, based on current market valuations, should be made from the strategic asset allocation. It is the third of the four tasks discussed in Chapter 1. Tactical asset allocation is a current fad in the US fund management industry, although investors have always tried to time markets. A number of articles have been written distinguishing tactical asset allocation from "old fashioned" market timing, but this writer fails to see the difference. True, the methods used differ to some extent, and there is now a greater emphasis on risk, but technology and attitude have changed throughout the fund management process. Many modern share selection techniques are a long way from the style of the old fashioned stock picker, but both aim to pick outperforming shares and are undertaking essentially the same activity. So too with tactical asset allocation and market timing. (For a contrary view see Phillips and Lee, 1989.)

We shall discuss whether tactical asset allocation is worthwhile and how an investor might go about it, but we first need to make a link between this chapter and the last. Tactical asset allocation will take place within ranges around the strategic weights. How are these ranges set? There is unfortunately no good answer. The range should be narrower, the greater the size of transaction costs and the more modest the timing skills possessed. This will often suggest quite narrow ranges. However, many clients expect their managers to possess timing skills. They often accept that short-term timing may be difficult but add a plea to the effect "but you will get us out if everything looks awful, won't you?" The clients then impose quite wide ranges to allow for their disaster scenario. This then gives managers a range which they either implicitly ignore and act well within, or they get bullied to act more aggressively than their skills warrant. A better solution might be to have relatively narrow ranges, with a clear understanding that in exceptional circumstances the clients will be contacted and asked if they will allow the manager to breach the range for specified reasons.

IS TACTICAL ASSET ALLOCATION IMPORTANT?

Asset allocation is generally accepted as *the* investment decision (see especially Brinson *et al*, 1991). This is only partly valid. The usual argument is based on the fact that the typical manager will have an equity return not too far adrift from the appropriate index and there are big differences in returns from different asset classes and international markets. Some investors go further and assert that the efficient market theory applies to security prices within markets and so the only way to win the performance game is to make bets between markets rather than within. It may be that classes of assets are more often mispriced relative to each other than are securities within an asset class. Additionally, there may be less information and smaller flows of money between countries so that international asset class inefficiencies may be even greater. But, even if the inefficiencies exist, it has to be shown that they can be exploited.

The practical argument about the differences in return between asset classes is, however, misplaced. It is true that there are often large differences in return, but there are even bigger differences in return within each equity market. Every year some shares will go bust and others soar. This will generate greater return differences than is usually observed between asset classes. This might suggest share selection is the most important decision. Of course, institutional investors have diversified portfolios and do not make the sort of stock bets necessary to achieve the potential returns. But if we shift the argument to checking actual returns from stock picking rather than possible returns, we ought to do the same for actual returns from actual asset shifts. Most funds do not make huge swings in asset allocation and so the realized return from tactical asset allocation is likely to be modest. If a fund switched from an 80/20 equity/gilt split to a 90/10 split, and equities outperformed gilts by 10%, the allocation change would result in a 1% gain in performance—before transaction costs. Now that is the sort of difference that is attainable by stock selection. Consultants Mercer Fraser (1988b) examined the performance of UK institutional funds for the period 1983–87 and found that there was indeed little difference in the returns from asset allocation versus stock selection. (See also Hensel *et al*., 1991.)

Note carefully what is *not* being said. It is not being denied that an all equity fund is likely to outperform an all bond fund over a long period. The strategic asset weights are very important in determining return. The tactical deviation from those weights, however, is likely to be modest in practice, and so the additional returns achieved will be more modest than is often implied.

Before focusing on what measures we might use to predict the level of an equity market and make tactical asset allocation decisions, it is worth looking at some of the academic research on what moves markets and whether they move too much, in other words, whether they are efficient with regard to level. (A useful discussion, which this chapter draws on, is Shleifer and Summers, 1990.)

THE LEMMING'S DILEMMA

Nobody doubts that there are some silly and naïve investors, but that would not stop market levels being efficient in the sense that we discussed earlier with regard to stocks. If there is a class of rational investors, with a reasonable amount of funds, market prices are likely to be driven towards some notion of fair value. This is especially likely if there is scope for arbitrage. This is the process whereby a simultaneous purchase and sale is made of two identical, or near identical, assets in the hope of a risk-free profit. This is easier to carry out in some markets than in others. In the option markets there are underlying securities to which the options are tied. Not surprisingly, options seem generally fairly priced: it is easy to trade in either stock or option and discrepancies get eliminated.

For the market as a whole, arbitrage is more difficult. Of course, if the market seems too expensive, an arbitrageur can sell the market and hold cash—and vice versa—but this is not a risk-free trade. There is a large role for judgement and the timing is more difficult than with short-lived options. A market judgement may take years to come right, if it ever does, adding to the risk. Moreover, professional fund managers, who have the funds to effect the trades, are generally measured on a short-time horizon. It would seem reasonable to assume that the market as a whole is more likely to deviate substantially from fair value than are individual stocks relative to each other.

This view is reinforced if one examines the way many investors behave. Many act as though "the trend is your friend", and they are likely to believe that a trend once started will continue for ever. Indeed, some professionals, such as chartists, publish stock advice which has a strong element of trend following. Finally, there is the psychological evidence which suggests that people pay too much attention to recent vivid news (the market is going up) and too little to general background information (there is always a cyclical downturn). Investors seem to face their own lemming's dilemma. It is said, (whether it is true or not), that lemmings lack sufficient body mass to survive in low temperatures. To overcome this, they are inclined to huddle together. The lemming's dilemma results from the tendency of other lemmings to throw themselves over cliffs. If investors find psychological warmth in doing what other investors are doing, it would not be surprising if equity markets deviated from fair value and were buffeted by changing sentiment.

One might expect rational professionals to bet against the trend followers. But how can they be sure that they are witnessing a short-lived trend? They do not know what the future holds and even professionals have emotions and may act just like the lemmings. Indeed, going with the trend may be a rational strategy even if it is self-evident that the trend will be eventually reversed. To be wrong with the crowd will not lead to a loss of clients, whereas to be wrong alone might.

VOLATILITY TESTS

Testing these arguments is difficult, because getting a handle on fair value is hard. A famous attempt was made by Shiller (1981). The dividend discount model assumes that the price of an asset will be the value of the discounted stream of dividends. We can apply this to the market as a whole. If we assume a constant discount rate and also that investors can forecast dividends perfectly, it is possible to use actual dividends to calculate the level the market should have been priced at in particular years and then compare it with the actual level. LeRoy (1990) transforms the argument slightly, and calculates simulated rates of return that would have been achieved if the market was priced by discounting dividends and he compares these returns with the actual returns the market delivered. Of course, investors did not know what future dividends would be but LeRoy assumed investors could forecast dividends perfectly for five years and that they then extrapolated dividends using a constant growth rate. His results are shown in Figure 25. The simulated rate of return is less volatile than the dividend growth rate. This is what should be expected if the market discounts future dividends, for this means stock prices should behave like a weighted average of dividends over time, and any average will always be less volatile than its components. Turning to the actual rate of return and dividend growth rate, we see that the rates of return are more volatile than the dividend growth rate: they are too volatile.

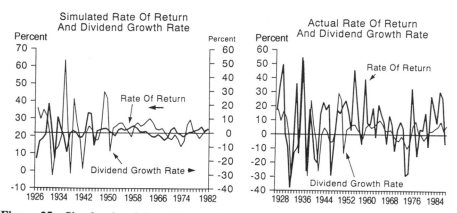

Figure 25 Simulated and Actual Rates of Return and Dividend Growth Rates. Source: LeRoy (1990, p. 35). Reprinted with permission from the *Federal Reserve Bank of San Francisco Economic Review*, Spring 1990

The type of tests proposed by Shiller and LeRoy to decide whether the market moves "too much" have been challenged by a number of writers (notably by Kleidon, 1986, and Marsh and Merton, 1986). The arguments are too complex for a full discussion in this book. However, we can note a couple of points. First, we would expect the discount rate to vary over time. It will depend on the risk-free rate and the riskiness of equities. Both will fluctuate. This will lead to fluctuations in the market greater than that justified by dividend fluctuations alone. Second, managers smooth dividends and this upsets the notion that stock prices and returns must be more stable than dividends. Imagine managers smooth dividends to the extent of not paying dividends at all, intending to do so only far into the future. The expected value of that future payout will surely fluctuate, so while dividends will follow a smooth path, stock prices and returns, which will reflect the present value of that future payment, will fluctuate. Yet, when all is said and done, when allowance has been made for all the criticisms, and the results modified, the outcome still appears to many observers to be that the market moves too much. The conclusion most academics reach seems to be more an indication of what they first believed rather than a consequence of the arguments. The majority US view is probably that the market moves too much. For the UK, Bulkley and Tonks (1989) have provided similar evidence that UK prices fluctuate too much.

A slightly different way of looking at the same issue is to see whether returns follow a pattern of reversals. If the market overreacts, we might expect good periods to be followed by bad periods and vice versa. Fama and French (1988b) examined monthly return data from 1926 to 1985 for NYSE firms. They regressed returns for various time periods on the previous time period of the same length (e.g., an 18 month period was related to the previous 18 months). The correlations were close to zero for short periods but generally negative for periods of 18 months or more and around -0.25 to -0.4 for three to five year returns. This implies that returns tend to reverse, good periods are followed by bad. The results are weaker than they appear, however, because: (a) the return reversal weakened over time (and the results disappear if the period 1926–40 is deleted); and (b) 60 years, using five-year sub-periods, is not a large sample. Moreover, the variation in returns could be caused by a changing equity risk premium rather than market overreaction, although that would not be without interest for investors.

Poterba and Summers (1988) examined the same issue but used US data for the period 1871–1985 and used a different statistical technique. Their results were consistent with finding negative autocorrelation of returns for periods from two to eight years. For periods of less than a year they found positive autocorrelations. They also looked at foreign countries, including the UK, for which they found evidence in the period 1939–86 of short horizon positive serial correlation and long horizon negative serial correlation. Using yet another statistical technique,

Jegadeesh (1991), found mean reversion (when returns move away from the mean return, they then revert back to it) in an equal-weighted index of NYSE stocks for the period 1926–88, but this was entirely concentrated in January. The January effect was strongest in the post-war period, although for all calendar months together there was no mean reversion. For the UK, for the period 1955–88, Jegadeesh found no evidence of mean reversion when the whole sample was examined, but there was a January effect.

REACTING TO NEWS OR NOISE?

If it is accepted that the market moves too much, and few practitioners would dispute it, the cause could either be investors overreacting to relevant information or investors reacting to information that is in some sense irrelevant. They probably do both. Certainly markets seem to react to irrelevant information. In a famous study, Roll (1984) examined US orange juice futures prices. These should reflect the spot prices investors expect when the future expires. Roll argued that the only thing that could give information about spot prices in the short run was the weather. A frost in Florida would be bad news for the orange crop. Other factors could not vary much in the short run—new trees cannot be planted and produce a crop in a year, it is unlikely that consumers suddenly get an urge for apple juice rather than orange juice, and so on. Roll found that low temperatures pushed up orange juice futures prices but only a few percent of futures' price variation could be explained by temperatures, and Roll could find no other important variables. In short, prices varied too much. Other studies paint a similar picture.

New information will cause prices to move. If public information drives the markets and information arrives all the time, prices should be as volatile when the markets are shut as when they are open. How do we know the price change when the market is shut? By comparing the closing price with the next opening price. Prices are more volatile when markets are open: the volatility during the hours of a typical market day is six times that of a typical weekend which is eleven times longer. Since company and economic information tends to be released when the markets are open, there will be more information when the markets are open, so the evidence may not seem very relevant. Yet the differences in volatilities seems excessive. It is worth noting that political news may be released when the markets are shut, earthquakes and storms may take place when the markets are shut, major economic news is often released when the markets are shut—devaluations tend to take place on weekends—and many companies release bad news after market hours. All this would make one suspicious of an explanation that only public information drives the markets and there is a study that supports this line of reasoning. The US stock market was closed on Wednesdays for a period in 1968, as back-offices tried to catch up with their paperwork. French and Roll (1986) found more price volatility on Wednesdays when the market was open, than when it was closed, yet the flow of public information should not have varied. In short, much trading takes place on the basis of private information—the market seems to generate its own news.

In a different approach, Cutler *et al.* (1989) tried to explain market movements by news. They tried to explain monthly US stock returns for the period 1926–85 by using seven measures of monthly macro-economic activity. They tried a number of approaches but concluded that a substantial portion of return variation—more than a half, perhaps as much as 80%—could not be explained by macro-economic news. What about non-economic news? Cutler *et al.* took important events from the *World Almanac* and selected those most likely to have an impact on the market and then those described in the *New York Times* as actually having had an impact on the market. The impact of events on prices was disappointingly small. Cutler *et al.* then tried to approach the issue from the other end. They selected days with large price movements and looked for the news that caused the movement. Generally they were unable to find significant news.

If it is hard to establish what news moves the market, this would seem to support the view that the market moves too much and that trends get overdone. The market seems to feed on itself. Investors make decisions on the basis of other investor's decisions. Trends can be self-perpetuating. But it is unlikely that trends go on for ever. After a period, the fundamentals will reassert themselves. If this argument is correct, good returns should be followed by poor returns, which takes us back to the mean reversion evidence. Excessive volatility and long-term price reversion are two different ways of looking at the same issue.

CAN TACTICAL ASSET ALLOCATION ADD VALUE?

Well, all of the above is interesting, but what value does it have for an investor? There is no simple answer. It seems the market is influenced by fundamentals but there is more to the market than that. Investors watch each other and the market as a whole; some investors chase trends. The market is too volatile—trends persist for too long, but they then reverse. This suggests that both a value and contrarian approach will eventually work because trends do reverse. This is one basis for tactical asset allocation, but it may be a painful approach for an investor if short-term results matter as well as the final outcome. Many investors in the 1980s felt the Japanese market was over-valued for a very long time before it corrected. A pure trend-following approach will work too, right up to the point it does not. Combining some measure of sentiment or momentum and some measure of value may be a sensible way of approaching market timing.

While in principle the evidence of this chapter suggests scope for market timing, there has been considerable scepticism in the past that investors could time the markets. Some early academic studies suggested mutual fund managers lacked timing skills. Some articles have argued that in principle it is unlikely that managers will perform well. They make two important points. First it can usually be shown for any period of years that if investors missed, say, the best 5% of the months for the equity market they would have achieved the same return from investing in cash. For example, Chandy and Reichenstein (1991) report that for the period 1926–87, the excess return from the S&P 500 over Treasury bills was achieved in 3.5% of the months. Because the market often moves quickly out of bear markets, a very high success rate has to be achieved in calling bull markets (see, for example, Jeffrey, 1984; Chua *et al.* 1987; and Droms, 1989). A fully invested position is always wrong in bear markets, but it is 100% correct in bull markets, and that is the important call—you have to be in it to win it. The second point relates to the variability of most measures used in making tactical asset allocation decisions. Methods that involve value assessed by yields, price-earnings ratios, risk premiums and so forth, use measures that have varied widely over time. (For some sample calculations see Carman, 1981.) Given the wide historical range, do investors have the skills to foretell which is the correct value for markets at any moment?

Despite these points, some studies have claimed some success for tactical asset allocation both in the US and UK either in terms of enhanced return or reduced risk (for example Vandell and Stevens, 1989; Weigel, 1991; Mercer Fraser, 1991; and Wagner *et al.*, 1992). Moreover, many studies of tactical asset allocation decision tools suggest the tools can be used to make profitable decisions.

TACTICAL ASSET ALLOCATION METHODS

What are the methods of tactical asset allocation? There are two basic approaches, top-down and bottom-up, and these can be further subdivided:

Top-down:

- business cycle anticipation;
- comparative valuation, e.g., aggregate dividend discount model, bond yield versus equity earnings yield, foreign versus domestic markets;
- liquidity and flow of funds, e.g., money supply, cash reserves;
- technical analysis.

Bottom-up:

- Numerous stock selection methods

The top-down approaches attempt to choose between asset classes. How can share selection (an intra-class decision) give a guide to the value of asset classes? There are two answers. One relates to intra-country decisions and the other inter-country.

Fund managers often say they cannot find anything to buy. This feeling can be used as an asset class decision rule. More formally, we have seen in Chapter 13 how the number of stocks that are cheap on a net asset basis might be a guide to the cheapness or dearness of the market. However, not many share selection techniques can be used in this way. Low price-earnings ratio stocks, for example, are low relative to other stocks, not low relative to other asset classes. Of course, sometimes investors feel that a particular absolute price-earnings ratio is too high, but at this point they seem to be making some comparative valuation of asset classes and have switched to a top-down approach. Some information about the value of the equity market as a whole probably can be obtained from some share selection techniques but, in general, for intra-country asset class decisions, the top-down approach seems preferable.

The bottom-up approach is more often used in selecting international equities. A manager may look for cheap shares on a world-wide basis and ignore the shares' national origins. Thus, if German chemical stocks look very cheap, German chemical stocks are purchased, either to add to other chemical stocks, or as the portfolio's sole chemical sector exposure. This results in country and currency exposure being determined by stock selection (although constraints in terms of maximum exposure to one country or maximum deviation from a country's index weighting may limit the impact of the bottom-up approach).

There is an empirical issue here. Do German chemical stocks behave more like world chemical stocks or other German stocks? The answer (see, e.g., Grinold et al., 1989) is that in most industries the national correlation is larger than the international industry correlation. Countries are more important than industries in determining returns although the returns to stocks in different countries are significantly influenced by global industry and common factors. Some industries are more global than others—e.g., banks, energy and health are more global than consumer goods, textiles and business services. All this suggests that even for international tactical asset allocation, a bottom-up approach should probably be a supplement to top-down approaches rather than be the sole method.

In general, it would seem that top-down approaches offer the most promise and this is what we mainly discuss. Economic analysis plays some part in some tactical asset allocation approaches: Chapter 24 discusses economic forecasting. Chapter 25 discusses business cycle anticipation and Chapters 26–27 discuss comparative valuation. Our discussion is selective and these chapters discuss only earnings- and yield-based valuation measures. Other measures, such as aggregate book-to-market, widely followed in the US, are not discussed. A brief treatment of a few aspects of liquidity, flow of funds and technical analysis is given in Chapter 28. Chapter 29 looks at aspects of international asset allocation. Chapter 30 pulls the tactical asset allocation chapters together.

Figure 26 Excessive Tactical Asset Allocation. Source: Illustration by Edward Sorel, *Wall Street Computer Review*, pp. 54–5, December 1989. (The *Wall Street Computer Review* is now called *Wall Street and Technology*.)

CONCLUDING COMMENTS

Tactical asset allocation determines what departures should be made from long-term strategic weights. The evidence on the success of tactical asset allocation is somewhat mixed, but it is probably worth the effort to try and make good tactical asset allocation decisions, although given the modest size of tactical bets that most managers make, managers with share selection skills who stick to their strategic asset weights would probably not come to grief in the performance stakes. Chapters 25–29 outline various methods of tactical asset allocation. Given the wide range of market valuations over time, it is probably sensible not to make assets switches in response to small price changes. Cheap markets can become cheaper. Extremes of valuation should be acted on. Extremes of valuation can be recognized by investment decisions being relatively insensitive to significant changes in assumptions. Figure 26 adds a reminder not to be too greedy.

24
Forecasting The Economy

The stock market is intimately linked to the economy. Changes in gross national product (GNP)—the nation's income—impact firms' sales and prices which in turn affect revenues, costs and profits. This, in turn, feeds through to dividends and retained earnings. Changes in GNP affect the general price level and interest rates. Dividends, growth and interest rates are all factors in determining share prices. Understanding and forecasting changes in the economy might be expected to be important for anyone wishing to forecast the stock market. At least, a fundamentalist might think so. A chartist would disagree.

Notice the qualifier "might" in the penultimate sentence above. There are two reasons for this. First, we would not expect an exact one-to-one correspondence between changes in the economy and changes in the stock market, if only because investors try to anticipate the economy's moves (on this, see Chapter 25). Thus, one has to forecast both the course of the economy and how much has been discounted by investors. Second, economic forecasting skills might be so poor that, in practice, there is no added value from forecasting. Remember, it is always possible to ignore the economy. For some investors, for example those whose liabilities lie far in the future and who are not worried by volatility, it would be perfectly sensible to have a strategy of, say, always being fully invested in small capitalization equities.

Despite these cautionary comments, a great deal of effort is made in the financial markets to forecast the economy. It therefore seems worth spending a few pages on the major forecasting methods. The author's experience is that the investors with the best understanding of economic issues, and best able to interpret the various forecasts that are available, have taken an economics course. It is beyond the scope of this book to try to give an understanding of how the economy works. Useful informal books, with masses of charts and written with a stock market orientation, include Carnes and Slifer (1991), Nelson (1987) and Mennis (1991). (Unfortunately, these three books deal with the American economy only.) All we can attempt here is to give the non-economist a better feel for the types of forecasts available and their advantages and disadvantages. There are five main forecasting methods:

- cyclical indicators
- survey data
- single equation models
- structural econometric models
- vector autoregressive methods

The poor record of forecasters in the last few years has caused some heart searching and there are signs of a shift in forecasting methods. Let's quickly run through the approaches.

CYCLICAL INDICATORS

Cyclical indicators, often called leading indicators, are more frequently referred to in the US than the UK, although UK data is readily available and is published by the Central Statistical Office. The idea of cyclical indicators is that as the economy passes through a business cycle, certain sequences are played out in roughly the same order as in previous cycles. Some events will lead the cycle, some will be coincident with the cycle and some will lag behind it. The Central Statistical Office cyclical indicators consist of four composite indexes: longer leading, shorter leading, coincident and lagging. The theory of the indicators is set out in *Economic Trends*, Numbers 257 and 271.

The composite indexes each have component series. These are listed below:

Longer leading:

- financial surplus/deficit of industrial and commercial companies;
- CBI quarterly survey: change in optimism;
- FT-A 500 share index;
- three month rate of interest;
- dwelling starts.

Shorter leading:

- change in consumer borrowing;
- gross trading profits of companies;
- new car registrations;
- CBI Quarterly Survey—change in new orders;
- CBI Quarterly Survey—expected change in stocks of materials.

Coincident:

- GDP factor cost;
- output of production industries;
- CBI Quarterly Survey: below capacity utilization;
- index of volume of retail sales;
- CBI Quarterly Survey: change in stocks of raw materials.

Lagging:

- adult unemployment index;
- employment in manufacturing industries;
- investment in plant and machinery in manufacturing industries;
- index of orders for engineering industries;
- level of stocks and work in progress, manufacturing industry.

Notice the substantial use made of survey information. Notice also that a stock market index is included in the leading indicators. We shall return to this below.

The longer and shorter leading indicators lead the economy by ten and four months respectively, and the lagging indicator lags by eleven months. These numbers are median values—the range is very wide: the longer leading indicator has led the cycle by as little as four months and as much as 39 months. Figure 27 shows the cyclical indicators at the end 1992. The first chart shows the then current values of the series and the second shows the series with the leads and lags applied.

It was noted above that the longer leading indicator includes the stock market. There is obviously an element of circularity here—the indicators are used to forecast the economy to help forecast the stock market and yet the stock market is being used to forecast the economy. Nonetheless, the indicators do have some value. First, the stock market is the shortest of the longer leading indicators. It leads with a median of seven months against the ten for the composite index. Second, if use of the stock market index improves the cyclical indicators, it would be pointless not to use this information. The stock market gives very noisy signals—prices jump around a lot—and using cyclical indicators provides additional information.

The cyclical indicators have had a bad press in the last year or two and the Central Statistical Office is apparently planning to overhaul them*. That they failed to forecast accurately the course of the recession of the early 1990s cannot be denied. But most other forecast methods failed too. Despite recent problems, the indicators have a generally good record. It is somewhat surprising that the cyclical indicators are relatively neglected. They are a painless forecasting aid for non-economists and have the advantage that similar series are available for other countries,

---

* While this book was in press the cyclical indicators methodology was changed. The new indexes are set out in B. Moore, 1993, A Review of CSO Cyclical Indicators, *Economic Trends*, 477, July, 99–102. Data using the new indexes became available from October 1993

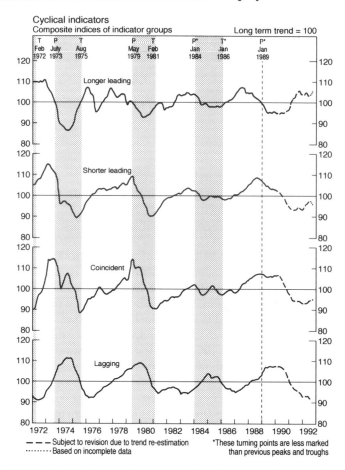

Figure 27 UK Cyclical Indicators. Source: reproduced by permission from Central Statistical Office *Economic Trends*, December, 1992, pp., 76 and 77)

especially the US. Unfortunately the variability of the indicators does not give an indication of the magnitude of the forecast boom or recession. In other words we can say we expect the economy to grow or decline next year, but we cannot say by what amount. And the indicators are restricted to economic growth—for inflation, etc., one has to turn to other sources. In the US, there are some readily available leading indicators of inflation (see, e.g., Cullity, 1987) and in both the UK and US some stockbrokers have developed leading indicators for inflation.

SURVEY DATA

As we have seen, survey data are included in the cyclical indicators. Survey data are important, if only because they are available sooner than other forms of data.

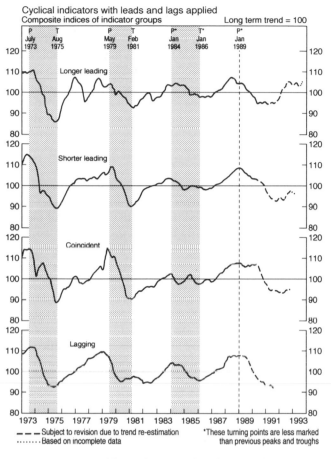

Figure 27 (*continued*)

There are many surveys available, but the most useful is the *CBI Quarterly Industrial Trends Survey*. Its data appear before more detailed Government surveys and it has a longer record than other surveys which makes it easier to establish its statistical properties. The CBI's business optimism measure is particularly useful for forecasting changes in national income. A wide range of information relating to inflation, consumer behaviour and growth is provided. Non-economists will find press reports of the CBI surveys easy to assimilate. Other surveys, covering exports, particular regions and other areas of special interest are reported in the press with varying degrees of coverage.

Probably the best of the US surveys is the National Association of Purchasing Management's *Report on Business*, which is widely followed. There is a UK sister organization which has been producing for a few years a comparable UK survey, the *Purchasing Managers' Report on Business*.

STRUCTURAL ECONOMETRIC MODELS

Most of the major UK stockbroking firms forecast the UK economy by means of a structural macroeconomic econometric model. A macroeconomic model is a simplified representation of the entire economy, expressed in equation form, and its goal is to forecast variables such as national output, inflation, and the balance of payments.

We can look at some of the issues involved in structural models by means of a simple example. If we view national income in terms of the nation's expenditures we might define it as follows:

$$Y = C + G + I + X - M$$

i.e., national income (Y) is made up of consumer expenditure (C), plus government expenditure (G), plus business investment (I), plus exports (X), minus imports (M). To forecast Y, we need to know the value of all the other variables, which the econometrician will attempt to forecast by a series of equations. Consumption, for example, might be forecast by an equation that includes income and interest rates, i.e., we spend more when we have more income and interest rates are low. Most variables in a model will be endogenous, i.e., determined within the model, but some will be exogenous, i.e., determined outside the model. For example, in a model of the UK economy, the level of exports will be partly determined by the level of world trade which will not be determined in the model but will be given a value assumed by the econometrician. Notice that in our example income depends partly on consumption and consumption in turn depends partly on income. A model is much better at keeping track of these simultaneous interactions than a human forecaster. Econometric models vary as to the number of equations they contain, ranging from a handful to hundreds. These equations are all based on appropriate economic theory.

The structural econometric approach appears to be very scientific and disciplined, but is less so in practice. There are similarities with a Punch and Judy show. At first sight Mr Punch appears to act as he pleases, but one soon realizes that a guiding hand is involved. So too with econometricians and their models.

Although economic theory is used to guide the specification of the model, there are sometimes competing theories to choose from. Moreover, theory seldom specifies the exact form of the equation to be used or, if it is thought that some effects take place with a lag, the length of the lags. For example, will 1% off interest rates when they are 15% have the same effect on consumption as 1% off rates when they are 6%, and will you spend more immediately a cut in rates has been made or will you wait a month or two? Usually the form of the equation and length of the lags is determined by playing with the data until the best fit is found. Behavioural equations (e.g., the consumption equation) will not provide an exact fit to the data, if only because not every relevant factor will be included in the equation. They will have a residual error term. Many theories involve expectations and it is unclear how these should be modelled. Usually expectations are assumed to be based on past and current values of a variable—e.g., expected inflation for 1994 will be low because it is now and has been in the recent past. But what would happen if there was a change in government, would expectations be formed on past data then? After the problems discussed have been resolved, the next stage is to estimate the model. At this stage, some theoretically relevant variables may not appear to be statistically significant and may be dropped from the model. Lag structures may be altered. There is a back-and-forth process between theory and the data.

If the model has been completed to the econometrician's satisfaction, a forecast can be made. This will require some exogenous values to be inserted by the econometrician. When the econometrician makes a forecast, the result may turn out to be implausible. At that point, the econometrician may tamper with the model by changing the residuals to get a more plausible forecast. The published forecast of a model may well owe as much to the econometrician's interventions as to the model's structure.

Clearly, a great deal of work goes into building a structural econometric model. How good are the results? The general feeling is that they are not very good. Davies and Shah (1992) give a typical gloomy assessment (Davies is one of the UK Chancellor's Seven Wise Men). They argue that the models are fine when not much changes, but they cannot cope with big changes in the economic environment such as oil price shocks and high inflation. They fail when they are most needed. This is because:

1. there is a large subjective element in model building, as we have seen;
2. the equation estimation is based on data that is frequently revised (i.e., the CSO publishes data which the econometrician uses and a year or two later the CSO revises—changes—the data, so the econometrician has used the wrong data when estimating a forecasting relationship);
3. many relationships are unstable, especially if economic policy changes. For example, consumption has recently been lower than most of the models forecast because of the effect of a new phenomenon, negative house equity.

All this may make some investors agree with Ezra Solomon, who apparently said: 'the only function of economic forecasting is to make astrology respectable.'

Despite these gloomy comments, there are numerous econometric forecasts produced by the UK Treasury, UK stockbrokers, and various commercial organizations. Moreover these forecasts are studied by investors. Which forecaster is best? Evaluating econometric forecasts is not simple, but the general finding is that there is no consistently best buy amongst forecasters. Combining forecasts leads to increased accuracy and, somewhat surprisingly perhaps, simple averaging of forecasts is useful (Clemen, 1989).

There is good news and bad news for investors on structural economic models. The good news is that non-econometricians can relax. They do not have to understand the details of structural econometric forecasts. They can simply look at the forecasts of a large group of forecasters and average them. This sort of information is periodically available in the *Financial Times* or available on subscription from organizations such as *Consensus Economics*. The bad news is that these average forecasts will not be very accurate.

SINGLE EQUATION MODELS

We have seen the complexity and the problems of structural econometric models and we have seen that simpler methods such as leading indicators or surveys provide some useful information. In the US there have been attempts to make econometric forecasts of single variables, such as GNP changes, or inflation, from a single equation which uses traditional leading indicators, survey data and financial spread variables.

Financial spread variables include the term spread, the difference between three month and ten year bond yields (see Estrella and Hardouvelis, 1991, for a very favourable review of the merits of this indicator) and the quality spread, the difference in yields on corporate and government bonds. What is the rationale for using financial spread variables? For the term spread, rising short rates relative to long suggests economic policy is being tightened and this signals a slow-down in GNP. For the quality spread, corporate bonds yield more than government bonds because corporate issues may default; when the spread widens, this signifies a belief that default is more likely, something associated with a slow-down in GNP. In the UK, the corporate bond market is not large and this statistic is not widely followed. Term spread data is readily available and do-it-yourself forecasters may be interested in Figure 28. This shows the transformation of the UK yield curve around the UK's exit from the ERM, with the spread changing from −1% to +1%. It is said that they never ring a bell at the top or bottom of the market. This dramatic transformation did seem to suggest that the market was ringing a bell for the end of the recession.

Davies and Shah (1992) claim good results for forecasting the annual change in the UK's GDP based on an equation which includes the following variables; (i) the 20 year gilt yield less the FT500 earnings yield; (ii) the 20 year gilt yield less the three month inter-bank rate; (iii) the annual change in real oil prices; (iv) the Central Statistical Office longer leading indicator. There are two problems with this type of equation. First, we are back to forecasting GNP for the financial markets by using the financial markets themselves. Second, many equations were tested and this one is used because it worked historically. The dangers of data-mining are clear enough. This is a general problem for single equation forecasts. They are likely to offer great promise because, freed from the necessity of specifying a detailed and consistent theory, the forecaster is set loose to find a good historical fit. Such fits can be found, but will they apply in the future? Even good out-of-sample historical fits are no guarantee of future fits. What does seem likely is that UK forecasters will make more use of financial spread forecasts, which do have some theoretical justification and have worked for long periods in a number of countries.

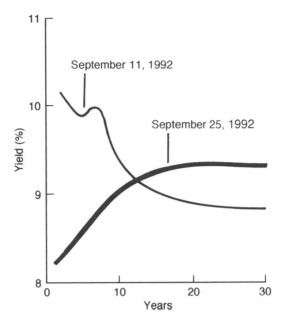

Figure 28   UK Gilt Yield Curves

VECTOR AUTOREGRESSIVE MODELS

We referred earlier to the macroeconometric models as structural. This means that the specific relationships between the variables are based on economic theory although, as we saw, in practice there is a back-and-forth movement from theory to data. Econometricians switch from theory to imposing their own beliefs or seeing which equation fits the data best. One could argue that the data should completely determine the forecasting equation. Vector autoregressions (VARs) are a means of doing this. The forecaster specifies the variables that are believed to be relevant on the basis of prior theory, and the largest number of lags required, and then lets the data speak. The model estimates how variables are related to lagged values of other variables and without restriction as to which variables affect which. VAR models are attractive in being easy to construct (by people who like that kind of thing!), require little subjective input from the forecaster and, because they can operate with few variables, are easy to update. There are, however, two major technical problems. First, macroeconomic series are highly correlated with their own past values and with other series, and this makes it hard to estimate parameters accurately and decide whether they are statistically significant. Also, if there are many lags, the number of estimates relative to the amount of data becomes large, and this makes the forecasts less reliable. One can overcome this by reducing the number of lags, but this undermines the approach of letting the data speak.

VAR models are a relatively recent development—interest in these models was sparked only a little over a decade ago by Sims (1980). A reasonably non-technical discussion is Schlegel (1985). The models are becoming increasingly popular and the academic journals carry an increasing number of articles on them. In the financial sector, the Bank of England has reported work on a VAR model of inflation (Henry and Pesaran, 1993) and stockbroker Goldman Sachs (Davies and Shah, 1992) has reported a VAR model of GDP. It is too early to assess the value of VAR forecasts.

CONCLUDING COMMENTS

There are many forecasting methods and none is foolproof. Combining forecasts, even by the simple procedure of averaging, is worthwhile. A workable strategy for non-economists would be to average the forecasts produced by econometric models and try to assess the likelihood of the forecasters being right and the direction in which they are likely to revise their forecasts by carefully following developments via the cyclical indicators and survey data. Structural economic models have often failed when big changes in the economy have taken place. If a major economic change takes place investors may be well advised to treat the models with an extra degree of scepticism. Problems with structural economic models have led to more interest in single equation models and VAR forecasts. It is too early to say whether these approaches will improve economic forecasts.

The problem of forecasting can lead investors in two divergent directions. One is to work hard at improving forecasting skills. The other is to take the view that forecasting the future is for astrologers and to devise investment strategies that minimize the use of forecasts. Both of these approaches are defensible. Not knowing which approach you believe in isn't.

25

Business Cycle Anticipation and Scenario Forecasting

As we saw in Figure 27, the course of the economy is not smooth: there are periodic fluctuations in economic activity, usually referred to as the business cycle. As the economy moves through a cycle, from recession to boom, profits rise and fall, as do interest rates, the rate of inflation and so forth. These factors are important in valuing securities, so it is not surprising that the financial markets move in response to the business cycle. But the economy and markets do not move in perfect unison, in fact the markets tend to anticipate the course of the economic cycle. If there is some regular pattern to the business cycle, and if the markets respond in some regular way to the business cycle, business cycle anticipation becomes a method on which tactical asset allocation can be based. Siegel (1991) reviewed US data and claimed that switching from stocks to bonds before business cycle peaks and back into stocks before business cycle troughs significantly improved returns.

Business cycles and their relation to the financial markets are much more intensively studied in the US than the UK. The average sequence of business cycle and financial market leads and lags in the US for the period 1920–82 is shown in Table 49. The same broad pattern may be expected in the UK.

Table 49 US Business Cycle and Financial Market Leads and Lags: 1920–82

Event	Months
Stock price trough to business cycle trough	5
Business cycle trough to bond yield trough	8
Bond yield trough to stock price peak	13
Stock price peak to business cycle peak	7
Business cycle peak to bond yield peak	1
Bond yield peak to stock price trough	6

Source: Moore and Cullity (1988, p. 62). Reproduced by permission of Dow Jones-Irwin

WHAT EXPLAINS THE MARKET/ECONOMY PATTERNS?

We can explain the general pattern shown in Table 49 as follows:

1. The story begins with the stock market anticipating, on average by five months, the end of recession. At this time interest rates are likely to be low, reflecting low demand for credit, falling inflation and monetary easing.

2. Once the economy starts to pick up, bond yields will begin to rise, on average eight months after the trough of the recession. Credit demands increase and bond purchasers will anticipate future inflation and expect higher nominal returns. The authorities will stop easing monetary policy and there will be expectations that the next move in short interest rates will be up.

3. Rising interest rates at first do not hurt the stock market. Investors will be focusing on large profit gains and equities will look attractive, especially against rising bond yields (i.e., falling bond prices and declining capital values). As time passes, rising credit demands, increasing inflation and tighter monetary policy will force up interest rates further, and this will start to slow the economy. The equity market will begin to focus on the competition from higher yields on bonds and cash. Prospects for profits will deteriorate as costs rise and margins can no longer be pushed up. Investment in plant and machinery may slow as a result of inadequate prospective returns caused by poorer profit prospects and a higher investment discount rate, resulting from higher interest rates. The stock market will peak.

4. The pressure from the authorities to slow the economy, and the natural slow-down resulting from reduced business investment, will cause the economic cycle to turn down. The stock market will fall.

5. The pressures pushing bond yields up when the economy was growing now operate in reverse and bond yields will start to fall.

6. The move into recession will continue, the authorities will start easing policy, inflationary pressures begin to dissipate and, after a period, the stock market will trough.

Now the above story is illustrative only and the exact same pattern will not be followed on every occasion. Also, the story focuses on monetary policy, but fiscal policy will be adjusted too. Sometimes recessions may be triggered by external factors, such as a world oil price hike. Booms can also be triggered by external factors. The general thrust of the story, however, seems valid enough. (For a detailed idealized economic cycle related to the stock market see McWilliams, 1984.)

One question often asked is whether the stock market forecasts the economic cycle or simply responds to concurrent events. The answer is probably a bit of both. Certainly investors do try to act in advance of the economic cycle. But they also respond to some concurrent events: for example market peaks and troughs are within a few months of profit peaks and troughs. The reason profits turn up as soon as the business cycle picks up is not so much a result of sales increases, but the fact that during the recession firms will have been struggling to reduce their costs, and they seem to achieve this just as the cycle turns.

IS THE PATTERN USEFUL?

A problem with business cycle anticipation as a timing strategy is that what has been described are averages within wide ranges: for example, while on average US bond yield troughs have led stock price peaks by 13 months, the range is 1 to 31 months. Further, the turning point in bond yields, the stock market and the economy do not always match up, so a sequence cannot always be recorded. Do these problems mean business cycle anticipation has no value for tactical asset allocation? Not necessarily.

First, some notion of a business cycle provides a useful framework around which investors can organize their views of the economy. Most investors probably use some version of the cycle to help them with their timing decisions. Second, although each business cycle is unique, this is not a problem if there are different causal factors which can be identified and which are simply combined in different amounts for each cycle. Of course, because stock prices lead the economy, what we need are factors that lead both the economy and stock prices. In the previous chapter, we discussed using leading indicators for forecasting the economy. In this section we are discussing using economic variables to form a leading indicator of markets. DuBois (1988) argues that measures of liquidity, interest rates, Federal Reserve policy and so on are important lead factors in the US. He has created a cyclical equity index combining four variables and claims high predictive ability for his index. The information coefficients claimed (e.g., 0.29 on a one month horizon and 0.46 on a 12 month horizon) are far higher than is typical in investment analysis and higher than DuBois found for valuation-based approaches. DuBois also has a bond cyclical index based on measures of economic, financial and inflation pressures, and again claims high information coefficients.

It is worth noting that the values for the variables used in DuBois' model are current values and not forecasts. The variables used, and the way of combining them, is not given. Unfortunately, many business cycle models are proprietary and the details are not published. An example of a simple system that has been published is provided by Zweig (1986). Zweig forecasts the equity market by combining monetary indicators and momentum indicators. There are three monetary indicators: changes in the prime rate, a measure of the Federal Reserve Bank's policy and an installment debt indicator. Each indicator is measured on a simple scoring system and the points are then added up. This aggregate score gives bullish, bearish or neutral signals. This is a perfectly straightforward approach which is based on business cycle anticipation and Zweig claims good results. Many brokers incorporate business cycle indicators in their market analysis. Elaine Garzarelli, of Shearson Lehman Brothers, and well known for forecasting the 1987 crash, uses a model that includes 10 economic and monetary indicators.

A recent interesting study by Boehm and Moore (1991) attempts to allocate between stocks, bills and bonds in five countries by use of leading indexes. For Australia, Japan, the UK, the US and West Germany, longer leading stock indexes have been developed. These are made up of four leading indicators—new housing permits or approvals, real M1 or M2, a price-cost ratio, and the yield on long-term bonds. Each index gives buy and sell signals based on the movements of the smoothed growth rate of the index. How well does this method work? Table 50 summarizes the investment experience in stocks and short-term securities during periods signalled by the long leading indexes for the five countries. Note that these are not true bull and bear market returns but returns achieved during periods designated as bull or bear by the indicators.

The first and second rows suggest the model can distinguish between periods of high and low returns, although modestly so in the case of the UK. Row three shows the return from holding stocks for the entire period—an equity buy and hold strategy—and row four shows the return from short-term bills. Section three shows the return from investing in equities in bull periods and bills in bear periods. Notice that in the UK a higher return would have been achieved by always being invested in equities and the difference between the buy and hold strategy and the bull/stocks and bear/bills strategy is modest for two other countries. Moreover, Boehm and Moore do not appear to allow for any costs. The standard deviation of returns is lower for the mixed strategy than the buy and hold strategy, so on a risk-adjusted basis the strategy appears slightly better. However, Boehm and Moore note that in the cheap money 1950s and 1960s, the buy and hold strategy outperformed in both Japan and the US.

What happens to the analysis if investment in bonds is permitted? Leading inflation indexes have been constructed for Australia and the US, which use measures of the proportion of the labour force in employment, commodity price movements, the growth of debt, and survey data on business price expectations (for details see Cullity, 1987). The indexes give about a six month lead in forecasting inflation. The smoothed growth rate of the index is used by Boehm and Moore as a signal for rising or falling interest rates.

Boehm and Moore argue that if a bear signal is given for the equity market and the inflation index gives a signal that interest rates and inflation will fall, bonds should be bought. But if interest rates and inflation are likely to rise, cash should be held. Unfortunately, the results for the US and Australia show no substantial difference between switching between stocks and bills and between stocks, bills and bonds.

Table 50 Summary of Investment Experience in Stocks and Short-term Securities During Periods Signalled by Long-Leading Indexes, Five Countries

	Australia 1970–89	Japan 1971–89	United Kingdom 1968–89	United States 1969–89	West Germany 1970–90
(1) *Stocks*					
(a) Total average annual rates of return:					
Bull-market periods	17.8	20.1	16.7	14.0	11.2
Bear-market periods	3.7	8.3	10.9	5.9	3.8
All periods	13.2	18.3	15.0	11.3	8.7
(b) Standard deviation of rates of return during:					
Bull-market periods	10.4	37.3	27.7	5.5	8.6
Bear-market periods	18.1	21.9	13.7	21.3	15.0
All periods	15.6	31.4	21.9	16.3	12.2
(2) *Short term securities*					
(a) Total average annual rates of return:					
Bull-market periods	11.5	6.1	10.1	6.9	5.2
Bear-market periods	12.2	10.5	9.8	8.8	8.3
All periods	11.7	6.8	10.0	7.6	6.1
(b) Standard deviation of rates of return during:					
Bull-market periods	3.2	1.0	3.0	3.9	0.9
Bear-market periods	3.5	2.1	3.5	2.3	1.8
All periods	3.4	1.9	3.3	3.4	1.5
(3) *Holding stocks during bull markets and short-term securities during bear markets*					
(a) Total average annual rates of return:					
All periods	16.3	18.7	14.6	12.2	10.3
(b) Standard deviation8.1	30.7	19.9	4.2	6.5	

Source: Boehm and Moore (1991, p. 367). Reproduced by permission of the authors and Elsevier Science Publishers BV

SCENARIO FORECASTING

We have looked in the above sections to see how we might use short-term business cycle anticipation to help in tactical asset allocation. In Chapter 22 we discussed asset-liability modelling. For such modelling, long-term historical averages would have been used. We might have used the data shown in Table 4 in Chapter 2. In this section we are going to look at medium term relationships and relate them to economic conditions. This is not exactly business cycle anticipation, but it is a natural extension.

Farrell (1983 and 1989) has discussed scenario forecasting, which is concerned with forecasting events over a three to five year period. If you look back to Figure 1 (p. 8), you will see that irrespective of the merits of the average as a descriptive statistic, the market spends an awfully long time at anywhere but the average. Is there some pattern to these departures from the average? Farrell has classified US equity return history by various periods, as shown in Table 51.

Table 51   US Historical Return Experience: 1929–86

Economic Environment	Deflation Without Recovery	Deflation With Recovery	Controls	Good Times	Inflation	Disinflation
Years	1929–33	1934–38	1939–45	1946–65	1966–80	1981–86
Stocks	–6.7%	15.3%	11.5%	15.0%	5.6%	15.3%
Bonds	6.2	7.8	3.5	2.3	4.6	18.1
Treasury Bills	1.9	0.2	0.2	1.9	5.7	9.6

Source: Farrell (1989, p. 35). Reproduced by permission

Farrell's classification is unfortunate in as much as he makes each environment historically unique. However, his data does suggest that far from being an inflation hedge, equities perform well in any period except inflationary periods and periods of deflation with no prospect of recovery. Other studies have shown equities perform poorly in inflationary periods (see especially Ibbotson and Brinson, 1987, p. 89 for US evidence for 195 years). For the UK, the evidence is similar, as shown in Table 52.

Table 52   UK Historical Return Experience: 1919–38 and 1946–91

Growth	Inflation	Number of years	Average real equity return %	Average real bond return %
greater than 7%	6% or less	9	+9.3	+1.0
+3% to +7%	6% or less	18	+17.1	+0.7
less than 3%	6% or less	25	+7.9	+8.4
all growth rates	above 6%	13	+4.9	–5.1

Source: Barclays de Zoete Wedd (1992, p. 7). Reproduced by permission

The evidence suggests that certain economic states, or scenarios, and asset returns may be related, as shown in Table 53.

Table 53 Possible Scenarios and Asset Class Performance

Scenario	Best Asset Class
High growth/low inflation	Common stocks
Disinflation/low growth	Bonds
Deflation	Bonds
Inflation	Cash equivalents

Source: Farrell (1989, p. 36). Reproduced by permission

What the data suggests is that it may be worthwhile to try and forecast the likely economic scenario that will prevail over the next few years. This would be useful for exercises such as asset/liability modelling where an investor might use historical return patterns associated with the anticipated environment, rather than long run averages. Asset allocation bets could also be made on the basis of scenarios. Of course, for this to be profitable, (a) future returns must relate to scenarios in the same way as they did in the past and, (b) the investor must be good at economic forecasting. You knew there would be a catch.

INFLATION AND EQUITIES

It is worth saying a little more about the relationship between inflation and equity returns. We will give some background here and discuss the issue again in Chapters 26 and 27.

There are three main reasons why equities might perform poorly in high inflation periods. Economic prospects may worsen, risk may increase and investors may make valuation errors. With inflation, firms may suffer adverse cost and price impacts. Some firms may not be able to achieve price increases as quickly as they suffer cost increases, and may face government pressure to restrain prices and be subject to increased international competition. Capital investments and stocks will be more expensive and affect cash flow. Company accounts will become more inaccurate. Investors may feel that prospects have been damaged and may demand a higher risk premium. We can illustrate these effects in terms of the constant growth dividend discount model, i.e.,

$$P = \frac{D}{k - g}$$

where P is the index value, D is the current dividend, k is the discount rate, required rate or expected return, and g is the growth rate of dividends. We can rearrange terms so that:

$$k = \frac{D}{P} + g \qquad \text{i.e.,}$$

expected return = dividend yield + dividend growth rate

In equilibrium, we would expect the returns from equities to equal the return from bonds (i.e., the redemption yield) plus an equity risk premium to compensate for the greater risk of equities, i.e.,

dividend yield + dividend growth rate = bond yield + equity risk premium

If something happens to affect one component of the expression, some adjustment must take place in another component to keep the expression true. If equities are seen as riskier, the equity risk premium will increase and the dividend yield will rise, i.e., prices will fall. If economic prospects deteriorate, dividend growth will be lower, and this too will lead to a higher dividend yield, i.e., share prices will fall again. These are two ways inflation can hurt equity returns.

We can use this framework to look at valuation errors. Imagine that inflation has no real effects on the economy. This may seem unlikely, and of course firms may find it difficult to adjust to a change in inflation, but after a while they ought to be able to do so. Let's make the assumption anyway. We would expect bond investors to focus on real returns, i.e., the redemption yield less the rate of inflation. If inflation were to rise by 1%, we would expect nominal bond returns to rise by 1% to offer the same real return. If inflation has no real effect on the economy, then firms should be able to raise their earnings by 1% and their rate of dividend growth by 1% too. Our expression would be back in balance without dividend yields rising. Bond returns have risen by 1% and dividend growth has risen by 1%. But, if investors focus on the nominal dividend yield and the nominal bond yield, they may demand an increase in the dividend yield when bond yields rise. Equity investors would be making a valuation error, because they will automatically be compensated for higher inflation through faster dividend growth. They would force down equity prices unnecessarily, and raise the equity risk premium. This valuation error argument has been propounded by Modigliani and Cohn (1979 and 1982), who argue that investors have underpriced equities during periods of inflation.

CONCLUDING COMMENTS

The course of the financial markets and the economy are linked. The stages of the business cycle may be discussed in idealized terms and this may be helpful in forecasting the equity market. Three studies were cited which involve use of leading indicators of the economy and market. The results suggest business cycle anticipation is worth attempting. However the study by Boehm and Moore carries the useful lesson that seemingly good forecasting ability does not necessarily translate fully into investment gains.

Economic scenario forecasting was briefly discussed. The relatively poor performance of equities in periods of high inflation was noted. There are at least three possible reasons for this: inflation may impair real economic activity, investors may see the outlook as being riskier and investors may make valuation errors.

26
Price-Earnings Ratio
Valuation Measures

Two of the most widely used market valuation measures are the market price-earnings ratio and the market yield. These may be considered on their own or in relation to other variables. In this chapter we review some approaches which use the price-earnings ratio as a market valuation method and we also look at how the market price-earnings ratio is forecast. We look at yield measures in the next chapter.

ABSOLUTE PRICE-EARNINGS RATIO

If we believe that the market swings about too much around some notion of fair value then, if we examine a measure of value, we might expect that when the

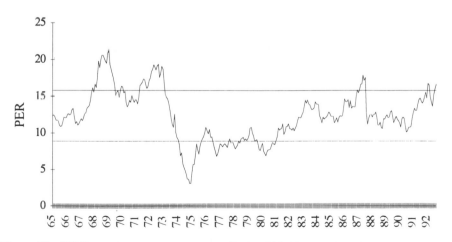

Figure 29 UK Equity Market Price-Earnings Ratio 1965–92. Copyright © 1993 Datastream International Ltd

market has moved away from the average level of the measure, it will move back towards it. The simplest valuation measure that can be derived from the market's price-earnings ratio is the absolute level of the ratio. Figure 29 shows the UK price-earnings ratio from 1965 to 1992.

The obvious decision rule is to sell at high price-earnings ratio levels and buy at low. But how useful would this approach really be? What exactly would the decision rule be? The two horizontal lines in Figure 29 are the plus one and minus one standard deviations. The location of these lines depends on how long a history we include in our calculations. One might argue that there appear to be two series, one before the early 1970s and one after. Of course, in the mid-1970s we would not have known that. Had we calculated the plus and minus one standard deviation lines based on data for 1965–74, and extrapolated that forward, even the peak of October 1987 would have fallen within the plus one standard deviation line. It is not self-evident that price-earnings ratios are useful and a detailed analysis is necessary. Bleiberg (1989) has carried out a useful analysis for the US market and we report some of his findings.

Bleiberg sorted quarterly US market price-earnings ratios for the period 1938–87 into quintiles. He then examined market performance by quintile. His data are shown in Table 54.

Table 54   US Market Index Performance by Price-Earnings Ratio Quintile: 1938–87

	P/E values		S&P 500: average % change over subsequent:		
P/E quintile	Low	High	6 months	12 months	24 months
1	17.81	22.43	−0.99	0.24	−0.68
2	14.29	17.77	5.82	6.96	8.86
3	11.23	14.28	3.34	8.09	16.57
4	9.04	11.19	4.20	8.99	25.57
5	5.90	9.01	7.99	16.21	29.79
Overall average			4.07	8.18	16.39

Source: Bleiberg (1989, p. 27). This copyrighted material is reprinted with the permission of the *Journal of Portfolio Management.*

The final column of Table 54 shows that over a two year period there is a clear relationship between quintiles and performance. Over shorter periods, the relationship holds for the extreme quintiles but either weakly, or not at all, for the intermediate quintiles. It must be stressed that the relationship shown is what happens on average—there is nonetheless plenty of scope for it not to hold true for any particular period. For example, the probability of the market rising in a six month period was 63%—there was a 73% probability for a market in the lowest price-earnings ratio quintile rising but also a 60% probability for a market in the highest quintile rising too. Or, another example, there is a one in four chance that the market will decline in the next six months even when the price-earnings ratio is low, and a three in five chance that it will rise even when the price-earnings ratio is high.

Over a two year horizon, the odds of a low multiple market falling are reduced and vice versa for a high multiple market.

It is likely that low market price-earnings ratios go hand in hand with high bond yields. If falling bond yields are part of the reason for a rising market, perhaps low multiple markets perform well, but bonds perform better because they start with a high yield, and then achieve capital gains as well. Bleiberg examined this possibility by relating the relative return of stocks over bonds to price-earnings ratio quintiles. The results were very similar to those just discussed. Low price-earnings ratio markets did best.

So far, so good, but what decision rules should we use for real world asset allocation? Bleiberg used all the available data in his analysis—what would be more interesting would be some kind of test using rules devised from part of the data and tested on the rest of the data. And that is what Bleiberg did. He determined the cut-off values for his quintiles by looking at the first 25 years of his data. He decided the portfolio would be invested in 50% stocks and 50% bonds if the market price-earnings ratio fell in the middle quintile and would shift more to equities if the market ratio was in the second lowest price-earnings quintile and even more if it was in the lowest. And vice versa for high multiple quintiles. The amount of the portfolio that was switched varied by 5% increments from 5% through to 25% in a test of five different allocation strategies.

The future wasn't the same as the past. First the multiples differed in the two periods: 40% of the observations of the market multiple in the period 1963-87 fell into the top quintile as defined by the 1938-62 observations. Second, the return relationships were a bit erratic. The lowest price-earnings ratio markets did perform best over six, twelve and twenty four months both in absolute terms and relative to bonds. But the other quintiles had an erratic relationship with returns over six and twelve months and also for the returns relative to bonds for the twenty four month period. The result was that none of the five active asset allocation strategies produced a higher return than a static 50/50 stock/bond mix and only one beat the 50/50 mix if both return and volatility of returns were considered.

Bleiberg's final comments (p. 31) provide a sensible conclusion:

"Is P/E useless as a valuation measure? No, not that. What I'm saying is that yes, the future will be like the past but only in broad outline .... On average, the return on stocks (both absolute and relative) will be higher in the periods following low P/E values than in periods following high P/E values.... But that's as far as we can go .... An 'overvalued' market can do well for quite a while. Historical P/Es are not graven in stone as valuation indicators. They tell us something about probabilities and expected returns, but it remains far from clear how portfolio managers can use that information profitably".

THE PRICE-EARNINGS RATIO RELATIVE TO GILTS

Although some investors look at the absolute price-earnings ratio alone, most relate it to bonds. A common way of making this relative valuation is to look at a

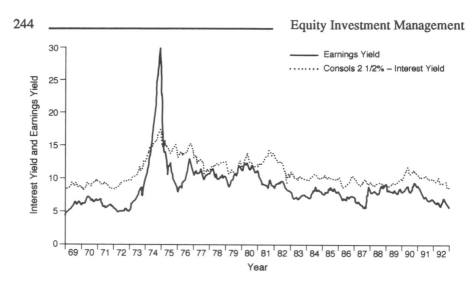

Figure 30 UK Earnings Yield and Bond Yield: 1969–92. Copyright © 1993 Datastream International Ltd

graph of the earnings yield (which is the reciprocal of the price-earnings ratio) and a long bond yield. Figure 30 shows the earnings yield for Datastream's UK Total Market Index and the yield on Consols 2 1/2%, an irredeemable gilt-edged stock.

Some analysts use the ratio of the two lines, some use the gap between them. We'll discuss the latter here. The procedure is a mixture of science and sorcery; it consists of deciding whether the gap between the lines, either current or prospective (i.e., taking either current values or using interest rate forecasts and earnings growth forecasts to project the lines forward twelve months) is appropriate or not, and the effect any adjustment will have on the market level and returns.

It is reasonable to ask why the gap between the two lines in Figure 30 has economic meaning. The dividend discount model and a little algebraic manipulation shed some light. Recall the constant growth version of the dividend discount model:

$$P = \frac{D}{k - g}$$

We want to manipulate this to see what the bond yield less the earnings yield relates to. To introduce bond yields into the equation we will replace k, the discount rate, by i plus z, where i is a bond yield and z is the equity risk premium. Let us also divide both sides by earnings, E. Then:

$$\frac{P}{E} = \frac{D}{E} \times \frac{1}{i + z - g}$$

The term D/E is the payout ratio. Rearranging terms:

$$i + z - g = \frac{D}{E} \times \frac{E}{P}$$

We are interested in the difference between the bond yield and the earnings yield, so if we rearrange terms once more:

$$i - \left(\frac{D}{E} \times \frac{E}{P}\right) = g - z$$

This tells us that the gap between the bond yield and earnings yield is related to the dividend growth rate and equity risk premium: specifically, the lower the required premium and the higher the growth rate, the greater will be the difference between the bond yield and the earnings yield. The gap will also be larger the lower is the payout ratio. If all earnings were paid out as dividends, we could simplify the last expression further since the payout ratio would be 1, i.e.:

$$i - \frac{E}{P} = g - z$$

While talking about the gap between two lines may appear to be unscientific, there would appear to be some theoretical justification which also has some empirical support, for example, Reilly, *et al.* (1983).

If we refer back to Figure 30 we see an interesting pattern. There would appear to be a roughly constant size gap between the two lines for the first few years. Then the gap disappears as equities are de-rated. It opens up again in the 1980s, narrows towards the end of the 1980s and then opens up again. We have already noted in Chapter 25 that real returns are lower in periods of high inflation. From 1973 to 1981, inflation was very much higher than it had been in the previous decades, and only in one year was it in single digits. Inflation did not appear in our equation above, but US and UK evidence suggests that as a practical matter it should be incorporated into investment decision making. The gap opened up again before inflation fell back to lower levels, but this is not too surprising. In 1979 Mrs. Thatcher became Prime Minister and the financial markets anticipated lower inflation. The narrowing of the gap at the end of the 1980s coincided with the crash of 1987 (which might be expected to lead to higher required risk premiums for a period), a steady increase and then decline in the rate of inflation (1987, +3.7%, 1988, +6.8%, 1989, +7.7%, 1990, +9.3%, 1991, +4.6%), and a change in the relationship of gilt yields to other yields. This was a consequence of a public sector surplus, when gilts were being bought-in by the Government, rather than being issued. As a result, gilt yields became expensive against other bonds.

The above discussion combines a view that the bond yield less the earnings yield is a meaningful statistic and that its size varies with factors that can be analysed. Essentially what we are doing is plotting the earnings yield against one variable, bond yields, but allowing for other variables by "guesstimating" the variation between the two graphed variables. To make asset allocation decisions an investor might go through the following steps:

1. forecast bond yields and calculate the one year total return;
2. forecast profit growth over the next year and calculate the prospective earnings yield;
3. decide whether the bond yield less earnings yield gap should widen or narrow based on factors such as inflation, stage in the economic cycle, political uncertainty, and so forth;
4. decide the change in the equity market required to make steps two and three consistent;
5. calculate the prospective total return on equities (i.e. capital change plus income) and compare this to the total return from bonds.

This sort of approach might be described as disciplined subjectivity and is typical of many approaches used in the UK. Because of the subjective inputs, both in terms of the variables used and the forecasts made for them, there is no evidence available as to whether investors are able to use it to outperform. But it should be noted that any relationships that exist have limited explanatory power. In the mid-1960s the earnings yield was more than the gilt yield, despite low inflation and steady economic growth, and inflation in 1970–72 was far higher than in the 1960s.

FORECASTING THE PRICE-EARNINGS RATIO

We saw above that we needed to forecast the prospective market price-earnings ratio which in turn required a forecast of profits for the next year or two. How is the profit forecast made? There are two main sources of such forecasts: from economists and from analysts. These two forecast sources influence each other—the analysts use economists' forecasts of the economy as background information and may be influenced by economists' profit forecasts, and economists tend to sneak a look at analysts' profit forecasts and may modify their own if the forecasts are too far apart.

Aggregating Analysts' Profit Forecasts

Using analysts' forecasts is much the easiest way of determining the prospective market price-earnings ratio. The usual procedure is simply to aggregate each sector analyst's company earnings per share forecasts and then aggregate each sector forecast to arrive at a forecast for the industrial sector—including or excluding oils—or the entire market. Not all companies have the same year end, so some rough and ready allocations of earnings from company years to calendar years have to be made.

Usually it is earnings per share rather than profits that are aggregated and it is earnings rather than profits that are of interest to investors. The earnings figures are very much affected by how companies treat various one-off items: write-offs have had a major impact in recent years, especially in the US. There has been a tendency in the last few years in the US to state the market's earnings before write-offs, on the grounds that this gives a better estimate of the long-term earnings power of companies. The new UK accounting regulations will require similar adjustments to be made in future in the UK.

A second advantage of using analysts' forecasts is that they relate to the stock market. Economists forecast profits for the entire economy and not all of the economy is quoted on the stock exchange (although after years of privatization this is less important than it was). Moreover national income profits are calculated on a different basis than stock exchange profits. The Central Statistical Office's annual profit figures for the economy are often 10 absolute percentage points different from those reported by stock exchange listed firms.

Economists' Profit Forecasts

Despite the above comments in favour of using analysts' forecasts it is worth looking at economists' forecasts because the analysts will have used at least part of the economists' forecasts in arriving at their own (e.g., interest rates, economic growth, the exchange rate, etc.) and there is a widespread suspicion—not well supported by the evidence—that analysts are generally too optimistic. It is said that company officers often give analysts a good guide to their prospects when all is going well, but they tend to be slow in passing on news about deteriorating prospects.

It is often argued that analysts not only tend to be optimistic in general but also tend to be too cautious in their forecasts of big profits changes. Economists, being more removed from contact with company executives, are more likely to make profit forecasts that reflect historical profit swings. And the swings have been large. Ignoring the recession that ended in 1992 or 1993, the previous five peaks in GDP growth have been followed by non-oil profit declines in the subsequent one and two years that have averaged over one-quarter and one-fifth respectively. Following troughs in GDP growth, profits have risen by a seventh in the first year and by a third in the second year.

Many economists do not forecast profits directly in their econometric model but obtain their forecast as a residual. Profits are what is left over after wages, rent and net interest, depreciation and indirect taxes are deducted from gross national product. For technical reasons it makes more sense to derive profits as a residual than to derive any of the other items as a residual. However, to the non-economist it may seem surprising to do this because profits are one of the driving forces of the economic system. Moreover, the residual will contain any statistical errors in any of the other variables so that profits derived as a residual may jump around erratically.

One way to improve the profits forecast is to modify the residual forecast by a non-econometric forecast or by a separate single forecasting equation. The former approach could be based on responses to CBI surveys. Goldman Sachs, for example, has derived a profits indicator from the *CBI Quarterly Industrial Trends Survey* which consists of a margins measure (derived from businessmen's responses to questions on prices and costs) which is then applied to the output response.

CONCLUDING COMMENTS

We have seen that the level of the market's price-earnings ratio may be helpful in deciding whether to increase or decrease equity weightings. A low price-earnings ratio increases the odds of good returns from equities but the definition of "low" varies from period to period and Bleiberg's study shows the difficulty in practice in using the rule. The rule might be improved by relating it to the level of inflation plus other factors such as growth rates. Most practitioners make some judgement about market levels in relation to the market price-earnings ratio and bond yields but the approach generally used is inherently subjective. One such approach was described. Finally, the use of analysts' and economists' profit forecasts for calculating the prospective market price-earnings ratio was discussed.

27
Yield and Dividend Valuation Measures

The format of this chapter is similar to that of the last. We look first at absolute yield, then yield in relation to bonds and finally we look at methods of forecasting yield.

ABSOLUTE YIELD

The simplest market yield valuation measure is the absolute value of the yield. Figure 31 shows the UK dividend yield since 1919. The yield has shown remarkable stability at around 5%—the mean value is, in fact, 5.13%—and the two horizontal lines are the plus and minus one standard deviation values. The US market has shown nothing like the same stability, with low yield periods in the mid-1950s through to the mid-1970s, and again in the last few years.

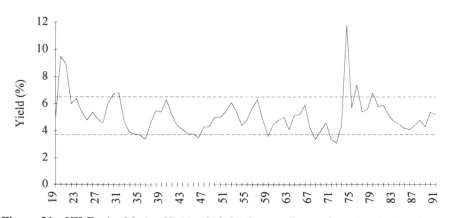

Figure 31 UK Equity Market Yield: 1919-91. Source: Drawn from data in Barclays de Zoete Wedd (1992, p. 68-9) by permission

The stability of the UK dividend yield may seem surprising given the wide range of economic and political circumstances that have prevailed since 1919. There have been booms and busts, war and peace; the rate of inflation has varied over a wide range and so too have bond yields; the private investor has been gradually displaced by tax-exempt institutional investors.

Swings in the dividend yield are a consequence of changes in the market index and changes in dividend payments. While there are a number of possible combinations of changes, since the Second World War cuts in the market's dividend payment have been rare. A decline in the market yield has almost always been the result of a rising market level.

Does the simple strategy of buying the market on high yields and selling on low yields work? There have been a number of US studies examining this (e.g., Rozeff, 1984; Fama and French, 1988a; Fuller and Kling, 1990). High dividend yields are related to subsequent high returns, but the same sort of problems noted by Bleiberg with regard to price-earnings ratios apply. Over long holding periods a yield-based strategy will work. Rozeff (1984) found in the US that over nine or ten year holding periods, returns increase continuously and monotonically as dividend yield in the prior year increases. In the UK the dividend yield has been much more stable than in the US, and it is a more powerful valuation tool.

EQUITY YIELDS RELATIVE TO BOND YIELDS

The above approach looks at equities in isolation. Many investors relate equity yields to bond yields. This can be done either as a difference or a ratio. In recent years the ratio has been the more useful measure and is shown in Figure 32.

Figure 32 UK Gilt/Equity Yield Ratio: 1970–92. Copyright © 1993 Datastream International Ltd

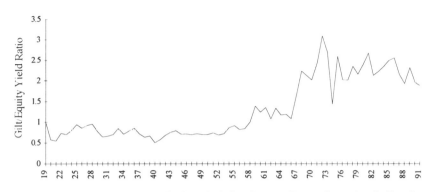

Figure 33 UK Gilt/Equity Yield Ratio: 1919–91. Source: Drawn from data in Barclays de Zoete Wedd (1992, p. 68–71) by permission

Based on consideration of diagrams such as Figure 32, various rules of thumb have been developed, such as investors should buy equities on yield ratios of less than 2 and sell on ratios of more than 2.6. Looking at the seven occasions between 1974 and 1991 when the yield ratio fell below 2, Wadhwani (1991c, p. 3) reports that for six of these, over the following 12 months, returns were superior to the average 12 month return over the entire period. Notice carefully that this is a statement about extreme values, it does not claim that less extreme values are helpful (recall Bleiberg's work).

Let us step back and look at a longer history. In Figure 33 we see that there appear to have been three distinct levels of the gilt/equity yield ratios. Equities used to yield more than gilts (to compensate for business risk) and then in the late 1950s gilts started to yield more than equities (because investors focused on the fact that equity yields grow over time but conventional gilt yields do not).

Some investors who have looked at this long run data are sceptical of rules such as buy at 2, sell at 2.6. They argue that the yield ratio has broadly reflected the level of inflation. Table 55 shows the yield ratio for three periods (selected on the basis of apparent shifts in the yield ratio in Figure 33) and the rate of inflation. There appears to be an obvious relationship. If inflation is set to fall in the UK, or even settle around 4-5%, it could be argued that the correct yield ratio should be much lower than it has been for the last 20 years.

Table 55 Average Yield Ratio and Rate of Inflation

Period	Yield Ratio	Inflation
1919–57	0.72	2.13%
1958–66	1.21	2.72%
1967–91	2.24	9.14%

Source: Calculated from data in Barclays de Zoete Wedd (1992, pp.68–71) by permission

Case	Dividend Yield %	+	Dividend Growth %	=	Redemption Yield %	+	Equity Risk Premium %	Gilt Equity Yield Ratio %
1	5	+	10	=	10	+	5	2
2	5	+	↑12	=	↑12	+	5	2.4
3	⇧6	+	12	=	12	+	↑6	2
4	⇧6	+	↑11	=	12	+	5	2
5	↑6	+	12	=	12	+	⇧6	2

Figure 34 The Response of the Equity/Yield Ratio to Inflation Changes

Should we expect a clear relationship between inflation and the gilt/equity yield ratio? Not necessarily, and to see this we will build on our discussion of inflation and equity returns at the end of Chapter 25. We will illustrate our discussion here with Figure 34. In this table the ↑ indicates which variable initiates a change and the ⇧ indicates which variable responds.

Case 1 sets out our initial conditions. This is a simple application of the constant growth dividend discount model and states that the dividend yield plus the dividend growth rate equals the redemption yield on gilts plus an equity risk premium. We have assumed that real growth is 3% and inflation is 7%, and that bonds are offering a 3% real yield. In Case 2 we assume inflation rises by 2% and bond purchasers demand the same real rate of return and that dividend growth automatically increases by 2%. Nothing else changes and, as a result, the gilt/equity yield ratio rises significantly. The real returns from equities and gilts are unchanged but the yield ratio implies that equities are less attractive. In this situation the yield ratio is misleading when inflation changes. In Case 3 we assume the same responses as in Case 2, but we also assume that investors believe risk has increased as a result of the higher inflation. They therefore demand a higher risk premium and our expression is kept in balance by the dividend yield rising. In this case there is no change in the yield ratio. In Case 4, we assume the same increase in inflation and the same response from gilts, but we assume that the real economy is adversely affected by inflation and dividend growth does not fully reflect the inflation increase. As a result, investors demand a higher dividend yield. Again the yield ratio does not change. In Case 5, we assume the same response as in Case 1, but we assume that investors also make a valuation error, and demand a higher nominal dividend yield because gilts offer a higher nominal yield. This forces up the equity risk premium. The yield ratio remains unchanged.

In the above examples, the unchanging yield ratio for Cases 3–5 is a consequence of the numbers chosen in our example. Had we begun in Case 1 with inflation at 5%, then all subsequent numbers would have come out differently. In fact the yield ratio would have been, reading down the last column, 1.6, 2.0, 1.67, 1.67, and 1.67. If we had assumed dividend growth of only 10% in Case 4, the dividend yield would have risen to 7% and the yield ratio would have fallen to 1.7. If we try more extreme inflation numbers for Figure 34 so that gilt yields move to, say, 15%, the yield ratio obviously would rise sharply in Cases 3–5 on the assumptions made above. But in such a situation it is likely that other assumptions should be changed so that the dividend yield rises to, say, 7%. At that level the yield ratio is not too far from 2. Despite the *ad hoc* nature of this discussion, a broad conclusion does emerge: if investors are rational and the real economy is unaffected by inflation, the level of the yield ratio is positively related to the rate of inflation (i.e., the higher the rate of inflation, the greater the yield ratio). This is because the numerator in the yield ratio will change by the change in the rate of inflation while the denominator will not change. If investors believe inflation harms the real economy, or increases risks, or if investors make valuation errors, there will be no clear relationship between the yield ratio and inflation. This is because the numerator in the yield ratio will change by the change in the rate of inflation and the denominator will also change. The outcome will depend on the size of the two changes and the starting values of the variables.

It would appear that whether there is a relationship between the yield ratio and inflation depends on how investors react to inflation and its real effects. On what would seem the most likely assumptions to most investors, there probably will not be a strong relationship. We saw in Table 55 data that might suggest this is incorrect. Wadhwani (1991c) has produced evidence that points in the other direction. He makes three observations.

First, the European Monetary System countries have achieved lower inflation levels over the period 1975–91, yet their yield ratios have risen and not fallen over this period. This change in rating, however, may reflect a change in factors other than inflation. The Continental European countries have been reluctant equity investors in the past but there has been more interest in equities in recent years both from within the countries and from international investors. Second, there is little relationship between inflation and yield ratios if one looks at different countries. For example, Spain and Italy have both averaged about 12% inflation over the period 1973–90, but Italy's yield ratio was more than twice Spain's. Finally, Wadhwani argues that the yield ratio does not generally move with inflation over time. The correlation between the five-year moving average inflation rate and the yield ratio is weak for both the UK and US.

Yet we are left with Table 55. The change in valuation in the late 1950s can be ascribed to factors other than inflation, such as "the cult of the equity", when equities were re-rated more favourably to bonds. But this is a label, not an explanation. Why was there a cult of the equity? Were growth prospects seen as better, or was the change related to inflation prospects?

Clearly the yield ratio poses some difficult issues. It has been a good timing tool when it has reached extreme values, but is less useful at other levels. It is probably only modestly affected by changes in the level of inflation, but a sensible precaution might be to put more weight on other allocation tools if inflation moves out of recent historical ranges. Despite the widespread use of the yield ratio, it is worth remembering that it relates the total return from bonds to only a component of equity returns. Let's now compare like with like.

THE PREMIUM APPROACH

The premium approach focuses on the size of the equity risk premium, i.e., how much extra return we may expect from equities relative to bonds. In terms of our constant growth dividend discount model:

equity risk premium = dividend yield + dividend growth rate − gilt yield

The premium approach is conceptually appealing but suffers from a practical problem. We know the gilt redemption yield and the dividend yield but we have to estimate dividend growth and the equity risk premium. The premium approach is dependent on some forecasting and model building skills.

The obvious way of forecasting dividend growth is to either extrapolate the most recent rate or to use a long historical average. We saw in Chapter 23 that the market moves too much to be explained by a dividend discount model except with some special assumptions. Most investors would probably accept that they overreact to recent events—when the economy is strong investors tend to be bullish and vice versa with recession. Investors don't believe that good or bad times will last for ever, and they try to anticipate turning points, but current conditions are probably weighted a bit more heavily in decision making than the long-term record would suggest is appropriate. What this suggests is that some mix of historical and recent conditions will probably be the best model of investors' expectations. Our discussion in the last two chapters has concentrated on equities relative to gilts, but other assets are also compared to equities. Here we shall give a US example of the premium approach involving cash and a UK example involving gilts.

DuBois (1988) discusses the use of the dividend yield and dividend growth approach in the US: he uses the current yield on the S&P 500 plus the expected nominal growth of dividends. DuBois derives the latter from inflation expectations and real growth expectations. Inflation expectations are based on an annualized 20 quarter exponentially-weighted moving average of inflation rates, measured by the GNP deflator. This is adjusted by the recent trend in wholesale prices, which picks up changes in inflation faster than the GNP deflator. Real growth is an assumed average of 2.8%, adjusted up or down when inflation is expected to be low or high. DuBois is using historical data for inflation, but it is recent history that he is using, and exponential weighting is a way of giving most weight to recent observations. His growth assumption is a long-term average, but modified by relatively recent historical inflation experience. From these measures, DuBois derives an expected return which he compares to the expected returns on bills and bonds. The expected return on bonds is assumed to be the redemption yield on long dated bonds. (One could forecast a one-year holding period return for bonds which could produce a very different benchmark return to that obtained from the yield to redemption.) The return on cash is taken to be the yield on a Treasury bill.

In Table 56, we show DuBois' data for equities and bills. The expected equity return less the three month Treasury bill yield is related to the excess return from stocks over bills. Table 56 shows that when the expected return from stocks relative to bills is high, stocks have returned more than bills over the following months with a high probability. The greater the premium, the greater should be the allocation to stocks.

Table 56 Stock/Bills Premium and Subsequent Performance US: 1951–85

Premium Range	# Mo. Obs.	Average Subsequent Excess Return (%)			Probability of Positive Excess Return (%)		
		1 mo.	3 mo.	12 mo.	1 mo.	3 mo.	12 mo.
>10	10	2.5	6.8	26.1	80	80	100
8–9.9	64	1.9	4.8	16.7	66	78	89
6–7.9	102	0.5	2.0	6.1	57	63	63
5–5.9	62	0.7	1.3	4.6	61	69	66
4–4.9	91	0.1	1.0	2.8	57	59	64
2–3.9	74	(0.2)	(1.1)	0.9	42	36	55
<2	16	(1.9)	(3.6)	(8.6)	31	19	38
	420	0.5	1.4	5.7	56	60	66

Source: DuBois (1988, p. 294). Reproduced by permission of Probus Publishing Co., Inc.

DuBois calculated information coefficients for the excess return approach for stocks/bills, bonds/bills and stocks/bonds. The average information coefficients for 1 month, 3 months and 12 months for the period 1951–85 were 0.18, 0.27 and 0.42 respectively. These all provide useful amounts of information. Because all the data seems to have been used to calculate these returns, they will overstate future correlations.

Turning to the UK, Davies and Wadhwani (1988) calculated risk premiums for UK equities relative to gilts. Instead of a simple constant growth model, Davies and Wadhwani used a two-stage dividend discount model. Specifically they used two growth rate assumptions, one for the first five years and the other thereafter. The first was based on the five-year growth rate of dividends centred on the year in question, and the second was based on a long-term measure. Using these growth assumptions and the market price, they derived the expected return. Given the gilt yield, the equity risk premium could be derived. Using this method and historical data, they derived equity risk premiums for the period 1923–87. The equity risk premium so derived was positively correlated with the inflation rate. Accordingly, they argued that a risk premium asset allocation decision rule should take account of the rate of inflation. If they ignored the rate of inflation, the average equity risk premium over the entire period was about 6%. If they allowed for the rate of inflation, the average risk premium was about 2.8% plus half the forward-looking inflation rate. They reported that the risk premium approach outperformed the yield ratio approach as an asset allocation tool. For the relationship of the equity risk premium and inflation based on a different set of calculations, see UBS Phillips and Drew's *Equity Market Indicators* (e.g., December 1992, p.11).

Although tactical asset allocation can be based on something as simple as the level of the dividend yield or market price-earnings ratio, commercial providers of tactical asset allocation advice appear to put most emphasis on the premium approach. While this is reasonable, it is worth pointing out that many of the simulated records used to promote the premium approach in the US oversell its capabilities. Track records based on the last 20 years incorporate an especially favourable period for the approach because during the 1980s the market fluctuated around the trend line of the equity risk premium.

Carman (1988) produced figures showing that asset allocation between US bonds and equities using the equity risk premium approach would have produced higher returns in the period 1951–87 than an all-equity portfolio. These results, however, depended on good performance in the 1970s and 1980s. The results were neutral in the 1950s and negative in the 1960s. Presumably most investors would have quit the method before they got to the good years. His simulation assumed that the average risk premium for the entire period (3.5%) was used as the guideline. But in the 1950s the premium was in the range 4%–11%: how would investors have anticipated the roughly four-decade average premium of 3.5%? Investors instead might have used a rolling five-year average for the premium. When this was used, tactical asset allocation, relative to being fully invested in equities, produced lower returns in the 1950s and 1960s, and higher returns in the 1970s and 1980s. There was no return advantage over the entire period. Tactical asset allocation is like many other valuation tools—it will produce poor results if there is a sea change in valuation standards.

THE DIVIDEND YIELD REVISITED

Just looking at the dividend yield seems rather low key compared to what we've just discussed. But it can be argued that the dividend yield is a rough guide to the equity risk premium (see Rozeff, 1984). Some economists argue that the real rate of interest and the real rate of growth will be the same over the long-term. If you refer back to Case 1 in Figure 34, you will see that we have plugged in that assumption. Notice what it implies—when the relationship holds, the dividend yield will equal the equity risk premium. You will see that in every case except Case 4, the dividend yield and the equity risk premium are the same. In the exception, we specifically broke the relationship by reducing real growth but keeping real interest rates unchanged. Too much should not be made of this argument, but it would perhaps be sensible for investors who do not calculate the equity risk premium to make sure they monitor the dividend yield.

QUANTIFYING THE EQUITY/BOND SPLIT

The output of tactical asset allocation tools can be used to give qualitative advice or can be processed to provide quantitative advice. There are a number of quantitative approaches: we shall give one example here of a method developed by Einhorn and Shangquan (1984).

Einhorn and Shangquan used a dividend discount model to calculate the S&P 500's implied annualized monthly return for the period 1961–67. By subtracting what they deemed the monthly required return (2.5% plus the five-year government bond rate) from the implied returns, they obtained five years of monthly excess returns. They then calculated the mean and standard deviation of these excess returns which turned out to be 0.8% and 5.6% respectively.

On the assumption that the historical data held for the period 1968–82, Einhorn and Shangquan came up with a decision rule. The positive and negative one standard deviation excess return for 1961–67 was 6.4% (i.e., 0.8% + 5.6%) and minus 4.8% (i.e., 0.8%–5.6%). Whenever the excess return was at the mean of 0.8%, 50% of cash flow went into equities. Whenever the excess return was equal or greater

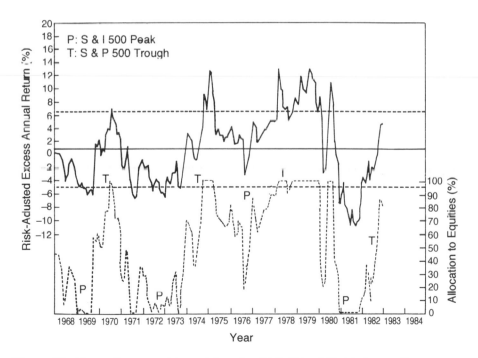

Figure 35 Excess Return and Asset Allocation S&P 500: 1968–82. Source: Einhorn and Shangquan (1984, p. 31). Reproduced by permission

than 6.4%, all cash flow was allocated to equities and whenever the excess return was less than 4.8% all cash flow remained in cash. Thus the range of 11.2 percentage points of excess return (i.e., 6.4% to minus 5.6%) covered a 100% allocation to equities through to a zero allocation. Every swing of 1% of excess return leads to a 8.9% (i.e., 100% divided by 11.2%) allocation swing to or from equities.

The application of the rule is shown graphically for the period 1968–82 in Figure 35. This Figure also shows monthly market peaks and troughs (P and T respectively). The results are encouraging. For three of the troughs, the model recommended high equity weights, and for three of the peaks, low weights. For one trough the model was lukewarm in its allocation and for one peak completely wrong.

FORECASTING DIVIDENDS

In some of the valuation methods we have looked at we used historical data while others have required dividend forecasts. We turn now to a more general discussion of forecasting dividends.

There are two main ways of forecasting the market's dividend growth—one is by aggregating analysts' individual company dividend forecasts and the other is by forecasting directly the market's dividend (or forecasting directly market profits, from which a dividend forecast may be obtained by means of a payout assumption). These approaches may lead to different forecasts.

Here we shall discuss forecasting the market dividend directly since most investors could do this themselves if they wished. Investors might use this as their sole forecast approach, but it would be more sensible to use it to check the reasonableness of aggregated company dividend forecasts produced by analysts.

Short-term Forecasts

In Chapter 12 we noted that companies appear to have target long-run payout ratios and that dividends follow profits in a smoothed manner. Companies resist dividend cuts but they will, nevertheless, cut dividends if circumstances warrant, as anyone following dividend payments in 1992 will have noticed. Chowdhury and Miles (1987) found that the percentage of companies cutting dividends can be high. For the period 1970–84, the number of companies cutting dividends varied from a low of 9% to a high of 47%. Despite the fact that companies will cut dividends if necessary, aggregate dividends have seldom fallen in the UK in recent decades.

How can we forecast dividends? First, we might look at how the payout ratio relates to past history—i.e., whether companies are close to or far from their desired payout ratio. This should be a forward looking measure that includes a profit forecast. Second, we might look at companies' ability to make increased dividend payments. Here we might look at the company sector's financial deficit, i.e., retained income less capital spending and also at income gearing, which is interest payments as a percentage of operating profits.

Had we been forecasting at the end of 1991, we would have found the payout ratio high, the financial deficit large and income gearing high. (Brokers' circulars frequently report these numbers or they can be found in government statistics.) Earnings were expected to fall. This background suggests that if we accept that companies smooth dividends, even firms making profits would probably have felt no pressure to raise them by more than the rate of inflation, if that. A few firms would be growing rapidly, despite the recession, or at least increasing their profits rapidly (for example the recently privatized electricity and water companies) and would pay more. Many troubled companies would omit their dividends or cut them sharply. Let's put some rough numbers on this. If we assume 20% of companies cut their dividends by 35%, 20% leave them unchanged, 10% raise them by 15% and the rest (i.e., 50%) raise them by 5%, the overall effect would be a 3% fall in dividends. These numbers are guesses made purely for illustration here, but the contentious one is the assumption that 20% of companies would cut dividends by 35%. The 20% is based on the distribution of cuts in the Chowdhury and Miles paper and the author's view of the course of the recession of the early 1990s. It does not seem worth cutting dividends by a few per cent, hence the assumption of a large cut. However, it will tend to be small firms that cut dividends so that the capitalization-weighted impact on aggregate dividends will be less than our calculation suggests. We might assume a reasonable forecast for aggregate dividends in respect of 1992 (i.e., dividends to be announced in Spring 1993 in respect of calendar 1992) would be for no change up to a fall of 3%.

We could have done a quick check on the plausibility of this analysis by looking at the trend in dividends. If we take the yield and index on the market at 12 month intervals we can calculate the implied growth of dividends. The calculation is:

$$\frac{(100 \times \text{yield at date of interest} \times \text{index at date of interest}) - 100}{\text{yield 12 months earlier} \times \text{index 12 months earlier}} = \frac{\% \text{ change in}}{\text{dividends}}$$

The first eight rows of Table 57 show the calculation that we could have made at the end of 1991, and the next six rows show what happened to dividend growth during 1992 and 1993. The figures are based on mid-month data and the May 1993 change is our best estimate of the change in dividends in respect of calendar year 1992. Dividends fell by 5% on April 5th 1993 because of the way the Index treated a tax change in the 1993 Budget. Apart from this, dividends fell by about 2.3%, so our rough calculation seems to have been in the right ballpark.

Table 57 Implied Dividend Growth for FT-A All-Share Index

12 Months Ending:	Annual Dividend Growth (%)
March 1990	18.5
June 1990	17.0
September 1990	16.6
December 1990	11.9
March 1991	7.4
June 1991	6.7
September 1991	5.4
December 1991	6.0
March 1992	4.2
June 1992	1.1
September 1992	−0.6
December 1992	−1.0
March 1993	−1.4
May 1993	−7.3

Source: Calculated from data in Table 13.7, *Financial Statistics*, 1993.

Long-term Dividend Forecasts

When we use dividend discount models for asset allocation we need long-term dividend forecasts. There are three main approaches:

● historical dividend growth
● sustainable internal growth
● the long-term growth of the economy

The historical growth of dividends can be measured in nominal or real terms. For example, since 1919 the real growth of UK dividends has been 1.7%. Investors could take this number and use it for their trend growth in dividends or they might wish to adjust this number based on some new information. For example the average growth rate for a more recent period could be used instead of the long-term rate.

The sustainable internal growth rate may be estimated based on the return on equity and the retention rate. For example, assume a return on equity of 10% and a retention rate of 40%. This would imply future dividend growth of 4% (i.e., 10% × 0.4 = 4%). Historical averages for the return on equity and retention rate may be used as a basis for the calculation. The calculation is, however, suspect. It implies that companies have complete control over their growth rates and gives no role to the economic environment. This is implausible.

The third approach is to relate dividend growth to the long-term growth rate of the economy. Two steps are necessary. First the long-run growth rate of the economy must be forecast and this may be based either on historical rates or on econometric forecasts. Second, a forecast must be made of the relationship between dividend growth and economic growth. In both the UK and US, dividends have not grown as fast as the economy. The simplest approach is to use the following relationship: the forecast economic growth rate times the past dividend growth rate, divided by the past economic growth rate. This relationship can be adjusted depending on the investor's view as to whether the historical relationship will hold.

Clearly, each method has subjective elements. The commonest approach in the UK would be to juggle the first and third approaches.

The third approach would normally be made in real terms and the first approach can be. To change the analysis into nominal terms one needs a forecast rate of inflation. This can be made on the basis of an economic forecast or can be deduced from bond market yields. If it is assumed that UK index-linked gilts and UK conventional gilts offer a similar real return, the real redemption yield on index-linked gilts can be subtracted from the redemption yield on conventional gilts and the expected inflation rate obtained.

CONCLUDING COMMENTS

When the equity market yield is high, future returns are likely to be high and vice versa when it is low. This relationship probably is most reliable at extreme values. Measures that relate equities to other assets include the gilt/equity yield ratio and the equity risk premium approaches. The gilt/equity yield ratio has proved useful in recent years and has been most reliable at extreme levels, but there are difficult issues to be faced as to whether it varies with inflation. Different investors have different views. The equity risk premium approach relates the total return from equities to the total return from other assets. It is probably superior to the yield ratio approach. Tactical asset allocation tools can be used to give qualitative advice or quantitative. A simple example of using a dividend discount model to provide quantitative advice was given. Finally, we looked at how the market dividend growth rate might be forecast.

28

Liquidity and Technical Titbits

Some analysts attempt to call the direction of the market by liquidity and technical indicators. These measures are usually directed to buy/sell signals rather than asset allocation between bonds and equities. We shall say a few words about liquidity, comment on technical indicators in general, and finally look at a couple of specific indicators.

LIQUIDITY

Liquidity is a term used in different ways. Sometimes liquidity refers to the money supply and sometimes to the cash position of institutional or private investors. We will look at money supply liquidity here.

A monetary portfolio balance theory could be used to support a case for believing that changes in the money supply precede changes in stock prices. Imagine that everybody in the economy has rationally balanced their portfolio of assets. Everybody will hold their desired amounts of cash, shares, bonds, consumer durables, houses, etc. If the money supply is increased, everybody will have more cash. This will upset their desired portfolio balance—they will have too much cash relative to other assets—so they will re-balance their assets by spending their extra cash. They will buy more consumer goods, add to their stocks and bonds and so on. Unfortunately, this just passes the cash around, and means that new individuals will have excess cash which they have to spend. The process will only come to an end, i.e., equilibrium will only be re-established, when prices rise or more goods are produced. Early studies, which looked mainly at graphs of relationships, suggested that increases in the money supply did lead to rises in stock prices.

However, is the portfolio balance theory really true, and is the evidence reliable? Even if we accept that the theory is true, why are changes in the money supply not discounted? After all, the action of the monetary authorities is one of the most closely examined factors in the market. A number of detailed econometric studies of the US market (e.g., Rozeff, 1974; Cooper, 1974; Kraft and Kraft, 1977;

and Rogalski and Vinso, 1977) claim that share prices do immediately reflect changes in monetary policy. Indeed, the stockmarket seems to lead money supply changes. Unless an investor has superior money supply forecasting ability, it would not be possible to outperform the market using money supply data.

In a more recent study, Stumpp and Scott (1991) looked at three measures of *excess* liquidity that relate money supply changes to changes in the real economy (for example, real M2 year-over-year rate of growth less the year-over-year rate of growth of industrial production). For the entire period studied, 1961–89, some measures of liquidity were correlated with market returns but it was not shown whether it was possible to make money on the back of the relationship after incurring transaction costs. For the period 1979–89, liquidity was unrelated to returns.

In Chapter 25 we noted studies which used some notion of liquidity or the money supply as part of a multi-variable economic analysis. Many brokers and technical analysts who talk of liquidity tend to rely on simple broad-based correlations such as those just discussed. The evidence is not very encouraging.

TECHNICAL INDICATORS

There are a large number of technical indicators that are used to assess the market's level in the US. We might classify technical indicators in terms of:

- contrary opinion rules: e.g., odd-lot short sales, mutual fund cash positions, credit balances in brokerage accounts, investment advisers' opinions and option put and call ratios;
- following the smart money: e.g., short sales by specialists and aggregate insider purchases and sales;
- chart patterns;
- general market analysis: e.g., Dow Theory and breadth of market.

Outside of the US, few of these measures are available, either because of lack of data or because of different institutional structures; and those that are, or could be calculated, do not appear to have been tested. We made some general comments on some technical analysis matters in Chapter 18. Here we shall simply comment on two measures, one a contrary opinion measure, and the other a smart money measure. Readers interested in other measures should consult Colby and Meyers (1988), Fosback (1991) and Zweig (1986).

SENTIMENT AND MARKET LEVELS

Anyone with contrarian instincts will want to know the market's sentiment—is it bullish or bearish? *Investors Intelligence* collects the views of a large number of

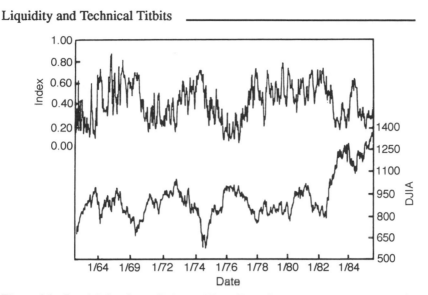

Figure 36 Bearish Sentiment Index and Dow Jones Industrial Average: 1963–85. Source: Solt and Statman (1988; p. 52). Reproduced by permission

US investment advisers and calculates a Bearish Sentiment Index. This is the ratio of the number of bearish advisers to all advisers expressing an opinion, i.e., bearish advisers divided by bulls plus bears. Investment advisers are bullish at the top and bearish at the bottom. Figure 36 relates their views to the Dow Jones Industrial Average.

Can an investor make money from this relationship? Alas no, according to Solt and Statman (1988). They estimated for the period January 1963 to September 1985, an equation of the following form:

$$\text{Return over four weeks} = a + b \times \left(\frac{\text{bearish advisers}}{\text{bulls + bears}} \right) + \text{random errors}$$

The sentiment ratio was calculated at the start of the four week period. The value for b turned out to be not statistically different from zero, i.e., there was no relationship between the ratio and returns. The equation was re-run for 26 and 52 week periods with the same result.

It is sometimes argued that it is at extremes of emotion that a contrary indicator will be of most use. Ratios of above 0.55 and below 0.15 on the Bearish Sentiment Index are said to be the most important for prediction purposes. Solt and Statman examined these extremes and their results are shown in Table 58: not much support is shown for the extremes of value argument.

Why should the Sentiment Index work? The argument is that advisers are trend followers—they will be bullish when the market has risen and when they should be switching tack. Solt and Statman checked to see if advisers really were trend followers. They re-ran the equation shown above, but this time they related return over a one month period to the Bearish Sentiment Index at the end of the period and discovered that there was a significant relationship. Now the important point is that if advisers tend to be trend followers, a graph of their sentiment is bound to be closely related to a graph of the market. A chart of the relationship will look great to the eye but will not be very useful. The advisers will tend to lag the market rather than lead it. Most of us will be unable to interpret the graph sensibly and will give too much weight to the seemingly strong relationship (recall the warning in Chapter 6).

Table 58 The Relationship between the Bearish Sentiment Index and Changes in the DJIA in the Subsequent 4, 26 and 52 Week Periods

	4 weeks	26 weeks	52 weeks
Number of observations where DJIA increased following Bearish Sentiment Index ratio above 0.55	37	12	11
Number of observations where DJIA decreased following Bearish Sentiment Index ratio above 0.55	37	9	3
Number of observations where DJIA increased following Bearish Sentiment Index ratio below 0.15	9	3	1
Number of observations where DJIA decreased following Bearish Sentiment Index ratio below 0.15	7	2	2

Source: Solt and Statman (1988; p.47). Reproduced by permission

INSIDERS AND THE LEVEL OF THE MARKET

It is widely believed that insiders' trades are a useful guide to forecasting the market's level. The justification for this is a belief that insiders act partly in response to firm-specific information but partly in response to general economic factors which impact their firms. If they react to such general information before it is widely known, they might provide a good guide to the market's likely level. Such a guide is unlikely to be infallible. Insiders may well just be taking a view on the market and expressing it by dealing in their own firm's shares. In that case their knowledge may not be "inside". Further, the economy and market do not have an exact correspondence. Businessmen might see surprisingly weak sales figures and believe a recession is continuing, while the market may have focused on a likely change in economic policy and the prospects of growth in, say, six months. The market might be looking further ahead than businessmen.

The popular view of knowledgeable insiders is supported by the tendency to focus on a few supporting instances. It is well known that US insiders bought heavily after the 1987 Crash and there were substantial numbers of corporate repurchases of shares authorized (see e.g., Seyhun, 1990 and Netter and Mitchell,

1989). The ratio of insider transactions rose to record levels during the week of October 19. Top executives were especially active. The insiders were a good guide after the Crash. But before the Crash they were a poor guide. Insiders were neither heavy buyers nor sellers during the first nine months of 1987 and in the week of October 12 the insiders started to buy. A reasonable interpretation would be that the insiders got it wrong before the Crash and right afterwards: about as good as a coin.

There have been a couple of attempts to study the value of insiders' aggregate trades more formally than the casual empiricism of the previous paragraph. Lee and Solt (1986) examined the period May 1971 to December 1982. They used data from Vickers Stock Research Corporation, which produces more timely disclosure of insider activity than the Security Exchange Commission. They related the ratio of total insider buying/total insider selling to market movements. They found that, on balance, aggregate insider trading followed market movements but market movements did not appear to follow insider trading. Lee and Solt looked at extremes of insider activity, tested various trading rules, and so forth, but found no case of statistically significant excess returns accruing from a strategy of following insiders.

Seyhun (1988) used SEC data and examined the period January 1975 to October 1981, i.e., part of Lee and Solt's sample. He used a different approach and concluded that future market returns are predictable to some extent after publication of insider trading information. Nonetheless, he concluded that this information could not be used to obtain a profitable switching strategy between Treasury bills and the stock market, even ignoring transaction costs.

It would seem that the aggregate activity of corporate insiders is not a useful forecasting guide for the US stock market: the author is not aware of UK research on this topic.

CONCLUDING COMMENTS

There is a large amount of US literature on liquidity and technical indicators. There are, however, few studies which relate these indicators to earning abnormal returns, especially for measures which are available outside the US. Casual inspection of graphs of market movements and a number of indicators appears to lead to the conclusion that there are exploitable relationships. Careful studies have often shown that the graphs are misleading. It is not clear that general money supply measures of liquidity, or technical indicators that are available outside of the US, beyond the rather intuitive and non-testable contrarian strategy discussed in Chapter 20, are useful for calling the market.

29
International Tactical Asset Allocation

Previous tactical asset allocation chapters have mainly, but not exclusively, discussed bonds versus cash versus equities asset allocation. Traditionally, this has been the most important set of decisions: it still is in the US, and many other countries. In the UK, however, bonds are now a small proportion of many institutional funds. Deciding between international and UK equities is a more important decision. Before we discuss how one might go about this, it is worth making a few points on why an investor might wish to go to all the extra trouble of investing in overseas assets.

The basic reason for international investing is that it is likely to improve the risk-return trade-off available to an investor. The major reason for this is not that foreign markets inevitably offer higher returns, but the low correlation of returns between international markets. The average correlation coefficient for the major markets with the UK over recent years has been about 0.47. Recall Figure 8b, which shows the effect of adding international stocks to US stocks. With continued growth of international investing, inter-market correlation of returns will probably increase, but there are always likely to be risk reduction opportunities. International stock markets will not all move together in perfect lock-step because they have, and will continue to have, different underlying industrial structures, different economic prospects, different monetary policies, different political systems, different currencies and so on.

Some investors invest internationally because they believe that certain countries have better economic prospects. These investors believe they will get better returns. Maybe they will, but the argument is analogous to only investing in growth stocks in the domestic economy. High growth stocks tend to sell on high price-earnings ratios and low yields: the growth is discounted by the market. It is not obvious why this would not apply to international markets too.

Some investors want to invest internationally because they think that most investors think primarily in terms of their home market and, as a result, inter-market mispricing is more likely than intra-market mispricing. The growth of international investing will have diminished such mispricing to some extent and is likely to do so increasingly in the future. However, because arbitrage will always be more difficult between markets than within markets, some mispricing may always remain.

There is a lively debate as to whether international investors should hedge currencies. If international currency volatility is high, it is possible that risks will not be reduced by international diversification unless currencies are hedged (see Kaplanis and Schaefer, 1991). However, even with the high currency volatility of recent years, unhedged international equity diversification would have reduced risks for investors from the major nations. Some analysts argue that investors should hedge their currency exposure completely, others that partial hedges are the solution, currency insurance is another option, and so is never hedging. Interested readers will find the four possibilities discussed in Aliber and Bruce (1991, Chapters 19–22). Because this area is subject to so much debate it must be noted, but will not be discussed here: we will simply echo the comment by Ibbotson *et al.* in relation to the four approaches we mentioned and pass on:

> "All four of these approaches to hedging are used—there is a clientele for each of them. Since most behavior is purposeful, we would have to have a very strong theoretical or empirical basis for saying that any of these approaches are irrational. We have no such evidence." (1991, p. 192)

The strategic international weighting decision can be handled within an asset-liability framework. Yet, anybody who looks at international weightings around the world will notice that there seem to be distinct national norms. Each country seems to have fixed on some acceptable strategic level of foreign exposure which appears to bear little relation to risks, returns and correlations. Americans invest very little abroad, British funds invest rather more, Hong Kong funds even more and the Middle East funds almost everything. There appear to be two broad patterns here. All countries have a bias towards investing at home, but the smaller the local market, the greater is the proportion likely to be invested abroad. Second, the amount invested abroad bears some relation to the amount of national income that is involved in foreign trade. Open economies invest more abroad. This makes sense. Pensioners will spend part of their income on imported goods. The more open the economy, the greater that percentage. To that extent, pensioners have overseas liabilities, and it is prudent to broadly match the liabilities with assets. This argument, incidentally, implies that currencies should not be hedged. Viewed in terms of the openness of the UK economy, a strategic international weight of around 25–30% would be defensible for UK pension funds.

APPROACHES TO ASSESSING MARKETS

A variety of approaches are used in deciding which international markets are the most attractive. Some investors:

- ignore countries and simply buy the cheapest stocks in the world, deriving their country allocation as a residual;
- compare markets as though they are simply different stocks within a market;
- treat each market separately and rate it cheap or expensive relative to its own history;
- forecast total returns;
- use international business cycle anticipation;
- use differences in international liquidity.

We shall comment on the first four approaches. We shall ignore the last two as we have little to add to our earlier business cycle analysis and scant evidence on international liquidity.

BUYING THE CHEAPEST STOCKS

Simply selecting the cheapest stocks in the world and ignoring international asset allocation appeals to many investors who believe they have stock selection skills. This approach could take the form of buying, say, the forty cheapest stocks in the world and, if they are all telephone companies, so be it. Usually, however, investors construct portfolios that are diversified by sector and they try to buy the cheapest oil company in the world, the cheapest chemical company and so on. Whether it is a sensible approach depends on whether stocks' returns are more correlated with their global industry's return or that of their national market. We have already seen in Chapter 23 that the national factor seems to predominate. The evidence cited there was global. If we narrow our focus and look at a region such as Europe, the same result is found. For example, Drummen and Zimmermann (1992) looked at 11 European markets over the 1986–89 period. They found that the country factor explained 19% of the average stock return variance, the world stock market 11%, overall European trends 8% and industry trends 9%. While picking cheap stocks may be a viable strategy, the evidence points to country factors as being the most rewarding starting point for international asset allocation.

SELECTING MARKETS AS THOUGH THEY ARE STOCKS

The argument for selecting markets as though they are stocks is that assets are assets and investors are investors. Presumably whatever the reason for low price-earnings stocks or small stocks performing well within a market should carry across to entire markets too. If investors concentrate too much on the past and reward past success, and that accounts for low price-earnings stocks tending to outperform, that should apply to markets too. And if poor liquidity is the explanation for small stocks performing, that should probably affect markets too. On this tack we should look for low price-earnings ratios, high yields, high book value, and so forth. Of course, there are vast differences between markets in terms of accounting policies, growth prospects, political risk, etc. But growth differences exist between stocks within a market, so there is nothing special about this at an international level. And while different countries do use different accounting methods (e.g., with regard to depreciation) one can reduce the effect of this (e.g., by looking at cash flow instead of earnings), as we shall see.

Let's look at some evidence. Two of the most basic stock attributes are the price-earnings ratio and dividend yield, and international data is readily available. These seem to be a good starting point for analysis. Some investors, however, argue for replacing the price-earnings ratio with a price-to-cash flow measure because of international accounting differences with regard depreciation policies. Germany and Japan, for example, over-depreciate relative to the US. Some investors argue that focusing on cash, i.e., profits plus depreciation, levels the playing field. This is only partly true. For example, a manufacturing plant in an industry with rapidly changing technology has to provide for substantial depreciation, whereas a property company or a bank does not. As the manufacturing/property/bank composition of world stock markets varies significantly, switching from price-earnings to cash-flow will result in changes in international rankings that are not just the result of ironing out accounting differences. Nonetheless, we'll look at price-to-cash flow here.

Keppler (1991a and 1991b), in two articles, looked separately at cash flow and at dividends as a basis for country asset allocation. In both studies he used the same procedure and we will discuss the studies together. He used 20 years of data drawn from Morgan Stanley Capital International (MSCI) country indexes, and he sorted the countries into quartiles based on their price-to-cash flow ratios and, separately, on their dividend yields. Quartile 1 had the lowest price-to-cash flow or the highest dividend yield and quartile 4 had the highest price-to-cash flow or the lowest dividend yield. For each variable he looked at six investment strategies, which consisted of investing in various quartiles, or groups of quartiles and these are listed in Table 59. The hypothetical portfolios were constructed with equal initial investments in each market, grouped according to the selection variable being studied, and rebalanced to equal investments at the end of each quarter. Returns were examined over rolling 1, 2, 3, 4 and 5 year periods. Keppler's benchmarks were the MSCI World Index with the countries (a) equally-weighted and, (b) capitalization-weighted.

By and large, the two selection criteria were successful in ranking portfolios by return, whether measured in local currency or a common currency. High yield countries and low price-to-cash flow countries produced the highest returns. If allowance is made for risk, in the form of the standard deviation of returns, the dividend yield approach partly achieved higher returns at the cost of higher risk. Table 59 shows returns per unit of risk for the two selection variables and the various strategies.

Table 59 Country Selection Based on Dividend Yield or
Cash Flow: Quarterly Returns

	Return Per Unit of Standard Deviation	
Strategy*	Dividend Yield	Cash Flow
1	0.52	0.61
2	0.58	0.57
3	0.54	0.56
4	0.48	0.43
5	0.35	0.31
6	0.19	0.15

*Strategy 1—quartile 1 stocks; Strategy 2—quartiles 1 and 2;
Strategy 3—quartiles 1, 2 and 3; Strategy 4—quartiles 2, 3 and 4;
Strategy 5—quartiles 3 and 4; Strategy 6—quartile 4. Source:
Keppler (1991a and 1991b)

Based on the above evidence, it would seem that treating countries as though they are stocks and using standard share selection screens has some value. Notice, though, that this approach is essentially a ranking approach, rather than a return forecasting approach. All we can say is that we prefer country X to country Y, not the return that we expect from each country.

SELECTING STOCKS BY LOCAL STANDARDS

The case for assessing markets on the basis of local standards is that despite the above evidence there is room for doubting that markets are directly comparable and, moreover, within each market the local investors are the dominant force. If local investors everywhere relate their own equity market more to local bonds and local cash than to other equity markets, then the sensible approach might seem to be to go native. International valuation then becomes a process of assessing markets on the basis of relative cheapness and dearness of each market based on its domestic valuation standard. These valuation standards may be based on simple measures such the price-earnings ratio in relation to its historical range and average, or more complex standards such as an equity risk premium comparison with local bonds.

There is surprisingly little published evidence on selection by local valuations. In an interesting article, Arnott and Henriksson (1991) give a clear statement of the local valuation approach. They note that if an equity risk premium is measured in any one country and compared with the normal risk premium for that country, an abnormal risk premium can be calculated (recall the discussion in Chapter 27). While normal risk premiums may differ from country to country and are not directly comparable, the abnormal premiums are directly comparable. The evidence they produce, however, does not prove that this approach actually leads to good portfolio selection in practice. Moreover the equity risk premium says something about potential *relative* performance within a market. It does not necessarily help an international equity investor to select just equities. For example, UK equities may seem cheap relative to UK gilts and Spanish equities may seem fairly valued against Spanish bonds. But if Spanish bond yields are very high and start to tumble, Spanish equities may well outperform UK equities while being only fairly valued relative to Spanish bonds. Nonetheless, the abnormal premium does seem a plausible approach and some brokers, e.g., UBS Phillips and Drew, publish equity risk premiums for a number of international markets.

Most international investors probably do make comparisons based on various local bond/equity measures, although most of these are unsophisticated and will simply take the form of noting that UK equities are, say, cheap against UK gilts whereas US equities are, say, dear against US bonds. Some investors look at graphical comparisons of international markets but these more often have some prima facie plausibility rather than a documented track record. For example Figures 37 (A) and (B) show the Japanese and US bond/equity yield ratios and Figure 37(C) shows the Japanese bond/equity yield ratio divided by the US bond/equity yield ratio. The charts show at the end of the period the Japanese ratio below its average and the US ratio above its average. This might suggest that Japan is cheaper than the US. The chart showing the relative yield ratio shows a clearer picture, with Japan becoming expensive in the late 1980s and then a remarkable change in relative value with the US becoming relatively expensive. Unfortunately this sort of chart has limited predictive value. In fact, for the example given, investors would have made awful tactical moves. They would have sold Japanese equities in 1986 and presumably bought in 1991. In dollar terms, the difference in returns between the two markets (+ shows a return that favours Japan) each year from 1986 to 1992 were approximately, +73%, +40%, +17%, −25%, −33%, −22% and −31%.

Some investors use different valuation measures for different markets. For example the book-to-price ratio might be thought to be especially relevant for Japan, or the gap between the earnings yield and long bond yield (see Chapters 31 and 32). In Hong Kong, however, there is no local long bond market—accordingly the earnings yield/long bond relationship is not appropriate. The stability of the dividend yield in the UK might indicate that the dividend yield would be more relevant in the UK than in other markets. We could go on, but the point is clear: there are some market idiosyncrasies so that different measures may be important in different markets. This may suggest a chalk and cheese problem: how can the cheapness/dearness of the UK on a yield basis be related to the cheapness or dearness ofJapan on a book value basis? One solution would be to measure each market's value in terms of the number of standard deviations it is from the mean of the

---

Figure 37 (A) Japanese Bond/Equity Yield Ratio; (B) US Bond/Equity Yield Ratio; and (C) Japanese/US Bond/Equity Yield Ratio: 1973–92. Copyright © 1993 Datastream International Ltd

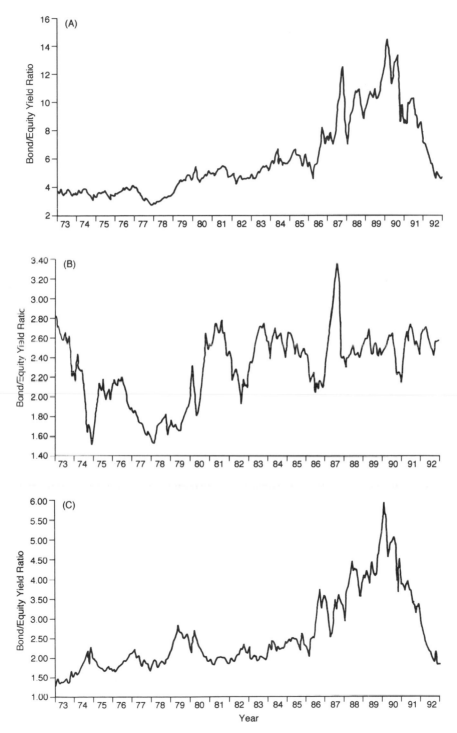

selection variable. Then, if the UK is one standard deviation above its average dividend yield, and Japan is half a standard deviation above its average book-to-price ratio, the UK would be cheaper. Some investors do use this sort of approach but the writer is not aware of any published evidence on its value.

The approaches discussed above rank markets rather than produce total returns. Of course, a premium approach involves making a total return forecast, but that is not the aspect focused upon. Some investors do make total return forecasts. This can be done in a number of ways, e.g., by the constant growth dividend discount model approach (yield plus growth) or by using price-earnings ratios. We will look at the latter here. For a UK investor investing abroad on an unhedged basis, four forecasts would be required for each market.

- expected change in market price-earnings ratio;
- expected change in profits;
- yield;
- change in foreign currency relative to sterling.

If £1million were invested in a market in which it was thought that in the next year the price-earnings ratio would rise from 10 to 12, that profits would rise by 20%, that the yield would be 5% and the currency would appreciate by 10%, then the annual total return in sterling would be:

$$((£1\text{million} \times 1.2 \times 1.2) + (£1\text{million} \times 0.05)) \times 1.1 = £1.64 \text{ million},$$

i.e., a total return of 64%.

Total returns can be produced in this, or other ways for all countries, and the returns compared. The problem with this approach is that international markets tend to be followed by a variety of analysts and it is often hard to get them to make their appraisals on a consistent basis. Ideally the currency forecast would be produced centrally (to ensure consistency of cross-rates, e.g., so that the dollar/sterling forecast and the dollar/yen forecast would be consistent with the yen/sterling forecast) and all country analysts would use the same global economic forecasts as background for their country analysis. Finally, the same analytical approach to deciding what determines the correct price-earnings ratio should be used for each market. In practice it is often difficult to get analysts and fund managers to act on consistent assumptions.

CONCLUDING COMMENTS

There are a number of approaches to international tactical asset allocation. Some investors simply choose the best stocks in the world, and their international asset allocation is a result of stock decisions. Investors who attempt to assess markets, may either calculate currency-adjusted returns or use ranking methods. Currency-adjusted returns are fine in principle, but it is often hard to obtain returns that have been produced on a consistent basis. Ranking methods fall into two broad categories, those based on treating markets much as though they are stocks and those that are based on evaluating markets on cheapness or dearness as measured by local standards. There has been far less research on international tactical asset allocation than on domestic.

30
Combining Tactical Asset Allocation Tools

In Chapters 25 to 29 we looked at various tools of tactical asset allocation. Some of the tools produce total return forecasts, while others offer some indication of relative attraction. The tools permit both qualitatively- and quantitatively-based tactical asset allocation. Decisions can be made for all asset classes simultaneously or for groups of assets. The first approach would determine the complete international and domestic bond, equity, cash, property, etc. allocation decision. A typical approach for groups of assets would be to allocate domestic assets within one group and international assets in another and separately decide the weights for domestic and international groups.

We will discuss first a quantitative approach that can consider all assets simultaneously and then a two-stage approach mixing quantitative and qualitative factors.

THE EFFICIENT FRONTIER CALCULATION

If investors have a set of total return forecasts, they can simply pick the markets with the highest returns. If, however, we recall the analysis of Chapter 2, we realize that this would be an inefficient approach. It would not achieve the best blend of risk and return because it would ignore the correlation of returns between markets. The efficient frontier traces out portfolios that offer the best return for a given level of risk and the least risk for a given return. In Chapter 2 we developed a graphical analysis of the efficient frontier. In this chapter we discuss this approach in practice. The process is usually called optimization and the computer software that does the calculations is called an optimizer.

In Chapter 2 we discussed Markowitz optimization and noted the large number of estimates required. In Chapter 3 we discussed Sharpe's simplification of relating each security's return to the market rather than to every other security. We saw that Sharpe optimization reduced the number of estimates required to calculate an efficient frontier. Nonetheless, in asset allocation work it is usual to undertake full Markowitz optimization because the number of asset classes is small and for small numbers there is not too great a difference in the number of estimates required for the two methods. For example, for 10 asset classes, a Sharpe optimization would require 32 estimates whereas a Markowitz optimization would require 65.

To calculate a Markowitz efficient frontier, an investor needs to know the expected return for all assets being considered, their variances and the correlation between their returns. The efficient frontier is then generated by a programming routine called quadratic programming, although there are approximate ratio methods as well, for example that were developed by Elton *et al.*, 1978. Fortunately, there are numerous commercial software products that will do the calculations. These are often discussed in trade journals such as *Wall Street & Technology* (see e.g., Bobseine, 1990 and Schmerken, 1987).

An example of a commercial optimizer is Sharpe's AAT or Asset Allocation Tools (Sharpe, 1985). This requires six inputs—upper and lower bounds for each asset's proportion in the portfolio, expected return forecasts, standard deviation of returns, correlation of the returns of each asset with every other asset, the risk tolerance of the investor and transaction costs. Investors can take historical values from databases provided with the AAT for the expected returns, standard deviations and correlations, or insert their own estimates. It is common for investors to provide forecasts of returns but accept historical standard deviations and correlations. Investors who believe that historical volatilities and correlations will not hold in the future should insert their own estimates. An investor's risk tolerance is expressed as a number from 0 to 100 that indicates the added risk an investor will accept to increase expected return by 1%. The risk tolerance can be roughly interpreted as the percentage of a portfolio that an investor would choose to have in equities if the only choice was equities versus Treasury Bills, i.e., a score of 70 indicates a 70/30 split.

Given all the required information, the program will crunch out either a single optimization, i.e., the portfolio which offers the highest utility for a particular risk tolerance, or multiple optimizations, i.e., portfolios for a range of risk tolerances. The latter is an especially useful feature. The estimation of risk tolerance is difficult and investors may find that quite large changes in their risk tolerance will not greatly affect the composition of the optimal portfolio. Most investors would find this reassuring. If modest changes in risk tolerance lead to large changes in portfolio composition, investors know that long and hard thought about risk tolerance is required. Investors can also easily check to see how changes in forecast values lead to changes in the optimal portfolio.

The AAT handles risk by calculating positive and negative utilities. Positive expected returns generate positive utility and this is reduced by the negative utility of transaction costs and the negative utility of risk. This negative utility is measured by dividing the variance of the expected return by the risk tolerance. An example of the calculation for an investor with a risk tolerance of 80, a portfolio with an expected return of 20%, a variance of 240 and transaction costs of 1% is shown in Table 60.

Table 60   Calculating Portfolio Utility

Contribution to utility		
Expected return		+20%
Decrements from utility		
Risk penalty (240/80)	−3%	
Transaction costs	−1%	
Portfolio net utility		+16%

The AAT will also print out a graph of risk and return in the style of the charts in Chapter 2.

An Example

Let's now turn to an example of the use of an optimizer by a UK firm which is given by Platt (1992). Her article is a case study of a proposal put by BZW to a Hong Kong fund. It was decided that an efficient frontier approach should be adopted with an aim of selecting a minimum risk position on the frontier and with a constraint of at least 60% of the portfolio being in real assets. The low risk objective was determined by the attitude of the trustees and the real asset constraint was based on both consideration of the liability structure of the fund and the asset allocation of competitors. The expected returns were forecast and the standard deviations were adjusted to reflect a view that the peg of the HK dollar to the US dollar might be broken.

Platt states that the efficient frontier will often generate a portfolio that invests in many markets. Because the fund being considered in this case was small, about £14 million, and BZW intended to use segregated index funds, it was felt that no more than six to eight markets should comprise the portfolio. Given the constraints, the recommended portfolio turned out to be at the extreme left of the efficient frontier. The asset allocation that was adopted is shown in Table 61.

Table 61   Asset Allocation for a Hong Kong Fund

Asset Category	%
Equities	
● Hong Kong	7.6
● US	17.3
● German	12.4
● Swiss	10.9
● Japanese	12.2
Bonds	
● US	4.7
● Swiss	3.3
● Japanese	11.8
Liquidity	19.8

Source: Platt (1992, p. 52). Reproduced by permission of the MacMillan Press Ltd and St. Martin's Press, Inc.

PROBLEMS WITH OPTIMIZERS

In Chapter 2 we examined the basis of the efficient frontier and in this chapter we have seen that optimizers are readily available and provide a convenient means of seeing the effect of changing return and variance assumptions, changing attitude to risk and so forth. Optimizers apparently efficiently utilize a lot of relevant information and can recalculate rapidly as conditions change. And yet most fund managers do not calculate efficient frontiers. Why? Optimizers present both practical and conceptual problems. (The following discussion draws, in part, on Michaud, 1989, to which mathematically inclined readers are referred: see also Frankfurter et al., 1971.)

Many fund managers resist any quantitative product because they fear they lack the necessary skills and, possibly, because they think quantitative products will eventually make them redundant. The senior people who sit on investment committees tend to lose power to the new process and to new people.

An optimizer requires information that a fund manager may not normally produce. For example, many managers resist producing expected returns. They often reason in a series of paired comparisons. They might decide that UK equities are cheap relative to gilts on the basis of a yield ratio or other valuation measure. What will equities return? Well, more than gilts. But what exact return? "Don't know" is likely to be the answer. Or, recall the Japanese market when the index was at its peak. Many managers felt happy to substantially underweight Japan because it seemed overvalued. How many would have forecast an expected return of minus 50%? They might have believed that was the extent of the overvaluation, but many, if forced to give a quantitative forecast, would probably have indicated a return of 0 to −10%. Fund managers simply don't say they expect a market to halve in value. Yet, when not forced to be specific on returns, many probably found it easier to underweight Japan to a degree that came close to reflecting their view on valuation.

Of course, fund managers can always be forced to produce return forecasts, so lack of data is seldom a critical problem, but if managers reason and act in the way described, an optimizer's output may not truly reflect their views. Bringing together the data required by the optimizer and the thought process of a manager can be a difficult, although not impossible, task.

A much more serious problem is what an optimizer does with data it is provided with. Optimizers are often derided for producing obvious or silly results. Consider the Hong Kong portfolio discussed above. If one aims to have the least risky portfolio and at least 60% of the portfolio in real assets it surely does not require an optimizer to suggest a 40% cash and bond and a 60% equity split. That bit is obvious, what about the rest? One notes that the portfolio is very mismatched against Hong Kong liabilities and even against Hong Kong and US liabilities (recall the currency tie between the HK$ and the US$). Nearly a quarter of the portfolio is invested in German and Swiss equities which on a world equity index capitalization-weighted basis would be about 4% of the portfolio. Further, these markets have a very restricted range of stocks. Is this a sensible allocation?

The usual reason that an optimizer produces strange results is that it will significantly overweight assets with large expected returns, negative correlation of returns with other assets and small variances. Yet these assets are likely to be the ones that have the largest errors in their estimates. If an asset looks too good to be true, it probably is. Optimizers are, in effect, estimation error maximizers. One would guess that in the above example that the German and Swiss markets had high expected returns and, judging by the other weights, the writer would guess that currency returns probably drove the allocation. The error estimation properties of optimizers mean that an "optimal" portfolio's risk is likely to be understated. The Hong Kong portfolio shown does not seem to be low risk on a common sense basis. The problem may seem to be a problem of poor forecasts, but it is more general than that. Simple random errors in estimation will always pose a problem because the program, in effect, goes looking for certain types of errors.

There are a host of other problems with optimizers. Often the optimizations are highly unstable in the sense that small changes in assumptions lead to quite different solutions. Again because of errors in inputs, the unique solution produced by the optimizer is better seen as highlighting an area on the efficient frontier within which the optimal portfolio may lie. Unfortunately, even quite close points on the efficient frontier can imply quite different combinations of assets.

Some of the disadvantages of optimizers can be reduced by setting constraints on the size of deviation from index or other benchmark positions (see e.g., Frost and Savarino, 1988). But with many constraints, one may wonder what exactly the optimizer is left to do and whether an experienced fund manager would not do as well by "eyeballing" the problem.

It is not surprising that optimizers have not been adopted by all fund managers although a little surprising that more do not keep the technique under review. After all, if we produce an allocation such as that shown for the Hong Kong fund and we don't like the outcome, we could reduce the forecast returns for the German and Swiss equities and re-run the optimization. There is no reason why an investor should not interact with the computer. This is especially the case now that some optimizers allow the approach to be used in reverse. We argued above that fund managers often rank markets without producing explicit return forecasts. They also produce asset allocations. Providing managers will specify their attitude to risk and will accept historical standard deviations and correlations, it is possible to take their portfolios and deduce the returns that they must be assuming if their portfolios are efficient. The managers can then be presented with their implicit forecasts and asked if they really believe them. Fund managers might be willing to consider their implicit forecasts and even change them, even though they would not initially produce forecasts. Alternatively they may still resist making an explicit forecast but change their asset allocation.

Optimizers can be useful, and they allow risk to influence asset allocation. But they can be dangerous when used in a mechanical manner because of their error maximization properties.

BLENDING QUANTITATIVE AND SUBJECTIVE ANALYSIS

More investment managers use an optimizer for tactical asset allocation than do for constructing a share portfolio. But most don't use an optimizer even for asset allocation. A non-optimizer approach can be quantitative or largely subjective. We will discuss a non-optimizer approach taking a two-stage approach. Investors might look at their intra-domestic tactical asset allocation and separately at the intra-international and then as another decision look at the domestic/international weight.

We reviewed a number of tactical asset allocation tools that might be used to help determine the domestic allocation in Chapters 25 to 28 and the same considerations as were discussed in share portfolio construction apply. To the extent that tactical asset allocation tools have some predictive value, and their forecasts are not perfectly correlated, it is worth using several tools. Most investors use a combination of business cycle analysis and valuation measures. Some managers use the same measures consistently whereas others look at a variety of indicators and subjectively combine them, giving different measures prominence at different times. Some tools involve estimating a total return (e.g., the equity risk premium) whereas others provide only a relative qualitative valuation (e.g., the yield ratio). Managers who use the same measures consistently, especially a measure such as the equity risk premium, are more likely to follow a quantitative rule for relating the degree of over- or underweighting of an asset class to its degree of mispricing (recall Figure 35).

Devising a sensible international equity mix is harder than devising a sensible domestic equity/bonds/cash mix. There is more of an *ad hoc* juggling of rules of thumb feel about the process. Most investors use a variety of inputs. These include elements of national business cycle anticipation such as the level and direction of inflation and interest rates, profits momentum and expected economic policy. Valuation measures are also used. These may consist of domestic comparisons— local equities versus local bonds—or inter-market comparisons, which may be based on absolute measures such as high dividend yields, low price-earnings ratios or relative measures such as country X's dividend yield relative to its own history compared with country Y's dividend yield relative. Less frequently used, are technical measures and liquidity factors.

The above factors may be pulled together in a formal or informal manner. An in-between approach is to produce some form of check list such as Table 62 (not all of the factors shown would be included, because many measure much the same thing). Each factor may be given a cheap or dear response or a rating on a five point scale for each country. Countries can then be rated by either the number of cheap responses, or the number of points awarded. Slightly more complex, each valuation measure could be given a different weight.

The tools used by a manager for making intra-domestic allocation and intra-international allocation may differ. For example total returns may be calculated for the domestic market and measures of relative value used in the international markets. One way of linking the two sets of analyses is to evaluate the domestic equity market in the same way as the international equity markets have been. Then, after deciding whether domestic equities are relatively cheap or dear, and after allowance for currency changes, a decision can be made on the weighting of domestic and international assets.

Table 62 Factors Involved in Rating International Markets

Factor	Ranking*
Earnings per share growth	Fast
Price-earnings ratio (PER)	Low
PER relative to own history	Low
Yield	High
Yield relative to own history	High
Bond yield/ dividend yield ratio	Low relative to own history
Bond yield relative to earnings yield	Low relative to own history
Trend in interest and bond yields	Down
Yield relative to world yield	High relative to history
PER relative to world PER	Low relative to history
Equity risk premium	High
Stage in economic cycle	Near end of recession; early growth
Currency trend	Strong
Long-term growth potential	High
Scenario forecasting	Growth and low inflation
Politics	Lack of uncertainty; pro-market government

* Description indicates direction for a favourable equity market rating

CONCLUDING COMMENTS

We have looked at two different approaches to tactical asset allocation. One, optimization, uses total return estimates (plus variances and covariances) and calculates an efficient frontier. This method blends risks and returns to produce efficient portfolios. This approach is used less often in practice than the textbooks imply. Many investors resist any quantitative approach but optimizers do pose genuine mathematical problems. In particular, they tend to be estimate error maximizers, focusing on those estimates most likely to be in error, thereby producing implausible allocations. Nonetheless, managers can improve the optimization process by interacting with it and changing estimates to produce more sensible outcomes.

The second approach to tactical asset allocation makes a series of comparisons without attempting to maximize the risk-reducing effects of diversification. To the extent that the tactical asset allocation tools discussed in Chapters 25 to 29 have predictive value and offer some independent information, using several tools will be advantageous. Some investors use the same tools consistently, while others look at many and give different tools prominence at different times. Some of the tools produce explicit return forecasts whereas others do not. Some tools can be used to derive specific asset weightings whereas others are used more subjectively.

PART FOUR
Further Aspects of
International Investment

International asset allocation is a large topic, albeit one that often gets only brief treatment in the standard textbooks. An intermediate position is adopted here—international asset allocation is discussed in several chapters but the coverage of topics is limited. Very little time is spent on general arguments about the case for international investing and the special risks an international investor faces. These topics are covered at length in the textbooks.

In Chapter 29 we looked at international tactical asset allocation. In this Part we look at two topics. The preceding discussion has used a mixture of UK and US evidence. The similarities between the markets seem greater than the differences. Of course there are differences, but a practical starting point for an investor in either country would be always to examine approaches that work in one country to see if they have relevance to the other. Other countries perhaps have more unique features, although this should probably not be overstated. Japan, however, is often seen as the most mysterious and irrational of the major markets and it is worth saying a little on the Japanese market. The US, Japan and the UK constitute about three-quarters of the world's equity markets on a capitalization-weighted basis. As we shall see in Chapters 31 and 32, Japan certainly has unique features, but Japanese asset pricing is not as odd as is often made out.

In Chapter 33 we discuss the small emerging markets. There is a tendency to omit these markets from institutional portfolios because they do not appear in the major equity indexes. Some of these markets, however, are in countries whose economies are larger than many of the Western industrialized nations. Further, the markets have interesting risk and return properties which make them excellent for diversification purposes. The markets are individually risky, but as a group they dramatically reduce risk when added to a traditional portfolio.

31
Selecting Japanese Stocks

A major issue international investors have to face is whether each market is unique and can only be understood by its own logic. While most investors believe that the various markets have some unique features, few would accept that markets have their own distinct logic. Nonetheless, in the second half of the 1980s the Japanese market tested many investors' beliefs. The market soared to what seemed to many to be overvalued levels and then crashed at the beginning of the 1990s. Figure 38 shows a 20 year history of the Japanese market. Is Japan different, or can it be analysed much like any other market? Many investors see the Japanese market as mysterious, irrational and rigged. Yet why should the market of such an economically successful nation not behave much like other large markets? Are there no profit-orientated investors, or is profit-orientated behaviour only manifested in the Japanese market by riding a trend and then jumping off?

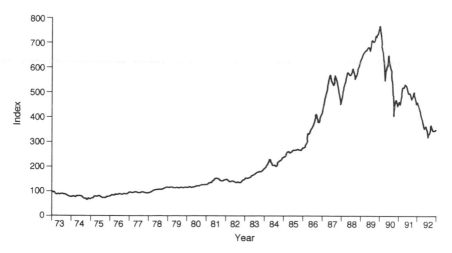

Figure 38   Japanese Market: Datastream Total Market Index, 1973–92. Copyright © 1993 Datastream International Ltd

The truth seems to lie somewhere between the view that the Japanese market is unlike any other and the view that it is just like any other large market. To give a flavour of the common characteristics and unique characteristics of international markets we discuss the Japanese market in this and the following chapter. In this chapter, unlike the rest of the book, some institutional details will be given, albeit on an informal basis. We will do this in terms of the Japanese market's "players" and their "games": we begin with the players.

MARKET PLAYERS

The Japanese equity shareholding and trading pattern is different from that in the UK and other major markets. In Britain, financial institutions dominate share registers. In Japan, industrial corporations own nearly a quarter of all shares, while banks, trust banks and insurance companies own over 40% and individuals over 20%. Foreigners and investment trusts hold the balance. In terms of market activity, individuals and foreigners are disproportionately active.

The company shareholdings and part of the banks' and insurance companies' holdings are especially interesting, being essentially cross-holdings based on extended families of companies called *keiretsu*. These consist of several firms associated with a banking group, and are a modern version of the pre-war *zaibatsu*, or holding company structure. Japanese firms have made more use of debt than Western companies and so have stronger relationships with their banks. Part of the banks' and insurance companies' shareholdings are cross-holdings and will not usually be traded. In addition, companies generally buy shares in their main suppliers and customers. These holdings are intended to cement relationships and induce business and the various *keiretsu* companies are expected to help each other.

It would be wrong to see all non-individual share holdings as *keiretsu* holdings and companies have been stock market players as well, especially in the mid-1980s, when they had excess liquidity and were uncertain about the business outlook. With poor profit prospects and low deposit rates, companies in search of better returns began engaging in *zaiteku*, or "financial engineering". Investments were made in land, bonds and the stock market. For a period, many companies were making more profits in the stock market than in their main business. However, with stronger economic growth towards the end of the 1980s, and the odd speculative abuse, *zaiteku* diminished. Following the 1990 market crash, *zaiteku* is not an important activity, although in early 1993 large losses from earlier *zaiteku* activities were still being reported.

Until the early 1980s banks accounted for less than 5% of all share trading but, following a change in tax regulations, in December 1980, banks began to be active traders in specified money trust accounts, or *tokkin* accounts. The tax change enabled companies to use their growing liquidity to trade equities in entirely segregated accounts without affecting the book cost of strategic holdings, incurring capital gains tax or disturbing corporate relationships. Despite the burst of *tokkin* activity it is generally thought that a least half the shares in the market are not traded but are effectively locked-in via cross-holdings. This estimate may be a little high but, whatever the exact percentage, cross-holdings are currently very important.

Because of the current strength of cross-holdings, the private investor is rather more important in determining individual share prices than the percentage share-holding suggests. Historically, the Japanese private investor has been a housewife; the Japanese family's purse being controlled by the wife. She accounts for a larger proportion of traded shares than the proportion of shares held. The private investor is also a major margin player. Consequently, housewives have been the target of the major stockbrokers which have large retail sales forces.

The broking industry is dominated by four firms—Nomura, Daiwa, Nikko and Yamaichi—which together account for half of market turnover. These brokers' views are widely disseminated and the brokers, therefore, have considerable power to move share prices, at least on a temporary basis.

However, one should not exaggerate the importance of the private investors. At the end of World War II the private investor held about 70% of all shares. Even in 1975 individuals were responsible for more than 70% of all share trades. There has been a post-war secular decline of the importance of the private investor and this is likely to continue, even with the demise of *zaiteku* and *tokkin* accounts. Pension funds, which will inevitably become more important with the ageing population structure of Japan, are restricted to having no more than 30% of their hold ings in equities. Were the regulations to change, institutional domination of the market would increase and the growth would be likely to be through institutions that would trade shares more actively. In the long run this might weaken the concept of non-traded cross-holdings.

One might expect individual shares, and possibly the entire market, to be volatile given that only part of the market is actually traded, that it is dominated by a few major brokers peddling well-publicized stories to private clients, and that even the professional investors appear (as we shall see) to be speculative players. Yet, until recently, the market has been one of the world's least volatile.

It is worth saying a few words about foreigners, or *gaijin*. Foreigners first became significant players in the Japanese market in the 1960s, attracted by rapid economic growth and low price-earnings ratios. Removal of UK exchange controls in 1979 freed the most adventurous of the large international investors to enter the market in a major way. There had been a general retreat by foreigners after the first oil crisis of 1973–74, but after the second oil crisis of 1979, foreigners were aggressive buyers, having seen how rapidly Japan could respond to shocks.

In 1984, as the Japanese market price-earnings ratio began to soar, foreigners turned net sellers, a position that continued through to 1990, apart from 1988 when they were effectively neither buyers nor sellers. In 1991 foreigners were net buyers. It has been argued, however, that the figures on which these statements are based are misleading. Japanese companies have issued a large proportion of new equity as foreign currency-denominated convertible bonds or bonds with warrants. Foreigners' purchases were classified as bonds, but eventual disposal after conversion or exercise was of the resulting equity. It is claimed that when this is allowed for, foreigners were net sellers only in 1986 and 1987.

MARKET GAMES

Having described the players in the stock market we now describe the games they play. Japanese investors can be classified as technical or fundamental, much as in the West. Technical analysis is very popular and a large number of chart books can be readily purchased in Japan. Fundamental analysis is also carried out and the brokers are prolific producers of economic and company research.

Japanese analysts carry out the same fundamental share analysis as Western analysts do, looking at balance sheet ratios, price-earnings ratios and so forth. The Japanese are becoming more analytical, and quantitative techniques are becoming more popular: Roll and Ross have been successful in selling their arbitrage pricing model in Japan and there has been a move to indexation. Foreign investors in Japan look at price-earnings ratios, and foreigners are still significant in terms of actively traded Japanese shares. However, it is also true that the reliance placed on price-earnings ratios by Japanese investors is less than that of Western investors in their own markets, and Japanese investors seem to be more story-driven than numbers driven. Some of the stories that drive Japanese stocks are listed below.

Incentive or speculative issues

The principal actor of the Japanese classical Noh theatre is known as the *shite* and this term is used to describe "operators" or "speculators" in the stock market. The stocks they are involved with are called *shite kabu*, incentive or speculative stocks. These stocks move on rumours of new developments and are the main interest of many private investors. Stocks bought on this basis are not long-term investments. Matsumoto (1989, p. 47), giving advice on how to deal in such stocks, notes:

> "It is also important to remember that it is a short-term action, and if as much as a month has gone by, it is usually a good sign to start getting out."

Restructuring stocks

Japanese industry has been adept at restructuring. Japan has transformed itself from defeat in the Second World War to become a major economic power. Industry has switched from low wages and copy-cat output to high wages and advanced technology. Companies have had to adapt to large changes in the value of the Yen and in oil prices. Subjected to these and other shifts, many firms have diversified. Given the success of Japanese industry at restructuring, it is not surprising that this is a popular stock market "theme".

Market themes

All stock markets have sectors that move in and out of favour as economic circumstances change. They also sometimes have "themes", which are broader than sectors. For example, a popular theme in the US in the first half of the 1980s was disinflation stocks. The Japanese market is unusual only in the enthusiasm with which *tema* are embraced. Roth's definition (1989, p. 81) of a theme is perhaps only a little too cynical:

> "A theme is a concept that is realistic enough to hold out the possibility of massive profits somewhere down the line for the companies involved, but is also sufficiently vague to encompass the greatest possible number of stocks."

Themes have focused on scientific developments, major projects such as the Tokyo Bay redevelopment and new stories such as AIDS. Themes are one reason for the very wide price-earnings ratio distribution to be found within Japanese sectors.

Latent assets

The preference of Japanese investors has been nicely captured by Yamashita, who states that they "prefer earnings to dividends, cash flow to earnings, and current replacement cost of net assets to cash flow". (1989, p. 83). Certainly, Japanese investors do not get much in the way of dividends—the yield on the Tokyo market is less than 1%. Management emphasis has been very much on sales growth and market share, minimizing tax payments, and increasing asset value while maintaining a high level of liquidity. Short-term profit has been rather less important and shareholders have accepted this orientation. Regulated companies have an additional incentive to keep reported profits down in order to get rate increases.

Whether Japanese firms will continue to seek market share rather than profits and whether shareholders will accept low payouts remains to be seen. Asset value has clearly been an important consideration for the Japanese investor, but why *latent* assets? This is largely a function of Japanese accounting practices which lead to hidden reserves or latent assets. Japanese accounting practices are heavily influenced by tax regulations: book-tax conformity is required, i.e., items claimed for tax purposes must be reflected in published accounts.

Three of the major causes of latent assets relate to land, investments and depreciation:

- Revaluation of property is not permitted (except on amalgamation when it is required) and, given the rapid rise in land prices, especially in Tokyo, many companies have latent land assets. This remains true, despite recent land price falls.

- Investments are shown at the lower of cost or market value. Given the rise in the Japanese stock market in the last decade, significant latent assets exist here. The Nikkei Average stood at 6570 at the start of 1980, 13 083 at the start of 1986 and 16 925 at the start of 1993.
- Accelerated depreciation can be made for tax purposes and since the depreciation rate can be greater than that used to write off the asset over its economic life, fixed assets can be understated.

It is easy to take a tough-minded view about latent assets. Since aggressive mergers and acquisitions are rare, although likely to become less so, what value are latent assets to the shareholder? Share investments are often cross-holdings so their value will not be realized. Further, if assets are so much larger than they appear, rates of return must be correspondingly lower: hardly a sign of efficiency. Alternatively, the asset values cannot be as high as assumed. Nonetheless, latent assets do attract the Japanese investor.

Tobin's q ratio

Tobin's q ratio is the market valuation of equities relative to the replacement cost of the physical assets they represent. Tobin used the ratio when trying to explain the transmission mechanism—how excess demand or supply of money feeds through to changes in aggregate expenditure. In Japanese practice, however, the q ratio is just another term for the concept of premium or discount to net asset value.

Speculative groups

Although aggressive take-over attempts are rare, there is sometimes pressure on companies to agree to a change in the management, or an agreed take-over. Certainly there are speculative groups—comprising companies or individuals—who try to corner the shares in a company and bring about changes or engage in greenmail. *Kaishime* speculators, i.e., corporate merger and acquisition speculators, usually do not intend to carry through their threats but hope the public will pile in and the speculators can then unload their shares at higher prices. The speculators are said to be "lighting lanterns". Ideal speculative stocks have a large free float of shares, management rifts and hidden assets.

In the past, the Japanese have viewed merger and acquisition activity with horror. Agreed take-overs and various speculative activities have been acceptable, but straightforward hostile take-over bids have been rare. There are, however, signs that this is changing. Merger and acquisition deals have increased in the last few years and Japanese firms have acquired foreign firms, while a small number of foreign firms have acquired Japanese firms. Changes appear to be underway, with the Ministry of Finance beginning to show signs of adopting a more Western approach to mergers and acquisitions. Pressure is being exerted by foreigners as a result of increased cross-border merger activities. Foreigners wishing to make take-overs of Japanese firms suffer more restrictive regulations than do Japanese firms seeking to acquire Western firms.

Political ramping

Because of the enormous costs involved in election campaigns, Japanese politicians have, in the past, been involved in ramping stocks to raise funds. The politician buys a stock and it is either ramped by a broker, or the politician, by virtue of his office, ensures contracts or other favours go the company's way. Recent scandals and their consequences suggest this is a game that may be played less frequently in the future.

Others

The above is by no means an exhaustive list of the "games" played in Japan. As in other markets, blue chips, growth stocks or small stocks are popular from time to time, as well as low price stocks and, unique to Japan, high absolute price stocks.

Having examined the players, and focused on some of their more colourful games, one might conclude that:

- There is a large speculative element in the Japanese market.
- While earnings are important, forming the ultimate rationale for many themes, it is difficult to argue that a very careful discounting procedure is always employed. It is earnings stories, rather than earnings numbers, that seem to be important.
- Investors clearly place a lot of reliance on net asset values. Unfortunately, while the analysis made in terms of any one share seems sensible, one cannot help but wonder if the analysis makes sense in aggregate. Investors and businessmen seem to get derisory returns from assets—if assets are a capitalized stream of earnings, can the assets really be worth what they are said to be worth?

BUT THINGS MAY NOT BE WHAT THEY APPEAR

We should be cautious of the value of general discussions of the type given above. Inevitably one tends to focus on the vivid and exotic, the things that seem unusual to a Westerner, and one tends to ignore more mundane fundamental analysis. Even if some investors play rather odd games, that does not mean that other investors do not exist who act to bring prices back to some Western notion of intrinsic value or produce similar anomalies. Several recent studies shed light on this.

Chan et al.(1991) studied the Tokyo stock market for the period 1971–88. Their sample drew from both manufacturing and non-manufacturing companies, and both First and Second Sections (i.e., large and small companies). They tried to explain cross-sectional differences in returns on Japanese stocks by four variables—earnings yield (i.e., the reciprocal of the price-earnings ratio), size, book-to-price ratio, and cash flow yield (i.e., earnings plus depreciation divided by price). Looking at each variable on its own, small stocks outperformed large, low price-earnings ratio stocks outperformed high, high cash flow yield stocks outperformed low and high book-to-price ratio stocks outperformed low. However, the variables were correlated, so Chan et al. undertook a multivariate analysis. They found that the book value and cash flow variables continued to be significant. Book value was the more important. The size effect was sensitive to the model specification and was often not significant. The price-earnings ratio effect was hard to disentangle—low price-earnings ratios in isolation had a favourable effect on returns, no effect once book-to-price was added and a negative effect when all four variables were included. These findings are a striking confirmation of Yamashita's views stated earlier in the sub-section on latent assets.

Elton and Gruber (1989) examined the effect of changes in analysts' forecasts of earnings and sales per share on the subsequent price perfomance of Japanese stocks. Their findings were very similar to US evidence:

> "earnings, not sales, drive stock prices in Japan. Analysts' estimates are incorporated with a lag. Because of this lag, extra returns can be earned by buying stocks immediately after an upward revision in analysts' earning estimates." (p. 401)

Rao et al. (1992) found that Japanese returns varied in exactly the same way as in the US in relation to dividend yield, i.e., the highest returns are for stocks with no yield, otherwise they increase with increasing yield. Ziemba (1991) reported that calendar effects in the Japanese market were quite similar to those in the US.

CONCLUDING COMMENTS

On the basis of our general discussion one has to conclude that the Japanese market is different in many ways from Western markets. But a general discussion inevitably focuses on the more colourful differences and this is reinforced by the tendency of Japanese brokers to promote the notion of Japan being unique. Turning to quantitative analysis, the way stocks appear to be priced according to Chan et al., Elton and Gruber, Rao et al, and Ziemba, does not appear to be unique or irrational. Indeed, a Westerner using screens of simple valuation measures should have some hope of achieving good performance. One can point to some irrational features of the Japanese market—for example we might ask how the Japanese could have believed the property values reported in Tokyo in the late 1980s. But the Japanese were not alone in misjudging property matters as we saw earlier in Chapter 18 and Western markets appear to have speculative bubbles too.

In the next chapter we continue our analysis of the Japanese market and discuss its level.

32
The Japanese Market Level

Many Westerners have taken one look at the level of the Japanese market's price-earnings ratio in recent years and decided that either there has been an enormous speculative bubble or the market is irrational. Yet the level of the Japanese market appears to be affected by many of the same variables that affect other markets, although the emphasis on some of these variables is a little different, reflecting the structure of the Japanese economy.

If it is to be argued that the Japanese market is "rational" in some sense, one would expect Japanese analysts to examine key macro-economic variables that affect dividends, earnings and interest rates, as these are the key components of any rational Western approach to valuing financial assets, such as the dividend discount model. In fact, Japanese analysts do a lot of research on these factors and favourable or unfavourable macro-economic influences often drive the entire market.

Indeed, there is some broad agreement as to what drives the market in terms of the variables investors discuss, and these are included in simple correlation studies and more complex econometric models. Most analysts see changes in GNP, inflation, interest rates, oil prices, the Yen/Dollar rate and the Marshallian K as important. Western arbitrage pricing theorists would presumably approve of the list. The importance of GNP, inflation and interest rates is obvious enough. Because Japan has to import its oil, oil prices affect the balance of payments, the exchange rate and the rate of inflation, which in turn affects the level of interest rates. Attention to some measure of the strength of the Yen is not surprising either, given the importance of exports to a number of Japanese industries and the impact of the value of the currency on inflation and interest rates. The Japanese appear to be the only investors in the world to focus on the Marshallian K, the reciprocal of the velocity of circulation.

Of course, all of this may be necessary for the market to be rational, but it is not sufficient. Two key questions need to be addressed. Why has the Japanese market sold on a higher price-earnings ratio than other markets and why did it soar in the mid-1980s and then fall?

There is no reason why all markets should sell on the same price-earnings ratio

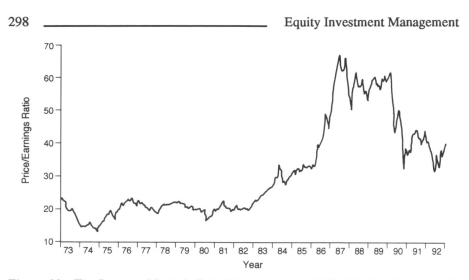

Figure 39   The Japanese Market's Price-Earnings Ratio: 1973–92. Copyright © 1993 Datastream International Ltd

any more than all stocks should sell on the same price-earnings ratio. Higher growth rates justify higher price-earnings ratios. Before one delves into this, however, one might ask whether the Japanese market has always sold on a high price-earnings ratio. Figure 39 shows the rise in the price-earnings ratio since 1973 (the start of Datastream's database). In the 1950s and 1960s the price-earnings ratio was lower, averaging less than 10 in the first period and about 15 in the second. On any simple comparison, the Japanese equity market from the mid-1980s appeared expensive relative to its own history.

Growth in Japan has averaged over 4% throughout the period shown in Figure 39 whereas in the period 1960–73 Japanese growth averaged over 9%. In the 15 years preceding the first oil crisis, Japan had very high economic growth compared to other countries, but reasonably high inflation. In the years following the first oil crisis Japan had more modestly superior growth; the biggest change was that Japan became a low inflation economy.

Possibly the sensible way to relate these changes to the stock market ratings is to argue that prior to the first oil crisis the Japanese market was simply undervalued. (Of course, this will not seem sensible to an efficient market theorist.) The Japanese had few surplus funds during that period and most investment was being channelled into physical plant and equipment, rather than the stock market. If one views the situation in these terms it is probably not the slow-down in Japanese economic growth after 1973 that one should be concentrating on but the dramatically lower inflation levels which began in 1982, and the effect on interest rates.

Popular approaches to explaining away the high price-earnings ratio of the last eight years have been to deny that the price-earnings ratio is relevant, because of latent assets, or re-work it so that it falls to Western levels. This approach involves a number of accounting adjustments, some of which seem legitimate—and some of which do not. Let us look at these issues.

RE-CALCULATING THE JAPANESE PRICE-EARNINGS RATIO

Asset values

In the stock selection discussion in the previous chapter we noted that the Japanese put less stress on profits than Westerners and are more concerned about asset values. We also noted that because of accounting conventions there are significant latent assets. One might argue, therefore, that the market price-earnings ratio is of little interest, as are stock price-earnings ratios, and some measure of book-to-price would be a better way of judging the Tokyo market. A feature of the pre-crash market was rising property values. Unfortunately it is hard to justify the rise in property values that took place in Japan. Prices soared in Tokyo yet rents did not (although see Ueda, 1990). It was inconceivable that an economic return could be made on property purchased during the boom (although the position is complicated by the tax treatment of real assets). It was claimed at one stage that the Imperial Palace grounds in Tokyo, if valued on the basis of prices for commercial property, were worth as much as California. Property appeared to suffer a speculative bubble and to base stock market prices on property prices essentially abandons an attempt at rational explanation. Nonetheless it should be noted that the property market's rise and fall has broadly coincided with the extraordinary rise and fall of the stock market.

Accounting Adjustments

If we focus on price-earnings ratios rather than asset values, there are several accounting adjustments which can be used to argue that Japanese price-earnings ratios are not as high as they appear. For instance, if half the shares quoted on the Japanese market are not likely to be traded and, because of *keiretsu* holdings, are held for reasons other than the dividend stream they generate, it could be argued that the cross-holdings should be eliminated from price-earnings calculations. This immediately halves the Japanese price-earnings ratio. It is hard to take this approach seriously. *Keiretsu* holders, if they hold enough shares, equity account them and they certainly bank their dividend cheques. There is, perhaps, some justification in arguing that if part of the market will never be traded under any circumstances, it is simply not available to foreigners and, therefore, a world index which is constructed on the investable stock principle (namely, stocks foreigners can actually invest in) should omit a large part of the Japanese market. On that basis the Japanese market would be much smaller than it is usually claimed to be. However, whatever the merits of this quite different argument, there seems to be little basis for reducing the price-earnings ratio on the basis of cross-holdings.

Legitimate accounting adjustments appear to be to allow for the non-consolidation of Japanese accounts, special reserves (which are not quantitatively very significant and will not be discussed here) and accelerated depreciation. The Ministry of Finance made the publication of consolidated accounts mandatory only in 1977. Parent accounts had to be lodged with the Stock Exchange within two months of the balance sheet date and with the Ministry of Finance within three months. Consolidated accounts appeared much later, so most analytical work used parent company data. From March 1989, companies have been required to present consolidated accounts together with parent accounts. In fact, many major companies with significant overseas interests have for many years presented additional accounting information showing consolidated accounts drawn up on Western accounting principles. For the market as a whole, given the change in regulations, non-consolidation will become less of an issue.

Consolidation of accounts could have produced a higher or lower price-earnings ratio, but most Japanese estimates suggested that consistent consolidation of accounts would have lowered the market price-earnings ratio by 10–15%. Some estimates suggest much higher numbers. For example, French and Poterba (1991) claim that the reduction is nearly a third. Non-consolidation of accounts will have had most effect in terms of overstating price-earnings ratios prior to 1977, but the degree of cross-holding has increased over time so that the net effect has probably been for a modest increase in the effect of non-consolidation over time.

A major accounting adjustment has to be made for the use of accelerated depreciation in Japan, because most other countries use straight-line depreciation. The Japanese approach is conservative by comparison and understates earnings as long as there is significant capital investment. Were investment to cease, then, as past asset purchases become fully depreciated, an accelerated depreciation nation would overstate earnings and artificially lower price-earnings ratios.

Contrary to the impression often given, especially by Japanese brokers in the late 1980s attempting to show Japanese price-earnings ratios were not really high, there is a very wide range of estimates of the impact of different depreciation methods. Estimates range from the Japanese price-earnings ratio being overstated by about 75% to it being understated by a few percent. A typical finding is that of a Prudential-Bache study which claimed that the Japanese price-earnings ratio was probably overstated by 10–15% (Schieneman, 1982).

The weight of the evidence appears to be that conservative Japanese depreciation generally understates earnings and, therefore, overstates the price-earnings ratio. The size of this overstatement is far from clear and varies from year to year but around 10% might be a sensible guess for the 1980s. Whatever the number, there is no reason to believe that the rapid rise in the market price-earnings ratio after the early 1980s can be explained by an increasingly greater depreciation bias, nor that Japanese or Western investors only noticed the depreciation policy of Japanese firms in the mid-1980s and made a one-off adjustment.

Pulling together adjustments for non-consolidation, special reserves and accelerated depreciation, it is doubtful if Japanese price-earnings ratios should be reduced
by more than 30%. (French and Poterba reduce the Japanese price-earnings ratio
by more, but they also adjust the US price-earnings ratio and the net effect is a
reduction of nearly 32%.) In short, it is possible to adjust the Japanese market
price-earnings ratio, but it still looks high in relation to other markets, and the
adjustments do not explain why it rose sharply in the 1980s.

SHOULD THE JAPANESE PRICE-EARNINGS RATIO BE HIGH?

A different approach to the Japanese price-earnings ratio is to consider it in the
context of a dividend discount model. If either the required return or the expected
growth rate change, this could have a big impact on the value of the market and
the price-earnings ratio. French and Poterba pursued this approach to explain the
changed price-earnings ratio in the 1980s. There is little evidence of a change in
expected growth in the 1980s, but the real yield on bonds fell by 1% in 1986.
Further, the Japanese tax reform of 1987 eliminated the tax break that private
investors enjoyed in *Maruyu* savings accounts. These two effects justified a higher
price-earnings ratio for the market, although not as high as it actually attained.

Investors more often use an earnings yield/long bond comparison than a dividend discount model to assess the value of a market, so let us move to that comparison. Figure 40 shows the Japanese earnings yield and the yield on long-dated
Japanese Government bonds since 1973. In broad terms, the two lines follow each

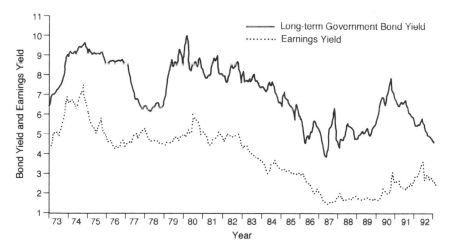

Figure 40 Earnings Yield and the Yield on Long-Dated Japanese Government Bonds:
1973–92. Copyright © 1993 Datastream International Ltd

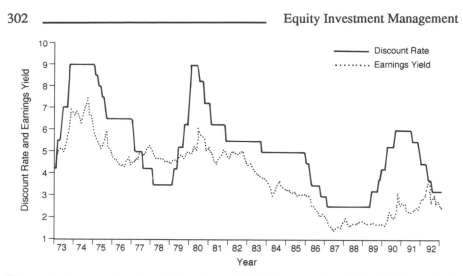

Figure 41 Japanese Earnings Yield and the Official Discount Rate: 1973–92. Copyright © 1993 Datastream International Ltd

other, although the correlation is far from perfect. Sometimes the two lines go in opposite directions or have quite disproportionate moves, and bond yields are rather erratic from 1986 onwards. Many investment models relate equities to bonds with an implicit assumption that bonds are correctly priced. There is no reason to assume this and it is often helpful to look at equities in relation to other indicators such as short rates.

Figure 41 shows the Japanese earnings yield and the Official Discount Rate and it is clear that in 1975 the Bank of Japan was giving a different signal than the bond market and again from 1987 onwards. It seems reasonable to argue that combining only a modest amount of judgement with the relationships shown in Figures 40 and 41, one can say something sensible about likely changes in the level of the market price-earnings ratio.

The gap between the earnings yield and bond yield has broadly averaged between 3 and 3.5% but has been subject to fluctuations which can be explained by the rate of growth (positive or negative) of mining and manufacturing production or a yield spread variable. Nomura, for example, uses a valuation model of the stock market which relates the market price-earnings ratio to the level of long bond rates and the slope of Japan's yield curve.

The above analysis suggests that the changes in the level of the Japanese price-earnings ratio were not as irrational as often portrayed. However, although the *change* in the market price-earnings ratio since 1983 can be explained by changing bond yields, that does not really answer the question of whether the *absolute* level of the price-earnings ratio was correct. The impression is that it was not, and the price-earnings appears to have been too high, although the accounting adjustments noted earlier would move the price-earnings ratio in the right direction.

FORECASTING THE MARKET LEVEL

Many investors have claimed that the Japanese market has been hard to forecast because of the valuation problem. This is only partially true. If investors use an approach such as that implied by Figure 40, they have to forecast profits, bond yields and the relationship between the two—i.e., whether the relationship will be above or below its average. There has been a tendency to assume that calling the Japanese market correctly has been all about forecasting the price-earnings ratio. In fact forecasting profits have often been more of a problem. For example, it seemed to the writer that Japan was poor value in 1988, and this was based on a widening gap between the bonds and earnings yield, the likelihood that the next move in the Official Discount Rate would be up and Japanese forecasts that profits would increase by only 10%. In fact profits increased by 25% and it was not surprising that the market continued to rise. At the start of 1992, Nomura thought the market was reasonable value around 20 000 on the Nikkei. But this was based on a view of no change in profits in 1992. At the end of 1992, first half profits for 1992 were reported to be down 41% in manufacturing and down 11% in non-manufacturing. Companies expected profits to be down by 25% for the full year—this would have suggested a Nikkei of 15 000 using Nomura's implicit price-earnings ratio. Clearly, there is more to forecasting the level of the Japanese market than simply forecasting the level of the price-earnings ratio.

CONCLUDING COMMENTS

In this chapter we have looked at the level of the Japanese stock market. For many years now, it has sold on a much higher price-earnings ratio than other major markets and at a much higher level than its own average historical level. Because of accounting differences, non-consolidation and special reserves, the Japanese price-earnings ratio is not directly comparable to Western price-earnings ratios but, even when adjustments are made for these differences, the ratio is still exceptionally high. Further, these factors would not have had a greater effect in the second half of the 1980s when the ratio soared. These factors cannot explain the change in the level of the rating. Part of the rating change can be explained in the context of a dividend discount model or an earnings yield/bond yield model. Part remains unexplained, presumably the effect of a speculative bubble. However, the Japanese market would not be the first market to have become overvalued. When forecasting the level of the market, careful attention should be paid to earnings forecasts as well as the earnings multiple. Clearly the Japanese market has unique characteristics, but it is far from clear that it has its own logic. Western analysis is helpful in understanding changes in the level of the Japanese market, although the actual level is perhaps slightly less understandable.

33
Emerging Markets

There has been increasing interest in "emerging markets" and it is worth saying a little about these markets. The components of International Finance Corporation's (IFC) Emerging Markets index are shown in Table 63.

Table 63   International Finance Corporation's Emerging Stock Markets: End 1991

Market	Market Capitalization (US$ billions)	Number of Listed Companies
Latin America		
Argentina	18.5	174
Brazil	42.8	570
Chile	28.0	221
Columbia	4.0	83
Mexico	98.2	209
Venezuela	11.2	66
East Asia		
Korea	96.4	686
Philippines	10.2	161
Taiwan	124.9	221
South Asia		
India	47.7	2556
Indonesia	6.8	141
Malaysia	58.6	321
Pakistan	7.3	542
Thailand	35.8	276
Europe/Mideast/Africa		
Greece	13.1	126
Jordan	2.5	101
Nigeria	1.9	142
Portugal	9.6	180
Turkey	15.7	134
Zimbabwe	1.4	60

Source: International Finance Corporation (1992, p. 4). Reproduced by permission

Most of the countries in the list are not included in the FT-A World Index or the Morgan Stanley Capital International (MSCI) World Index; they are developing economies and the markets are relatively small, limited in marketability and are less regulated than more mature markets. They may have only recently opened to outside investors or may still have significant restrictions. But other markets have similar characteristics and could reasonably be included, e.g., Costa Rica, Trinidad and Tobago, China, Papua New Guinea, Sri Lanka, Cyprus, Hungary, United Arab Emirates and Botswana. Indeed, with the demise of communism, there is a new group of emerging markets in Eastern Europe. Let's agree that we know what an emerging market is without being dogmatic about the correct index.

It is worth bearing in mind that the current size of these markets is not necessarily a good guide to the size of the underlying national economy. Indeed, the use of market exchange rates to calculate national income seriously understates the true size of some developing economies. If national income is calculated on the basis of purchasing power parity, to allow for international differences in prices, India has a larger economy than four of the G7 Group of industrial nations, i.e., France, Italy, the UK and Canada. Brazil and Mexico also have larger economies than Canada. China, which does not appear in the index at all, is probably the second largest economy in the world. The emerging markets will be very important in the long-term, but they already have interesting characteristics.

THE INTERESTING RISKS OF EMERGING MARKETS

From an investor's viewpoint, emerging markets have three interesting characteristics: they are very risky, they have offered high returns, they have low correlation of returns with each other and also with more developed markets. Measuring returns as annualized compound returns in US dollars over the five years ending June 30, 1991, and risks as the annualized standard deviation of sixty monthly returns, the US market returned 12.9% with a risk of 18.8% and the IFC's Composite Emerging Market Index returned 18.3% with a risk of 28.2% (Wilcox, 1992b, p. 52). Individually, the emerging market countries are very risky indeed. Nearly all have risks far higher than the US. But taken as a group the risk is greatly reduced—although still high. The reason risk falls so much by taking all the markets together is that their returns have a very low correlation with each other. The emerging markets are quite different from one another.

There are many ways of looking at these differences: size, political stability, growth rates and so forth. Jordan is a small country while Indonesia, with a population of 180 million, is one of the largest in the world. Zimbabwe is a tiny market while the market capitalization of Taiwan is about the same as that of Austria, Denmark, Finland, Ireland and Norway combined. Emerging market growth rates are on average higher than for developed countries but the spread of rates is much wider amongst emerging markets than among developed countries. There are few trade ties between the various emerging markets although there are, of course, some ties between countries in the same geographical area. And, from a strictly stock market viewpoint, the restrictions on investment that have existed, or still exist, tend to isolate the markets from each other.

Some investors have expressed concern that as developing countries become more tied into the world economy and investment restrictions disappear, the correlation of returns within the emerging markets and between them and the other markets will increase (see especially Speidell and Sappenfield, 1992). This may well happen, but the speed with which it will happen is probably overstated. European Community countries have been moving closer together for 40 years but their stock markets still don't move in lock-step. Wadhwani (1991b) examined the intra-European correlations for the periods 1973–79, 1980–85 and 1986–91. Short interest rates and bond yields showed increasing intra-Europe correlations over the three periods while equity correlations showed a dip in the middle period and a large rise in the most recent period. However, it turned out that US and European stock market correlations had risen over the three periods. Once this was allowed for, it appeared that the European markets were not becoming more similar to each other except through their increased correlation with the US. The increased correlation with the US was explained by Wadhwani to be a result of the increased percentage of European profits earned in the US, increased cross-border investment and a general "sentiment" factor.

If the European experience is a guide it seems likely that intra-emerging market correlations are unlikely to increase except via an increased correlation of each market with the rest of the world. Investment into the US from emerging market economies is likely to be trivial, so any increased correlation with the rest of the world may be modest. For the five years to the end of the first quarter of 1991 the correlation was 0.35.

Divecha et al. (1992) trace out the risk-return relationship obtained by varying the proportion of a portfolio invested in the FT-A World Index and the IFC Emerging Markets Index. This is shown in Figure 42. Starting from a 100% exposure to the world index we see that despite the higher risk of the emerging markets, adding emerging markets reduces risk—up to the point at which 20% of the portfolio is in emerging markets. The risk reduction is a result of the low correlation of returns between the two indexes. Because the emerging markets produced a higher return over the period to which the data relate, there was an increase in return as well as risk reduction.

What is the "best" mix? The efficient frontier between 20% in emerging markets through to somewhere between 30% to 40% dominates the 0% to 20% segment. If the risk level of the world index is acceptable, a fund should be at least 30% to 40% invested in emerging markets for a significantly enhanced return, i.e., it should be at that point on the efficient frontier directly above the world index. At that point higher return is achieved for no extra risk. Beyond that point, extra return comes at the cost of extra risk. At a common sense level these weightings

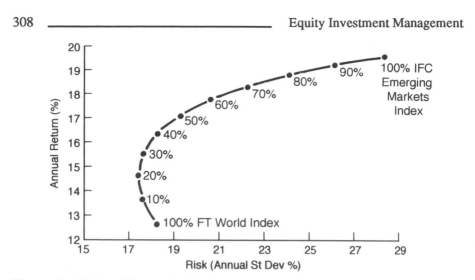

Figure 42 Risk and Return for Varying World and Emerging Market Mixes. Source: Divecha *et al.* (1992, p. 49). This copyrighted material is reprinted with the permission of *The Journal of Portfolio Management*

seem excessively high and they are very sensitive to the correlations assumed and the excess return earned by the emerging markets. But exposure to emerging markets does seem warranted.

SELECTING EMERGING MARKETS PORTFOLIOS

An investor can form an emerging markets portfolio in three ways:

- by selecting stocks
- by selecting markets
- by diversifying broadly

Arguments can be put forward for all three approaches. A few years ago it was possible to purchase stocks that were very mispriced based on asset value or other straightforward valuation techniques. This is less easy now. Nonetheless, some analysts argue that simplistic valuation rules have worked well both in the US and internationally in the past. While they may not have worked so well in the US in recent years, they have worked better in less mature markets. Referring to emerging markets, Wilcox (1992a, p.16) states that

> "judging from their enormous volatility, I hypothesize that they lack enough value-oriented investors. With computer-readable public data on hundreds of stocks in emerging markets, a global value-oriented investor could logically hope to enjoy superior returns ..."

A different approach would be to stress country selection. There are two reasons why this might be appropriate (see Divecha *et al.*, 1992). First, the low intra-emerging market return correlations, which offers scope for outperforming. Second, individual stock returns in emerging markets are more homogeneous than in developed markets. This is partly because the largest stocks and sectors in the emerging markets account for a large share of each market than is the case in the developed markets. More important is the high volatility of the emerging markets—for example, when the market goes up by a large amount in a short period, it is likely that most stocks will move up. The country selection approach would justify buying mutual funds or perhaps a few large stocks in each market. For the smaller investor, funds will often be an appropriate route.

The third approach to selecting emerging markets is to adopt the broadest possible diversification. Although fund managers may be tempted to pick the "better" markets and countries, the political and economic issues they will have to deal with are not the usual ones they face or have expertise in. Ibbotson and Brinson (1987, p. 114), discussing a different age, point out the dangers:

> "Eighteenth- or nineteenth-century investors who bet on the United States, Canada or Britain would have been prodigious forecasters of the world economy. ... In 1900, an international investor might well have bought Austro-Hungarian, Russian, and German stocks instead of US and British issues. The Austro-Hungarian equities would have lost all their value by the end of World War I. The Russian equities would have been rendered worthless by the communist government, which nationalized firms not long after the Russian Revolution of 1917. And German equity claims were wiped out by World War II."

To avoid these sort of risks an investor would diversify broadly in the emerging markets.

CONCLUDING COMMENTS

Managers who are measured against a standard world index benchmark may be tempted to omit emerging markets which are not included in such an index. So too might managers who just tag along with the median manager asset distribution. However, this would seem unwise if one focuses on the historical pattern of risk and return, and the client's interests. Emerging markets have good diversification characteristics and probably offer high returns.

A case can be argued for constructing an emerging market portfolio by stock picking, country selection or broad diversification. For most managers with only a small exposure to emerging markets, broad diversification via funds would seem sensible.

PART FIVE
Winning

In the previous parts of this book we have discussed theories and evidence relating to investment. Learn the theory, know the evidence, act in a disciplined manner and success will be yours. That is not stated anywhere, but the reader will inevitably have assumed something like that, both for this and for other investment books. Yet we all know that of the many people taught how to play golf, for example, only a few will really get the hang of it. And what could be easier than golf? Raise the club, swing, hit the ball, follow through. Winning seems to be more complicated than simply knowing the rules.

In Part Five we take a look at some winning stocks, winning investors, winning psychology and finally, at winning organizations. There is nothing definitive in this section as we merely touch on some important issues without exploring them in depth. Nonetheless it should stimulate your thoughts.

34
Winning

In this chapter we look at different aspects of winning—winning stocks, winning investors, winning psychology and winning organizations.

WINNING STOCKS

In Part Two we focused on outperforming—picking winners—but in a slightly indirect manner. The studies have looked at the results of constructing portfolios according to various attributes. Happiness is a portfolio that yields a few more per cent than the market. Some stocks will have done badly, some well, but if on average the portfolio is ahead, academic researcher and investor have made an interesting discovery. But why not simply examine winning stocks? Marc Reinganum (1988) did just that.

Reinganum took his list of winners from a William O'Neil + Co publication, *The Greatest Stock Market Winners: 1970–1983*. The book lists 272 stocks most of which at least doubled in value in a year. Not all stocks that doubled were included and not all included stocks doubled. The companies covered traded on the NYSE, AMEX and OTC markets. Reinganum selected 222 winners for which he could obtain data. To compute the price appreciation of the winners he assigned hypothetical buy and sell dates, selected *ex post facto*. The average price increase was 349%, the median 237%.

Reinganum classified each variable contained in the Datagraph files into one of five categories. We shall look at each in turn.

- *Smart money*—this category considers the behaviour of professionally managed funds and corporate insiders. These people did not appear too smart: they did tend to own the winners, but only as prices began to escalate: "professional money managers may participate in, but do not prophesy, extraordinary price appreciation." (p. 19).

- *Valuation measures*—this category included (a) price-to-book ratio; (b) price-earnings ratio; (c) stock price level, i.e., low or high price, (d) capitalization;

and (e) beta. The winners seem to have a low price-to-book ratio. Among the 222 winners, 164 were selling for less than book value in the buy quarter and the median ratio was 0.6. The average beta was 1.14 which suggests above average riskiness, but not enough to justify the returns. Low price-earnings ratio, low price and small capitalization were not characteristics of the winners. It is not clear how O'Neil staff chose their winners: to insure institutional interest they may have had a bias against small stocks.

- *Technical indicators*—these were relative strength and O'Neil's proprietary Datagraph ratings. Both were related to winners. For relative strength, one should look for high relative strength and a positive change in relative strength.

- *Earnings and profitability measures*—the winners appeared to have three factors in common in this category: (a) positive pre-tax margins; (b) prior to the buy quarter, there was a positive change in quarterly earnings, i.e., an acceleration in quarterly earnings; (c) positive five-year quarterly earnings growth rates.

- *Miscellaneous measures*—two measures were relevant here: (a) nearly 90% of the winners had less than 20 million shares in issue; (b) the winners were not contrarian picks: most stocks were close to their highest price in the previous two years, in fact 80% were within 15% of their highest price in the past two years.

Using the nine indicators of a winner that have been mentioned in the five categories discussed, Reinganum returned to the O'Neil database of 2279 NYSE and AMEX firms for the 1970–83 period. He then excluded the 222 winners and selected stocks from the remaining 2057 stocks. Note carefully that while Reinganum went datamining to find his selection criteria, he did so on an unusual sample—winners—and tested the criteria on a different, wider, universe. His criteria generated 453 buy signals for 319 different companies. The results are shown in Table 64.

Table 64 Cumulative Excess Returns from Nine Screen Strategy

Quarter	Mean (%)
Buy + 1	5.97
Buy + 2	11.56
Buy + 3	18.20
Buy + 4	23.71
Buy + 5	30.20
Buy + 6	37.80
Buy + 7	44.09
Buy + 8	50.65

Source: Reinganum (1988, p. 25). Reproduced by permission

Quarter Buy+1 is the first quarter following purchase: the return shown for Buy+8 is therefore the two year holding period excess return. Excess return is defined as the difference between the holding period return on the security and the holding period return on the S&P 500 index over the same period. These results were not generated by a few exceptional stocks—79% beat the S&P 500 over the two years. Nor was high risk the explanation, as the selected firms had betas similar to the market.

Whether an institutional investor could use the nine screen strategy would depend on how many stocks the investor felt obliged to hold. On average only a little over 30 stocks a year were selected and presumably in some years far fewer stocks were selected. Of course the database was limited to just over 2000 stocks and there are far more US stocks that could be considered. In the UK, however, 2000 stocks is close to the total investable universe. But what would happen if the number of selection factors were reduced? This should increase the number of eligible stocks. Fortunately Reinganum reported the results of using four screens. They were: (a) price-to-book ratio of less than 1.0; (b) accelerating quarterly earnings; (c) a relative strength rank of the stock in the current quarter greater than the rank in the previous quarter; and (d) fewer than 20 million shares in issue. The four screen approach generated 10 543 buy signals, and produced excess returns as shown in Table 65. These are high excess returns, albeit not as high as in Table 64.

Table 65 Cumulative Excess Returns from Four Screen Strategy

Quarter	Mean (%)
Buy + 1	3.04
Buy + 2	8.19
Buy + 3	12.65
Buy + 4	16.67
Buy + 5	20.84
Buy + 6	26.10
Buy + 7	31.13
Buy + 8	37.14

Source: Reinganum (1988, p. 27). Reproduced by permission

A large amount of space has been spent on a single study, especially one that may have no relevance for the UK, for two reasons. First, the approach is unusual for an academic study but likely to strike a chord with practitioners. It probably seems sensible to most practitioners to try and find the secret of success by examining success. Second, Reinganum's conclusion is worth pondering. He notes that most of the factors usually associated with outperformance were not favoured—no small stocks, low price-earnings ratio stocks and so forth. "This suggests that there may be more than one way to skin the performance cat!" (p. 27).

Following Reinganum's approach of studying winning stocks directly, why not study winning investors and see how they skin the performance cat?

WINNING INVESTORS

There are many books on "great" (i.e., very successful) investors (e.g., Talley, 1987; Train, 1981; Schwager, 1990) and a few by great investors (e.g., Lynch, 1989). Can one learn from these books? Yes, but perhaps not what one expects. One certainly can learn a great deal about market folklore and since great investors tend to be in love with investing some of the enthusiasm might rub-off onto the reader. But will most of us be better investors as a result?—the enthusiasm may rub off, but will the winning way? There are a number of problems one may encounter when reading about, or reading a great investor. Let's look at some of the problems.

First, are all the great investors truly great? A good five to ten year record may confer riches but it is not necessarily a sign of greatness. Some people do flip ten heads in a row. And even if an investor's record is a result of skill, that does not necessarily make his views interesting. For example small stocks have substantially outperformed large stocks. Any investor who stuck to a small stock strategy for a long period would have a great record. Clearly one decision—the key decision—was a good one, but does that make the investor's views on investment in general worth listening to?

The author knows an investor who has made himself a multi-millionaire. He is not a famous investor but he illustrates a problem that applies to the greats. This investor is very active, thoughtful and interesting. But how instructive his views are is open to doubt because he admits he has made his fortune from about six decisions. Is his record a result of his investment style, or a consequence of being constantly involved with markets (he is a broker) and simply grabbing a few significant opportunities?

Related to the above point, it is not obvious in general which part of a professed investment style is really the critical part. For example, Warren Buffett's record clearly makes him a great investor. He puts himself in the Graham and Dodd camp of fundamental value investing and cites his record as proof that the general approach works (Buffett, 1984). But, according to Train, while Buffett is influenced by Benjamin Graham, he has modified some of the principles. He gives more emphasis to the uniqueness of any situation and the strength of a business franchise. He looks at subjective issues that Graham would have ignored. (Train, 1981, pp. 19–21 lists 11 items Buffett feels makes a wonderful business.) Judging by many of the stocks Buffett has made a lot of money in, business franchises are important to him. So what accounts for Buffett's success—good fundamental accounting analysis and a value orientation, or shrewd strategic analysis of companies and industries?

Peter Lynch had a spectacular record when he managed the Magellan Fund. He has set out his views on successful investing in his book (Lynch, 1989). But which views are the really important ones? It is convenient to put stocks into categories which are homogeneous with regard to expected performance and the kind of analysis needed. Lynch classifies stocks into six categories which he discusses at some length. The categories are: (a) slow-growth; (b) stalwarts; (c) fast-growth; (d) cyclical; (e) asset plays; and (f) turnarounds. A recent US textbook (Smith *et al.*, 1992) spends six pages on Lynch and concentrates on Lynch's stock classifications. But are these categories the essence of Lynch's style, or is it better captured by his chapter on the perfect stock? That chapter's side-headings (pp. 122–36), which we quote below, indicate that the perfect stock has 13 attributes:

- it sounds dull—or, even better, ridiculous;
- it does something dull;
- it does something disagreeable;
- it's a spin-off;
- the institutions don't own it, and the analysts don't follow it;
- the rumours abound; it's involved with toxic waste and/or the Mafia;
- there's something depressing about it;
- it's a no-growth industry;
- it's got a niche;
- people have to keep buying it;
- it's a user of technology;
- the insiders are buyers;
- the company is buying back shares.

Perhaps Lynch's style is better captured by a list of his homilies (pp. 234–35) some of which we quote below:

- Big companies have small moves, small companies have big moves.
- Avoid hot stocks in hot industries.
- Long shots almost never pay off.
- Look for companies with niches.
- Companies that have no debt can't go bankrupt.
- Be patient. Watched stock never boils.
- When in doubt, tune in later.

So, what exactly is the essence of Lynch's style? Even if we can pin it down, we can find another great investor with a different orientation—as anybody who reads the books listed in the first paragraph of this section will observe. Some like dull stocks selling cheaply, some like growth stocks and are willing to pay up: some invest for the long-term, whereas others trade rapidly. To paraphrase some comments made by Herbert Simon in another context, the investment principles of the great investors are like proverbs, they occur in pairs. For almost every principle one can find an equally plausible contradictory principle and one has no means of choosing between the principles. Given the great investors' different analytical techniques and orientations it might seem that if the greats have anything in common it is more likely to be psychological traits and work practices and that it is these that distinguish them from the rest of us. Schwager, after interviewing successful traders, came to a similar conclusion. Common features he found frequently included:

> "a driving desire to become successful traders....Confidence that they could continue to win over the long run....[A consistently applied style] discipline was the word most frequently mentioned....Rigid risk control....Having the patience to wait for the right trading opportunity....The importance of acting independent of the crowd....Losing is part of the game....They all love what they are doing." (pp. 439–40)

Perhaps we should read about the great investors to remind ourselves that it is possible to be an investment winner, read the investment textbooks to learn the mechanics and study the psychology of investing to try and act more like a great investor. It is to psychology we now turn.

WINNING PSYCHOLOGY

There is surprisingly little written in the academic and professional finance literature about the psychology of investment given the frequent assertion by investors that the key to understanding the stock market is psychology rather than economics. There are two psychological aspects of investment that might be studied. One is the psychology of individual or group decision making and the other is the psychology of superior investors. The latter is the topic of this section.

When we watch sports we find no difficulty in spotting the great sportsmen. They obviously have good physical skills but they have something else—confidence, commitment, a special attitude. Everyone recognizes this: sports reporters tend to talk as much about psyching up as warming up. Most of us who saw Linford Christie's face before the Olympic 100 metres final knew the reason he was there and that we were couch potatoes was at least as much to do with mental factors as physical. Maybe it is the same in investing, maybe there is a winner's psychology.

Interesting work on the psychology of successful trading has been carried out by Van K. Tharp. Unfortunately the writer has been unable to trace any of his many books which are held neither by the Library of Congress nor by the British Library. The discussion here is based on a single interview in Schwager (1990). Tharp believes that to achieve success it is necessary to learn to do things in an effective manner. For success one needs the right beliefs, mental states and mental strategies. One also needs a model of how to trade that has been tested in some way.

According to Tharp, the sort of beliefs winners have include: money is not important; trading is a game; it is OK to lose on some transactions; mental rehearsal is important; and the game is won before it has started. Losers, on the other hand, believe that money is important and find it hard to take losses. Whether this is true or not is difficult to say, but certainly there is evidence that people in general (as well as investors) treat losses and gains in a different way. There is a tendency to run losses and cut winners. Successful investors appear to cut losses and run winners.

Turning to mental states, many people blame other people or events for mistakes that they had a part in bringing about. Tharp claims that successful traders accept responsibility for problems they have created. When this is done one may discover that certain mental states are the cause of the problem, for example being too impatient with the markets, being afraid at the wrong time, and so forth. But what should one do if one realizes at the trading desk that one has the wrong mental state? Tharp advises

> "Get up out of the chair. Walk away about four feet and then look at how you looked in that chair. Notice your posture, your breathing, your facial expressions. Then imagine how you would look if you had the sort of mental state you would like. When you can see that clearly, sit down in the chair again and assume the position that you just imagined." (Tharp in Schwager, p. 425)

Mental strategies relate to the sequence in which we think. For example if an investor uses an investment system that gives signals, one mental strategy might be: "See the signal. Recognize that it is familiar. Tell yourself what might go wrong if you take it. Feel bad about it." Another mental strategy might be: "See the signal. Recognize that it is familiar. Feel good about it." (Tharp in Schwager, p. 426). The second mental strategy would allow a trading system to be implemented successfully while the first would not.

Tharp paints a picture of a loser's personality which will typically show some of the following features: highly stressed, negative outlook on life, lots of conflict within his personality, blames others when things go wrong, tends to follow the crowd, disorganized and impatient. Let's look at one of those problems, that of stress. If someone is preoccupied with worries, that takes up decision space and narrows focus, according to Tharp. This may lead the stressed investor to excessive reliance on very simple decision rules and become a crowd follower. One approach to handling stress is to tackle it directly and send the investor on a stress management programme. However it may not be necessary to overcome all negative aspects if an investor can learn to invest in an effective manner. And that takes us back to our starting point of having a sensible system and the right beliefs, mental states and strategies.

The above approach seems to have an air of plausibility. That does not make it correct and there may be better psychological analyses: nonetheless some time spent on this sort of work rather than yet another study on book-to-market or price-earnings ratios may be a sensible allocation of time. Tharp's teaching seems to involve a significant amount of visualization. If you already have a well thought out investment system, maybe the next time you are in a bookstore you should walk past the investment section and stop at the "New Age" section and pick up something on visualization.

WINNING ORGANIZATIONS

Most institutional investors do not operate on their own or even in a fund management boutique, but in a large organization. There are a number of articles in the investment literature about building good investment organizations. These articles imply that good performance and certain organizational designs go hand in hand. There is usually an implicit assumption that there are organizations that outperform consistently, although the evidence for this is somewhat sparse. Perhaps the articles should be viewed as saying good performance would be found if the organizational principles were followed. In fact, it is likely that different organizational styles will be appropriate for different segments of the fund management industry.

Lakonishok *et al.* (1992) split the US fund management industry into two segments. (This split is less appropriate for the UK, but probably will become more appropriate in the future.) One segment consists of the large banks and insurance companies providing generic products such as index funds, immunized and dedicated bond portfolios and so forth. This segment stresses stability, can achieve economies of scale, and tends to become dominated by a few big firms. The performance orientated segment consists of smaller firms with varying styles which "seems to need a concept and a story as much as it needs good past performance" (p. 363). More service is required than in the generic sector, performance is elusive and therefore there are fewer economies of scale. This is a

"service-oriented industry for which perceptions of the qualities of individual firms vary widely over time and across customers. The structure of this industry is not unlike that of hair salons or trendy restaurants." (p. 364)

Much of the literature describing "good" organizations relates to the performance, rather than the generic, segment. We will say a little about the performance segment.

Are there winning organizations? Let's see. If the market consists mainly of professionals competing against each other they cannot all beat the index. Indeed, after allowing for costs, they must on average do a little worse than the index. The way to tell if some managers are winning is to look for consistency of performance.

One UK performance measurement service, Combined Actuarial Performance Services, or CAPS, shows the number of managers who have been in the top half of the performance league over a five-year period. A manager could appear in the top half every year, for four years, three years and so on down to no years. If there are no winning organizations, the distribution of managers will be exactly the same as the number of heads observed if a coin is flipped five times. In Table 66 we show the probability distribution for coin flipping and the percentage of managers outperforming for various periods for their entire fund and also the UK equity component.

Table 66 Fund Management Performance Compared to Distribution of Heads in Coin Tossing

	Fund Managers		Coins	
Number of years of above average performance	Percentage of managers: Total Fund Excl. Property	Percentage of managers: UK Equities	Number of heads	Percentage Probability
0	3	5	0	3
1	17	16	1	16
2	29	28	2	31
3	32	30	3	31
4	17	17	4	16
5	2	4	5	3

Source: Columns 1–3 are from Combined Actuarial Performance Services (1992, p. 27). Reproduced by permission

The distributions are very similar, although the tails of the UK equity distribution are a little fatter than the random coin distribution. This might suggest that there may be a few winning organizations, but this is wishful thinking: it is unlikely to be significant. Urwin (1990 and 1991) produced slightly different data and claimed that there was a suggestion of modest persistence of performance. For the US, the evidence is mixed. For example, Lakonishok *et al.* (1992), found that relative performance from year to year was not consistent, but over two, and especially three-year periods, there did appear to be some consistency of performance. However the data used could have a bias towards finding consistency and the expected returns even for the good managers, net of fees, were below the S&P 500. Grinblatt and Titman (1992) claim that there is evidence that there is persistence in mutual fund performance. Troutman (1991), on the other hand, cites a number of studies which relate relative performance over five-year periods to subsequent five-year periods and which suggest that past performance is not related to subsequent performance. Well, are there winning organizations? Possibly, but not many.

If there are winning organizations, what special characteristics will they have? Urwin (1991, p. 10) has argued that three important factors in identifying a winning organization are:

> "First, the quality of the individuals will be paramount. Secondly, first class investment processes are vital and involve a clear philosophy, and strong disciplines. Thirdly, investment management houses also require sound management just like any other business."

The investment processes, apparently, should be quantitative. Few would disagree with these three points (although many would dispute the necessity for a quantitative process) but the problem with this sort of list is that one wonders if it says more than "get good people, do good things". Good things, of course, are identified retrospectively. Many a US firm will have appeared to have been a winning organization having built a business around investing in smaller stocks. In the second half of the 1980s, such a firm would have stayed a winner in organizational terms and been buried in the performance tables.

It is perhaps easier to identify the characteristics of a losing organization. One of the problems managing fund management companies is that they bruise easily. Firms can be reasonably well organized and then quickly fall apart. Clearly a losing organization might simply be one that failed to satisfy the factors listed above. However, Urwin (1990, p. 28) produced some interesting general observations that are of a different nature. He found:

> "There appears to be a slight link between the number of individuals in the team and the results produced which supports the idea that strength in depth is helpful.... There is a stronger link between changes in the team and performance. The negative impact of staff leaving an organization is statistically significant. On the other hand, growth in staff is positively associated with performance....[But] there was a clear inverse link between *fast* new business growth and future performance."

These factors are similar to the negative factors that consultants involved in fund manager selection have traditionally focused upon. They have been concerned when one or more key investment managers quit; when assets under management decline; when assets under management increase dramatically; when a firm gets a poor reputation for communicating with clients; and when ownership of the firm is changed. (See e.g., Owen, 1990, p. 117ff.)

It is a difficult feat to keep investment managers acting together as a team and adhering to a common investment style. If key individuals depart or the organizational style is changed by merger or acquisition, morale can decline quickly. Fund management firms are often poor at managing their business because superior investment managers often end up in the key executive positions and retain some investment role. With steady growth this can work, but rapid growth forces these executives to neglect their investment role to cope with the business growth.

The best staff tend to want to be part of a winning team, enjoying good performance, good internal relationships and winning funds. When things start to go wrong, investment firms can decline rapidly. Some accounts may be lost and consultants will not offer the opportunity to present for new business. Some firms will begin a stream of retail product launches in a probably futile attempt to offset the declining institutional business. This entire process is quickly and accurately assessed by the better fund managers who will shift their focus from fund performance to getting another job. Morale declines, and the firm moves swiftly from winner to loser.

Despite the scepticism expressed above of the value of "do good things" lists, here is one. An organization that will have a chance of winning and continuing to win is probably one that has good people, a clear investment discipline, is well managed in a general business sense, grows at a steady and manageable rate, probably does not get involved in mergers, keeps its staff together (but gets an injection of new blood by the requirements to recruit for growth). Although it is not essential that investment firms be partnerships, it is probably ideal if they are, or can act as though they are, with a profit share for the managers and with the sole focus on investment management. It hardly needs adding that the scope for problems is enormous when a bank or insurance company acquires a performance salon but thinks in generic terms, terms which it is familiar with in its other businesses.

CONCLUDING COMMENTS

In this chapter we have looked at various aspects of winning. We looked at winning stocks and found that these stocks had some, but by no means all of the characteristics we might have expected based on earlier chapters. This does not mean that earlier chapters are misleading. Extreme observations (e.g., big winners) may well have different characteristics than less extreme observations (e.g., the better-performing half of an entire universe). For example, many stunningly attractive people seem to have characteristics that are different from those of merely pretty or good looking people. Nonetheless, Reinganum found that he could select outperforming portfolios on the basis of the characteristics of the big winners. It seems there are many ways to pick winners.

What do great investors do? It is hard to pin down the key elements of the great investors' styles. But they do seem to use incompatible styles. Some take big risks, some are cautious, some are value investors while others are growth investors. This suggests there is more to being a successful investor than the actual style used. It is easy to believe that there is a winners' psychology. There is not much evidence on this in the investment field, but winners do seem to be in love with what they do, have a belief that they will win over the long-term, act in a disciplined way, control risks, be willing to accept losses and act independently of the crowd. It is easy to believe that investment winners could win in other fields too.

Finally we looked at winning organizations. The characteristics of winning organizations will vary depending on the segment of the industry they are in. In the performance segment, an organization that wins and keeps on winning is probably one that has good people, a clear investment discipline, is well managed in a general business sense, grows at a steady and manageable rate, probably does not get involved in mergers, keeps its staff together (but gets an injection of new blood by the requirements to recruit for growth). All this may be necessary, but it may not be sufficient.

Will *you* be a winner? Reading this book is a start. It provides some of the tools of the trade. But do you now have an investment system, a winning psychology and do you (or, in the case of students, will you) work for a winning organization? A negative answer is OK, providing you read the final chapter on indexing.

PART SIX
Passive Investment Management

Active investment management has been the major theme of this book but it is worth spending the last few pages on passive investment management. Active investment management attempts to outperform the return on indexes by selecting underpriced shares and asset classes. Passive management involves holding securities to match the return on an index. Because of this tie to an index, passive management is often referred to as indexation or index fund management. Both bonds and equities may be indexed but the discussion in Chapter 35 relates to equities. There are three reasons for discussing passive management here. First, passive management has grown rapidly in the US and UK, and even committed active managers should know something about the passive approach as part of their general financial knowledge. Second, active managers have not been very successful at outperforming indexes and some investors and trustees may conclude that their best chance of outperforming other managers is by indexing. While there are many active strategies that appear to offer the prospect of outperformance, either they are unstable over time, or most investment managers are not sufficiently disciplined to use these strategies successfully. In the light of this, a passive strategy may be the best active strategy! Third, investment does not have to be all or nothing; it may make sense for active managers to index parts of their portfolios.

35
Index Funds

The first equity index fund was created by Wells Fargo in the US in 1971. Since then indexing has grown rapidly in both the US and the UK. Indexing is generally associated with institutional investment: although a number of retail unit trust products are available, these have a small market share. Greenwich Associates conducts research on the institutional investment market and examines mainly large funds. For its universe (Greenwich Associates, 1991 and 1992), more than 18% of UK institutional funds' UK equities were indexed. In the US the comparable figure for US equities was nearly 35%. About 25% of US institutional funds' international equities were indexed and about 14% of their bond portfolios.

What has accounted for the rapid growth of index funds? First, a growing acceptance of aspects of modern portfolio theory. Second, the increasing power and decreasing cost of computer facilities. Third, the introduction of negotiated commissions in the US and UK which enabled index fund managers, who do not require brokers' research, to deal at low cost.

SELECTING AN INDEX TO TRACK

When setting up an index fund the first issue that has to be tackled is which index will be the benchmark. This will depend upon the objective of the investor. For example, investors who wished to index their entire UK and US equity investments would probably choose broad indexes such as the FT-A All-Share and the S&P 500. The former index covers over 800 shares while the latter covers 500. Indeed it might be felt that 500 shares is not a very broad coverage for an economy as large as the US and involves too much of a big company bias. In that case the Wilshire 5000 might be thought appropriate. If investors think they have skill in selecting large stocks they might wish to actively manage the large stocks and only index small stocks. In the UK such an investor might choose a smaller companies index such as the Hoare Govett Smaller Companies Index, or the FT-SE SmallCap Index, as the benchmark.

Clearly there is no correct answer to the question of which index to track. It depends on the objective. But some indexes are better for tracking than others. Some indexes have a large number of non-investable stocks. A non-investible stock is one in which the index fund cannot invest. For example, some countries do not allow foreigners to buy certain types of stocks or certain classes of equity. If a non-investible stock is included in the index, an index fund run by a foreigner will inevitably be subject to tracking error. The size of the inevitable tracking error can be calculated and allowed for, but it might be thought better to select a different index that does not have this problem—e.g. the FT-Actuaries World group of indexes.

METHODS OF INDEXATION

Having chosen an index, the next step is to select a method of indexation. There are four main methods, listed below, and each will be discussed in turn:

- full replication
- stratified sampling
- optimization
- synthetic funds

Full Replication

Full replication involves buying all the stocks in the index, and in the same proportion. This can involve tedious administrative chores. A large number of stocks may have to be bought (and some of the smaller ones may be difficult to buy) and a large number of dividends handled. These dividends have to be re-invested in the correct proportions. The fund has to be adjusted for rights issues, acquisitions and changes in the index.

A fully replicated fund will track an index closely, but not exactly, because the index does not have the costs associated with setting up the fund, re-investing dividends and custody. Moreover calculations of the index with dividends re-invested usually assume that dividends are re-invested on the ex-dividend date although the income will not be received by a fund for some time.

Stratified Sampling

Instead of holding all the stocks in an index, the stratified sampling approach aims to track the index by holding only a sample of stocks in the index. There are a variety of sampling techniques.

If an investor aimed to track the FT-A All-Share Index, all stocks above a certain size, say 0.25% of the index, might be purchased, and in proportion to their market capitalization. Further stocks might then be purchased to bring the sector distribution of the sample into line with the index. This approach will inevitably have a large stock bias and, if there is a small stock effect, lead to large tracking errors.

An alternative approach is to set each sector weight in the sample equal to the index sector weight. Each sector then might be split into large, medium and small stocks and samples drawn from each of these subcategories. One could go even further and try to ensure that the sector samples broadly match the index with regard to a few variables such as price-earnings ratio, yield and beta. This introduces a modest degree of optimization, which is discussed below.

Generally the tracking error from stratified sampling will be good, albeit a little worse than full replication, although if some individual stocks or small stocks as a group do exceptionally well the tracking error can be substantially greater. For example, the small stock effect was a particular problem for funds tracking the FT-Actuaries Japan Index in 1989. If all costs are allowed for in calculations of tracking errors, a stratified sample index fund could track better than a fully replicated fund if brokerage commissions or custody costs have a sliding scale (i.e., higher proportionate fees for small deals) or include a fixed sum per transaction.

Optimization

Optimization is a sample method based on the view that the return from a stock is determined by its exposure to certain attributes such as size, price-earnings ratio, volatility, growth, etc. In the UK, proprietary optimization models sold by BARRA use about 40 variables in the optimization procedure, which attempts to ensure that the sample has the same characteristics as the index with regard to these variables.

This seems rather hard conceptual work compared to stratified sampling, but optimization adherents argue that stratified sampling:

> "is unsophisticated in that the only control of tracking error is by minimizing the deviations of portfolio holdings from index holdings along the two dimensions of, usually, capitalization and industry groups. Unfortunately, the intuition that keeping the differences in holdings small will cause the tracking error also to be small is frequently erroneous." (Rudd, 1980, pp. 60–61)

Stratified sampling adherents criticize optimization, in turn, on the grounds that it involves some data interpretation so that there is a blurring of the distinction between passive and active management. Moreover the optimization model assumes that historical risk and return relationships will hold in the future, which is not necessarily true. Also, as the characteristics of the market and stocks change, portfolio rebalancing will be required. Tracking errors can vary from year to year and user to user.

Despite these concerns, in the UK optimization dominates the indexation market. About 75% of the indexation market uses optimization techniques against about 10% in the US. This UK bias towards optimization is probably a result of the ready availability of off-the-peg optimization software rather than a result of intellectual arguments.

Synthetic Index Funds

It is possible to construct synthetic index funds by using a derivative product, a stock index future. A future is a contract that requires investors to buy or sell a given quantity of a specified asset on a specified future date at a specific price. Futures have traditionally been important for agricultural products but now cover financial instruments and stock market indexes. A rapidly increasing number of indexes are now traded on futures markets, both on their local market and in the US (for a list, see, e.g., Abbott, 1991). Because no physical commodity underlies an index, stock index futures are settled by cash when the contract expires.

Futures are bought and sold on margin. Only a small part of the total value of the future changes hands when the trade is made. The price of a future will be the current index value plus an allowance for interest earned on the cash that can be deposited because of the margined nature of the transaction, less the value of dividends that would be received on the underlying stock. Futures trade at close to the theoretical value, but not always exactly at it.

It is possible to construct an index fund by buying futures. A single transaction would suffice to index the S&P 500 by stock index futures. Apart from the simplicity, futures involve much lower costs. Bid/ask spreads are lower, commissions are lower and stock exchange taxes are often avoided. Liquidity is often better in the futures markets than the underlying markets and execution may be easier. For funds with inflows and outflows of money, it is easier to adjust exposure in the futures market than in the equity market. (For more details of the advantages of futures, see Bruce and Eisenberg, 1992.)

Against these advantages it must be noted that futures are not available for all indexes—for example there is a future on the FT-SE 100 but not on the FT-A All-Share. However it would be possible to track reasonably well a broad index such as the MSCI EAFE or the FT-Actuaries World Index by combining various local indexes (see Meier, 1991).

There are a number of tracking risks with synthetics. First there is the possibility that the future will be mispriced against stocks at the time of purchase. The FT-SE 100 future has been mispriced by as much as 2% although the S&P 500 has seldom been more than ½% mispriced. Second, futures contracts are short-dated and managers wanting to buy large positions will have to operate with the most liquid contracts which usually are those expiring in three to six months. This means the manager must roll-over the contracts periodically to a longer date. At each roll-over there is a pricing risk. Third, in calculating the theoretical price for a future, both dividends and interest rate assumptions have to be made. If the forecasts are incorrect, there will be tracking error. Fourth, cash-settled stock index futures are on a daily market-to-market basis, i.e., any gain or loss on a future must be settled daily. This means that in a falling market the futures investor will have to pay away cash, thereby earning less interest than anticipated. This will lead to underperformance. In a rising market the fund will outperform.

In practice, there are few synthetic index funds outside the US.

THE MISPLACED EMPHASIS ON TRACKING ERROR

It is worth saying a little more about tracking error, that is the amount an index fund deviates from its benchmark index. Many investors become obsessed with tracking error—the smaller, the better, they argue. However it should be noted that for a sampling approach the tracking error can be reduced by increasing the sample size. (Examples of tracking statistics and trade-offs are included in a series of publications by Mossaheb, e.g., 1988a and 1988b.) There will always be a trade-off between administrative chores and tracking error and the investor must decide the optimal blend.

Further, it is worth asking whether the size of the tracking error, within reason, really matters. Is the real objective of an index fund to exactly match the index or to avoid the unpleasant surprises that can result from an active manager underperforming by a very large amount? If the latter, a tracking error of, say, 0.5% rather than 0.35%, does not seem very important.

The tracking error is important as a control measure. If the change in the index and the change in the portfolio are measured daily, one can check whether the tracking error is behaving randomly. Some days the fund should outperform the index and some days it should underperform. Based on historical data, the standard deviation of the historical tracking error can be calculated and the size of the tracking error can be related to historical experience. If the tracking error is behaving non-randomly, or growing in size, the index fund should be rebalanced, that is to say stocks should be bought and sold to get a closer match to the index.

There is an important point here. The tracking error based on market prices and ignoring costs is the best way of seeing if the fund is correctly structured. However what interests the investor is the tracking error after costs and this may affect indexing tactics, especially for smaller company funds. Sinquefield (1991) shows that in practice it may be better to be as much concerned with achieving good trades as attempting to always have the exact index weights. It is important that the quantitative staff and the traders for an index fund work closely together.

THE FUTURE

What of the future? The UK will probably follow the US in developing a number of "enhanced" index funds. Such funds are tilted to stress attributes thought to lead to outperformance, such as low price-earnings ratios. Funds may also engage in arbitrage by holding stocks or futures depending on which is cheap relative to the other. Passive funds are also likely to be held alongside active funds to gain exposure to areas where the manager lacks expertise, such as small stocks or emerging markets, or for practical reasons.

A good example of a practical reason for indexing concerns small overseas stocks. Many fund managers' foreign holdings have underperformed the local indexes. There may be many reasons for this but one is surely the small company effect. A manager running a UK pension fund might invest, say, 8% of the fund in Continental Europe. With the prospect of investing in perhaps 10 countries, the number of holdings in each country is going to be fairly limited in a smallish fund. Even in France and Germany no more than five or six stocks might be held and fewer in the other, smaller, countries. Where a manager holds one to six stocks in a country it is unlikely that a top-down manager will invest in small stocks: to do so would be to take a stock rather than a country bet. Moreover the manager may not have the time to follow smaller stocks in ten markets. Inevitably, such a manager's fund will have a rather blue chip bias. This could kill performance. One solution would be to invest part of this European exposure in a European smaller companies index fund. This would seem to be a sensible blend of active and passive management.

CONCLUDING COMMENTS

Index funds are here to stay. They give up the chance to outperform an index for the security of not underperforming. In practice, index funds have often outperformed the average active fund manager. There are four main methods of managing an index fund: each has advantages and disadvantages. Somewhat oddly, the UK market is dominated by the optimization approach, which has a small US market share. Managers tend to be either for or against index funds yet there is no reason why predominately active managers should not hold index funds for areas where they lack expertise, or for practical reasons.

Further Reading

In this book some of the current approaches and empirical evidence relating to managing equity investments have been outlined. Not all aspects of analysing equities have been covered and derivative instruments and the bond markets have been entirely omitted.

Readers wishing information on these matters or more discussion of matters covered in this book should consider the following works. A textbook which manages to achieve a real world feel is: Cohen, J. B., Zinbarg, E. D. and Zeikel, A. (1987), *Investment Analysis and Portfolio Management*, 5th ed. Homewood, Irwin.

Excellent, more rigorous, textbooks include: Alexander, G. J., Sharpe, W. F. and Bailey, J. V. (1993), *Fundamentals of Investments*, 2nd. ed. Englewood Cliffs, Prentice Hall. Radcliffe, R. C. (1992), *Investment: Concepts, Analysis, and Strategy*, 3rd ed. HarperCollins.

Graham and Dodd's textbook is now a bit old-fashioned but it is packed with good sense and is still required reading. The latest edition is: Cottle, S., Murray, R. F. and Block, F. E. (1988), *Graham and Dodd's Security Analysis*, 5th ed. New York, McGraw-Hill.

An 1800 page handbook of useful articles is: Levine, S. N. (1988), *The Financial Analyst's Handbook*, 2nd ed. Homewood, Dow Jones-Irwin. It contains an introduction to statistical concepts and regression analysis.

Anyone wishing to keep up-to-date should read the major professional journals and, if they have the necessary statistical and mathematical skills, the academic journals. The best publications are American.

The two major professional journals are:

Financial Analysts Journal, Association for Investment Management and Research, PO Box 7947, Charlottesville, VA 22906 and *The Journal of Portfolio Management*, Institutional Investor Inc., 488 Madison Avenue, New York, NY 10022

There are no equivalent British journals. British research is sparse by comparison to American: few practitioners publish original research or even thoughtful reviews. British research is mainly produced by academics and published in a variety of academic journals, e.g., British accounting or economics journals or in the American academic journals. The following British academic journal probably publishes more on investments than any other, although a lot of it is by Americans about the US market: *Journal of Business Finance and Accounting*, Journals Department, Basil Blackwell Ltd, 108 Cowley Road, Oxford OX4 1JF

The leading US-edited academic journals publishing articles on investment are:

Journal of Finance, American Investment Association, 100 Trinity Place, New York, N.Y. 10006 and *Journal of Financial Economics*, Elsevier Sequoia SA, POB 564, CH-1001, Lausanne 1, Switzerland

As computer software becomes increasingly important to fund management operations, fund managers, as well as their computer specialists, might wish to read a computer trade journal: *Wall Street & Technology*, PO Box 7626, Riverton, NJ 08077-7626

Academic literature on investment topics is occasionally surveyed in the publications of the US regional Federal Reserve Banks at a less mathematically demanding level than in the academic journals. These publications are free and also cover economic topics which often will be of interest to investment managers or students. They make a useful addition to department libraries. The publications and their addresses are:

Economic Review, Public Affairs Department, Federal Reserve Bank of Kansas City, 925 Grand Avenue, Kansas City, Missouri 64198-0001. *Business Review*, Publications, Federal Reserve Bank of Philadelphia, Department of Research and Statistics, Ten Independence Mall, Philadelphia, PA 19106-1574. *Review*, Research and Public Information Department, Federal Reserve Bank of St Louis, PO Box 442, St Louis, Missouri 63166. *Economic Review*, Public Services, Federal Reserve Bank of Richmond, PO Box 27622, Richmond, Virginia 23261. *Economic Review*, Public Affairs Department, Federal Reserve Bank of Atlanta, 104 Marietta St N.W., Atlanta, Georgia 30303-2713. *Quarterly Review*, Research Department, Federal Reserve Bank of Minneapolis, PO Box 291, Minneapolis, Minnesota 55480-0291. *Economic Perspectives*, Public Information Center, Federal Reserve Bank of Chicago, PO Box 834, Chicago, Illinois 60690-0834. *New England Economic Review*, Research Library-D, Federal Reserve Bank of Boston, PO Box 2076, Boston, MA 02106-2076. *Economic Review*, Public Information Department, Federal Reserve Bank of San Francisco, PO Box 7702, San Francisco, California 94120. *Quarterly Review*, Public Information Department, Federal Reserve Bank of New York, 33 Liberty Street, New York, New York 10045-0001.

Glossary of Investment Terms

Abnormal Rate of Return Return earned on an asset less its risk-adjusted return. May be distinguished from excess return (see below) but often it is not.

Accounting Standards Board Main accounting standard-setting board in the UK. Replaced the Accounting Standards Committee. The Board is developing a set of Financial Reporting Standards (FRS). These are established after consultations and after circulation of a Financial Reporting Exposure Draft (FRED). An associated body, the Financial Reporting Review Panel can ensure compliance with the standards, ultimately by going to Court.

Active Investment Management Investment management process which aims to purchase mispriced securities and assets and thereby earn a positive abnormal rate of return.

Alpha Used in a number of different senses including the y-intercept of the characteristic line and also as the difference between a security's expected return and the equilibrium return predicted by the capital asset pricing model.

American Stock Exchange (AMEX) Second largest US stock exchange. Its listed firms tend to be smaller than NYSE firms and larger than NASDAQ firms. Sometimes abbreviated as ASE.

Anomaly An empirical regularity not predicted by an asset pricing model, e.g. calendar effects, low price-earnings effect, small capitalization effect.

Arbitrage Simultaneous purchase and sale of identical or similar assets in different markets for different prices. The aim is to earn a risk-free return.

Arbitrage Pricing Theory An equilibrium asset pricing model which states that the expected return of a security is a linear function of the security's sensitivity to various common factors.

Arithmetic Mean Return A measure of central tendency calculated by summing period returns and dividing by the number of periods.

Asset Allocation   The process of selecting the best allocation of an investor's portfolio among various asset classes.

Attribute Screening   Process of searching through stocks seeking those possessing attributes that are thought to be associated with positive abnormal returns, or avoiding stocks possessing attributes thought to be associated with negative abnormal returns.

Autocorrelation   See serial correlation.

Benchmark Portfolio   A portfolio against which investment performance can be evaluated.

Beta   A measure of the sensitivity or responsiveness of an asset's return to an underlying factor or index. The most common beta is a market beta where the underlying factor is the market. See also Arbitrage Pricing Theory.

Blue Chip Stock   Shares of a large company with a record of steady growth of earnings and dividends over a long period.

Book-to-Market   Book value divided by market capitalization.

Book Value   Aggregate value of ordinary shareholders' equity, i.e., ordinary share capital plus reserves.

Book Value per Share   Book value divided by issued ordinary shares.

Buy and Hold Strategy   A strategy whereby assets are purchased and held without any trading or asset rebalancing to the original mix.

Calendar Effects   The effect of the time of the year, week, day, etc. on security returns.

Capital Asset Pricing Model (CAPM)   An equilibrium asset pricing model which states that the expected return of a security is a linear function of the security's sensitivity to changes in the market's return.

Capital Market Line   The set of portfolios obtained by combining the market portfolio with risk-free borrowing and lending. It is a tangent from the risk-free rate to the efficient frontier of risky assets.

Capitalization-Weighted (or Value-Weighted) Index   A market index in which each security is weighted according to its market capitalization.

Central Tendency   The typical value in a set of data, usually represented by the mean, mode or median.

Characteristic Line   The linear relationship between the expected return on a security and the expected return on the market portfolio.

Chartered Financial Analyst (CFA)   US professional qualification awarded by the Association for Investment Management and Research.

Closed-end Investment Company   US name for an investment trust. An investment company that is traded on the stock market at the market clearing price which may be above or below the company's net asset value. It will seldom issue new shares and is unlikely to repurchase its own shares.

Closet Indexing   The practice, unwittingly or otherwise, by active managers of keeping their portfolio close to the asset distribution of a benchmark index.

Coincident Indicators   Economic indicators which move at the same time as the business cycle.

COMPUSTAT Data Tape   Data source providing profit and loss, balance sheet and other data on a large number of US stocks.

Contrary Opinion   Investment strategy based on trading against the crowd.

Correlation Coefficient (R)   A measure of the degree to which two variables move together. Correlation coefficients range from -1.0 to $+1.0$. A coefficient of $+1.0$ means the variables move in perfect lockstep, -1.0 means they move in perfect negative lockstep and 0.0 implies that they are completely unrelated. Correlation coefficients measure the strength of a relationship but do not imply causality. The correlation coefficient squared (R^2) is called the coefficient of determination and measures the percentage of variance of one variable explained by its relationship with the other.

Covariance   A measure of the degree to which a pair of variables move together. Covariance is related to, but not the same as, the correlation coefficient.

CRSP Data Tape   A standard source for investment research. The Center for Research in Security Prices (CRSP) at the University of Chicago provides stock price, dividend and return data for all stocks on the NYSE from 1926.

Datastream Total Market Index   Datastream is an on-line financial information service. It has constructed capitalization-weighted indexes for many of the world's equity markets, e.g., the Datastream UK Total Market Index.

Day-of-the-Week Effect   See Weekend Effect.

Dedicated Portfolio   A bond portfolio that has been designed to insulate the portfolio from the effect of interest rate changes by matching the asset's cash flows to the liabilities' cash flows.

Derivative Security   Security such as option or future whose value derives from an underlying asset.

Diminishing Marginal Utility   Utility is the satisfaction we get from a good or money. If additional satisfaction diminishes with additional increments of a good, there is diminishing marginal utility. If wealth is subject to diminishing marginal utility, this will imply risk aversion because additional wealth produces less utility than a loss of the same quantity of wealth.

Discount Rate   The rate of interest used to discount a stream of cash flows to a present value. The discount rate reflects both the time value of money and the riskiness of the cash flows.

Dispersion   Extent to which observations of a sample deviate from the sample's measure of central tendency (e.g., its mean). The standard deviation is the most common measure of dispersion.

Diversification   The adding of assets to a portfolio to reduce its unsystematic risk and thereby its total risk.

Dividend Discount Model (DDM)   A valuation model for equities which assumes that the intrinsic value of a stock is equal to the discounted value of its future stream of dividends.

Dividend Payout Ratio   Percentage of earnings paid out as dividends - it equals one minus the retention rate.

Dow Jones Industrial Average (DJIA)   Best known US index. A price-weighted index of 30 leading industrial shares with a divisor which is adjusted for stock splits: its construction makes it of limited relevance for portfolio analysis or for judging the trend of the market.

Earnings Multiplier Model   Model for estimating the value of a stock or a market as a multiple of its earnings.

Earnings Per Share (EPS)   A company's earnings divided by its number of issued shares. The earnings used in the calculation may be the last reported earnings (sometimes called historic or trailing) or forecast earnings (sometimes called prospective).

Earnings Surprise   Difference between reported earnings and analysts' prior expectations.

Earnings Yield   Earnings per share divided by the price per share: reciprocal of the price-earnings ratio. Also called earnings/price ratio.

Efficient Frontier   The locus of all efficient portfolios, i.e., portfolios that have varying combinations of risk and return such that no other portfolio can offer the same return for less risk or the same risk for more return.

Efficient Market Theory   The theory states that security prices fully reflect all available information. It is sometimes stated in three versions. The weak-form of the theory states that prices reflect all past price information. The semi-strong version states that prices reflect all publicly available information. The strong-form states that prices reflect all information, both public and private.

Efficient Portfolio   A portfolio with the highest expected return for a given level of risk or the lowest level of risk for a given return.

Equally-Weighted Index   A market index which weights each share equally. This means a small company will have as much impact on the index as a large company. See also Capitalization-Weighted Index.

Equity Risk Premium   The difference between the return on equities and a riskless asset. Often used in the UK by practitioners as the difference between equity and gilt returns.

Event Study   Analysis of the reaction of stock price movements to new information.

Excess Return   The difference between the return on a security and the return on a risk-free asset. May be distinguished from abnormal return (see above), but often is not.

Expected Return   The return anticipated by an investor over a particular holding period.

Factor   Aspect of the investment environment which affects the returns of assets. Some factors affect only a few assets while others affect many—these are referred to as common, pervasive or systematic.

Factor Analysis   Factor analysis refers to a group of statistical techniques used to analyse intercorrelations within a set of variables. It is often used to uncover underlying factors determining security returns.

Factor Beta   A measure of the variation of a factor with the return on the market portfolio.

Factor Loading or Sensitivity   A measure of the sensitivity of an asset to a particular factor.

Factor Risk   That part of a security's total risk which derives from common factors and cannot be diversified away.

Federal Reserve (Fed)   The US government agency that controls monetary policy.

Financial Analyst   Usual US name for a person who analyses the risk and return characteristics of financial assets in order to identify mispriced assets. Usually called an investment analyst in the UK.

Financial Reporting Exposure Draft (FRED)   See Accounting Standards Board.

Financial Reporting Standards (FRS)   See Accounting Standards Board.

Fourth Market   US name for the secondary market in which investors trade directly with each other.

FT-A All-Share Index   The major UK capitalization-weighted index consisting of over 800 shares and broadly representative of the UK market.

FT-A World Indices Group of capitalization-weighted indexes for individual countries and groups of countries. Includes only investable stocks.

FT-SE 100 Index Capitalization-weighted index of the 100 largest London-listed stocks.

FT-SE SmallCap Index Capitalization-weighted index consisting of all companies in the FT-A All-Share Index not large enough to be in the largest 350 shares. It comes in two versions, one including, and the other excluding, investment trusts.

Fundamental Analysis Evaluation of firms and markets and possible security mispricing based on analysis of economic and financial factors.

Geometric Mean Return The nth root of the product of n observations. It is that rate of return which makes the initial value of an investment equal to its end period value.

Generally Accepted Accounting Principles (GAAP) The accounting practices authorized in the US by the Financial Accounting Standards Board.

Gilts or Gilt-Edged Securities Fixed interest securities issued by the UK government. Interest payments may be quarterly or semi-annually, and some issues have no redemption date.

Graham or Graham and Dodd Benjamin Graham pioneered fundamental security analysis in the US and, with Dodd, wrote the major textbook of the 1930s to 1950s. Still worth reading, see the "Further Reading" chapter.

Growth Stock The shares of a company expected to achieve above average growth.

Hoare Govett Smaller Companies Index (HGSCI) Index comprising the lowest 10% by capitalization of the main UK equity market.

Holding Period Return (HPR) The total return from an investment over a specified holding period expressed as a percentage.

Idiosyncratic Risk See unsystematic risk.

Immunization A bond portfolio strategy that aims to minimize the impact of interest rate changes and lock in a known yield to maturity.

Implied Volatility The risk of an asset in the form of the standard deviation of returns derived from an options valuation model.

Index-Linked Gilts A special class of UK gilt which has both coupon payments and principal indexed to the retail price index.

Index Arbitrage Simultaneous purchase (sale) and sale (purchase) of stock index futures and the stocks in the index to earn a risk-free return resulting from pricing differences.

Index Fund A passive investment strategy which aims to achieve the performance of a particular index.

Index Option An option based on a market index.

Information Coefficient Term used to describe the correlation between ex ante predictions and ex post results.

Initial Public Offer (IPO) The initial offer of a company's shares to the public.

Insider and Inside Information Insider and inside information have specific legal meanings in the UK and US and trading on the basis of inside information is illegal. However the research studies use the terms in a more general sense to assess the activity of investors (such as company directors) with access to information not generally available to the public.

Internal Rate of Return The discount rate which equates the present value of future cash flows from an asset to the cost of that asset.

Investment Analyst See Financial Analyst.

Investment Horizon The period over which an investor makes investment plans.

January Effect Empirical regularity observed in the US and other countries that stock returns appear to be higher in January relative to other months.

Jensen's Index A portfolio performance measurement which is the difference between the actual return on a share or portfolio and the expected return given its beta and the market return.

Lagging indicators Economic indicators which follow movements in the business cycle.

Leading Indicators Economic indicators which lead movements in the business cycle.

Marketability The degree to which stocks can be traded without significantly affecting the price.

Market-Maker A company or individual who facilitates trades by acting as a principal and holding an inventory of stocks. The market-maker attempts to make a profit by the difference in the bid and ask prices and by being long or short of stocks when the market rises or falls.

Market Model Describes the relationship between the rates of return on securities and portfolios and the rate of return on the market.

Market Portfolio Contains all risky assets in proportion to their market value.

Mean Reversion   The process by which an asset's returns revert to an average value or an equilibrium value. Thus, returns above an average are expected to decline and vice versa.

Modern Portfolio Theory   Widely used term, but without precise definition. Usually implies a belief in the efficient market theory and the capital asset pricing model or some other asset pricing model which quantifies the relationship between risk and return.

Momentum Indicator   An indicator that provides information about the rate of change of a variable of interest (eg., earnings or share prices).

Morgan Stanley Capital International (MSCI) Indexes   Group of capitalization-weighted indexes for individual countries and groups of countries.

Multicollinearity   The tendency for the independent variables in a multiple regression to be correlated with each other. This may lead to poor regression estimates.

Multifactor CAPM   An extended version of the capital asset pricing model that includes factors such as size and liquidity as well as systematic risk.

Multifactor Model   Model which relates the return on a security to movements in various common factors.

Multiple Regression Analysis   Regression analysis that estimates the linear relationship between a dependent variable and more than one independent variable. See Regression Analysis.

NASDAQ (National Association of Securities Dealers Automated Quotations)   US electronic stock market providing bid-ask quotes from at least two market makers on OTC securities.

Neglected Firm Effect   Empirical regularity that stocks neglected by analysts or investment institutions provide positive abnormal returns.

Net Asset Value   Ordinary share capital plus retained reserves divided by the number of ordinary shares in issue.

New Issue   Initial stock sale by underlying firm.

New York Stock Exchange (NYSE)   The largest US stock exchange.

Nonsynchronous Trading   Not all securities trade at the end of every return interval, e.g., every day. Return data for different securities thus may relate to different periods and this is referred to as nonsynchronous trading. This leads to various statistical problems, in particular, securities which trade infrequently will have underestimated betas, unless a correction is made.

Normal Probability Distribution   Bell-shaped probability distribution whose properties are completely described by its mean and standard deviation. The normal distribution is frequently used in making statistical inferences from measures derived from samples.

Normalized Earnings The earnings one would expect in a 'normal' year or a mid-cycle year.

Odd-lot Theory US investors who trade in less than 100 shares are said to trade in odd-lots. Odd-lot theory presumes that these small investors are ill-informed and provide a contrary investment indicator.

Open-end Investment Company A mutual fund (in the US) or a unit trust (in the UK) which stands ready to issue or redeem new shares at net asset value (possibly subject to a sales load).

Optimal Portfolio The portfolio lying on the efficient frontier which offers the best expected return to an investor given the investor's attitude to risk.

OTC (Over-the-Counter) Market The market in stocks not listed on the recognized exchanges. Some listed stocks are also traded on the OTC market. The security dealers act as market-makers.

Out-of-Sample Data Data which has not been used in the estimation of a statistical relationship. Also called a holdout sample.

Overpriced Security A security whose expected return is less than its required return.

Overreaction Hypothesis Hypothesis that investors tend to overreact to news causing asset prices to deviate from their intrinsic value.

Overweight A fund is said to be overweight in an asset when it holds more than the appropriate index or benchmark weight.

Passive Investment Management An investment strategy that does not involve trying to find mispriced assets. Usually will involve use of an Index Fund.

Percentiles Measures of the distribution of data given by ranking data from lowest to highest. The percentile of a given number is the percentage of other numbers that are less than that number.

Portfolio The collection of assets held by an investor.

Present Value The present value is the equivalent value today of future income streams. It is calculated by discounting future income by an appropriate discount rate.

Price-Earnings Ratio Share price divided by earnings per share.

Price-to-Book Value Ratio Share price divided by the book value of assets.

Price-to-Cash Flow Ratio Share price divided by cash flow, usually calculated as earnings plus non-cash expenses, the largest of which is depreciation.

Price-to-Sales Ratio   Share price divided by company's sales.

Programme Trading   The purchase or sale of a basket of securities as though the trade were a single security: e.g. a trader may agree to supply a basket of shares at the closing mid-market London price plus a 1% fee. The trader may effect the trade either as a principal trade or as an agency trade.

Quality Spread   The difference in yields on corporate and government bonds.

Random Walk Theory   When applied to share prices the theory asserts that the next percentage price change of a stock cannot be deduced on the basis of past changes.

Rate of Return   The percentage return from an investment, over a specified holding period, which includes both income and capital gains or losses, whether realized or unrealized.

Real Return   The inflation-adjusted return on an investment.

Redemption Yield   The discount rate which equates the present value of all future cash flows from a bond to the current price. In the US this is called yield-to-maturity.

Regression Coefficient   Indicates the responsiveness of one variable to changes in another. The regression coefficient between a security's rate of return and the return on the market is called beta.

Regression Equation   An equation that is fitted by statistical methods and which attempts to explain the level or changes of a variable of interest, the dependent variable, as a function of one or more independent variables.

Regression to the Mean   Tendency of extreme observations to become more like the average over a period of time.

Relative Strength   Measure of the price performance of shares or sectors relative to an appropriate index. Technical analysts believe that past high relative strength predicts good future performance.

Required Rate of Return   The minimum expected return necessary to induce an investor to invest.

Retention Ratio   The percentage of a firm's earnings not paid out as dividends but retained by the firm: it equals one minus the payout rate.

Reward-to-Variability Measure   See Sharpe's Index.

Reward-to-Volatility Measure   See Treynor's Index.

Risk   The uncertainty that an asset will earn its expected return. Usually measured by the variability of past returns.

Risk-averse   Investors are said to be risk-averse if they dislike risk and will choose from two investments with equal returns the one with least risk. They will incur additional risk only if they expect additional return. Consequence of diminishing marginal utility.

Risk-adjusted Return   The return on an asset adjusted for the risk it bears.

Risk-free Asset   An asset whose holding period return is known with certainty. Treasury bills are usually used as a proxy for this rate.

Risk-free Rate   The return on a risk-free asset.

Risk-Neutral Investor   Investor who is indifferent between investments that have the same expected return but varying levels of risk.

Risk Premium   Rate of return above the risk-free rate required as compensation for bearing risk.

Runs Test   A test that looks for series or runs of positive or negative price changes for a security greater than would be expected in a random series.

S&P 500   US capitalization-weighted share index published by Standard and Poor consisting of 500 shares. The 400 industrial shares included also form a separate index, the S&P 400.

Securities and Exchange Commission   US federal agency which regulates security issuing and trading.

Security Market Line   The linear relationship between the risk of a security as measured by its beta and its expected return.

Semistrong-form Efficient Market Theory   See Efficient Market Theory.

Separation Theorem   A theorem which states that the selection of the optimal portfolio of risky assets is separate from an investor's attitude to risk and return.

Serial Correlation   The relationship between one period's observation and a subsequent period's observation. A positive relationship, i.e., positive serial correlation, indicates the presence of trends while a negative relationship, i.e., negative serial correlation indicates the presence of reversals.

Sharpe's Index   Portfolio performance measure over an evaluation period of the excess return of the portfolio divided by the portfolio's standard deviation of returns.

Single Factor (or Index) Model   Model which relates the returns on a stock to the return on the market.

Size Effect   Empirical regularity that over long periods small capitalization stocks have outperformed large stocks on a risk-adjusted basis.

Small Stock Effect   See Size Effect.

Soft Commission   UK name for process of paying commission on security trades with a pre-agreed proportion of that commission being used by the broker to purchase fund management products on behalf of the fund manager. US name is soft dollars.

Soft Dollars   See Soft Commission.

Specific Risk   Another name for unsystematic risk.

Standard Deviation   A measure of dispersion calculated as the square root of the difference between each observation and the mean of the data, divided by the number of observations.

Statements of Standard Accounting Practice (SSAPs)   Statements of recommended accounting practice issued by the UK's Accounting Standards Committee and adopted by the Accounting Standards Board. Accounts which depart from the standards have had to justify the departure.

Statistically Significant   Term used to describe a research finding when the outcome of a statistical test indicates that the probability of the result occurring by chance is small, usually less than 5%.

Strategic Asset Allocation   Asset allocation that is appropriate given an investor's liabilities and objectives. The benchmark portfolio from which tactical asset allocation may be made.

Strong-form Efficient Market Theory   See Efficient Market Theory.

Structural Macro-economic Econometric Model   A statistical model of the economy based on economic theory, and used to test economic theory and make forecasts.

Systematic Risk   That part of a security's total risk which is related to moves in the market portfolio and therefore cannot be diversified away.

t-test   A tool of inferential statistics that allows the probability to be determined that the difference between the means of sets of data occurred by chance.

Tactical Asset Allocation   Tactical asset allocation determines what departure, based on current market valuations, should be made from the strategic asset allocation.

Technical Analysis   A form of security and market analysis which uses past price movements and volume levels plus other indicators to forecast future price movements.

Term Spread   The difference in yield between bonds with different maturities, e.g., three month and ten year bond yields.

Third Market   US term for the trading of exchange listed securities on the OTC market.

Total Risk   Consist of both systematic and unsystematic risk. Usually measured as the standard deviation of the return on an asset or portfolio.

Treasury Bill   A security issued by the UK or US government which has a maximum maturity of one year. The bills are issued at a discount and pay interest and principal of redemption.

Treasury Bond   A US government fixed income security with a term to maturity of over ten years. Income is paid semi-annually and the principal is returned at maturity.

Treasury Note   A US government fixed income security with a term to maturity of between one and ten years. Income is paid semi-annually and the principal is returned at maturity.

Treynor's Index   Portfolio performance measure over an evaluation period of the excess return of the portfolio divided by the portfolio's beta.

Underweight   A fund is said to be underweight in an asset when it holds less than the appropriate index or benchmark.

Unlisted Securities Market (USM)   UK market for smaller stocks, traded on the London Stock Exchange. Listing requirements were less onerous than those required for a full listing.

Unsystematic Risk   That portion of total risk unrelated to a specific factor and which can therefore be diversified away.

Value Line   A firm which publishes various financial analysis including the Value Line Investment Survey, a weekly service which rates 1700 US stocks.

Value-Weighted Market Index   An index whose components are weighted on the basis of their market capitalization.

Variance   A measure of the volatility or dispersion of a variable. It is the squared value of the standard deviation.

Vector Autoregressive Models   Vector autoregressive economic forecasting models use variables selected on the basis of economic theory but allow the data to determine the interrelationships between the variables and the lags.

Volatility   The variability of an asset's return over time, usually measured by the standard deviation of returns.

Weak-form Efficient Market Theory   See Efficient Market Theory.

Weekend Effect   Empirical regularity that stock returns appear to be lower on Mondays in the US and some other countries.

Wilshire 5000 Index   Value-weighted equity index consisting of all NYSE and AMEX common stocks plus the most active OTC stocks.

Yield Curve   A graph of the redemption yield of fixed income securities of various maturities.

Yield Spread   The difference in the redemption yields of two fixed income securities with different attributes such as maturity or issuer (e.g. five and ten year securities and corporate and government securities).

Yield-to-Maturity   The discount rate which equates the present value of all future cash flows from a bond to the current price. In the UK this is called the redemption yield.

Bibliography

Abbott, S. (1991) Stock market indexes opening in every direction. *Futures*, **20**, August, 40–42.

Abeysekera, S. P. and Mahajan, A. (1987) A test of the APT in pricing UK stocks. *Journal of Business Finance and Accounting*, **14**, 377–91.

Affleck-Graves, J. and Mendenhall, R. R. (1992) The relation between the Value Line enigma and post-earnings-announcement drift. *Journal of Financial Economics*, **31**, 75–96.

Aharony, J., Jones, C. P. and Swary I. (1980) An analysis of the risk and return characteristics of corporate bankruptcy using capital market data. *Journal of Finance*, **35**, 100–116.

Aharony, J. and Swary, I. (1980) Quarterly dividend and earnings announcements and stockholders' returns: an empirical analysis. *Journal of Finance*, **35**, 112.

Akemann, C. A. and Keller, W. E. (1977) Relative strength does persist! *Journal of Portfolio Management*, **4**, Fall, 38–45.

Alexander, G. J., Sharpe, W. F. and Bailey, J. V. (1993) *Fundamentals of Investments*, 2nd. edn. Englewood Cliffs, Prentice Hall.

Aliber, R. Z. and Bruce, B. R.(eds.) (1991) *Global Portfolios: Quantitative Strategies for Maximum Performance*. Homewood, Business One Irwin.

Altman, E., Haldeman, R. and Narayanan, P. (1977) ZETA Analysis: A New Model to Identify Bankruptcy Risk of Corporations. *Journal of Banking and Finance*, **1**, 29–54.

Altman, E. I. (1968) Financial ratios, discriminant analysis and the prediction of corporate bankruptcy. *Journal of Finance*, **23**, 589–609.

Altman, E. I. and Brenner, M. (1981) Information effects and stock market response to signs of firm deterioration. *Journal of Financial and Quantitative Analysis*, **16**, 35–51.

Altman, E. I. and Spivack J. (1983) Predicting bankruptcy: the Value Line relative financial strength system vs. the Zeta bankruptcy classification approach. *Financial Analysts Journal*, **39**, November–December, 60–67.

Ambachtsheer, K. (1974) Profit potential in an 'almost efficient' market. *Journal of Portfolio Management*, **1**, Fall, 84–87.

Ambachtsheer, K. P. (1977) Where are the customer's alphas? *Journal of Portfolio Management*, **4**, Fall, 52–56.

Ambachtsheer, K. P. and Farrell, J. L. (1979) Can active management add value? *Financial Analysts Journal*, **35**, November–December, 39–47.

Amihud, Y. and Mendelson, H. (1991) Liquidity, asset prices and financial policy. *Financial Analysts Journal*, **47**, November–December, 56–65.

Andrews, C., Ford, D. and Mallinson, K. (1986) The design of index funds and alternative methods of replication. *Investment Analyst*, **82**, 16–23.

Arbel, A. (1985a) Generic stocks: an old product in a new package. *Journal of Portfolio Management*, **11**, Summer, 4–13.

Arbel, A. (1985b) *How to Beat the Market with High-Performance Generic Stocks*. New York, Morrow.

Arbel, A., Carvell, S. and Strebel, P. (1983) Giraffes, institutions and neglected firms. *Financial Analysts Journal*, **39**, May–June, 57–63.

Arbel, A. and Strebel P. (1983) Pay attention to neglected firms! *Journal of Portfolio Management*, **9**, Winter, 37–42.

Ariel, R. A. (1987) A monthly effect in stock returns. *Journal of Financial Economics*, **17**, 161–74.

Ariel, R. A. (1990) High stock returns before holidays: existence and evidence on possible causes. *Journal of Finance*, **45**, 1611–26.

Arnold, J. and Moizer, P. (1984) A survey of the methods used by UK investment analysts to appraise investments in ordinary shares. *Accounting and Business Research*, **14**, 195–207.

Arnold, J., Moizer, P. and Noreen, E. (1984) Investment appraisal methods of financial analysts: a comparative study of US and UK practices. *International Journal of Accounting*, **19**, 1–18.

Arnott, R. D. (1979) Relative strength revisited. *Journal of Portfolio Management*, **5**, Spring, 19–23.

Arnott, R. D. (1980) Cluster analysis and stock price comovement. *Financial Analysts Journal*, **36**, November–December, 56–62.

Arnott, R. D. (1985) The use and misuse of consensus earnings. *Journal of Portfolio Management*, **11**, Spring, 18–27.

Arnott, R. D. and Copeland, W. A. (1985) The business cycle and security selection. *Financial Analysts Journal*, **41**, March–April, 26–32.

Arnott, R. D. and Fabozzi, F. J. eds. (1988) *Asset Allocation: A Handbook of Portfolio Policies, Strategies and Tactics*. Chicago, Probus.

Arnott, R. D. and von Germeten, J. N. (1983) Systematic asset allocation. *Financial Analysts Journal*, **39**, November–December, 31–38.

Arnott, R. D. and Henriksson, R. D. (1991) A disciplined approach to global asset allocation, in R. Z. Aliber and B. R. Bruce, (eds). *Global Portfolios: Quantitative Strategies for Maximum Performance*. Homewood, Business One, Irwin.

Arnott, R. D., Kelso, C. M., Kiscadden, S., and Macedo, R. (1989) Relative strength revisited. *Journal of Portfolio Management*, **16**, Fall, 28–35.

Aron, P. H. (1984) *Japanese Price Earnings Multiples Revisited*. New York, Daiwa Securities America.

Aron, P. H. (1989) *Japanese Price Earnings Multiples*. New York, Daiwa Securities America.

Arrow, K. J. (1982) Risk perception in psychology and economics. *Economic Inquiry*, **20**, 1–9.

Ball, R. (1978) Anomalies in relationships between securities' yields and yield surrogates. *Journal of Financial Economics*, **6**, 103–26.

Ball, R. (1989) What do we know about stock market 'Efficiency' in R. M. C. Guimaraes, *et al.* (eds.) *A Reappraisal of the Efficiency of Financial Markets*. Berlin, Springer-Verlag.

Band, R. E. (1989) *Contrary Investing for the '90s*. New York, St. Martin's Press.

Bannister, B. B. (1990) In search of excellence: a portfolio management perspective. *Financial Analysts Journal*, **46**, March–April, 68–71.

Banz, R. W. and Breen, W. J. (1986) Sample-dependent results using accounting and market data: some evidence. *Journal of Finance*, **41**, 779–93.

Barclays de Zoete Wedd (1992) *The BZW Equity-Gilt Study 1992*. London, Barclays de Zoete Wedd Research Limited.

Barry, C. B. and Brown, S. J. (1986) Limited information as a source of risk. *Journal of Portfolio Management*, **12**, Winter, 66–72.

Bartley, J. W. and Cameron, A. B. (1991) Long-run earnings forecasts by managers and financial analysts. *Journal of Business Finance and Accounting*, **18**, 21–41.

Basu, S. (1975) The information content of price-earnings ratios. *Financial Management*, **4**, Summer, 53–64.

Basu, S. (1977) The relationship between earnings' yield, market value and return for NYSE common stocks—further evidence. *Journal of Finance*, **32**, 663–81.

Basu, S. (1983) The relationship between earnings' yield, market value and return for NYSE common stocks. *Journal of Financial Economics*, **12**, 129–56.

Bauman, W. S. and Dowen, R. (1988) Growth projections and common stock returns. *Financial Analysts Journal*, **44**, July–August, 79–80.

Beaver, M. and Morse, D. (1978) What determines price-earnings ratios? *Financial Analysts Journal*, **34**, July–August, 65–76.

Beaver, W. H. (1968) Market prices, financial ratios, and the prediction of failure. *Journal of Accounting Research*, **6**, 179–92.

Beenstock, M. and Chan, K. (1986) Testing the arbitrage pricing theory in the United Kingdom. *Oxford Bulletin of Economics and Statistics*, **48**, 121–41.

Beenstock, M. and Chan, K. (1988) Economic forces in the London Stock Market. *Oxford Bulletin of Economics and Statistics*, **50**, 27–39.

Benesh, G. A. and Peterson P. P. (1986) On the relation between earnings changes, analysts' forecasts and stock price fluctuations. *Financial Analysts Journal*, **42**, November–December, 29–39, 55.

Bergstrom, G. L. and Frashure, R. D. (1977) Setting investment policy for pension funds. *Sloan Management Review*, **18**, Spring, 1–16.

Bernhard, A.: n.d. *How To Use The Value Line Investment Survey: A Subscriber's Guide.* New York, The Value Line Investment Survey.

Berry, M. A., Burmeister, E. and McElroy, M. B. (1988) Sorting out risks using known APT factors. *Financial Analysts Journal*, **44**, March/April, 29–42.

Bhandari, L. C. (1988) Debt/equity ratio and expected common stock returns: empirical evidence. *Journal of Finance*, **43**, 507–28.

Bhaskar, K. N. and Morris, R. C. (1984) The accuracy of brokers' profit forecasts in the UK. *Accounting and Business Research*, **14**, Spring, 113–24.

Biddle, G. and Lindahl, F. (1982) Stock price reactions to LIFO adoptions. *Journal of Accounting Research*, **20**, 551–88.

Bidwell, C. M. (1981) SUE/PE. Revista. *Journal of Portfolio Management*, **7**, Winter, 85–87.

Biggs, S. F. (1984) Financial analysts' information search in the assessment of corporate earning power. *Accounting, Organizations and Society*, **9**, 313–23.

Bjerring, J. H., Lakonishok, J. and Vermaelen, T. (1983) Stock prices and financial analysts' recommendations. *Journal of Finance*, **38**, 187–204.

Black, F. (1973) Yes, Virginia, there is hope: tests of the Value Line ranking system. *Financial Analysts Journal*, **29**, September–October, 10–14.

Black, F., Jensen, M. C. and Scholes, M. S. (1972) The capital asset pricing model: some empirical tests, in M. C. Jensen (ed.) *Studies in the Theory of Capital Markets*. New York, Praeger.

Black, F. and Litterman, R. (1992) Global portfolio optimization. *Financial Analysts Journal*, **48**, September–October, 28–43.

Black, F. and Scholes, M. S. (1974) The effects of dividend yield and dividend policy on common stock prices and returns. *Journal of Financial Economics*, **1**, 1–22.

Bleiberg, S. (1989) How little we know—about P/Es, but also perhaps more than we think. *Journal of Portfolio Management*, **15**, Summer, 26–31.

Blume, M. E. (1980) Stock returns and dividend yields: some more evidence. *Review of Economics and Statistics*, **62**, 567–77.

Blume, M. E. and Husic, F. (1973) Price, beta, and exchange listing. *Journal of Finance*, **28**, 283–99.

Blume, M. E. and Siegel, J. J. (1992) The theory of security pricing and market structure. *Financial Markets, Institutions and Instruments*, **1**, no. 3.

Board, J. L. G. and Sutcliffe, C. M. S. (1988) The weekend effect in UK stock prices. *Journal of Business Finance and Accounting*, **15**, 199–213.

Bobseine, M. (1990) Software simplifies asset allocation strategies. *Wall Street Computer Review*, **8**, November, 55, 56, 58, 61, 62, 64.

Bodie, Z. (1991) Shortfall risk and pension fund investment policy, in A. W. Sametz (ed.) *Institutional Investing: Challenges and Responsibilities of the 21st Century*. Homewood, Business One, Irwin.

Boehm, E. A. and Moore, G. H. (1991) Financial market forecasts and rates of return based on leading index signals. *International Journal of Forecasting*, **7**, 357–74.

Bohan, J. (1981) Relative strength: further positive evidence. *Journal of Portfolio Management*, **8**, Fall, 36–39.

Boldt, B. L. and Arbit, H. L. (1984) Efficient markets and the professional investor. *Financial Analysts Journal*, **40**, July–August, 22–34.

Bomford, M. D. (1968) Changes in the evaluation of equities. *Investment Analyst*, **22**, 3–12.

Born, J. A., Moser, J. T. and Officer, D. (1988) Changes in dividend policy and subsequent earnings. *Journal of Portfolio Management*, **14**, Summer, 56–62.

Bouwman, M. J., Frishkoff, P. A. and Frishkoff, P. (1987) How do financial analysts make decisions? A process model of the investment screening decision. *Accounting, Organizations and Society*, **12**, 1–29.

Bower, D. H., Bower, R. S. and Logue, D.E. (1984) A Primer on Arbitrage Pricing Theory. *Midland Corporate Finance Journal*, **2**, Fall, 31–40

Brealey, R. A. (1986) How to combine active management with index funds. *Journal of Portfolio Management*, **12**, Summer, 4–10.

Brealey, R. A. (1990) Portfolio theory versus portfolio practice. *Journal of Portfolio Management*, **16**, Summer, 6–10.

Brinson, G. P., Singer, B. D. and Beebower, G. L. (1991) Determinants of portfolio performance II: an update. *Financial Analysts Journal*, **47**, May–June, 40–48.

Brown, B. and Rozeff, M. S. (1978) The superiority of analyst forecasts as measures of expectations: evidence from earnings. *Journal of Finance*, **34**, 1–16.

Bruce, B. and Eisenberg, A. (1992) *Global Synthetic Index Funds*. Chicago, Chicago Mercantile Exchange Strategy Paper Series.

Brush, J. S. (1986) Eight relative strength models compared. *Journal of Portfolio Management*, **13**, Fall, 21–28.

Buffett, W. E. (1984) *The Superinvestors of Graham-and-Doddsville*. Talk given at Columbia University and reprinted in B. Graham (1973) *(SIC) The Intelligent Investor*, 4th edn. New York, Harper and Row.

Bulkley, G. and Tonks, I. (1989) Are UK stock prices excessively volatile? Trading rules and variance bounds tests. *Economic Journal*, **99**, 1083–1098.

Cadsby, C. B. and Ratner, M. (1992) Turn-of-month and pre-holiday effects on stock returns: some international evidence. *Journal of Banking and Finance*, **16**, 497–509.

Campbell, J. Y. (1987) Stock returns and the term structure. *Journal of Financial Economics*, **18**, 373–99.

Campbell, J. Y. and Shiller, R. J. (1988) Stock prices, earnings, and expected dividends. *Journal of Finance*, **43**, 661–76.

Campbell, J. Y. and Shiller, R. J. (1991) Yield spreads and interest rate movements: a bird's eye view. *Review of Economic Studies*, **58**, 495–514.

Capaul, C., Rowley, I. and Sharpe, W. F. (1993) International value and growth stock returns. *Financial Analysts Journal*, **49**, January–February, 27–36.

Carman, P. (1981) The trouble with asset allocation. *Journal of Portfolio Management*, **8**, Fall, 17–21.

Carman, P. (1988) *Tactical Asset Allocation: Have We Finally Found an Acceptable Name for Market Timing?* New York, Sanford C. Bernstein.

Carnes, W. S. and Slifer, S. D. (1991) *The Atlas of Economic Indicators*. New York, Harper Collins.

Carter, R. B. and Van Auken, H. E. (1990) Security analysis and portfolio management: a survey and analysis. *Journal of Portfolio Management*, **16**, Spring, 81–85.

Carvell, S. A. and Strebel, P. J. (1987) Is there a neglected firm effect? *Journal of Business Finance and Accounting*, **14**, 279–90.

Central Statistical Office, *Economic Trends*, March, (1975), No. 257; May, (1976), No. 271; and December, (1992), No. 470.

Chan, K. C. (1988) On the contrarian investment strategy. *Journal of Business*, **61**, 147–63.

Chan, K. C. and Chen, N. (1991) Structural and return characteristics of small and large firms. *Journal of Finance*, **46**, 1467–84.

Chan, K. C., Chen, N. and Hsieh, D. A. (1985) An exploratory investigation of the firm size effect. *Journal of Financial Economics*, **14**, 451–71.

Chan, L. K. C., Hamao, Y. and Lakonishok, J. (1991) Fundamentals and stock returns in Japan. *Journal of Finance*, **46**, 1739–64.

Chandy, P. R. and Reichenstein, W. (1991) Timing strategies and the risk of missing bull markets. *AAII Journal*, **13**, August, 17–19.

Chant, P. D. (1980) On the predictability of corporate earnings per share behavior. *Journal of Finance*, **35**, 13–21.

Chen, N. (1988) Equilibrium asset pricing models and the firm size effect in E. Dimson (ed), *Stock Market Anomalies*. Cambridge, Cambridge University Press.

Chen, N. (1991) Financial investment opportunities and the macroeconomy. *Journal of Finance*, **46**, 529–54.

Chen, N., Roll, R. and Ross, S. A. (1986) Economic forces and the stock market. *Journal of Business*, **59**, 383–403.

Chopra, N., Lakonishok, J. and Ritter, J. R. (1992) Measuring abnormal performance. *Journal of Financial Economics*, **31**, 235–68.

Chowdhury, G. and Miles, D. K. (1987) *An Empirical Model of Companies' Debt and Dividend Decisions*. London, Bank of England Discussion Paper No 28.

Choy, A. Y. F. and O'Hanlon, J. (1989) Day of the week effects in the UK equity market: a cross-sectional analysis. *Journal of Business Finance and Accounting*, **16**, 89–104.

Chua, J. H., Woodward, R. S. and To, E. C. (1987) Potential gains from stock market timing in Canada. *Financial Analysts Journal*, **43**, September–October, 50–56.

Chugh L. C. and Meador, J. W. (1984) The stock valuation process: the analysts' view. *Financial Analysts Journal*, **40**, November–December, 41–48.

Chui, A., Strong, N. and Cadle, J. (1992) The empirical significance of tax effects on the valuation of dividends: the UK evidence. *Journal of Business Finance and Accounting*, **19**, 515–32.

Clare, A. D. and Thomas, S. H. (1992) International evidence for the predictability of bond and stock returns. *Economic Letters*, **40**, 105–112.

Clark, S. E. (1991) Practising what they teach. *Institutional Investor*, 116–21.

Clark, T. A. and Weinstein, M. I. (1983) The behavior of the common stock of bankrupt firms. *Journal of Finance*, **38**, 489–504.

Clayman, M. (1987) In search of excellence: the investor's viewpoint. *Financial Analysts Journal*, **43**, May–June, 54–63.

Clemen, R. T. (1989) Combining forecasts: a review and annotated bibliography. *International Journal of Forecasting*, **5**, 559–83.

Cohen, K. and Pogue, J. (1967) An Empirical Evaluation of Alternative Portfolio Selection Models. *Journal of Business*, **40**, 1203–32.

Colby, R. W. and Meyers, T. A. (1988) *The Encyclopaedia of Technical Market Indicators*. Homewood, Dow Jones-Irwin.

Cole, J. A. (1984) Are dividend surprises independently important? *Journal of Portfolio Management*, **10**, Summer, 45–50.

Collins, W. A. and Hopwood, W. S. (1980) A multivariate analysis of annual earnings forecasts generated from quarterly forecasts of financial analysts and univariate time series models. *Journal of Accounting Research*, **18**, 340–406.

Combined Actuarial Performance Services (1992) *CAPS General Report 1991*. Leeds, Combined Actuarial Performance Services.

Condoyanni, L., O'Hanlon, J. and Ward, C. W. R. (1987) Day of the week effects on stock returns: international evidence. *Journal of Business Finance and Accounting*, **14**, 159–74.

Cook, T. and Rozeff, M. S. (1984) Size and earnings/price ratio anomalies: one effect or two? *Journal of Financial and Quantitative Analysis*, **19**, 449–66.

Cooper, R. (1974) Efficient capital markets and the quantity theory of money. *Journal of Finance*, **29**, 887–908.

Cooper, T. (1984) Stockbrokers' earnings forecasts: a résumé. *Investment Analyst*, **73**, 19–26.

Cooper, T. and Taylor, B. (1983) How good are stockbrokers' earnings forecasts? *Investment Analyst*, **67**, 14–23.

Copeland, T. E. and Mayers, D. (1982) The Value Line enigma (1965–1978): a case study of performance evaluation issues. *Journal of Financial Economics*, **10**, 289–321.

Corhay, A., Hawawini, G. and Michel, P. (1987) Seasonality in the risk-return relationship: some international evidence. *Journal of Finance*, **42**, 49–68.

Corhay, A., Hawawini, G. and Michel, P. (1988) The pricing of equity on the London Stock Exchange: seasonality and size premium in E. Dimson (ed), *Stock Market Anomalies*. Cambridge, Cambridge University Press.

Costello, E. (1992) How to spot a company going bust. *Investors Chronicle* (Supplement), **26**, 12–13.

Cottle, S., Murray, R. F. and Block, F. E. (1988) *Graham and Dodd's Security Analysis*, 5th edn. New York, McGraw-Hill.

Coulson, D. R. (1987) *The Intelligent Investor's Guide to Profiting From Stock Market Inefficiencies*. Chicago, Probus.

Cragg, L. and Malkiel, B. (1968) The consensus and accuracy of some predictions of the growth of corporate earnings. *Journal of Finance*, **23**, 67–84.

Cross, F. (1973) The behavior of stock prices on Fridays and Mondays. *Financial Analysts Journal*, **29**, November–December, 67–69.

Cullity, J. P. (1987) Signals of cyclical movements in inflation and interest rates. *Financial Analysts Journal*, **43**, September–October, 40–49.

Cutler, D. M., Poterba, J. M. and Summers, L. H. (1989) What moves stock prices? *Journal of Portfolio Management*, **15**, Spring, 4–11.

Davies, G. and Shah, M. (1992) New methods for forecasting GDP growth in the UK. *The UK Economics Analyst*, June, London, Goldman Sachs.

Davies, G. and Wadhwani, S. (1988) *Valuing UK Equities Against Gilts—Theory and Practice*. April, London, Goldman Sachs.

De Bondt, W. F. M. and Thaler, R. (1985) Does the stock market overreact? *Journal of Finance*, **40**, 793–808.

De Bondt, W. F. M. and Thaler, R. (1987) Further evidence on investor overreaction and stock market seasonality. *Journal of Finance*, **42**, 557–81.

De Bondt, W. F. M. and Thaler, R. (1989) A mean reverting walk down Wall Street. *Journal of Economic Perspectives*, **3**, Winter, 189–202.

Dhrymes, P. J., Friend, I., Gultekin, M. N. and Gultekin, N. B. (1985) New tests of the APT and their implications. *Journal of Finance*, **40**, 659–74.

Diacogiannis, G. P. (1986) Arbitrage pricing model: a critical examination of its empirical applicability for the London Stock Exchange. *Journal of Business Finance and Accounting*, **13**, 489–504.

Diermeier, J. I. (1988) Asset allocation strategies, in S. N. Levine *The Financial Analyst's Handbook*, 2nd edn. Homewood, Dow Jones-Irwin.

Dimson, E. (ed.) (1988) *Stock Market Anomalies*. Cambridge, Cambridge University Press.

Dimson, E. and Fraletti, P. (1986) Brokers' recommendations: the value of a telephone tip. *Economic Journal*, **96**, 139–59.

Dimson, E. and Marsh P. (1984) An analysis of brokers' and analysts' unpublished forecasts of UK stock returns. *Journal of Finance*, **39**, 1257–92.

Dimson, E. and Marsh P. (1985) Stock pickers: chumps, chimps or champs? *Investment Analyst*, **75**, 26–35.

Dimson, E. and Marsh P. (1986) Event study methodologies and the size effect: the case of UK press recommendations. *Journal of Financial Economics*, **17**, 113–42.

Dimson, E. and Marsh P. (1989) The smaller companies puzzle. *Investment Analyst*, **91**, 16–24.

Dimson, E. and Marsh P. (1992) *The Hoare Govett Smaller Companies Index 1992*. London, Hoare Govett.

Divecha, A. B., Drach, J. and Stefek, D. (1992) Emerging markets: a quantitative perspective. *Journal of Portfolio Management*, **19**, Fall, 41–50.

Donnelly, B. (1985) The dividend discount model comes into its own. *Institutional Investor*, March, 157–59, 162.

Dowen, R. J. and Bauman, W. S. (1986) A fundamental multifactor asset pricing model. *Financial Analysts Journal*, **42**, July–August, 45–51.

Dowen, R. J. and Bauman, W. S. (1991) Revisions in corporate earnings forecasts and common stock returns. *Financial Analysts Journal*, **47**, March–April, 86–90.

Dreman, D. (1982) *The New Contrarian Investment Strategy*. New York, Random House.

Droms, W. G. (1989) Market timing as an investment policy. *Financial Analysts Journal*, **45**, January–February, 73–77.

Drummen, M. and Zimmermann, H. (1992) The structure of European stock returns. *Financial Analysts Journal*, **48**, July–August, 15–26.

DuBois, C. H. (1988) Tactical asset allocation: a review of current techniques, in R. D. Arnott and F. J. Fabozzi (eds) *Asset Allocation: A Handbook of Portfolio Policies, Strategies and Tactics*. Chicago, Probus.

The Economist, (1992) The prophet of profit. August 22, **59**.

Edmister, R. O. and Greene, J. B. (1980) Performance of super-low-price stocks. *Journal of Portfolio Management*, **7**, Fall, 36–41.

Edwards, R. D. and Magee, J. (1984) *Technical Analysis of Stock Trends*, 5th ed. Springfield, John Magee.

Einhorn, S. G. (1978) *Risk, Return, and Equity Valuation: A Quarterly Service*. New York, Goldman Sachs.

Einhorn, S. G. (1990) The perplexing issue of valuation: will the real value please stand up? *Financial Analysts Journal*, **46**, July–August, 11–13, 16.

Einhorn, S. G. and Shangquan, P. (1984) Using the dividend discount model for asset allocation. *Financial Analysts Journal*, **40**, May–June, 30–32.

Elliott, J. A. and Philbrick, D. R. (1990) Accounting changes and earnings predictability. *Accounting Review*, **65**, 157–74.

Elton, E. J. and Gruber, M. J. (1972) Earnings estimation and the accuracy of expectational data. *Management Science*, **18**, 409–24.

Elton, E. J. and Gruber, M. J. (1989) Expectational data and Japanese stock prices. *Japan and the World Economy*, **1**, 391–401.

Elton, E. J., Gruber, M. J. and Grossman, S. (1986) Discrete expectational data and portfolio performance. *Journal of Finance*, **41**, 699–714.

Elton, E. J., Gruber, M. J. and Gultekin, M. (1981) Expectations and share prices. *Management Science*, **27**, 975–87.

Elton, E. J., Gruber, M. J. and Gultekin, M. N. (1984) Professional expectations: accuracy and diagnosis of errors. *Journal of Financial and Quantitative Analysis*, **19**, 351–63.

Elton, E. J., Gruber, M. J. and Padberg, M. W. (1978) Optimal portfolios from simple ranking devices. *Journal of Portfolio Management*, **4**, Spring, 15–19.

Elton, E. J., Gruber, M. J. and Rentzler, J. (1983) A simple examination of the empirical relationship between dividend yields and deviations from the CAPM. *Journal of Banking and Finance*, **7**, 135–46.

Estep, T., Hanson, N. and Johnson, C. (1983) Sources of value and risk in common stocks. *Journal of Portfolio Management*, **9**, Summer, 5–13.

Estrella, A, and Hardouvelis, G. A. (1991) The term structure as a predictor of real economic activity. *Journal of Finance*, **46**, 555–76.

Fama, E. F. (1970) Efficient capital markets: a review of theory and empirical work. *Journal of Finance*, **25**, 383–417.

Fama, E. F. (1991) Efficient capital markets: II. *Journal of Finance*, **46**, 1575–1617.

Fama, E. F., Fisher, L. and Roll, R. (1969) Adjustment of stock prices to new information. *International Economic Review*, **10**, 1–21.

Fama, E. F. and French, K. R. (1988a) Dividend Yields and Expected Stock Returns. *Journal of Financial Economics*, **22**, 3–26.

Fama, E. F. and French, K. R. (1988b) Permanent and Temporary Component of stock Prices. Journal of Political Economy, **96**, 246–73.

Fama, E. F. and French, K. R. (1989) Business conditions and expected returns on stocks and bonds. *Journal of Financial Economics*, **25**, 23–49.

Fama, E. F. and French, K. R. (1992) The cross-section of expected stock returns. *Journal of Finance*, **47**, 427–65.

Fama E. F. and MacBeth, J. D. (1973) Risk, return and equilibrium: empirical tests. *Journal of Political Economy*, **81**, 607–36.

Farrell, J. L. (1974) Analyzing Covariation of Returns to Determine Homogenous Stock Groupings. *Journal of Business*, **47**, 186–207.

Farrell, J. L. (1982) A disciplined stock selection strategy. *Interfaces*, **12**, October, 19–30.

Farrell, J. L. (1983) *Guide to Portfolio Management*. New York, McGraw-Hill.

Farrell, J. L. (1985) The dividend discount model: a primer. *Financial Analysts Journal*, **41**, November–December, 16–25.

Farrell, J. L. (1989) A fundamental forecast approach to superior asset allocation. *Financial Analysts Journal*, **45**, May–June, 32–37.

Ferson, W. E. and Harvey, C. R. (1991) Sources of predictability in portfolio returns. *Financial Analysts Journal*, **47**, May–June, 49–56.

Fields, M. J. (1931) Stock prices: a problem in verification. *Journal of Business*, **4**, 415–18

Fields, M. J. (1934) Security prices and stock exchange holidays in relation to short selling. *Journal of Business*, **7**, 328–38.

Fielitz, B. D. and Muller, F. L. (1983) The asset allocation decision. *Financial Analysts Journal*, **39**, July–August, 44–50.

Finnerty, J. E. (1976) Insiders and market efficiency. *Journal of Finance*, **31**, 1141–48.

Fisher, K. L. (1984a) Price-sales ratios: a new tool for measuring stock popularity. *AAII Journal*, **6**, June, 13–17.

Fisher, K. L. (1984b) *Super Stocks*. Homewood, Business One Irwin.

Fogler, H. R. (1990) Common stock management in the 1990s. *Journal of Portfolio Management*, **16**, Winter, 26–35.

Forbes, W. P. and Skerratt, L. C. L. (1992) Analysts' forecast revisions and stock price movements. *Journal of Business Finance and Accounting*, **19**, 555–69.

Fosback, N. G. (1991) *Stock Market Logic: A Sophisticated Approach to Profits on Wall Street*. Chicago, Dearborn Financial Publishing.

Foster, G. (1979) Briloff and the capital markets. *Journal of Accounting Research*, **17**, 262–74.

Fouse, W. L. (1976) Risk and liquidity: the keys to stock price behavior. *Financial Analysts Journal*, **32**, May–June, 35–45.

Fouse, W. L. (1992) Allocating assets across country markets. *Journal of Portfolio Management*, **18**, Winter, 20–27.

Frankel, J. A. and Froot, K. A. (1990) Chartists, fundamentalists, and trading in the foreign exchange market. *American Economic Review*, (Papers and Proceedings), **80**, 181–85.

Frankfurter, G. M., Phillips, H. E. and Seagle, J. P. (1971) Portfolio selection: the effects of uncertain means, variances, and covariances. *Journal of Financial and Quantitative Analysis*, **6**, 125–62.

French, K. R. and Poterba, J. M. (1991) Were Japanese stock prices too high? *Journal of Financial Economics*, **29**, 337–63.

French, K. R. and Roll, R. (1986) Stock return variances: the arrival of information and the reaction of traders. *Journal of Financial Economics*, **17**, 5–26.

Fried, D. and Givoly, D. (1982) Financial analysts' forecasts of earnings. *Journal of Accounting and Economics*, **4**, 85–107.

Friend, I., Westerfield, R. and Granito M. (1978) New Evidence on the Captital Asset Pricing Model. *Journal of Finance*, **33**, 903–20.

Fritzemeier, L. H. (1936) Relative price fluctuation of industrial stocks in different price groups. *Journal of Business*, **9**, 133–54.

Frost, P. A. and Savarino, J. E. (1988) For better performance: constrain portfolio weights. *Journal of Portfolio Management*, **15**, Fall, 29–34.

Fuller, R. J. and Hsia, C. (1984) A Simplified Common Stock Valuation Model. *Financial Analysts Journal*, **40**, September–October, 49–56.

Fuller, R. J., Huberts, L. C. and Levinson, M. (1992) It's not higgledy-piggledy growth! *Journal of Portfolio Management*, **18**, Winter, 38–45.

Fuller, R. J. and Kling, J. L. (1990) Is the stock market predictable? *Journal of Portfolio Management*, **16**, Summer, 28–36.

Fuller, R. J. and Wong, G. W. (1988) Traditional versus theoretical risk measures. *Financial Analysts Journal*, **44**, March–April, 52–57, 67.

Gerstein, M. H. (1986) Timeliness ranks: how they're computed and why they change. *Value Line: Selection and Opinion*, **41**, September 19, 871–75.

Givoly, D. and Lakonishok, J. (1980) Financial analysts' forecasts of earnings: their value to investors. *Journal of Banking and Finance*, **4**, 221–33.

Givoly, D. and Lakonishok, J. (1984) The quality of analysts' forecasts of earnings. *Financial Analysts Journal*, **40**, September–October, 40–47.

Givoly, D. and Palmon D. (1985) Insider trading and the exploitation of inside information: some empirical evidence. *Journal of Business*, **58**, 69–87.

Glascock, J. L. *et al.* (1986) When E. F. Hutton Talks.... *Financial Analysts Journal*, **42**, May–June, 69–72.

Goldstein, M. L., Sommer, M. and Pari, R. A. (1991) *The Bernstein Multifactor Optimization Model*. New York, Sanford C. Bernstein.

Gooding, A. E. (1978) Perceived risk and capital asset pricing. *Journal of Finance*, **33**, 1401–21.

Goodman, D. A. and Peavy, J. W. (1983) Industry relative price-earnings ratios as indicators of investment returns. *Financial Analysts Journal*, **39**, July–August, 60–65.

Goodman, D. A. and Peavy, J. W. (1986) The interaction of firm size and price-earnings ratio on portfolio performance. *Financial Analysts Journal*, **42**, January–February, 9–12.

Goodman, S. H. (1980) Who's better than the toss of a coin? *Euromoney*, September, 80, 83, 85–6, 89.

Grace Jr., W. J. (1985) *The Phoenix Approach*. New York, Bantam.

Graham, B. (1973) *The Intelligent Investor*, 4th rev. edn. New York, Harper and Row.

Granatelli, A. and Martin, J. D. (1984) Management quality and investment performance. *Financial Analysts Journal*, **40**, November–December, 72–74.

Gray, D. and Walton, P. (1992) *Accounting Matters: The Impact of New Accounting Standards on UK Company Analysis*. London, James Capel & Co.

Greenwich Associates (1991) *Coming Challenges, Growing Sophistication*. Greenwich, Greenwich Associates.

Greenwich Associates (1992) *Strengthening Relationships, Improving Performance*. Greenwich, Greenwich Associates.

Grinblatt, M. and Titman, S. (1992) The persistence of mutual fund performance. *Journal of Finance*, **47**, 1977–84.

Grinold, R., Rudd, A. and Stefek, D. (1989) Global factors: fact or fiction? *Journal of Portfolio Management*, **16**, Fall, 79–88.

Gropper, D. R. (1985) Mining the market's inefficiencies. *Institutional Investor*, July, 80–81, 84–86, 90, 94.

Grossman, S. and Stiglitz, J. (1980) On the impossibility of informationally efficient markets. *American Economic Review*, **70**, 393–408.

Guerard, J. B. (1989) Combining time-series model forecasts and analysts' forecasts for superior forecasts of annual earnings. *Financial Analysts Journal*, **45**, January–February, 69–71.

Gultekin M. N. and Gultekin, N. B. (1983a) Stock market seasonality: international evidence. *Journal of Financial Economics*, **12**, 469–81.

Gultekin M. N. and Gultekin, N. B. (1983b) Stock return anomalies and the tests of the APT. *Journal of Finance*, **42**, 1213–24.

Hagin, R. (1990) What practioners need to know ...about t-tests. *Financial Analysts Journal*, **46**, May–June, 17–20.

Hall, T. W. and Tsay, J. J. (1988) An evaluation of the performance of portfolios selected from Value Line rank one stocks: 1976–1982. *Journal of Financial Research*, **11**, Fall, 227–40.

Hand, J. (1990) A test of the extended functional fixation hypothesis. *Accounting Review*, **65**, 740–63.

Harris, L. (1986) How to profit from intradaily stock returns. *Journal of Portfolio Management*, **12**, Winter, 61–64.

Harris, T. and Ohlson, J. (1990) Accounting disclosures and the market's evaluation of oil and gas properties. *Accounting Review*, **65**, 764–80.

Hawkins, E. H., Chamberlin, S. C. and Daniel, W. E. (1984) Earnings expectations and security prices. *Financial Analysts Journal*, **40**, September–October, 24–38, 74.

Healy, P. M. and Palepu, K. G. (1988) Earnings information conveyed by dividend initiations and omissions. *Journal of Financial Economics*, **21**, 149–75.

Henry, S. G. B. and Pesaran, B. (1993) VAR models of inflation. *Bank of England Quarterly Bulletin*, **33**, May, 231–39.

Hensel, C. R., Ezra, D. D. and Ilkiw, J. H. (1991) The importance of the asset allocation decision. *Financial Analysts Journal*, **47**, July–August, 65–72.

Holloway, C. (1981) A note on testing an aggressive investment strategy using Value Line ranks. *Journal of Finance*, **36**, 711–19.

Holmes, G. and Sugden, A. (1990) *Interpreting Company Accounts* 4th edn. Cambridge, Woodhead-Faulkner.

Huberman, G. and Kandel, S. (1990) Market efficiency and Value Line's record. *Journal of Business*, **63**, 187–216.

Hughes, M. (1992) *UK Equity-Gilt Study 1918–1991*. London, Barclays de Zoete Wedd Securities Limited.

Ibbotson, R. G. (1989) On the cheap. *Financial Analysts Journal*, **45**, September–October, 8–11.

Ibbotson, R. G. and Brinson, G. P. (1987) *Investment Markets*. New York, McGraw-Hill.

Ibbotson, R. G. and Brinson, G. P. (1993) *Global Investing*. New York, McGraw-Hill.

Ibbotson, R. G., Sindelar, J. L. and Ritter, J. R. (1988) Initial public offerings. *Journal of Applied Corporate Finance*, **1**, Summer, 37–45.

International Finance Corporation (1992) *Emerging Stock Markets Factbook*. Washington, International Finance Corporation.

Jackson, P. D. (1986) New issue costs and methods in the UK equity market. *Bank of England Quarterly Bulletin*, **26**, December, 532–42.

Jacobs, B. I. and Levy, K. N. (1988a) Disentangling equity return regularities: new insights and investment opportunities. *Financial Analysts Journal*, **44**, May–June, 47–62.

Jacobs, B. I. and Levy, K. N. (1988b) On the value of 'value'. *Financial Analysts Journal*, **44**, July–August, 47–62.

Jacobs, B. I. and Levy, K. N. (1988c) Trading tactics in an inefficient market in W. H. Wagner,(ed.) *The Complete Guide to Securities Transactions*. New York, Wiley.

Jacobs, B. I. and Levy, K. N. (1989) How dividend discount models can be used to add value in H. R. Fogler and D. M. Bayston, (eds.) *Improving Portfolio Performance With Quantitative Models*. Charlottesville, Institute of Chartered Financial Analysts.

Jaffe, J. F. (1974) Special information and insider trading. *Journal of Business*, **47**, 410–28.

Jaffe, J. and Westerfield, R. (1985) The week-end effect in common stock returns: the international evidence. *Journal of Finance*, **40**, 432–54.

Jaffe, J., Keim, D. B. and Westerfield, R. (1989) Earnings yields, market values, and stock returns. *Journal of Finance*, **44**, 135–48.

Jaffe, J. and Westerfield, R. (1989) Is there a monthly effect in stock market returns? Evidence from foreign countries. *Journal of Banking and Finance*, **13**, 237–44.

Jaffe, J. F., Westerfield, R. and Ma, C. (1989) A twist on the Monday effect in stock prices: evidence from the US and foreign stock markets. *Journal of Banking and Finance*, **13**, 641–50.

Jahnke, G., Klaffke, S. J. and Oppenheimer, H. R. (1987) Price-earnings ratios and security performance. *Journal of Portfolio Management*, **14**, Fall, 39–46.

Jahnke, W. W. (1990) The development of structured portfolio management: a contextual view in B. R. Bruce, (ed.) *Quantitative International Investment*. London, McGraw-Hill.

Jain, P. C. and Joh G. (1988) The dependence between hourly prices and trading volume. *Journal of Financial and Quantitative Analysis*, **23**, 269–83.

Jameson, M. (1988) *A Practical Guide to Creative Accounting*. London, Kogan Page.

Jegadeesh, N. (1991) Seasonality in stock price mean reversion: evidence from the US and the UK. *Journal of Finance*, **46**, 1427–44.

Jeffrey, R. H. (1984) The folly of stock market timing. *Harvard Business Review*, **62**, July–August, 102–10.

Jensen, M. C. and Bennington, G. A. (1970) Random walks and technical theories: some additional evidence. *Journal of Finance*, **25**, 469–82.

Johnson, R. S., Fiore, L. C. and Zuber, R. (1989) The investment performance of common stocks in relation to their price-earnings ratios: an update of the Basu study. *Financial Review*, **24**, 499–505.

Jones, R. C. (1989) A long term relationship in *3rd Annual Institutional Investor Money Management Forum*. New York, Institutional Invetor.

Jones, R. C. (1989) Group rotation from the bottom up. *Journal of Portfolio Management*, **15**, Summer, 32–38.

Jones, R. C. (1990) Designing factor models for different types of stock: what's good for the goose ain't always good for the gander. *Financial Analysts Journal*, **46**, March–April, 25–30, 50.

Joy, O. M. and Jones, C. P. (1986) Should we believe the tests of market efficiency? *Journal of Portfolio Management*, **12**, Summer, 49–54.

Kahn, A. E. (1971) *The Economics of Regulation. Vol. II*. New York, Wiley.

Kalay, A. and Loewenstein, U. (1986) The informational content of the timing of dividend announcements. *Journal of Financial Economics*, **16**, 373–88.

Kaplan, R. and Roll, R. (1972) Investor evaluation of accounting information: some empirical evidence. *Journal of Business*, **45**, 225–57.

Kaplanis, E. and Schaefer, S. M. (1991) Exchange risk and international diversification in bond and equity portfolios. *Journal of Economics and Business*, **43**, 287–307.

Karpoff, J. M. (1987) The Relationship between Price Changes and Trading Volume: A Survey. *Journal of Financial and Quantitive Analysis*, **22**, 109–26

Katz, S., Lilien, S. and Nelson, B. (1985) Stock market behavior around bankruptcy model distress and recovery predictions. *Financial Analysts Journal*, **41**, January–February, 70–74.

Keane, S. M. (1986) The efficient market hypothesis on trial. *Financial Analysts Journal*, **42**, March–April, 58–63.

Keane, S. M. (1989) Seasonal anomalies and the need for perspective. *Investment Analyst*, **91**, 25–30.

Keasey, K. and Short, H. (1992) The underpricing of initial public offerings: some UK evidence. *Omega*, **20**, 45766.

Keim, D. B. (1983) Size-related anomalies and stock return seasonality. *Journal of Financial Economics*, **12**, 13–22.

Keim, D. B. (1985) Dividend yields and stock returns: implications of abnormal January returns. *Journal of Financial Economics*, **14**, 473–89.

Keim, D. B. (1986) Dividend yields and the January effect. *Journal of Portfolio Management*, **12**, Winter, 54–60.

Keim, D. B. (1987) Daily premiums and size-related premiums: one more time. *Journal of Portfolio Management*, **13**, Winter, 41–47.

Keim, D. B. (1988) Stock market regularities: a synthesis of the evidence and explanations in E. Dimson, (ed.) *Stock Market Anomalies*. Cambridge, Cambridge University Press.

Keim, D. B. (1990) A new look at the effects of firm size and E/P ratio on stock returns. *Financial Analysts Journal*, **46**, March–April, 56–67.

Keim, D. B. and Stambaugh, R. F. (1986) Predicting returns in the stock and bond markets. *Journal of Financial Economics*, **17**, 357–390.

Kemp, A. G. and Reid, G. C. (1971) The random walk hypothesis and the recent behaviour of equity prices in Britain. *Economica*, **38**, 28–51.

Kendall, M. G. (1953) The analysis of economic time-series. Part I: prices. *Journal of the Royal Statistical Society*, **116**, 11–25.

Keppler, A. M. (1991a) The importance of dividend yields in country selection. *Journal of Portfolio Management*, **17**, Winter, 24–29.

Keppler, A. M. (1991b) Further evidence on the predictability of international equity returns. *Journal of Portfolio Management*, **18**, Fall, 48–53.

King, M. and Roell, A. (1988) *Insider Trading*. London, LSE Financial Markets Group Special Paper Series, No 4.

Kirscher, J. C. (1990) Machine 'seer' handicaps stocks for customer portfolios. *Bank Management*, **66**, 54–56.

Kleidon, A. (1986) Variance bounds tests and stock price valuation models. *Journal of Political Economy*, **94**, 953–1001.

Klein, R. W. and Bawa, V. S. (1977) The effect of limited information and estimation risk on optimal portfolio diversification. *Journal of Financial Economics*, **5**, 89–111.

Klemkosky, R. C. and Miller, W. P. (1984) When forecasting earnings, it pays to be right. *Journal of Portfolio Management*, **10**, Summer, 13–18.

Kolodny, R., Laurence, M. and Ghosh A. (1989) In search of excellence ... for whom? *Journal of Portfolio Management*, **15**, Spring, 56–60.

Kosmicke, R. (1986) The limited relevance of volatility to risk. *Journal of Portfolio Management*, **13**, Fall, 18–20.

Kraft, J. and Kraft, A. (1977) Determinants of common stock prices: a time series analysis. *Journal of Finance*, **32**, 417–25.

Kritzman, M. (1991) What practitioners need to know ... about uncertainty. *Financial Analysts Journal*, **47**, March–April, 17–21.

Kritzman, M. (1993) What practitioners need to know ... about factor methods. *Financial Analysts Journal*, **49**, January–February, 12–15.

Kritzman, M. and Ryan, J. C. (1980) A short-term approach to asset allocation. *Journal of Portfolio Management*, **7**, Fall, 45–49.

Kross, W. (1985) The size effect is primarily a price effect. *Journal of Financial Research*, **8**, 169–79.

Lacey, N. J. and Phillips-Patrick, F. J. (1992) Source of the Value Line enigma. *Applied Financial Economics*, **2**, 173–178.

Lakonishok, J. and Shapiro, A. C. (1984) Stock returns, beta, variance and size: an empirical analysis. *Financial Analysts Journal*, **40**, July–August, 36–41.

Lakonishok, J., Shleifer, A. and Vishny, R. W. (1992) The structure and performance of the money management industry. *Brookings Papers on Economic Activity: Microeconomics*, 339–79.

Lakonishok, J., Shleifer, A. and Vishny, R. W. (1993) *Contrarian Investment, Extrapolation, and Risk*. Faculty Working Paper No. 93–0128, College of Commerce and Business Administration, University of Illinois at Urbana-Champaign.

Lakonishok, J. and Smidt, S. (1988) Are seasonal anomalies real? A ninety-year perspective. *Review of Financial Studies*, **1**, 403–25.

Lanstein, R. J. and Jahnke, W. W. (1979) Applying capital market theory to investing. *Interfaces*, **9**, 23–38.

Lee, W. Y. (1990) Diversification and time: do investment horizons matter? *Journal of Portfolio Management*, **16**, Spring, 21–26.

Lee, W. Y. and Solt, M. E. (1986) Insider trading: a poor guide to market timing. *Journal of Portfolio Management*, **12**, Summer, 65–71.

Lehmann, B. N. (1990) Fads, martingales, and market efficiency. *Quarterly Journal of Economics*, **105**, 1–28.

Leibowitz, M. L. and Langetieg, T. C. (1990) Shortfall risks and the asset-allocation decision in F. J. Fabozzi (ed.) *Managing Institutional Assets*. New York, Harper and Row.

LeRoy, S. F. (1990) Capital market efficiency: an update. *Federal Reserve Bank of San Francisco: Economic Review*, Spring, 29–40.

Levine, D with Hoffer, W. (1992) *Inside Out*. London, Arrow.

Levine, S. N. (1988) *The Financial Analyst's Handbook*, 2nd edn. Homewood, Dow Jones-Irwin.

Levis, M. (1985) Are small firms big performers. *Investment Analyst*, 76, 21–27.

Levis, M. (1989) Stock market anomalies: a re-assessment based on UK evidence. *Journal of Banking and Finance*, 13, 675–96.

Levis, M. (1990) The winner's curse problem, interest costs and the underpricing of initial public offerings. *Economic Journal*, 100, 76–89.

Levis, M. (1993) The long-run performance of initial public offerings: the UK experience 1980–88. *Financial Management*, 22, Spring, 28–41.

Levy, R. A. (1967) Relative strength as a criterion for investment selection. *Journal of Finance*, 22 , 595–610.

Litzenberger, R. H. and Ramaswamy, K. (1979) The effect of personal taxes and dividends on capital asset prices: theory and empirical evidence. *Journal of Financial Economics*, 7, 163–95.

Lloyd, W. P. and Modani, N. K. (1983) Stocks, bonds, bills, and time diversification. *Journal of Portfolio Management*, 9, Spring, 7–11.

Lo, A. W. and MacKinlay, A. C. (1988) Stock market prices do not follow random walks: evidence from a simple specification test. *Review of Financial Studies*, 1, 41–66.

Loeb, T. F. (1991) Is there a gift from small-stock investing? *Financial Analysts Journal*, 47, January–February, 39–44.

Lofthouse, S. (1990) A guide for the Gaijin to the Japanese market, *Professional Investor*, 1, April, 20–26.

Lynch, P. with Rothchild J. (1989) *One Up On Wall Street*. New York, Simon and Schuster.

MacDonald, R. and Power, D. (1991) Persistence in UK stock market returns: aggregated and disaggregated perspectives in M. P. Taylor (ed.) *Money and Financial Markets* Oxford, Blackwell.

MacDonald, R. and Power, D. (1992a) Persistence in UK stock market returns: some evidence using high-frequency data. *Journal of Business Finance and Accounting*, 19, 505–14.

MacDonald, R. and Power, D. (1992b) Persistence in UK share returns: some evidence from disaggregated data. *Applied Financial Economics*, 3, 27–38.

McEnally R. W. (1985) Time diversification: surest route to lower risk? *Journal of Portfolio Management*, 11, Summer, 24–26.

McEnally, R. W. and Todd, R. B. (1992) Cross-sectional variation in common stocks. *Financial Analysts Journal*, 48, May–June, 59–63.

McWilliams, J. D. (1984) 'Watchman, tell us of the night!' *Journal of Portfolio Management*, 10, Spring, 75–80.

Maital, S., Filer, R. and Simon, J. (1986) What do people bring to the stock market (besides money)? in B. Gilad and S. Kaish (eds.) *Handbook of Behavioral Economics*. Volume B. Greenwich, JAI.

Malkiel, B. G. (1963) Equity yields, growth, and the structure of share prices. *American Economic Review*, 53, 1004–31.

Malkiel, B. G. (1990) *A Random Walk Down Wall Street*, 5th edn. New York, Norton.

Malkiel, B. G. and Cragg, J. G. (1970) Expectations and the structure of share prices. *American Economic Review*, 60, 601–17.

Markese, J. (1986) The stock market and business cycles. *AAII Journal*, 8, November, 30–32.

Markowitz, H. M. (1952) Portfolio selection. *Journal of Finance*, 7, 77–91.

Markowitz, H. M. (1959) *Portfolio Selection*. New York, Wiley.

Marsh, P. (1992) *Dividend Announcements and Stock Price Performance*. Working Paper, London Business School, 5/8/92.

Marsh, T. A. and Merton, R. C. (1986) Dividend variability and variance bounds tests for the rationality of stock market prices. *American Economic Review*, **76**, 483–98.

Matsumoto, T. (1989) *Japanese Stocks: A Basic Guide for the Intelligent Investor*. Tokyo, Kodansha.

Mayers, D. and Rice, E. M. (1979) Measuring portfolio performance and the empirical content of asset pricing models. *Journal of Financial Economics*, **7**, 3–28.

Meier, J. P. (1991) Tracking global equities with stock index futures. *Futures*, **20**, January 34, 36.

Melnikoff, M. (1988) Anomaly investing in S. N. Levine *The Financial Analyst's Handbook*, 2nd edn. Homewood, Dow Jones-Irwin.

Mennis, E. A. (1991) *How the Economy Works: An Investor's Guide to Tracking the Economy*. New York, New York Institute of Finance.

Mercer Fraser, W. M. (1988a) *Index Matching in the UK*. London, Mercer Fraser.

Mercer Fraser, W. M. (1988b) *Where Does Performance Come From?* London, Mercer Fraser.

Mercer Fraser, W. M. (1988c) *Tactical Asset Allocation Performance Survey*. London, Mercer Fraser.

Mercer Fraser, W. M. (1990) *The Gilt-Equity Yield Ratio*. London, Mercer Fraser.

Mercer Fraser, W. M. (1991) *The UK Equity Dividend Yield*. London, Mercer Fraser.

Michaud, R. O. (1985) A scenario-dependent dividend discount model: bridging the gap between top-down investment information and bottom-up forecasts. *Financial Analysts Journal*, **41**, November–December, 49–59.

Michaud, R. O. (1989) The Markowitz optimization enigma: is 'optimized' optimal? *Financial Analysts Journal*, **45**, January–February, 31–42.

Michaud, R. O. and Davis P. L. (1982) Valuation model bias and the scale structure of dividend discount returns. *Journal of Finance*, **37**, 563–73.

Mintzberg, H. (1979) *The Structuring of Organizations*. Englewood Cliffs, Prentice Hall.

Mintzberg, H. and Quinn, J. B. (1992) *The Strategy Process: Concepts and Contexts*, 2nd edn. Englewood Cliffs, Prentice Hall.

Modigliani, F. and Cohn, R. (1979) Inflation, rational valuation and the market. *Financial Analysts Journal*, **35**, March–April, 24–44.

Modigliani, F. and Cohn, R. (1982) Inflation and the stock market in J. A. Boeckh and R. T. Coghlan (eds.) *The Stock Market and Inflation*. Homewood, Dow Jones Irwin.

Modigliani, F. and Pogue, G. A. (1988) Risk, return, and CAPM: concepts and evidence in S. N. Levine *The Financial Analyst's Handbook*, 2nd edn. Homewood, Dow Jones-Irwin.

Moizer, P. and Arnold, J. (1984) Share appraisal by investment analysts—portfolio vs. non-portfolio managers. *Accounting and Business Research*, **14**, 341–348.

Moore, G. H. and Cullity, J. P. (1988) Security markets and business cycles in S. N. Levine, (ed.) *The Financial Analyst's Handbook*, 2nd edn. Homewood, Dow Jones-Irwin.

Moses, O. D. (1990) On analysts' earnings forecasts for failing firms. *Journal of Business Finance and Accounting*, **17**, 101–118.

Mossaheb, N. (1988a) *Index Portfolios for FT-SE 100*. Edinburgh, James Capel and Co.

Mossaheb, N. (1988b) *Index Portfolios for EAFE*. Edinburgh, James Capel and Co.

Murphy, J. M. (1977) Efficient markets, index funds, illusion, and reality. *Journal of Portfolio Management*, **4**, Fall, 5–20.

Nagorniak, J. J. (1985) Thoughts on using dividend discount models. *Financial Analysts Journal*, **41**, November–December, 13–15.

Naser, K. and Pendelbury, M. (1992) A note on the use of creative accounting. *British Accounting Review*, **24**, 111–18.

Neiderhoffer, V. and Regan, P. J. (1972) Earnings changes, analysts' forecasts and stock prices. *Financial Analysts Journal*, **28**, May–June, 65–71.

Nelson, C. R. (1987) *The Investor's Guide to Economic Indicators*. New York, Wiley.

Netter, J. M. and Mitchell, M. L. (1989) Stock-repurchase announcements and insider transactions after the October 1987 stock market crash. *Financial Management*, **18**, 84–96.

Nicholson, S. F. (1960) Price-earnings ratios. *Financial Analysts Journal*, **16**, July–August, 43–45.

Nunn, K. P., Madden, G. P. and Gombola, M. J. (1983) Are some insiders more 'inside' than others? *Journal of Portfolio Management*, **9**, Spring, 18–22.

Ofer, A. R. and Siegel, D. R. (1987) Corporate financial policy, information and market expectations: an empirical investigation of dividends. *Journal of Finance*, **42**, 889–911.

O'Hanlon, J. (1988) Days of the week returns over trading and non-trading periods: UK evidence. *Investment Analyst*, **90**, 3–15.

O'Hanlon, J. and Papaspirou, P. (1988) The daily behaviour of national equity markets: seasonal patterns and inter-relationships. *Investment Analyst*, **89**, 26–35.

O'Hanlon, J., Poon, S. and Yaansah, R. A. (1992) Market recognition of differences in earnings persistence: UK evidence. *Journal of Business Finance and Accounting*, **19**, 625–39.

O'Hanlon, J. and Ward, C. W. R. (1986) How to lose at winning strategies. *Journal of Portfolio Management*, **12**, Spring, 20–23.

O'Hanlon, J. and Whiddett, R. (1991) Do UK security analysts over-react? *Accounting and Business Research*, **22**, 63–74.

O'Hanlon, J. *et al.* (1992) Market recognition of differences in earnings persistence: UK evidence. *Journal of Business Finance and Accounting*, **19**, 625–39.

Oppenheimer, H. J. (1984) A test of Ben Graham's stock selection criteria. *Financial Analysts Journal*, **40**, September–October, 68–74.

Oppenheimer, H. J. (1986) Ben Graham's net current asset values: a performance update. *Financial Analysts Journal*, **42**, November–December, 40–47.

Oppenheimer, H. J. and Dielman, T. E. (1988) Firm dividend policy and insider activity: some empirical results. *Journal of Business Finance and Accounting*, **15**, 525–41.

Owen, J. P. (1990) *The Prudent Investor: The Definitive Guide to Professional Management*. Chicago, Probus.

Peavy, J. W. (1992) Stock prices: do interest rates and earnings really matter? *Financial Analysts Journal*, **48**, May–June 10–12.

Peavy, J. W. and Goodman, D. A. (1983) The significance of P/Es for portfolio returns. *Journal of Portfolio Management*, **9**, Winter, 43–47.

Peel, M. J. (1985) Directors shareholdings in failed companies and insider dealing controls. *Investment Analyst*, **77**, July, 24–28.

Peel, M. J., Peel, D. A. and Pope, P. F. (1986) Predicting corporate failure—some results for the UK corporate sector. *Omega*, **14**, 5–12.

Peters, T. J., and Waterman, R. H. (1982) *In Search of Excellence: Lessons from America's Best Run Companies*. New York, Harper and Row.

Peterson, D. R. (1987) Security price reactions to initial reviews of common stock by the Value Line Investment Survey. *Journal of Financial and Quantitative Analysis*, **22**, 483–94.

Phillips, D. and Lee, J. (1989) Differentiating tactical asset allocation from market timing. *Financial Analysts Journal*, **45**, March–April, 14–16.

Pinches, G. E. (1970) The random walk hypothesis and technical analysis. *Financial Analysts Journal*, **26**, March–April, 104–10.

Pines, H. A. (1983) A new psychological perspective on investor decision making. *AAII Journal*, **5**, September, 10–17.

Platt, J. (1992) Asset allocation: a case study in T. E. Cooke, *et al.* (eds.) *Risk, Portfolio Management and Capital Markets*. London, Macmillan.

Poon, S. and Taylor, S. J. (1991) Macroeconomic factors and the UK stock market. *Journal of Business Finance and Accounting*, **18**, 619–35.

Pope, P. F., Morris, R. C. and Peel, D. A. (1990) Insider trading: some evidence on market efficiency and directors' share dealings in Great Britain. *Journal of Business Finance and Accounting*, **17**, 359–80.

Poterba, J. and Summers, L. (1984) New evidence that taxes affect the valuation of dividends. *Journal of Finance*, **39**, 1397–415.

Poterba, J. M. and Summers, L. H. (1988) Mean reversion in stock prices: evidence and implications. *Journal of Financial Economics*, **22**, 27–59.

Power, D. M. *et al.* (1991) The over-reaction effect—some UK evidence. *British Accounting Review*, **23**, 149–70.

Pratt, S. P. and DeVere, C. W. (1968) Relationship between insider trading and rates of return for NYSE common stocks, 1960–66 in L. Lorie and R. Brealey (eds.) (1972) *Modern Developments in Investment Management*. New York, Praeger.

Pruitt, S. W. and White, R. E. (1988) The CRISMA trading system: who says technical analysis can't beat the market. *Journal of Portfolio Management*, **14**, Spring, 55–58.

Rao, R. P., Aggarwal, R. and Hiraki, T. (1992) Dividend yields and stock returns: evidence from the Tokyo stock market. *Journal of Economics and Business*, **44**, 187–200.

Rea, J. B. (1977) Remembering Benjamin Graham—teacher and friend. *Journal of Portfolio Management*, **3**, Summer, 66–72.

Regan, P. J. (1981) The cover story syndrome. *Financial Analysts Journal*, **37**, January–February, 12–13.

Regan, P. J. (1991) Insider transactions: watch what they do. *Financial Analysts Journal*, **47**, January–February, 13–15.

Reilly, F. K., Griggs, F. T. and Wong, W. (1983) Determinants of the aggregate stock market earnings multiple. *Journal of Portfolio Management*, **10**, Fall, 36–45.

Reinganum, M. R. (1981) Misspecification of capital asset pricing: empirical anomalies based on earnings' yields and market values. *Journal of Financial Economics*, **9**, 19–46.

Reinganum, M. R. (1983) Portfolio strategies based on market capitalization. *Journal of Portfolio Management*, **9**, Winter, 29–36.

Reinganum, M. R. (1988) The anatomy of a stock market winner. *Financial Analysts Journal*, **44**, March–April, 16–28.

Reinganum, M. R. (1992) A revival of the small firm effect. *Journal of Portfolio Management*, **18**, Spring, 55–62.

Rendleman, R. J., Jones, C. P. and Latané, H. A. (1982) Empirical anomalies based on unexpected earnings and the importance of risk adjustments. *Journal of Financial Economics*, **10**, 269–87.

Renshaw, E. F. (1985) A risk premium model for market timing. *Journal of Portfolio Management*, **11**, Summer, 33–35.

Renshaw, E. (1990) Five simple rules for identifying bear markets. *AAII Journal*, **12**, July, 7–10.

Ricks, W. (1982) The market's response to 1974 LIFO adoptions. *Journal of Accounting Research*, **20**, 367–87.

Ritter, J. R. (1984) The 'hot issue' market of 1980. *Journal of Business*, **57**, 215–40.

Ritter, J. R. (1991) The long-run performance of initial public offerings. *Journal of Finance*, **46**, 1–27.

Rock, K. (1986) Why new issues are underpriced. *Journal of Financial Economics*, **15**, 187–212.

Rogalski, R. J. (1984) New findings regarding day-of-the-week returns over trading and non-trading periods: a note. *Journal of Finance*, **39**, 1603–14.

Rogalski, R. J. and Tinic, S. M. (1986) The January size effect: anomaly or risk measurement. *Financial Analysts Journal*, **42**, November–December, 63–70.

Rogalski, R. J. and Vinso, J. (1977) Stock returns, money supply and the direction of causality. *Journal of Finance*, **32**, 1017–30.

Rogers, R. C. (1988) The relationship between earnings yield and market value: evidence from the American Stock Exchange. *Financial Review*, **23**, 65–80.

Rohrer, J. (1985) Are asset allocation models a rip-off? *Institutional Investor*, October, 118, 120.

Rohrer, J. (1989) The Bernstein formula. *Institutional Investor*, November, 143, 144, 147, 149, 151, 152.

Rohrer, J. (1991) Has value investing lost its value? *Institutional Investor*, June, 91–94, 97, 98.

Roll, R. (1977) A critique of the asset pricing theory's tests; Part I: on past and potential testability of the theory. *Journal of Financial Economics*, **4**, 129–76.

Roll, R. (1978) Ambiguity when performance is measured by the securities market line. *Journal of Finance*, **33**, 1051–69.

Roll, R. (1984) Orange juice and weather. *American Economic Review*, **74**, 861–80.

Roll, R. (1992) Talk given at 'Volatility in US and Japanese stock markets: a symposium.' in *Journal of Applied Corporate Finance*, **5**, Spring, 4–35.

Roll, R. and Ross, S. A. (1980) An empirical investigation of the arbitrage pricing theory. *Journal of Finance*, **35**, 1073–1103.

Roll, R. and Ross, S. A. (1988) The arbitrage pricing theory approach to strategic portfolio planning in S. N. Levine *The Financial Analyst's Handbook*, 2nd edn. Homewood, Dow Jones-Irwin.

Rosenberg, B., Reid, K. and Lanstein, R. (1985) Persuasive evidence of market inefficiency. *Journal of Portfolio Management*, **11**, Spring, 9–16.

Ross, S. (1976) The Arbitage Theory of Capital Asset Pricing. *Journal of Economic Theory*, **13**, 341–60.

Ross, S. A. (1985) On the empirical relevance of APT: reply. *Journal of Portfolio Management*, **11**, Summer, 72–3.

Roth, M. (1989) *Making Money in Japanese Stocks*. Rutland, Tuttle.

Rozeff, M. S. (1974) Money and stock prices: market efficiency and the lag in effect of monetary policy. *Journal of Financial Economics*, **1**, 245–302.

Rozeff, M. S. (1984) Dividend yields are equity risk premiums. *Journal of Portfolio Management*, **11**, Fall, 68–75.

Rozeff, M. S. and Kinney, W. R. (1976) Capital market seasonality: the case of stock returns. *Journal of Financial Economics*, **3**, 379–402.

Rudd, A. (1980) Optimal selection of passive portfolios. *Financial Management*, **9**, 57–66.

Samuelson, P. A. (1989) The judgement of economic science on rational portfolio management: indexing, timing, and long-horizon effects. *Journal of Portfolio Management*, **16**, Fall, 4–12.

Saunders, A. (1990) Why are so many new stock issues underpriced? *Business Review: Federal Reserve Bank of Philadelphia*, March/April, 3–12.

Schieneman, G. (1982) *International Accounting and Investment Review*. New York, Prudential Bache.

Schlegel, G. (1985) Vector autoregressive forecasts of recession and recovery: is less more? *Economic Review: Federal Reserve Bank of Cleveland*, Quarter II, 2–12.

Schmerken, I. (1987) Optimization package draws on modern portfolio theory. *Wall Street Computer Review*, **4**, January, 8, 11–14.

Schultz, P. (1983) Transaction costs and the small firm effect: a comment. *Journal of Financial Economics*, **12**, 81–88.

Schwager, J. D. (1990) *Market Wizards: Interviews with Top Traders*. New York, Harper and Row.

Schwert, G. W. (1983) Size and stock returns, and other empirical regularities. *Journal of Financial Economics*, **12**, 3–12.

Senchack, A. J. and Martin, J. D. (1987) The relative performance of the PSR and PER investment strategies. *Financial Analysts Journal*, **43**, March–April, 46–55.

Seyhun, H. N. (1986) Insiders' profits, costs of trading, and market efficiency. *Journal of Financial Economics*, **16**, 189–212.

Seyhun, H. N. (1988) The information content of aggregate insider trading. *Journal of Business*, **61**, 1–24.

Seyhun, H. N. (1990) Overreaction or fundamentals: some lessons from insiders' response to the market crash of 1987. *Journal of Finance*, **45**, 1363–88.

Sharpe, W. F. (1963) A simplified model for portfolio analysis. *Management Science*, **9**, 277–93.

Sharpe, W. F. (1964) Capital asset prices: a theory of market equilibrium under conditions of risk. *Journal of Finance*, **19**, 425–42.

Sharpe, W. F. (1982) Factors in New York Stock Exchange security returns, 1931–1979. *Journal of Portfolio Management*, **8**, Summer, 5–19.

Sharpe, W. F. (1984) Factor models, CAPMs, and the ABT (*sic*). *Journal of Portfolio Management*, **11**, Fall, 21–25.

Sharpe, W. F. (1985) *AAT—Asset Allocation Tools*. Palo Alto, Scientific Press.

Sharpe, W. F. and Cooper, G. M. (1972) Risk-return classes of New York Stock Exchange common stocks 1931–1967. *Financial Analysts Journal*, **28** March–April, 46–52.

Shaw, A. R. (1988) Market timing and technical analysis in S. N. Levine *The Financial Analyst's Handbook*, 2nd edn. Homewood, Dow Jones-Irwin.

Shefrin, H. and Statman, M. (1985) The disposition to sell winners too early and ride losers too long: theory and evidence. *Journal of Finance*, **40**, 777–90.

Shiller, R. J. (1981) Do stock prices move too much to be justified by subsequent changes in dividends? *American Economic Review*, **71**, 421–36.

Shiller, R. J. (1984) Stock prices and social dynamics. *Brookings Papers on Economic Activity*, 457–98.

Shleifer, A. and Summers, L. H. (1990) The noise trader approach to finance. *Journal of Economic Perspectives*, **4**, Spring, 19–34.

Siegel, J. J. (1991) Does it pay stock investors to forecast the business cycle? *Journal of Portfolio Management*, **18**, Fall, 27–34.

Sims, C. A. (1980) Macroeconomics and reality. *Econometrica*, **48**, 1–48.

Sinquefield, R. A. (1991) Are small-stock returns achievable? *Financial Analysts Journal*, **47**, January–February, 45–50.

Slovic, P. (1972) Psychological study of human judgement: implications for investment decision making. *Journal of Finance*, **27**, 779–99.

Smith, R. K., Proffitt, D. L. and Stephens, A. A. (1992) *Investments*. St Paul, West.

Smith, T. and Hannah, R. (1991) *Accounting for Growth*. London, UBS Phillips and Drew.

Solnik, B. H. (1974) Why not diversify internationally rather than domestically? *Financial Analysts Journal*, **30**, July–August, 48–54.

Solnik, B. (1984) Stock prices and monetary variables: the international evidence. *Financial Analysts Journal*, **40**, March–April, 69–73.

Solt, M. E. and Statman, M. (1988) How useful is the sentiment index? *Financial Analysts Journal*, **44**, September–October, 45–55.

Sorensen, E. H. and Arnott, R. D. (1988) The risk premium and stock market performance. *Journal of Portfolio Management*, **14**, Summer, 50–55.

Sorensen, E. H. and Burke, T. (1986) Portfolio returns from active industry group rotation. *Financial Analysts Journal*, **42**, September–October, 43–50.

Sorensen, E. H. and Williamson, D. A. (1985) Some evidence on the value of dividend discount models. *Financial Analysts Journal*, **41**, November–December, 60–69.

Speidell, L. S. and Sappenfield, R. (1992) Global diversification in a shrinking world. *Journal of Portfolio Management*, **19**, Fall, 57–67.

Stambaugh, R. F. (1982) On the exclusion of assets from tests of the two-parameter model. *Journal of Financial Economics*, **10**, 237–68.

Stickel, S. E. (1985) The effect of Value Line Investment Survey rank changes on common stock prices. *Journal of Financial Economics*, **14**, 121–43.

Stoll, H. R. and Whaley, R. E. (1983) Transaction costs and the small firm effect. *Journal of Financial Economics*, **12**, 57–79.

Strebel, P. and Carvell, S. (1988) *In the Shadows of Wall Street: A Guide to Investing in Neglected Stocks*. Englewood Cliffs, Prentice-Hall.

Stumpp, M. and Scott, J. (1991) Does liquidity predict stock returns? *Journal of Portfolio Management*, **17**, Winter, 35–40.

Sunders, S. (1975) Stock price and risk related to accounting changes in inventory valuation. *Accounting Review*, **50**, 305–15.

Taffler, R. J. (1983) The assessment of company solvency and performance using a statistical model. *Accounting and Business Research*, **15**, Autumn, 295–307.

Taffler, R. J. (1984) Empirical models for the monitoring of UK corporations. *Journal of Banking and Finance*, **8**, 199–227.

Talley, M. D. (1987) *The Passionate Investors: Secrets of Winning on Wall Street from Bernard Baruch to John Templeton*. New York, Crown.

Taylor, S. J. and Ward, C. W. R. (1985) Relative accuracy of earnings forecasts made by UK stockbrokers. *Investment Analyst*, **75**, 15–17.

Tepper, I. (1977) Risk vs. return in pension fund management. *Harvard Business Review*, **55**, March–April, 100–107.

Thaler, R. H. (1987a) Anomalies: the January effect. *Journal of Economic Perspectives*, **1**, Summer, 197–201.

Thaler, R. H. (1987b) Anomalies: seasonal movements in security prices II: weekend, holiday, turn of the month, and intraday effects. *Journal of Economic Perspectives*, **1**, Fall, 169–77.

Tinic, S. M. and West, R. R. (1986) Risk, return, and equilibrium: a revisit. *Journal of Political Economy*, **94**, 126–47.

Tobin, J. (1958) Liquidity preference as behavior toward risk. *Review of Economic Studies*, **67**, 65–86.

Train, J. (1981) *The Money Masters*. Harmondsworth, Penguin.

Troutman, M. L. (1991) The Steinbrenner syndrome and the challenge of manager selection. *Financial Analysts Journal*, **47**, March–April, 37–44.

Tseng, K. C. (1988) Low price, price-earnings ratio, market value, and abnormal stock returns. *Financial Review*, **23**, 333–43.

Tversky, A. and Kahneman, D. (1981) The framing of decisions and the psychology of choice. *Science*, **211**, 453–58.

UBS Phillips and Drew (1992) *Equity Market Indicators*. London: UBS Phillips and Drew.

Ueda, K. (1990) Are Japanese stock prices too high? *Journal of the Japanese and International Economies*, **4**, 351–70.

Urwin, R. (1990) *Identifying Tomorrow's Successful Manager Today*. Paper Presented to The Institute of Actuaries Staple Inn Society, November 20th.

Urwin, R. (1991: Managers. in: *Notes to Accompany: Investment Success in the 1990s Seminar*. Reigate: Watsons Investment Consultancy.

Value Line Publishing, Inc. (1993) *Value Line Investment Survey: Part 2, Selection and Opinion*. 22 January.

Vandell, R. F. and Stevens, J. L. (1989) Evidence of superior performance from timing. *Journal of Portfolio Management*, **15**, Spring, 38–42.

Vu, J. D. (1988) An empirical analysis of Ben Graham's net current asset value rule. *Financial Review*, **23**, 215–25.

Wadhwani, S. (1991a) *The Interest Rate Sensitivity of Stocks*. London, Goldman Sachs.

Wadhwani, S. (1991b) *Are European Stock Markets Converging?* London, Goldman Sachs.

Wadhwani, S. (1991c) *The Outlook for UK Equities in 1992*. London, Goldman Sachs.

Wadhwani, S. (1992) *A Sector Selection Strategy for the UK*. London, Goldman Sachs.

Wagner, J., Shellans, S. and Paul, R. (1992) Market timing works where it matters most…in the real world. *Journal of Portfolio Management*, **18**, Summer, 86–89.

Watts, R. (1986) Does it pay to manipulate EPS? in J. M. Stern and D. H. Chew (eds.) *The Revolution in Corporate Finance*. Oxford, Blackwell.

Weigel, E. J. (1991) The Performance of Tactical Asset Allocation. *Financial Analysts Journal*, **47**, September–October, 63–70.

Whitbeck, V. S. and Kisor, M. (1963) A new tool in investment decision-making. *Financial Analysts Journal*, **19**, May–June, 55–62.

Wilcox, J. W. (1992a) Global investing in emerging markets. *Financial Analysts Journal*, **48**, January–February, 15–19.

Wilcox, J. W. (1992b) Taming frontier markets. *Journal of Portfolio Management*, **19**, Fall, 51–56.

Yamashita, T. (1989) *Japan's Security Markets: A Practitioner's Guide*. Singapore, Butterworths.

Zaman, M. A. (1988) Market inefficiency and insider trading: new evidence. *Journal of Business*, **61**, 25–44.

Zarowin, P. (1989a) Does the stock market overreact to corporate earnings information? *Journal of Finance*, **44**, 1385–99.

Zarowin, P. (1989b) Short-run market overreaction: size and seasonality effects. *Journal of Portfolio Management*, **15**, Spring, 26–29.

Zavgren, C. V., Dugan, M. T. and Reeve, J. M. (1988) The association between probabilities of bankruptcy and market responses—a test of market anticipation. *Journal of Business Finance and Accounting*, **15**, 27–45.

Zielinski, R. and Holloway, N. (1991) *Unequal Equities: Power and Risk in Japan's Stock Market*. Tokyo, Kodansha.

Ziemba, W. T. (1991) Japanese security market regularities: monthly, turn-of-the-month and year, holiday and golden week effects. *Japan and the World Economy*, **3**, 119–46.

Zweig, M. E. (1986) *Martin Zweig's Winning on Wall Street*. New York, Warner.

Index

Indexed terms may appear in figures and tables on the indicated pages, as well as in the text. For some frequently used statistical and technical terms only the glossary entry has been indexed.